NATIVE INFORMANT

NATIVE INFORMANT

□

Essays on Film, Fiction, and Popular Culture

Leo Braudy

New York   Oxford

OXFORD UNIVERSITY PRESS

1991

Oxford University Press

Oxford   New York   Toronto
Delhi   Bombay   Calcutta   Madras   Karachi
Petaling Jaya   Singapore   Hong Kong   Tokyo
Nairobi   Dar es Salaam   Cape Town
Melbourne   Auckland

and associated companies in
Berlin   Ibadan

Copyright © 1991 by Leo Braudy

Published by Oxford University Press, Inc.,
200 Madison Avenue, New York, New York 10016

Oxford is a registered trademark of Oxford University Press

Library of Congress Cataloging-in-Publication Data
Braudy, Leo. Native informant : essays on film, fiction,
and popular culture / Leo Braudy.
p. cm.   ISBN 0-19-505274-9
1. Motion pictures.   2. Fiction.   3. Popular culture.
I. Title. PN1995.B719   1991
814'.54—dc20   90-32975

1 3 5 7 9 8 6 4 2

Printed in the United States of America
on acid-free paper

For Jerry, Lee, Stan, and Stephen—
and several very good years

Acknowledgments

Perhaps, like Michelangelo's "Slaves," some writing is preformed, ready to spring forth at the proper touch. But certainly any collection of this sort owes much to the individuals who have helped to call some works into being by assignment, suggestion, or request. This is especially true of those pieces in this volume that began life as book reviews, but it also holds for those originally written as lectures, contributions to conferences, or tributes. For help in the process of engendering, I would especially like to thank Richard Locke, Ernest Callenbach, John Gross, Christopher Ricks, Leonard Michaels, Peter Brooks, Kai Erikson, George Slusser, Laurence Goldstein, Richard Macksey, Martin Price, Mary Price, Christie Vance, Jack Beatty, Peter Biskind, Naomi Schor, Ronald Gottesman, Richard Poirier, James W. Johnson, and Brigitte Weeks.

The newspapers, magazines, and journals in which most of these pieces first appeared have kindly granted permission to reprint them. I would therefore like to thank *Yale French Studies* for "Zola on Film: The Ambiguities of Naturalism"; *Yale Review* for "Popular Culture and Personal Time" and "Mad in Pursuit"; the Regents of the University of California for "Succeeding in Language" (from *The State of the Language*, 1980); *Film Quarterly* for "Newsreel: A Report," "The Sacraments of Genre: Coppola, DePalma, Scorsese," "Hitchcock, Truffaut, and the Irresponsible Audience," and "The Difficulties of *Little Big Man*"; Southern Illinois University Press for "Genre and the Resurrection of the Past" (from *Shadows of the Magic Lamp: Fantasy and Science Fiction in Film*); the *Times Literary Supplement* (London) for "Western Approaches" and "The Rise of the *Auteur*"; the *New York Times Book Review* for reviews of *Maidstone: A Mystery* by Norman Mailer, *Stargazer* by Stephen Koch, *We Are Your Sons* by Michael and Robert Meeropol, *G.* by John Berger, *Regiment of Women* by Thomas Berger, and *Winter Kills* by Richard Condon; *Michigan Quarterly Review* for "Framing the Innocent Eye: *42nd Street* and *Persona*"; The Johns Hopkins University Press for "The Double Detachment of Ernst Lubitsch" *(Modern Language Notes)* and "Providence, Paranoia, and the Novel" *(ELH); Studies in English Literature* for "Lexicography and Biography in the *Preface* to Johnson's *Dictionary*"; *Eighteenth-Century Studies* for "*Fanny Hill* and Materialism"; *Genre* for "Daniel

Defoe and the Anxieties of Autobiography''; *The New Republic* for ''A Genealogy of Mind''; *Novel* for ''The Form of the Sentimental Novel''; Columbia University Press for ''Penetration and Impenetrability in *Clarissa*'' (from *Approaches to Eighteenth-Century Literature,* 1974); *Prose Studies* for ''Edward Gibbon and 'The Privilege of Fiction' ''; *American Film* for ''In the Criminal Style''; *Washington Post Book World* for ''Grime on the Glitter: Hollywood and McCarthyism.''

I would also like to thank the many individuals at *Film Quarterly,* the *Michigan Quarterly Review,* the Larry Edmunds Bookshop, the American Film Institute, the Margaret Herrick Library of the Academy of Motion Picture Arts and Sciences, and the Museum of Modern Art Film Archive who were of such help in assembling the film illustrations. Victor Ingrassia, of the slide library at the University of Southern California School of Art and Architecture, once again put his fine skills at my disposal and furnished some of the other images.

Finally, deep and perpetual thanks are especially extended to David St. John, Molly Bendall, Peter Manning, Jane Tompkins, and Jerry McGann, who gave wise and open counsel about the separate sections of the manuscript and the shape in which they could best appear.

Los Angeles L. B.
April 1990

Contents

Introduction   3

I. Principles

Popular Culture and Personal Time   13

Succeeding in Language   26

Being a Teacher   37

II. Authors and Audiences

The Rise of the *Auteur*   43

Hitchcock, Truffaut, and the Irresponsible Audience   51

Maidstone: A Mystery by Norman Mailer   60

Stargazer by Stephen Koch [on Andy Warhol]   64

The Double Detachment of Ernst Lubitsch   67

III. Body and Text

Fanny Hill and Materialism   79

Zola on Film: The Ambiguities of Naturalism   95

Lexicography and Biography in the *Preface* to Johnson's *Dictionary*   107

Daniel Defoe and the Anxieties of Autobiography   111

A Genealogy of Mind [on Susan Sontag]   126

Adulation and Revenge   132

IV. Fictions of Feeling

Providence, Paranoia, and the Novel   137

Penetration and Impenetrability in *Clarissa*   152

The Form of the Sentimental Novel   169

Edward Gibbon and "The Privilege of Fiction"   179

Mad in Pursuit   193

V. The Sway of Genre

Framing the Innocent Eye: *42nd Street* and *Persona*   201

Genre and the Resurrection of the Past   214

Newsreel: A Report   225

In the Criminal Style   230

Western Approaches   235

The Sacraments of Genre: Coppola, DePalma, Scorsese   240

VI. Myths of History

G. by John Berger   255

Grime on the Glitter: Hollywood and McCarthyism   258

We Are Your Sons by Michael and Robert Meeropol   262

Regiment of Women by Thomas Berger   265

Winter Kills by Richard Condon   268

The Difficulties of *Little Big Man*   271

Afterwords

Democracy and the Humanities   279

California Criticism: From Tweed Jacket to Wet Suit   288

Credits   292

Index   295

NATIVE INFORMANT

When I make an interpretation, I always watch my dreams to see if they agree. If they do, then I know that the interpretation is as good as I can make it—that in relation to my own nature I have interpreted the material satisfactorily.

MARIE-LOUISE VON FRANZ, *Interpretations of Fairy Tales*

. . . the confession of incapacity which in polite studies is the only authorized way to claim capacity; the forbearing to insist as the only polite tone of insistence.

RAYMOND WILLIAMS, *Writing in Society*

Introduction

I am an American, Philadelphia-born—the third city when I was young, now sunk. My father's parents came over from Eastern Europe and Russia in the late 1890s, and my mother's in the early twentieth century. My parents were born here and, aside from going to synagogue for family ceremonies and a few inescapable holidays, they practiced an essentially secular Judaism. Most of their closest friends were gentiles and my mother never made an issue of keeping kosher. Although my father would occasionally say that ham or bacon just tasted bad, other varieties of pork, especially those in Chinese food, were fine. Yet I, born in 1941, was brought up with enough of a feeling about being Jewish that I had nightmares over the execution of the Rosenbergs. After seeing a picture of their sons in the paper, I asked my mother if they were going to kill the kids, too. It was a paranoia that spawned as well a desire to submerge whatever obvious ethnic identity I retained into the multiple worlds of American culture. I went to the movies constantly, and the polio I contracted at four, pre-gamma globulin and pre-Salk, made me a reader as well, unable to participate in any sports requiring the strenuous use of legs, sitting in my chair on late summer afternoons, as the shouts of my friends on the way to the park to play touch football drifted up from the back alley.

My father was a civil engineer and the first in his family to go to college. But he retained a deep suspicion of higher education and somehow thought that I should become a businessman and make a family fortune that the Depression had put out of his own reach. His dream even included a change of name, from the frequently misspelled and mispronounced "Braudy" to something clearer, and he would sketch the "Broad E" logo of this unspecified business in the quick strokes of his blueprint-trained calligraphic style.

But this rarely spoken yet deeply felt vision of who he thought I ought to become could not compete with my own eager embrace of a world of books, movies, and rock and roll. Much to the disgust of my father, who was given to sarcastic asides about the "perpetual student," I wanted to make the contemplation of these pleasures my profession. In other words, I wanted to be an English teacher. He threatened that if I didn't get a scholarship I couldn't go to college, and he constantly pointed out how poorly teachers were paid. Underneath his anger, I now wonder if there wasn't also a sense of defeat before some new version of the enshrouded talmudic scholar his own more active life had rejected. For my own part, I hardly knew what being an English teacher really meant, aside from its being an official passport into a world I already had entered as an amateur and an enthusiast. The heroes of my high school crowd were George Orwell, Edmund Wilson, and Albert Camus, with a touch of Jack Kerouac and Lenny Bruce. What I wanted to imitate in this unlikely pantheon was their passion for thinking, observing, experiencing, and understanding the world through language.

Teaching English has always been to me the most protean of academic disciplines. Most of the arguments over the decline of the university, literacy, and the generally educated American finally come down to the study of literature, which usually isn't what the commentator thinks it ought to be—as defined by his or her undergraduate education. Yet in each era it has meant something different. In the 1950s and 1960s much of that undergraduate education in literature was concerned with the need to define specializations and boundaries, canons and exclusions, all in a misconceived effort to make humanistic truths resemble scientific ones and thereby seem more eternal. Neither the observer nor what was observed counted for as much as the method of observation. It was an activity comparable to that of a physician who doesn't know or care whether his patient is male or female, tall or short, black or white, so intent is he on the abstract generality of cure.

In the face of an older style of literary criticism that emphasized social snobbery and noblesse oblige, this approach did boast an energetic egalitarianism about the powers of thought. But I could not get over its falsity to my own experience of the many realms of the aesthetic. What was considered worthy of being discussed as well as the terms in which discussion had to be carried on seemed equally unrelated to the pleasures that had drawn me into the study of literature at the start: the mysteries and slippages in the aesthetic rather than its accessibility to orderly analysis; its status as a ground of conflict within culture, the place of negotiation and argument. I thought then as now that "both/and" was a more alluring approach to art than "either/or." Without believing that questions of relative value were empty, I was more interested in problems of inclusion than of exclusion. It's easy to have good taste if you have high standards. The challenge is to have good taste with low standards.

The literary critical orthodoxy of the 1950s—an emphasis on the work itself and the empirical demonstration of its value—reflected a basic trend in American education. The belief that specialization meant professional progress had been gathering steam since the organization and rise of professions in the nineteenth century. My father's personal decision to study engineering at the University of Pennsylvania in 1921 had echoed a century-long democratic hope that numbers and technology could erase the inequities of the past. Similarly, my own undergraduate study at Swarthmore almost forty years later was still part of the aftermath of World War II, which brought an enormous influx of new people and new groups into the university. Even more than in previous eras of careers open to talent, academic training and advanced degrees in the 1950s represented an escape from one's personal history through a professional training that was in effect essentially uninterested in speaking to a general public.

In this world where impersonal "scientific" knowledge was the prime goal, usefulness was often considered an intellectual blind alley. Replacing the personal tones of the general practitioner with an impersonal tone of voice defined the specialist as merely the instrument of his or her own knowledge. In the search for truth, "I" was too assertive, a throwback to a sloppier and more intellectually willful world. Warmth and enthusiasm undermined the critical faculties, and so had to be banished from literary discourse. Somehow a passive voice, an invisible critical presence, would be untainted by the distortions of ego. "I believe" was to be replaced by "all men of sense and judgment agree."

That such a phrase substitutes an illegitimate but Godlike authority for the corruptible personal reference was somehow overlooked. Its goal was to embody an ideal of intellectual victory not only over social marginality but also over physical and emotional frailty, and its heroic texts were Hume's writings on empiricism, Freud's introductory lectures on psychoanalysis, and A. J. Ayer's *Language, Truth, and Logic:* rationality and a positivistic approach to experience were the only stay of individual freedom.

Such standards were necessary because without them the self was adrift, prey to its demons and its past, ready to be snared by every spellbinder who came along. On the one hand historical study was barely tolerated, and on the other few academic literary critics thought that much could be learned from popular culture. In the cold light of professional analysis, such study was assumed to be either trivial or escapist—material for the sociologist and social psychologist, but not for the student of literature. Words were to be our armor against the assaults of both invisible and visible demons. Some critics even considered an interest in art history suspect, let alone a taste for movies or television. Only the verbal could be truly complex.

But I had brought myself up on movies, comic books, trash fiction, rock and roll, as well as the classics and whatever else I could find. Now contemplating a career in literary study, I wondered how I fit into this world that seemed to reject virtually everything that had nurtured me. I wondered how I could write about what interested me without either asserting that my own experience was the sole criterion of value or banishing it from consideration altogether. Was it possible to acknowledge a personal perspective as the armature of connection without either affirming a falsely coherent self or rejecting the existence of any reality—call it history, spirit, the unconscious, or what you will—outside the individual perception of it? During my student years I felt isolated because I favored both feeling and history, and later—during the vogue of structuralism, semiotics, and other critical theories—because I believe that character and personality still mediated language and experience. My urge was to express an empathy and sympathy for what had been usually considered the anomalies and contradictions of culture and art rather than the roster of classics recommended by the more impersonal and rational method. In my engagement with the reader or the student, I didn't want to minimize my special knowledge and interests in the subjects. Yet I also tried not to forget that I was someone very like that reader: curious about the general meaning of this special knowledge, uninterested in handing down authority from above, willing to give up a Mosaic pipeline to the truth for a sensitivity to the mosaic of variety and difference.

While I was in graduate school, and later when teaching at Yale from 1963 to 1968, these untested attitudes assumed firmer shape, as my individual interests tried to come to terms with the practical need to establish my professional credentials. Yale in those years was virtually synonymous with the New Criticism and its polemical emphasis on the literary work as object—in Cleanth Brooks's metaphor "the well-wrought urn" and in W. K. Wimsatt's "the verbal icon." (I explore these literary attitudes and their impact on someone who wanted to be an English teacher more fully in "Succeeding in Language.") Yet at the same time many of the students and the younger Yale literature faculty were passionately committed to both reading and interpretation not only in class but in the outside world as well: arguing about the movies, transposing ideas of pastoral to baseball, denouncing the distortions of language in the official version of the Vietnam War.

But these passions were not what you received degrees or were promoted for pursuing. In the face of an academic division of labor that defined certain subjects as not real knowledge, I wondered again if it were possible to draw upon both my training and my enthusiasms, my particular interests as a specialist and scholar, along with my curiosity as an amateur and general reader. Like many of my friends, I found it difficult to separate what I was writing from the life within me or the life around me. This doesn't mean that what I wanted to write was mere autobiography, as if that could exist. But I wanted to find an angle of personal vision that might also engage others, in the way that my mother was always noticing strange cornices on old buildings otherwise unnoticed by the walkers in the streets below.

In 1968 I left Yale for a job at Columbia. It was a movement toward New York (where my first wife, a free-lance journalist, could find more work) and to a university noted for a faculty who could combine a social perspective with the most rigorous intellectual analysis. As at Yale, however, where the New Critical public image quickly dissolved to reveal people like Martin Price and Eugene Waith, whose definition of literature I found much more embracing and congenial, so at Columbia I discovered that people like Lionel Trilling and F. W. Dupee in Columbia College looked down on the more scholarly professors in the Graduate School as narrow-minded, while they were themselves dismissed by their antagonists as superficial journalists. Neither side of this argument seemed totally convincing to me, although I was overjoyed to be in a place where trying to write for a larger public wasn't automatically considered intellectually suspect. I stayed at Columbia until 1976, when I moved to Johns Hopkins, which was then at the center of the new methods of interpretation that were swiftly dethroning the New Criticism. In 1983 I moved again, this time to the University of Southern California, a university similar to Columbia, with its face turned more directly toward the challenges of a complex urban world.

In retrospect I realize that this pattern of emphasizing first the intensity of literary study as an academic discipline and then its expansiveness as a way of looking at the world has been the source of most of my intellectual energy. The great burden of our world is information. All our obvious triumphs in knowledge and understanding seem to have made life more and more difficult to grasp as a whole. In the midst of this incoherence, we may wonder how we ourselves cohere and make sense of what we see around us in present, past, and future. What is our own competence as native informants—about ourselves, our world, and our place in it? We "know" so much more than any society in human history. Yet all our knowledge seems only to have deprived us of the sense of at-homeness in the world that is the birthright of the most primitive tribe. While most of our professions surge onward to greater refinement, we have culturally lost the ideal of the general practitioner who had a spiritual as well as practical relation to those who consulted him.

The process of professionalization leads to the hardening of boundaries, emphasizing procedures rather than content or context. Its sense of mastery comes from contemplating objects isolated from their connection to the rest of the world. As Edward Hall remarks in *Beyond Culture,* "modern classification methods provide me with a lot of information that is difficult to integrate into a usable, intelligible pattern." Too much commerce with the outside, goes the implication, and you warp the purity of the phenomena you ought to be only observing. Usually this detachment is considered to be the exclusive property of academics, who turn away from the real world. But in fact it is potentially true of all professions. Every locksmith tends to think the world is made up of people who have either lost or broken their keys. The tunnel vision of professionalism proceeds from the assumption that there is too much that is irrelevant going on; let's clear the decks.

In line with this definition of expertise as insulation, one of the most intriguing intellectual phenomena of the past few decades has been the flight to monocular points of view. To protect the experts from the annoying discovery of variation and change, the search is for the restrictive pattern, the single issue, by which all can be explained and all processed. Desperate for a quick fix, bureaucrats tell us that the teaching of a canon of great books or a list of cultural catchwords will balance the professional necessities that force teachers to concentrate on "advancing the field." But they ignore the importance of a more embracing perspective on what is to be learned and how. Minimalism as a movement in contemporary art has some of the same quality: an effort to renovate the vision and validate the profession by making the work pure and uncontaminated.

My own prejudice is obviously toward more contamination. I have always enjoyed reading books in other fields—anthropology, political theory, social history, art history especially—to take the kernel of general ideas and let the chaff of special pleading and professional chitchat go. Similarly, even before I began writing and teaching about film, I was not able to separate my interest in film from my interest in literature. Nor can I readily tell what medium came first in directing my attention to particular problems or fascinations. The study of eighteenth-century fiction helped me formulate questions about narrative and characterization that guided me in the study of film, although perhaps it was the experience of film that raised those questions to begin with. Literary study had a well-established tradition of interpretation and analysis, but film and television offered instances and contexts that sharpened those questions immeasurably and introduced issues of affective structure, the social collaboration between maker(s) and audience, and the shaping context of cultural expectation. Both eighteenth-century fiction and twentieth-century film are popular forms that not only successfully meet a cultural need but also may stand apart from that contemporary context to become "classics." And in both, the issue of canonized greatness—what purpose is served by the institutionalization of aesthetic value?—is crucial. Just as the older, more internally self-justifying theories of film form were opened up to generic questions of intertextuality, economic questions of studio influence, and biographic questions of career, so theories of literary production came to acknowledge more frankly the inspiration they have received from models of film production, with their intricately tangled webs of art and commerce.

In my cultural see-saw, minimalism's twin is therefore collage and assemblage, where the artist for the moment sweeps everything from the closet onto the canvas. The crucial link between these extremes—the intense and the expansive, the purified separation from distraction and the indulgence in it—may be autobiography. Oscar Wilde once said—I may be misquoting—that literary criticism is the most sincere form of autobiography: most sincere, I suppose, because the critic, in contrast to the autobiographer, denies having an explicit design on the reader's self-awareness. He therefore seems more likely to tell the truth, unlike those artists who give more interviews than they complete works.

But the danger in such displacement is that it may still involve selling the work as an inferior version of the self, a distinction whose implications Wilde himself discovered were neither so simple nor so benevolent. Without the focal point of personal perspective, expertise becomes stultifying; without the material of reality, "autobiography" becomes self-indulgent. A better version of the synthesis is proposed by Oliver Sacks, only one of a number of people in many fields who are trying to bring the language of professional learning in touch with a larger human context. As Sacks says in *The Man Who Mistook His Wife for a Hat,* "We have, each of us, a life-story, an inner narrative—whose continuity, whose sense, *is* our lives. It might be said that each of us constructs and lives, a 'narrative,' and that this narrative is *us,* our identities."

Some of the fruits of my own version of this search over a period of some twenty years are on display in what follows: a group of essays, lectures, and reviews about contemporary culture, eighteenth-century literature, and the movies that are held together by some constant themes and by the fact that I wrote them all. The earliest was published in 1968 and the most recent in 1989. I have not changed anything materially—except for obvious inaccuracies, tangle-footed moments in arguments, and some sentences whose length or rhythm I could no longer live with—because I wanted to keep the essays in their own time and context, as part of a continuity of thinking about issues that for me are deeply related.

During the time these shorter pieces were written, I published several books whose preoccupations are intimately connected with them. First came *Narrative Form in History and Fiction* (1970), a study of the histories of David Hume and Edward Gibbon and the novels of Henry Fielding that argued the connection between the ways the historians and the novelist tried to make a story of human events, and the difficulty of making any absolute distinction between their methods. Written between 1966 and 1969, it was heavily marked by its era's characteristic meditation on the place of individual will (as actor, observer, storyteller) amid the supposedly impersonal forces of public history. At one point I wanted to dedicate it to Norman Mailer and William Sloane Coffin, Jr., but it wound up being dedicated to my parents and my first wife, while I later put together an anthology about Mailer's work (1972). After *Narrative Form* came two books on film, first *Jean Renoir* (1972), then *The World in a Frame* (1976); a short anthology dealing with François Truffaut's *Shoot the Piano Player* (1972); and, in 1979, a coedited anthology called *Great Film Directors,* and a long essay for *The Harvard Guide to Contemporary American Writing,* called "Realists, Nautralists, and Novelists of Manners," that tried to make sense of the immensely varied tradition of American fiction since World War II that could not be characterized as ethnic or regionalist, feminist or fabulist.

In 1986 came *The Frenzy of Renown: Fame and Its History,* on which I had been working for about ten years. In it I explored how the historical styles of fame in Western civilization have varied according to the political system, the available media, and each culture's idea of a perfect person. The history of fame was a human-centered continuity undermining the assumption that impersonal political, economic, or social factors were the primary causes of historical change, as well as the excessive emphasis placed on individual will in "great man" theories of history. Instead of a heroic molder of history, the famous person was a heightened version of every individual's effort to mediate general forces; and *The Frenzy of Renown* was similarly an elaborate gesture of professionally responsible amateurism, in which I tried to trace the history of fame across a variety of disciplines and eras in all of what Marie-Louise von Franz might call its "chronic manifoldness."

As I read over these pieces of writing, with their different occasions and intensities, I am therefore struck by how often I am drawn to the border where artistic forms impinge upon each another, and to works that define themselves against the "classic' and the "masterpiece." Sometimes they break the traditions of detachment and autonomy by introducing autobiographical impulses; sometimes they experiment with forms of popular entertainment that employ repetition and pattern and genre; sometimes they bring into art the unwritten and the unpremeditated as ways to connect with an audience itself unpersuaded by premeditation. "The Form of the Sentimental Novel," for example, situates the beginnings of this subversive potential in the growth of an eighteenth-century popular audience looking for literature that acts upon the feelings and sensibility rather than on the mind, while "*Fanny Hill* and Materialism" shows how a work usually perceived only as "pornography" accomplishes its effort to stir through a distinctive polemic about the nature of character and identity. "Popular Culture and Personal Time" explores the way in which television and the kinds of stories it tells influence our understanding of both public and private history, while "Succeeding in Language" meditates on the history of the academic study of literature conceived as suppressed autobiography.

Just as some of these essays overlap with the longer works, so a few of the essays themselves overlap, with sentences even migrating between them. I haven't pruned these few repetitions because I feel they emphasize the interconnectedness of my concerns. The great lie of the professional essay is that it makes its typographical linearity seem like a necessary causality of ideas. But in fact, ideas develop in many different directions. My own interest is in exploring surprising continuities, constellations of relationship between ideas. Part of that exploration involves searching for new forms of expression, more suggestive than limiting or defining—sparks to strike the reader's mind rather than a solid argument to enclose it permanently in language. In this effort to stand between the scholarly and the amateur, then, many of these essays are aslant from specific concerns of the discipline of literary studies, although rooted in a literary perspective, while others are more demonstratively "professional," although infused with themes of general relevance. Many also first saw life as book reviews—which I have always found to be a good place to try out ideas—where one can be suggestive without the burden of being exhaustive or conclusive. Accordingly, I have divided the collection that follows into several major topics that cut across areas of literature, film, and cultural analysis. Within each section the pieces are generally in chronological order, although that may vary as well. All have common elements: the nature of genre and the familiar in art; the interrelation of authors and their audiences; the reflective relationship between the book and the author's own body and character, which lie behind it; and the double effort to control through art one's own feelings as well as the history that swirls around us, authors and readers alike.

There are two essays in progress that might bind these others even more firmly together. One might be called "Character in Fiction and Film." It is based on a 1979 lecture I gave in the wake of teaching an NEH Summer Seminar. The thesis of both seminar and lecture was that the development of the presentation of character in the history of film closely paralleled that in the eighteenth-century English novel—a coincidence that suggested a general paradigm for how an art form views the interconnection between "innate" human nature and its social display. The other would be an essay on the prevalence in American culture for the last ten years or so of a quest after the meaning of innocence, the redemptive quality of the primitive and the natural, that is reflected in films and fiction, as well as in such social issues as the environment, genetic engineering, increased sensitivity to child molestation and abuse, and abortion. But neither is complete yet. After this effort to pull together in retrospect what in prospect had no single goal, I am waiting to see how they will turn out.

I
PRINCIPLES

Popular Culture and Personal Time

I feel somehow fraudulent writing on the question of culture because I have never been formally trained in the analysis of culture, like an anthropologist or a sociologist, nor do I know deeply enough any theory of culture to be willing or able to adopt a systematic view of its nature. Furthermore, most of my academic training has been in the study of literature, notoriously the preserve of so-called "high" culture, whose canons and standards have been under attack for the way they arbitrarily designate certain works and certain ways of understanding those works as true culture, while calling everything else low, ersatz, or false.

My credentials for writing on behalf of popular culture, therefore, are roughly equivalent to those of anyone else: I live in the world and therefore can hardly be immune to the rush of movies, television, radio, newspapers, magazines, posters, advertising, T-shirts, department store displays, graffiti, and all the other fragments that make up the culture of immediacy. Therefore, as any of us might, I self-consciously nominate myself as native, if not naive, informant.

Implicit in the concept of culture is the position of separation from what one studies. The awareness of the observer has become one of the chief investigative clichés of the present and is often dealt with by a pro forma piece of epistemological autobiography that poises uneasily between ignoring the author's presence and quantifying it as a cautionary maxim: "my personal nature should be kept in mind as a possible variable in my interpretation of what I study." Yet the desire to interpret is itself rarely questioned, nor is it usually the focus of study, unless we are contemplating past interpreters in order to exhibit their biases or attraction to certain kinds of interpretation, often without much sense of what those biases allowed them to see.

Most varieties of interpretation, because they are aimed toward posterity, present themselves as calmly aslant from the cultural moods of the present, their surfaces unruffled by the awareness that later interpretive generations will see their obviously close connection to the general trends of their times. I take the anthropological view of culture, at least as an amateur like me understands it, to be the basic model of this detachment. That view is virtually predicated on a looking outward from the observer, *at* something, in the same way that, by necessity, we view the cultures of the past—assuming that their inhabitants, no matter how perceptive and articulate, cannot be aware of the cultural array the outsider will be able to discern. Thus opens the familiar wound of observation that is nowadays bandaged with methodological self-consciousness, although in the eighteenth century it could be magisterially ignored by Samuel Johnson: "Let observation with extensive view, / Survey mankind, from China to Peru."

But if anything distinguishes the study of popular culture, it is its habit of teetering between external description (and sometimes theory) on the one hand and internal sympathy and emotional connection on the other. The study of popular media and entertainment is preeminently the kind of cultural study, or at least cultural awareness and apprehension (in both senses), in which the interpreter is a part of what he studies. It implies a perception that one's own world can, with a slight crossing of the eyes, be seen as exotic—in the same way that artists and writers suddenly realize that the immediate world around them, what is most familiar, can be turned into art. So Hogarth brought together the artistic tradition he had been taught with the world he saw, and so Norman Mailer discovered in James T. Farrell and other novelists of the 1930s the possibility of a literature not then part of the Harvard undergraduate curriculum.

The study of immediate and popular culture is therefore not so much an objective witnessing, marred by personal involvement, as it is an introspection and a witnessing intricately paired. It thus appeals very much to someone like me, who tries usually to wrestle together a theoretical habit of mind with a descriptive, empirical, and generally nontheoretical sensibility. Anthropology itself, again as it appears to the sympathetic observer, also has become much more sensitive to such problems. In a totally unsystematic way, I mark out several phases. The first is exemplified by George P. Elliott's 1958 story "Among the Dangs," in which a struggling black academic anthropologist periodically revisits a South American tribe to exploit for his career their belief that he is an inspired prophet. In the next phase, which I will localize in the late 1960s, a graduate student in anthropology at the University of Chicago decides to take the somewhat daring step of writing her M.A. thesis on drag queens. With some hesitation and embarrassment, she finally approaches one that she believes will be sympathetic and begins explaining the project and anthropology itself in some detail. "Sure I'll cooperate," he interrupts, "I was an anthro major at U.C.L.A." By our own time, of course, sociology and anthropology freely mingle, and the study of popular culture has become prominent. Thus we move through the contemplation of the exotic, the anthropologist himself as an exotic, the exotic contemplating himself, the contemplation of the exotic features of one's own culture, and finally the study of what is familiar in one's own culture—with the possibility of making it unfamiliar and exotic. Each stage in a different way explores the connection between interpretation and cultural power, and each takes another angle on the problem of the observer, not by banishing him or relegating him to a footnote, but by making him a sympathizer, a co-conspirator in the study itself.

Because the kind of interpretations made in the name of the study of popular culture so often deal with immediate phenomena and trends, they are easy targets for either the long-view cultural interpreters or up-close journalists who dismiss them as "pop culture" or "pop sociology" and, perhaps soon, "pop anthropology." The long-viewers are upset by the lack of interest in "lasting value" and the canon of great works, while the up-closers resent academic poaching on what they consider to be their private domain. On one side, then, poor pop gets it from the more measured and detached grandfathers, and on the other from the more engaged and nuance-obsessed sons. Yet the lure of focusing one's interpretive abilities, fostered by the analysis of cultures very different from one's own, on the more emotionally laden phenomena of the present nevertheless has some historical justification. The preoccupation with the present, the search for its patterns, and the exposure of its imagery are recurring compulsions. I associate them with cultural moments—like England and France in the late seventeenth and early eighteenth centuries, or the end of Republican and the beginning of Imperial Rome—when the signals are unclear and cultural self-awareness becomes the prime way to get control over events. Such control can be exerted by rulers and artists who self-consciously manipulate and create an imagery of syncretism and coherence. But the impulse to control is also expressed by that kind of control all critics uniformly favor, the control we call interpretation. When there seems to be no cultural coherence, only an oppressive weight of accumulation, self-consciousness presses forward. The edges of forms are searched to discover where they end and what lies beyond them. For the central questions at those moments are: where does cultural authority now reside, and what are the signs, images, tracks in the snow by which we can know it? At such times, mistakes of interpretation—if "mistake" is ever a word usefully applied here—can occur honestly or purposely. The point is rather that the effort has been made.

The study of the popular and immediate culture around us thus allows a unique emphasis on the way culture in general *moves*, rather than the usual preoccupation with its static patterns. Images are effective so long as they can be reinterpreted, even in the most seemingly contradictory ways. Culture in this perspective is not a group of related images but a search for such images and the stories to hold them together. If, as I think, we are now in a floundering or fermenting period, then our interpretive relation to our own culture requires that we investigate the mechanisms of its changes of direction, the breakdown of old images and the growth of new. But I must confess that most theoretical models evolved by the study of popular culture do not help me to understand my own culture any better. So much of the interpretation that takes place in a discipline or a department called popular culture is in fact just stray shots—the discerning of motif, the explication of iconography—the spadework of cultural archaeology, dusting the fragments while we wait for enough time to perceive the edifice (or its rubble) as a whole. Some writers concentrate on the producers of popular culture and others on the audience. But it is success that binds the two together in an ongoing negotiation. Yet both Marxist theories of cultural production and semiotic or structuralist theories of cultural reception, as well as the more literary or art-historical arraying of imagery, invite the reader to stand outside the chaos. The rule of thumb of cultural interpretation, like most species of interpretation fostered by an academic discipline, is to search out coherences and coordinations. But how often does that habit of mind blind us to the flux of imagery and its different degrees of solidification? Perhaps I am looking for the impossible, an understanding that allows both detachment from and involvement in the culture that swirls around us. But I would like to see if some attention to the present might revive the militantly premeditated definitions that preoccupy the study of popular culture. Like many theories, at least in the humanities, they too often seem primarily designed to offer conceptual stencils for the unimaginative but professionally eager graduate students to process whatever comes their way. In much of what follows, therefore, although the urge to generalization is strong, I will speak in the spirit of two of my favorite titles for academic works: Erwin Panofsky's *Studies in Titian, Mostly Iconographic* and W. K. Wimsatt's "In Praise of *Rasselas:* Four Notes (Converging)."

❏   ❏   ❏

In times of cultural crisis, the interpretation of culture frequently presents itself as a species of storytelling. A group of stories that appeared towards the end of the seventeenth and the beginning of the eighteenth centuries so much summarized the essential story of how an individual tries to understand his own culture that they have remained with us in the form of children's tales. I'm thinking about John Bunyan's *Pilgrim's Progress,* Daniel Defoe's *Robinson Crusoe,* and Jonathan Swift's *Gulliver's Travels,* as well as those stories designed for children but springing from the concerns of adults, like Charles Perrault's *Cinderella* and *Sleeping Beauty.* In part such works extend earlier efforts—by Rabelais, Montaigne, Robert Burton, and others—to create a book that mediates in some way between the individual assembling it and the vast pile of cultural material on which he has been nurtured; or, as in the case of *Don Quixote,* they may seek to resurrect from the rust and ashes of the present the formerly glorious age of gold to correct a world that has ignored and therefore fallen from its ideals.

But the three later English works I mention above also share the common feature of being first-person and pseudoautobiographical. The focus of each narrative is very different: Christian's journey to the Heavenly City, Crusoe's tale of survival on a desert island, Gulliver's tour of a variety of maniacally plausible societies. But all continually underline the belief (validated by their success with their readers) that an individual story makes sense of the world by the exemplary coherence of its perspective. And that point of view is precisely most useful for taking a distance from one's home culture, in order to hew a personal coherence out of what otherwise appears as a jungle of competing cultural authorities. Bunyan's Christian must wend his way through the many lures of life in a very recognizable section of rural England, constantly alert to what lies beneath the individuals and places he sees and constantly attuned to the significance of their "true" names in the spiritual order of the universe. His interpretation therefore aims to cut through the oppressive variety of secular culture and individual nature in order to find the straight line of sacred truth that will lead him to his salvation. The shipwrecked Crusoe, on the other hand, despite his preoccupation with God's providence, discovers not that culture is only a phantom, but that neither culture nor religion requires a geographic still point, a peculiar language, a national identity, or any group of social institutions into which the individual must fit. Culture is as portable for Crusoe as the tools he rescues from the ship and as personally valid as the ability that he finds within himself to make a boat, build a barricade, bake bread, or fight a war—just as Socrates' slave boy discovers he already knew the Pythagorean theorem. Gulliver similarly sets sail for exotic ports, but, unlike Crusoe, he concludes his journeys by coming back to England, where he purifies the message of his experiences into a rod to chastise national immorality. Like an inept anthropologist (or is a social satirist a proto-anthropologist?), Gulliver sees in other cultures only those aspects that can favorably or unfavorably be compared to life at home. His increasing isolation as the only man who has been able to see and make those comparisons finally drives him to the exclusive company of horses. Christian rejects culture in order to affirm religion and find God. Gulliver is obsessively burdened by the cultural impurities he discovers in himself and demands a moral cleansing of his homeland. Crusoe discovers that an accommodation between religion and culture can be made within himself that facilitates his personal freedom, unbounded by the historical institutions of either religion or culture.

I summon up these three still familiar works from the dawn of the modern period because once again we seem to be in similar straits, with kindred interests in the individual processing of cultural data and in the personal witness of events, with kindred uncertainties about the relation between personal and social identity, spiritual integrity and public fame, and with a similarly paired urge and inability to decide what our culture is and where its authority may be in the crowd of petitioners all waving projects, poems, world views, and their precious selves for our judgment, attention, and fealty. The air is filled with faces and voices who aspire to mediate for us with great events, famous personalities, and the meaning of existence. Everyone is a member of many audiences, and there is no movie star left who was not once a fan. Yet still there is an urge to coherence, which such mediators never satisfy, a seeking of the story that will tie all this together or at least allow us to trace a calmer path through the many stories spun out every day.

Ever since shortly after the Second World War, we have been in a period obsessively intent on telling stories to itself about the connections of the world and in search of crystallizing images by which to embody and subdue its complexity. The academically trained students of culture do it in one way, the teenagers who thought they had discovered Paul McCartney's death through minute "clues" do it another, and the Cold War politicians, fundamentalist preachers, and Hollywood scriptwriters only begin to embody the variants. While high culture was destroying its traditional genres and avant-garde theater was breaking the proscenium and virtually every other formal assumption, national and international life were aching to return to the unities. Paranoid stories have especially taken center stage as the most visible and the most popular, because they are the tightest and most logically and aesthetically satisfying—what the mathematicians would call the most elegant solutions—comprehending the largest number of actors, events, and objects in the least amount of time and space. The corollary of such elegance is that the construct is believed to exist in nature and society rather than at all in the mind of the constructor. Relief comes from the pattern in which the interpreter is the center. Structure in art, theory in interpretation, paranoia in psychological life—all express, and frequently with benevolence, a hypersensitivity to variety and the innumerable tugs at eyes and elbows for attention that is characteristic of the modern world. Paranoia particularly is an extreme version of the desire to control by story, to find the right order for information otherwise confusing and overwhelming. In American culture at the present I would say that there are two prime ways of achieving that order—the single story forever true and the continuing story always evolving, the mode of the significant moment and the mode of the endless narrative—catastrophic time and soap-opera time.

❑ ❑ ❑

The Second World War decisively dramatized both the individual's obligation to make sense of the world and the impossibility of ever finally doing it. I was recently on a panel that playfully, but with an undertone of anxiety, discussed the question "If something like a modern-day Vesuvius buried the United States, what would our excavators find?" Ever since the 1950s science-fiction novels and films, and now "futurologists" as well, in the process of projecting the future, have also implicitly wondered what about the present will still resonate after we're all gone. In the past, if you did not live in the area of fighting, war was a dim echo, fought by special groups on mutually agreed-upon days. But modern war is so total that it rips across the continuity of history, unmistakably affecting entire cultures even at a distance, and incessantly proclaiming that Vesuvius can occur in the next ten minutes. And, unlike the Vesuvius of the past, the man-made disaster to come will neither freeze nor preserve, but destroy entirely.

Yet soothingly enough, in the wake of the Second World War, there also appeared television, a technology that had previously been available but awaited refinement until its enwrapping continuities were suitable to the culture at large. Not that television became itself immediately. Like all new shapers of cultural imagery, it carried with it (and still does) innumerable allusions to previous forms, particularly films and theater, and it owed much to the general formats of radio and vaudeville. But it heightened these precedents enormously, and by now its infectious way of structuring imagery and experience has become our dominant national mode. This is what I've called soap-opera time—ongoing stories that absorb all drama into an endless unraveling of relationship and event. There are no crucial moments, or, more accurately, there are many, many crucial moments. But such moments do not structure the action in terms of any Aristotelian beginning, middle, and end, or rising and falling action, or any other of the narrative formats so amply repeated in the literary criticism of the 1930s through 1950s. Stories in soap operas have innumerable crises, but all those significant moments are subordinated to the format of continuity itself.

Beyond its actual soap operas, situation comedies, and variety shows, television presents culture, public event, and even character itself as collage, complete with interpretation attached. Without the penumbra of television's ceaseless cultural curating, it would be hard to understand a "high" art situation like the installation of Larry Rivers's *History of the Russian Revolution* at the Hirshhorn in Washington. Around this work of intricate mixed media construction—covered with books, photographs, portraits, newspapers, words, maps, guns, and more—is a detailed en horror films become welcome treats for the fan, and fright, as on the Six 'Clock News, becomes another variation of familiarity. Unlike earlier horror ms, whose endings often featured the dawn of a bright new day, many of the rror films of the present leave the viewer inside, the horror for the moment gone t obviously not for long. Sequels will come. Yet the knowing audience is more illated than afraid. If in fact there is any pure genre still afoot right now, it is e genre of self-consciousness about genre, the genre of accummulation and collage. There the knowing audience allows the flattery of its interpretive sophistiation to compensate for its emotional indulgence in the aesthetic experience. It atefully accepts the badge of professional in one's own culture, and soap opera sorbs catastrophe once again.

❑ ❑ ❑

have spoken of the knowing audience. But there is another audience that militntly does not want to be numbered among the knowing. Its members are not nknowing, but with similar self-consciousness they reject the whole movement ward a continuous unfolding of history, the reduction of sharp edges between rms, and the belief that there is no canon but only a group of constantly shifting xts of equal or of no didactic value. The group easiest to spot in this audience , that which calls itself the Moral Majority, and, as I have said, what interests e most here about its members is their conception of time. In the face of the ovement toward soap-opera time, they seek to specify significant moments, significant events, and at least one significant text. Like their frequent companions, e antievolutionists, they want to return to the catastrophism of the nineteenth entury, because it emphasizes the crucial intervention of God in history and therefore akes individual action significant. In place of the multiple authorships and unertain authority of the present, they seek again the single author, the single cretor, who validates man's favored uniqueness. In place of the layers of genre selfonsciousness, irony, and endless revaluation, they establish the single, literal iblical text: at least one work will have a different status from all the rest. And, s antiabortionists, they assert similarly that life begins at one special moment, efore which it did not exist and after which it cannot be threatened. If the mother or any reason rejects this created life, it would be as absurd as if God, having reated them, rejected man, woman, and the world together. For the believers in atastrophic time there are beginnings and ends, but no middles; significant moents but no connecting history; no change or growth, only the possibility of eing born again.

Irony is therefore anathema to them, and their recent public agitations indicate deep antagonism to the growth of a culture without clearly significant moments, ital texts, or unquestionable imagery. In response, the Moral Majority and their ellow travelers have attempted to fill seemingly empty sociocultural universals ike patriotism, marriage, and the family with their own discontent, each pressing orward to be the representative, intermediary, and interpreter who will make sure hat every aspect of American life corresponds to his version of divine authorship. Often such people are cultural terrorists, for their beliefs about time precisely mirror those of political terrorists, who think that once one man is killed, then

explanation of what the painting means and how the artist put it together. Burdened by information, walleyed with the volley of competing ideologies, Rivers seeks to lead us and himself out of the maze of events by a creative juxtaposition—which then has to be explained itself. The impulse seems purely modern. In the late sixteenth-century portrait of Sir Henry Unton, now hanging in the National Portrait Gallery in London, the events of the subject's life, his achievements, and the procession of his death surround Unton himself. It is a sufficient message to his family, to his friends, and to posterity, and the National Portrait Gallery's annotations are clearly a modern addition. But in Rivers's work the surrounding annotations are meant to be part of the meaning. *History of the Russian Revolution* has no central figure, no clear focus of meaning, nor does it follow older historical painting by dramatizing a crucial moment of history. Instead, it is like a novel, or an essay on its own engendering, a textbook to be studied and explicated with the help of the right curators. Everyone wondered why Nixon tape-recorded all the conversations that occurred in the Oval Office, no matter how potentially embarrassing. But embarrassment is a question of audience, and Nixon was no doubt biding his time for the right curators to come along. With facts and opinions piling up everywhere, who can be sure what future generations will think is significant and what disposable? Better to record everything.

Writers for newspapers and magazines still try to assert that a certain event is the most important, most significant, etcetera, of modern times, history, the last twenty years, etcetera. But this is the vestige of an older interpretation of history that is disappearing in the face of the realization that, while there may be upsetting or sad or happy or joyous events, there are really no central events anymore. The biggest news items of the last ten or fifteen years have all been ongoing stories— the Vietnamese War, the economy, the hostage crisis, the conflicts in the Middle East—that have forced both print and visual journalists to reorganize their techniques. By calling such a narrative and epistemological approach to events soap opera, I don't want to minimize its importance, only to point to what I think is the prime model for the change. The soap-opera perspective is valuable because it undercuts the confrontational and hero-oriented view of politics and history by reinforcing the endless interconnection between plots rather than any simplistic causalities. By depicting a world in which there are many small victories and defeats but few absolute or final resolutions, soap-opera time enforces a more complex view of how events actually occur. But its success can also be the danger it poses. It increases our understanding even as it decreases our scope for action, simultaneously inviting and then deflecting involvement by ''wrapping up'' the ''big story'' for tonight in the smiles and weak banter of the pseudofamily of the Eleven O'Clock News (so reminiscent of the multiethnic patrol in movies made about the Second World War), after which—if you live in Baltimore—you are told ''That's what friends are for'' and ''Channel 13 likes YOU!'' The interpreters have done all the work for us. Soap opera, like interpretation in general, domesticates even as it complicates.

Television itself, of course, is the arch soap opera, an unending envelope in which everything is covered both immediately and retrospectively, in specials, reruns, revivals, and rebroadcasts. Like its ancestors, radio and vaudeville, television maintains a constant level of high energy by trying to introduce discrete acts each at the top of their professional polish. And television, even more than radio, has elaborated what is perhaps vaudeville's greatest contribution to the shadowy intersection of economics and aesthetics—the continuous performance, the brainchild of Benjamin Franklin Keith (the K of RKO), which made its immediately successful debut on July 6, 1885. Commercials seem to disrupt this continuity, but actually are the training grounds for irony, returning us to the show at hand with newly sensitized layers of reaction. Sometimes it is a challenge to figure out what is in fact being advertised; it takes so long for the demure product to appear. More quickly than the actual programs, commercials pick up new techniques and imagery for their own uses. Shortly after the inauguration the friendly druggist who recommends the right deodorant began to resemble Ronald Reagan (the product, of course, was ARRID), and recently someone strongly resembling Alexander Haig has been standing in front of a map of the world and telling me to get the same kind of protection against burglars that world leaders get against terrorism.

The usual attack on television for its homogenization of experience therefore misses the real importance of television's constant contextualizing of virtually everything. In the 1940s and 1950s the beginning of each chapter of an adventure serial would shift our point of view slightly to show that the fatal end of the previous chapter wasn't so bad after all. Tarzan didn't really fall directly into the river with a thousand alligators; he fell into a part of the river where there was only one or two that he could polish off easily. Now, however, in the constant serial world of television, we are told it's exactly as bad as we thought it was last week. But it's not the end. Science-fiction novels and films of the 1950s would often feature a scene in which a television face or radio voice, professional to the last, would sign off by saying "this is it, the end of the world." But if that last gasp of journalistic integrity could have been envisioned then, it can be no longer. There will be no apocalypse on television. "The whole world is watching" means "join the show." There is always another program, another season, another bridge of music, voice, and computer graphics to make the audience feel it is not alone in the void. Virtually every aspect of television experience can be reexperienced, if some audience has liked it sufficiently. There are no ends in television, only cancellations, and even they may be rescinded.

With video-tape recorders, television can also now be stored for future consumption, one show watched and another taped at the same time. What can possibly be appealing in having more television to watch? Perhaps it is the lure of selectivity itself, which television has brought into being. The process of sifting and assorting that takes generations and centuries in the growth of historical culture takes hardly a decade in television, and the medium has begun to honor its roots barely thirty years after they were planted. This process has created an enormous sophistication of formal appreciation in the television audience, most markedly in the forms of international and domestic public events, even though it is television that is usually attacked for pouring events into such forms. After Anwar el-Sadat's assassination, for example, the fact that he was not nearly so popular

or respected within Egypt as he had been in America was news [to] United States audiences. But it also formed an important part of the re[ality of his] assassination. Thus the disparity between image and reality—itsel[f a staple of] television reporting and the prior fitting of Sadat into the Great State[s narrative] became part of the next generation's definition of the great foreign [leader who,] to all appearances, well understood how to deal with the media [when they] were available. But the media themselves were ready and eager [to find a] knowing employer of their means. To talk about the media manipu[lation in] the Kennedy or Nixon Presidential races could ten years ago seem [a revela]tion. With Carter and Reagan the manipulation itself became part [of the news,] just as soap-opera audiences are invited to immerse themselves in [the intricacies] of the *Dallas* plot even as they watch Larry Hagman on talk shows [discuss the] nature of the character he plays or read fan-magazine articles abou[t what] ("J.R.") Hagman is really like.

The audience that can appreciate all those nuances without the [self-]conscious twitch has become skilled in forms rather than content, or [(to depart] from that ancient and ill-founded distinction) skilled in the content [and forms] that come from an internalized awareness of the rapid variation and [play of] cultural forms. It is an audience that thinks of itself as *knowing*, an [audience that] is in on the ironies of the relation of performer and character, and [of the] relation of plots behind the camera to plots in front of the camera[, for] which the medium congratulates itself and its audience for being [in the charmed] circle. The irony generated by such awareness is not savage or sati[ric,] just as it is in recent Hollywood genre films. For this formally sophi[sticated tele]vision audience has influenced filmmaking tremendously, until we hav[e what] could be called a genre bombardment, in which past forms are repea[ted] and revaluated not to purge their effect but to envelop the audience [in them.] Films generate sequels because their stories, built on a core of chara[cter, never] really end. Thus, in the case of *Star Wars,* we have a film that seems [to be set in] the future but we're told is set in the past, and seems to be self-co[ntained but] we're told is the middle section of an array of interlinked stories. Ma[ny such] genre films are, of course, produced and created by men and wome[n versed in] the literary critical strategies of the 1950s and 1960s, and so it is not s[urprising to] find them making films and television that include a tone of ironic[, knowing] distance as part of their format. In the 1950s no horror film required th[at you had] seen other horror films; that experience might enhance your appreciatio[n and help] you to interpret the film, but it wasn't necessary. Now, every horror[, science-] fiction or other genre film virtually insists that you be aware of preexi[sting forms] so that you can savor the particular film's relation to its tradition. In [this respect,] as in the supposed resurrection of traditional political values à la Reaga[n, the past] weighs heavily on the present, either because it has been ignored or [because it] has been treated too seriously, with the requisite distance and irony. B[ut this au]dience's beliefs as well as its ironies are always superior to those of the c[haracters.] Such viewers are not necessarily wiser or closer to "reality." They ar[e merely] only more learned in film form and thereby adept practitioners of an unself[-conscious] detachment that is neither satirical nor demystifying but oddly consol[ing.]

something decisive will happen, to themselves and to the world. People who assassinate are the ultimate believers in hierarchy and heroes. Muddled by the examples of the past, they believe that by killing or attacking individuals, they can change the system. There is no past or future, no history or continuity, only the white-hot crucible of immediacy and apocalypse, now and forever. Thus the desire of the Moral Majority to pressure television stations and sponsors to keep sex and violence out of their shows seems to be not an essential part of their ideology but the hangover of an older puritanism with which they would honorifically like to associate themselves. Of course it does imply with what attention the Moral Majority's target audience watches television, and their view of its essential importance to the fabric of national culture and virtue. But in terms of their concept of time, violence on television is much more suitable to the fundamentalist view of the world. It is the enwrapping, soap-opera context of television itself that they should more logically be against, for these are people who take prime time seriously.

In this distinction between the catastrophic and the ongoing view of time, I believe we can glimpse something of the variety of present reactions to the question of cultural authority, particularly as the search is carried on in popular culture and in reaction to it. In cultures whose traditions are wrapped tightly into history, the conflict may arise as well. But in America, a culture assertedly born not from history but from the brow of nature, the conflict lies always just below the surface. A friend of mine is a social worker in a clinic for schizophrenics. One day a man appeared carrying a suitcase and asking to be admitted to the program. "Can you tell me why you think you have a psychiatric problem?" asked my friend. "I can't tell you, but I can show you," he said, and opened the suitcase. Inside was a collection of significant objects precisely arranged: a picture of the man's son, a book called *America in the 80s,* a small statue of Ronald Reagan, and many others. This was his brain, he explained, and the suitcase was his effort to keep in in order. "Where do you live?" asked my friend. "I live in my car," he answered, "1971 Buick Drive." A few days later he returned with yet another collage of his life, an enormous chart of all the American presidents and significant dates in American history, interwoven towards the end with events from his own life. On the back of the chart he had first assembled and then pasted permanently together a jigsaw puzzle map of America.

This man was simultaneously trying to solve America and himself, or to solve himself by assembling America, through the most advertised emblems of his immediate culture and the most celebrated facts of national history. Together they would help him connect his own disheveled life with the great American story in a coherent personal myth. Like popular culture itself, he was searching for a group of personal symbols and images that would yet be valid to others as well. But even in the midst of his search he also very self-consciously considered himself to be suitable material for attention in a mental hospital.

One of the most intriguing and peculiar elements of American identity is the extent to which it pretends to be a nonsocial concept, as if each person were Crusoe on his island, bent on spawning a world of his own. In such a mood, the American owes nothing to tradition, beginning history for the first time in his country and his own life, the past, like the present, at most a suitcase of images. But the urge either to leave the world behind, as does Bunyan's Christian, or to lash ferociously its shortcomings, as does Gulliver, is also strong. Culture in America has less of the historical in it than the pastoral, and those attempts like *Roots* to validate a particular culture by its historical continuity often have ambiguous results. Authenticity in America comes more often from passion than from history. As Emerson wrote, *"Do you love me?* means, Do you see the same truth?" Thus popular culture in twentieth-century America has become a medium of emotional exchange: since we both like Humphrey Bogart, we probably like each other. Are we therefore caught fatally between the debased social pluralism of soap-opera time and the asocial and millennial purity of catastrophic time? Or is there some way to merge soap opera's inclusive exuberance with catastrophe's sensitivity to moral significance and utopian promise?

Of course every group has its own ideals as well as its own vision of what America is, and recently many literary critics have been busily at work dismembering the idea of a canon of generally approved works. But often they attack the old hierarchy in order to promote new members. In the proliferation of popular culture, we might see instead a redefining of that hierarchy itself. To what end, I am not very sure. Today, in the same movie or television show, we can observe both a wallowing in past forms and a skepticism about them, an homage and a cannibalistic destruction. We are now, I believe, in the process of completing an important period of culturally spawned cultural evolution, which when it faced outside America might be called imperialism, but when it faced inside could be known as the New Deal, the GI Bill of Rights, feminism, and so on. In the floundering that typically follows a period of such wide-reaching and energetic changes, many retreat to what they think of as older, simpler values, while others plunge even further into the sea of troubles, just as the Reagan administration seems to be the worst possible combination of soap-opera smarminess with catastrophic adventurism.

But, to the extent that popular culture continues to stage and restage everyone's conflicting visions of America, it supplies the occasion for insights very unlike the codified and canonized perception of traditional "high" culture. Even at its most rudimentary, it embodies the prime possibility for community among the descendants of many older cultures, whose moments of nostalgia are expressed through ancient popular songs, the personnel of old films, and sports statistics. When such information is exchanged, momentary warmth and even friendship arises as well, and for the time it seems that there is a unified American culture after all. This is the great legacy of the 1960s, which is most apparent in the interest in popular culture—the refusal to exclude any subculture as "not American," the insistence on reforming and reshaping America into something like her ideal form. In the cultural enfranchising of so many groups who surged forward to demonstrate and demand their place in the creation of America, popular culture with its constant assertion of pastoral individualism played a central role. Its saving grace was and still is its own uncertain depiction of the individual trying to step back from his world and make some personal and perhaps public sense of it. Like so much about popular culture, this too takes us back to the beginnings of

America, and the ambiguous interplay between the child of Nature, justified by merely being American, and the member of the Elect, who can never be quite sure that he won't discover that the voice of God in his ear in only an echo of his own.

[1982]

Succeeding in Language

Pedagogy is the queen of all the arts, but in teaching we unavoidably must use an enormous amount of words as go-betweens, which creates confusion, because those who listen must transform the words into concepts and ideas.

COMENIUS, as quoted by Roberto Rossellini

More words, and then nausea.

INGMAR BERGMAN. *Persona*

. . . Hello. Duffy's Tavern, where the elite meet to eat. Archie the manager speakin'. Duffy ain't here. . . . Oh, hi, Duffy, I didn't know it was you.

ED GARDNER on the radio show *Duffy's Tavern*

When I was in graduate school studying English literature at Yale University from 1963 to 1967, I often thought of myself as a football player, huddled over my precious cargo, facing a line of granite-chested bruisers. Beyond them was not just the goal, but the outside, and I was determined to break through, taking the punishment on my head and shoulders, looking up every so often to check directions, preserving whatever it was I carried within my arms until I could set it free.

Since I never played football and rarely watched it, the image could itself run free, until it threatened to become lost in its flourishes. But in those years it was constructed from pure self-preservation. "Try to run, try to hide, / Break on through to the other side." sang the Doors, and all around me, in the faces of my friends and acquaintances, my colleagues in the calling of language and literature, I could see what I hoped to evade: the despair or bravado of failure, the shell-shocked look of those who would find jobs but no comfort, and, most disconcerting, the twitching signs of success disfiguring those who had before seemed quite different. We had all come to study English through a combination of inward conviction, the insistence of favorite teachers, and the evidence of talent. Success would arise from a special relation to language and its uses, validated by the imprimatur of a university that still awarded its degrees in Latin. We were at Yale to learn, to search, to compound insight and labor into a name that would get a job—whereupon we would teach and the cycle would begin again.

Every profession, I knew, has its particular techniques and its special language, and I thought those students naive who had been horrified to discover that the literature they had loved as undergraduates had in graduate school often turned into a matter of footnotes, research, and lengthy papers. I knew already that part of my professional responsibility would be to take up what has been called, without irony, a custodial relation to language. But I was hardly more than dimly aware of the particular difficulties of a profession that had evolved special critical languages in order to discuss equally special literary languages. Nor had I yet experienced that enhanced sense of self a professional language can give, when a normal adult discovers he is faced with an English teacher and reduces himself to an insecure child: "That was my worst subject."

As a graduate student, I had little time to appreciate this power to exact instant subjection, although the status in being able to speak, master, and even teach English must not have been too far from my conscious mind, since my grandparents spoke Yiddish almost exclusively. My parents, both born in America, spoke it primarily when they wanted to talk about matters they didn't want my sister and me to understand. Far from being a childhood language, then, Yiddish to me was a language of ritualized adult control, even though the secrets it veiled were usually arguments over when we should be put to bed. But I did carry with me other languages, neither those of my parents nor those of my teachers, and, in the interpreting style at which Yale was making me expert, I identified my protected football with those solitary languages of feeling salvaged desperately from my youth, that were considered irrelevant to the struggle for professional mastery and unworthy of professional tribute: the visual–verbal language of films and the musical–verbal language of popular songs. I may have realized that *Middlemarch* meant more to me married at twenty-three than it did when I wrote a paper on its imagery as a sophomore of nineteen. But it would be some time before I could see how the language of emotional connection might supplement, correct, or contradict my new professional language. Marriage, like literature, would organize the potential disruptiveness of emotion into social and linguistic forms easily subordinated to the more pressing business of vocation. Meanwhile, alone in my room on Chapel Street, I sat at my typewriter, a plug in my ear attached to a small portable radio, Fr. Klaeber open before me, translating *Beowulf* with the Beatles singing in my head.

Once again, the image crystallizes a time of defensive self-containment, when a comforting solipsism both complemented and tried to allay the forced atomization of graduate school itself. Appropriately enough, Old English (required then) was the only class first-year students took in common, and therefore the only ground of cooperation and community. Otherwise, New Haven was a world of library carrels and tiny apartments. I have since been told that, whereas the typical scientists looks back on graduate study with fondness and warmth, the typical humanist remembers only isolation and anxiety. While the embryonic scientist can enjoy the camaraderie of the laboratory, where teachers and students may even work together to create a group product, the budding humanist, in a discipline celebrated for its ability to transmit history, tradition, and "shared values," discovers a world of sharp and fragmenting competition. But the only difference may be that scientists must face later what humanists find out almost immediately, unburdened by impractical longings for collegiality and intellectual openness.

Initiatory rituals are of course a feature of all professions and many occupations as well. But how seriously one takes them should be determined by the extent to which they advance or erode the ostensible values of the profession. In the nineteenth-century evolution of professions, the founding of professional societies aimed to define who was a member, who was not, and how the change in status was to be regulated. The raising of professional standards answered well to the Napoleonic formula of careers open to talent, even while it also allowed the policing of charlatans, the ostracizing of failure, and the restriction of titles. Somewhat earlier, Samuel Johnson may have spoken slightingly of "the shelter of academic bowers" in his preface to the *Dictionary*. But he did not reject the protection his honorary degree might give him from the anxiety of eighteenth-century intellectual free-lancing

Anyone who spends even a small amount of time in professional training begins to learn how intimately the power of a special language to define, and thereby to cure or solve, connects with the power to intimidate, and the authority of professional knowledge acquires a social dimension, where vocabulary implies class as clearly as does any Back Bay or Main Line accent. The intimidation is enhanced by the extent to which the professional views his special language as a kind of superself, an authority beyond the frailties of the immediate, a costume of eternity the otherwise inadequate individual can don and thereby escape his unpremeditated and merely personal vocabulary. To dwell on a word, to invent a language for talking about words, is to insist that your audience admit the deficiency of their own language (and their reality). Only then can they begin to measure up to the transcendent standard that you have defined but which, you must imply, exists apart from you in some rarefied common room, where the Forms take tea.

Although I have been talking about professions in general, I have in the last sentence strayed again into the special problems of the profession of literature. It is of course the profession that I know the best. But also, by its special commitment to the study of language, it can provide a focus for the ways in which all professions fortify their borders and consolidate their social and economic positions by codifying their languages. Academic disciplines, like professions, are tribes in which everyone believes in the importance of the same set of terms, but insists on wrangling endlessly over their meaning. To the extent that the terms are literally the same, the field has an ethics or a theology; to the extent that they must be continually redefined, the field has a politics and a history. The language of the academic literary critic, like the language of most humanistic disciplines, contains a group of words to be endlessly vexed in the attempt to reconcile their ambiguities, in much the same way that Edmund Leach has described the genealogies of the Old Testament as a framework within which otherwise rigid definitions of who is Jewish and who isn't can be effectively qualified. The irreconcilable urges are toward comfort and toward adventure. New people are inducted less because they are perceived to be capable of treating the field or tribe politically or historically—and therefore capable of change—than because they are perceived as being innately of the same sensibility, speaking a birth-language rather than an acquired language. The manufacture of new terms is therefore always a political act.

Before World War II, in the humanities division of the most prestigious institutions (and many farther down the ladder), one either spoke some approximation of the birth-language or one couldn't get in the door. Those nongenealogical humanists whose origins were outside the university definition of the acceptable classes had therefore to tailor their manners, style, and speech to the traditional form. Later their ideas, their personal energy, and even a small portion of their new language might get a hearing, once an acceptable professional image had been established. But a process was beginning in the 1930s, then urged quickly forward by World War II, that was reminiscent of what happened in eighteenth-century England, when outsiders like the Catholic Alexander Pope, the Irish Jonathan Swift and Edmund Burke, the Scots Tobias Smollett and David Hume, the non-Londoners and nonaristocrats Laurence Sterne and Samuel Johnson, began to teach the English about their heritage, history, and values. Instead of justifying cultural authority through lineage or wealth, they in their different ways insisted on a continuity and community of cultural sensibility that owned little to economic or political power and might even be opposed to them. If this tradition were traced to its roots, one would also see parallels in the way men as different as Dryden and Richelieu helped create a cultural climate in which literary history could be considered an alternative source of values in the face of a declining aristocratic tradition. Already within its own history, literary studies in the 1920s and 1930s had responded somewhat petulantly to the sciences by asserting the possibility that its methods and conclusions could similarly be codified and therefore "objective." In a related effort that first gathered strength in the more socially conscious 1930s, professors of literature defined their mission less in terms of the analysis and interpretation of specific texts than in terms of the values they were preserving and inculcating by the mere enterprise of teaching literature.

After World War II this interlocking emphasis on linguistic analysis and moral interpretation, energized by the admission of new people from new classes to the American university system, helped raise a defense of literary studies against any charges of conceptual archaism, historical irrelevance, or slackening social authority. In great part the presiding Zeus of the transformation was Samuel Johnson, not the Johnson who said that no one but a blockhead writes except for money, but the Johnson who through both his life and work implied that writing, the control of language, could preserve the writer (and thereby help him preserve his culture) from the willfulness and self-indulgence of aristocratic culture. To rise in class through one's mastery of language meant first to identify with the language and concerns of those whom one was joining and of necessity with the ethics of interpretation that language implied. But birth was no longer a criterion for interpretive accuracy. The glory of the postwar period in literary criticism was its insistence that special knowledge and privileged background were insufficient and even irrelevant to the discovery of meaning in literature. Johnson had amassed his own *Dictionary,* and we all had the OED. Everyman his own interpreter was the message. All worked individually, but all also worked implicitly toward the common verifiable end of the "complete reading."

But how does one recognize and distinguish the authentic inheritor of a tradition from the con man? The public horrors and propagandistic verbiage of World War II had brought in their wake a revulsion against language pressed into either the service of the state or the interests of demagogic individuals. In a manner reminiscent of the period after the English civil wars of the seventeenth century, postwar literary criticism attempted at once a greater precision of language and a new affirmation of timeless literary values. Pedagogy, in the form of the spellbinder or "great teacher," had traditionally used the trappings of classical oratory, and the new rhetoricians just as traditionally dismissed the orators as manipulators without any convictions of their own, suspect because they used language to persuade rather than to clarify. So, in their classic essay of 1954, "The Affective Fallacy," William K. Wimsatt and Monroe C. Beardsley included in their gamut of villains both Hitler and William Lyon Phelps. The style of self as part of the content of presentation was ruled out for both author and critic. Only by deemphasizing the self in the classroom could the democratization implied by the New Criticism be effective. The enemy to truth was personality, the excrescence that American etiquette had always been out to cure in the rising new classes. Now that literary study had been effectively separated from its class roots, the new autonomy required an etiquette of interpretation as well. If intellectual ability were to be translated into social mobility, some separation from one's prior languages was still needed, a willingness to be molded at least visibly into the preexisting forms of the chosen profession. The most important postwar development in academic politics was therefore the increasingly strong allegiance of the professor to his field rather than to his university. Scientists had long had such connections; humanists, aided by their new professional self-definition, were learning how to assert them. But the assertion of profession required the submergence of self. Class was to be shed in the service of the classroom, and along with the costume of self-effacement went an insistence on the "purity" of the play of ideas, a turning away from politics and toward ethics. The only spellbinders who might be acceptable were those who cloaked their language in the rhetoric of objectivity, withdrew their presences, and implied that their results could be verified and vindicated in the carrel of any student who cared to try.

New Criticism especially made this detachment a principle of interpretation. The self-contained critic would contemplate the self-contained work. If, as Hobbes had argued, without language there would be no society, then the mastery of language might hold off the barbarians at home and abroad, as well as repress the untoward and antisocial impulses from within. For the best practitioners, of course, mastery of language and mastery of knowledge were twin ideals. But as the new ideology was disseminated, the pose of pseudoanonymity and pseudo-objectivity became more pronounced. Verbal analysis, it seemed, could keep the text under a control that was impossible if one allowed affective responses. By making critical language more specific and dispensing with any ambiguity that could not be encased as "tension" or "irony," the linguistic pattern was praised at the expense of other, less specifiable, modes of connection. E. B. White has remarked that "a good many of the special words of business seem designated more to express the user's dreams than to express his precise meaning."[1] For literary study in the postwar period the dream was often a dream of precision, in which linguistic power would replace social power, and the prerogatives of a class would be transformed into the privileges of a profession. Words clarified, specified, ordered, and arranged. Self-enclosed, "sufficient" formal interrogation could discover secrets emotion could not, because, while feelings were always the same and primitive, intelligence and language evolved. Johnson had said that he was so upset by the end of *King Lear* that he could not bring himself to read it a second time until he came to edit it. So too the New Critical faith in the superiority of the work to its fallible creator concealed a fear of the power of art and its ability to excite the imagination of the reader and upset his carefully composed sense of self. The validation of the power to determine the meaning of literary language had shifted decisively from social lineage to professional commitment. But the implications and paradoxes of that new power often remained unexamined.[2]

The democratic faith of New Criticism accorded well with the general postwar fascination with both documentary evidence and religious belief. "America is a political reading of the Bible," announced an article by Richard Nixon, while at the other end of the spectrum of public politics Edward R. Murrow created a series called *This I Believe,* in which a variety of Americans formulated their personal testaments. For the nonbelievers, empirical philosophy, with its positivistic and depersonalizing mode of analysis, emphasized verifiability of interpretation. Thinking and believing occupied their mutually exclusive and mutually dependent universes. In this Pyrrhonist world, only feeling had no coterie. In 1950 my fourth-grade teacher spent many classes explaining why we should avoid *I* in expository writing. In 1964 a graduate-school teacher corrected "Thomson feels that" to "Thomson thinks that" and commented in the margin, "Poor fellow. Doesn't he know how to think?" Together the encouragement toward the passive voice and the primacy of thought were meant to subdue the ego and bow the head before truths larger than the individual. But in retrospect they seem less pure, like the operations of those priests who know that levers behind the statue can make the god roar. e. e. cummings was celebrated in the 1950s for his playful use of language and the small letters with which he wrote *i* and his own name. With similarly back-handed assertion, analytic and objective criticism was creating impersonality cults as elaborate as the belletristic charismas of the past.

Under the democratic marquee, where intelligence was the only price of entrance, stood an increasingly long life of aspiring professors. Once inside the precincts, however, they discovered that the proud claim of the purity of true knowledge barely veiled a competition for preeminence in areas of learning and literary theory that were increasingly opaque to all but the proto-professional. The democratic impulse of the GI Bill was no match for the occupational mystique of the literary scholar, which "was calculated to appeal to a powerful scribal minority, for whom linguistics still had a strong tinge of exclusive magic, and the very fact of literacy alone symbolized knowledge, authority, power."[3] In the manner of late-arriving torchbearers, the new initiates often showed their commitment by elaborating the ritual. Power was defined as the influence over word usage and word interpretation. Language therefore became at once more sanctified and more remote. Like the scholar–pornographers of the nineteenth century, such critics claimed both the privilege of being closest to the sacred material and the burden of denaturing it for the faithful who would be unable to face it without screens of critical terminology and antiquarian learning. Like the elaborate system of pulleys by which technicians handled atomic material, the literary criticism spawned by the cold war maintained life by staying at a distance.

Once the study of literature takes on the trappings of religion, then the choice of critical language becomes a moral issue, with its cults and heresies. When the critic–teacher defines himself as the master of language, then the reader–student becomes a tentative, woefully unprepared novice in the mysteries. If he falters for a second, he will not only fail to understand, but also prove himself unworthy of the time taken to instruct him. Since the time of the democratic and deindividual-izing etiquette of the New Criticism, the intellectual hegemony of American lit-erary criticism has passed through many capitalized phases, including Archetypal Criticism, Structuralism, Semiotic Criticism, Reader Response Criticism, Decon-structive Criticism, and other poststructuralist hybrids. In an important sense the field of literary study has become more permeable to perspectives and terminology from a host of other disciplines: anthropology, linguistics, philosophy, economics, art. But with this seeming intellectual expansionism has come a narrowing of vision that preserves the old hierarchies and continues to recast new energies into the images of their adoptive forefathers. New critical formal analysis, in its effort to release literary criticism from the socially restrictive sensibilities of the past, had set the stage for the professor of the humanities to reassume his emblematic social role as a representative of "Western civilization." By banning ideology and personality from the concerns of literary criticism, the investigators of literary language had created new ideologues of their own.

But, while the New Critics at least assumed that there was a writer who had presented them with the opportunity to create a critical language that excluded the writer's importance, later criticism would attack the "illegitimately privileged" text itself, complaining of a sanctity that was unearned and authoritarian. The only necessary person was the critic who, like Berkeley's God, validated what he saw because he saw it. Saying that a literary work was a "text" allowed such a critic to manipulate it for his own ends, to create from it his own text, more privileged because more detached—the iconoclast in his turn creating, or becoming, an icon. New Critics may have assumed the intelligibility and therefore the specifiability of literary language, while many of their descendants now assume its final unin-telligibility. But they are the optimistic and the pessimistic sides of the same well-rubbed coin, a critical solipsism that may indeed be the necessary first step away from the undue pressures of society and history, but should hardly be the last. The secular priesthood Coleridge had called the "clerisy" clearly appealed to those who had grown up on movie-nurtured images of the professional as an isolated moral hero who faced alone a hostile or indifferent town. As French critics already knew, and American critics were ready to learn, those who wish to be part of a romantic outlaw group of the truly moral must first create an argot which the leaders will recoin at ritual moments: woe to the counterfeiters, outer darkness for the uninitiated.

In the hierarchies of the anointed, success naturally implies succession. Al-though the postwar emphasis on critical depersonalization led the way, it does seem appropriate that the schools of the newer criticisms have arisen in the past ten years, at a time when the baby boom of the war years has passed through the university. With a newly contracting student population, the university itself was changing, the open field for academic jobs that characterized the period from about 1950 to 1970 was increasingly crowded, and the competition becoming more cutthroat. The possession of one of the new languages therefore offered to the graduate student an efficient passport to security. Although his own thoughts might be inchoate, and what he wanted to say or contribute uncertain, his sense of where the professional winds were blowing might accompany but hardly required intelligence, understanding, or accomplishment. Professional language, critical jargon, could supply the necessary stilts to get the ambitious student over otherwise baffling hurdles. The process may not substantially differ from the traditional way the apprentice entered a profession; yet the social mobility that previously had been the reward of talent and intelligence was now often bestowed for the possession of a hermetic and ritualized vocabulary into which the world could be processed. The student armed with such a language could sell himself as the newest product of a literary profession that seemed more akin to an industry or a business, in both its standards of analysis and the social behavior of its practitioners. Efficiency was the watchword: the efficiency of landing a job by an efficient method of interpretation that employed a preexisting terminological framework, to such separate but equal ends as teaching language by computer or analyzing literature by decoding.

The concept of profession, with its emphasis on merit and a coherent body of knowledge, has, since the beginning of the nineteenth century, had a key role in the creation of both the opportunities and the barriers of the modern world. But when professions define themselves as priesthoods interested primarily in their own perpetuation, they can irretrievably stunt both their social and their intellectual vitality. Much insight has come from the efforts of those who took the study of literature away from the sole possession of a genealogical elite, and revealed its mysteries through a language literature itself rarely spoke. But more damage results when critical and interpretive language becomes so self-adoring and self-perpetuating that it offers its audience few if any new ways to open up or expand the understanding of any particular author, work, or period. Still laboring under the imperatives of postwar retrenchment, American literary criticism has distinctly failed to help bring cultural insight up to the level of the political, social, or economic insight available in the worst popular magazines. The benefits that have come from the concentrated investigation of literary language and procedures have rigidified into a variety of competing authoritarianisms of interpretation. The specificity of literature and its potential to deal with ungeneralizable situations are faced and often defeated by the critic's desire to extract generalizations that testify to his moral nature and professional insight. The writer's desire to create a work that is unique and intense is faced and often defeated by the critic's desire to "raise" its importance by showing how similar it is to other works or to point out that its real subject is criticism and interpretation.

To the extent that contemporary literary criticism has replaced a social elite with a language elite, it has confirmed and extended the worst aspect of the old hier-

archies, institutionalizing an exclusionary view of knowledge that brandishes sac-
erdotal metaphors of initiation, mystery, and the passing on of the flame. Generalization is an essential part of the humanistic enterprise. But it should not be
forgotten that the very nature of humanistic culture is in its incompleteness, its
basic unwillingness to come to an end in its attempt to describe and to understand
the possibilites open to human nature and human understanding. Those professions who pride themselves on their sensitivity to language have an obligation to
distinguish between the generalizations that intensify meaning and those that dis-
place attention to their own systems of incantation. *Theory* originally means "to
take a view of" and *theoroi* were at first tourists who traveled to view the local
celebrations of another city. Later, it is true, they had become official sacred
emissaries, although one might assume that they did not view disdainfully, whatever the provocation, unlike those acolytes of professional language who are now
sent out from the great centers to bring the message to the barbarians.

To the more common proposition that professions combine a practical theory
with an ideal of service, William J. Goode has added a third element: the necessary trust between "client" and professional.[4] In these terms, although medicine
is considered by sociologists to be the model profession, it is teaching that relies
much less catastrophically and therefore more pervasively on bonds of social trust.
The teaching of literature intensifies even that situation by its preoccupation with
the way emotions and personal energies have been shaped by language and embodied in a variety of verbal forms. While the scientist may rule emotion out of
his studies by definition, and the social scientist include emotion in order to quan-
tify it, the student of literature considers it his prime subject matter—the emotions
and thoughts of the past as they have been preserved for us by language. Lawyers
connect us with social norms, doctors with the demands of nature, and clergymen
with the realm of the spirit. But teaching—including the teaching of law, medicine, and theology—tends to deal with the variety of human languages and how
to understand them and their relation to each other.

Of all the academic professions, literary criticism especially labors to steer between a flexible and an authoritarian use of its special language, between an open
and a coercive attitude toward its subject matter. When the demands of professionalization create not teachers but salesman for special languages that will supposedly unlock the doors of employment, the atomization process I first experienced in graduate school will have become the norm. The sensitivity to language
will not have made teachers of literature like Odysseus—able to speak to anyone
in their own language—but like hermits, each desperately peering from his professional enclave.

Authoritarianisms of all sorts flourish on the isolation of their subjects. It has
been a phenomenon of twentieth-century life that the increasing professionalization of work has created a society in which economic and psychic hardships are
freely visited on those outside the pale. But democracy in our world seems less
and less to be the flatly egalitarian order that so many of its proponents and its
detractors claim than a vital context in which a growing number of groups display
their languages and make their demands. Since, in each of us, a good many of
those groups overlap, is it possible that autonomy and interdependence, like Duffy

the forever absent owner and Archie the garrulous manager, need each other for definition?

Language is the prime tool by which we understand the world, and the process of statement, correction, and adjustment is endless. Since it is an essential part of the social role of language specialists to teach how language unexamined becomes language as authoritarian truth, it seems hardly worthy that so many critics and scholars merchandise their own languages as stencils for the world. The privileges of the literary text are less dangerous than the privileges of the text about the text. Literary criticism needs as much replenishment by experience as does literature itself. Those who follow the professsion of language should be less concerned with mandarin restrictions and distinctions than with creating a situation in which all languages might have equal entry and be subject to equal scrutiny. Otherwise the teaching of language and literature will have taken up a somewhat shorter place in social history than that of manciple. The learning of language, as Odysseus knew, is both an exploration of self and a journey through the world, a series of successive releases from the authority of static gurus and self-important oligarchies. The way in which, since World War II, special languages have first helped to insulate and then to stifle literary criticism may show us what elite learning in a democracy might be, rather than what it has been: not a self-protective professional group with little sense of its relation to the rest of society and its languages, but a special group among many special groups, each with its training and its goals—ours to describe the struggle of language to articulate without controlling, and to foster a creative uncertainity amid competing truths. But when the categories of literary criticism ignore the emotions without which their patterns do not work, they create a self-contained process in which the critic discovers only the pattern of his own confinement. Writing, even writing about language, can be as much a response as a purification, for discrimination hardly requires the invocation of absolute hierarchies of moral and aesthetic value. Too often the fate of warriors has been to become inseparable from their armor, frozen in the stances of battle. Professional and personal defensiveness may make it difficult to unhunch one's shoulders, even after the ball has long since been carried across the line.

[1980]

Notes

1. William Strunk, Jr., and E. B. White, *The Elements of Style,* 3rd ed. (New York, 1979), p. 83.

2. Compare, for example, Arthur Engel's remarks about the effort of the Tractarians in nineteenth-century Oxford to establish teaching as a lifetime career rather than merely a prelude to the clergy: "They saw that power was in the hands of a tight oligarchy of heads of houses, most of whom were hostile to their ideas. The Tractarians therefore wished to undermine the power of the present rulers of the university, while still preserving its autonomy." "Emerging Concepts of the Academic Profession at Oxford, 1800–1854," in Lawrence Stone, ed., *The University in Society,* vol. I (Princeton, 1974), p. 319.

3. So Peter Green, in an article about classical studies, describes the survival of humanistic edu-

cation in rhetoric and linguistics from the late Roman Empire through the Middle Ages and into the Renaissance. "The Humanities Today," in Peter Green, *Essays in Antiquity* (London, 1960), p. 4.

4. For a concise statement of Goode's views, see "The Professionalizing Occupations," in *Professionalism and Humane Values,* Columbia University General Education Seminar Reports, vol. 4 (Fall 1975): 97–104.

◻

Being a Teacher

For me at least, any worry about the future of the humanities involves three areas: the future of individual values, both moral and aesthetic, in a mass culture; the future of the teaching of those fields of knowledge usually called the "humanities"; the future of the cultural critic as a force within society and culture.

I say "for me" because I also believe that understanding any of these issues necessarily involves some awareness of the relation of individuals to their own sensibilities as well as to the culture that helped form them. One definition of the role of the teacher in the classroom requires the ruthless exposure of fallacies of student thought, and there have been frequent analogies made with the relation of critic to culture, and of the individual to society. This is the adversary definition of the intellectual that was current in the period from 1930 to 1960, with its roots in Romantic artistic isolation and antibourgeois mandarinism. In its turn it helped create the counterculture of the 1960s, where opposition often seemed more vital than synthesis, and every group trumpeted its own idea of what was truly culture, politics, arts, health, and truth.

Such attitudes were the fruit of a pedagogical tradition in which teachers, convinced of the necessary opposition between true art and the society around it, sought out disciples and protégés who could receive the message (i.e., become majors) and pass that message on to generations yet unfledged: mass culture and mass society should always be opposed; their messages and satisfactions are always degraded and degrading, always corrupt and corrupting.

Like the adversary style of teaching, the adversary view of culture need not be liberal or conservative, radical or reactionary. It is essentially an exercise in self-definition by exclusion. Of course exceptions will be made: certain films will be canonized, certain popular novelists will be shown to possess atypical value. But what persists is an image of the critic and teacher as one who conveys value by

In the spring of 1974 the Rockefeller Foundation organized several conferences on that perennial subject, "The Future of the Humanities." I was invited to attend a session hosted by *Partisan Review* and later made these observations for a symposium that never found its way into print.

notice, preserving what is inside to defend against the contamination from without.

"Cooptation" is a word that frequently comes up when contemporary politics and culture are discussed. From the Left, it refers to the inability of individuals to maintain a critical perspective once tainted by working in any way within the "system." From the Right, it usually implies their inability to maintain "true" standards of value once tainted by any connection to mass culture.

Although the implication of "cooptation" purports to be political, the meaning is essentially psychological. It assumes a conception of personal nature in which the self must sleeplessly police and repress the inconsistencies and irrationalities that threaten to destroy its fragile integrity. This Jekyll–Hyde critic does not fear his inner sexual nature so much as his inner desire for entertainment.

If, on the other hand, we consider our ideas and attitudes to be part of a constantly changing but stable self, we might define a more truly subversive and creative role for the critics and teachers, able now to criticize culture and society from within, while acknowledging their own pleasure and complicity. The minority position taken by intellectuals over the past thirty or forty years can no longer be maintained, when American society is defining itself as a collection of overlapping minorities, each demanding that we all recognize its claim as a central human and social possibility. To respond to this variety, we need to evolve a more selfish criticism, selfish in its ability to respond to all the pleasures of culture, not merely those sanctioned by tradition. By accepting a mandarin view of culture at the same time that we believe in an egalitarian view of society, we fall into the values of social hierarchy without realizing it; we assert merely that our hierarchies are better, and we become institutionalized outsiders whose opposition is tolerated only because it is so limited and powerless.

Growing from such a broadened personal response, the teaching and the criticism of the future should emphasize inclusion rather than exclusion. The teacher and the critic should attempt to improve taste and understanding in general rather than establish an elite list of "classics" as touchstones of value. Instead of defining a point of view from which all others are deficient and meretricious, such a criticism will seek to synthesize, to appreciate the mingled roots of feeling and intelligence that create all art, to move away from self-aggrandizing evaluation and closer to a more communal sense of the process of understanding.

How could such an expansive and inclusive criticism be aided by structural change? The concept of the academic department, with its careful delineation of subject matter and field, corresponds to what I have described as the exclusive view of culture. It institutionalizes barriers not only between different kinds of knowledge but also between knowledge and feeling. Pleasure is a crucial part of humanistic education, and pleasure does not exclude hard work and critical discrimination; it may even demand them more thoroughly than do the adherents of preordained and professional knowledge.

Nor does pleasure exclude history, for the imaginative understanding of the past allows the responses of the present to become more vital and free. The reader connects to the critic and the student connects to the teacher through a simultaneous appreciation of both the quality of thought and the involvement in the subject matter. To exclude large areas of culture from such a process walls out worlds of emotional satisfaction and intellectual development in the individual as well as in the culture at large. Nothing improves until self-consciousness allows us to leave styles and modes of thought behind so that we can move on to the untested and the untried. The great changes in American society in the last ten or fifteen years have not really been understood or effectively criticized (to improve rather than oppose) by the old methods of humanistic criticism. We all have culture within us. Let us allow it to emerge, and thereby make both it and ourselves into something new.

[1974]

II

AUTHORS AND AUDIENCES

The Rise of the *Auteur*

The defining characteristic of the New Wave, and its ambiguous legacy to all films made since 1958–61, was self-consciousness: of the act of making a film, of the individual film within the history of film, and of the director as the controlling creative force, the *auteur* of the film. Except for such carefully constructed celebrities as Eisenstein, Welles, and Hitchcock, the film director had previously been a kind of anonymous popular artist, hidden in the collectivity of technicians and scriptwriters, and fronted for by his actors and actresses, whose glossy surfaces simultaneously reflected and inspired the dreams of their audience. But the New Wave brought the film director to the public's immediate attention as a potential cultural hero, a Byronic adventurer whose fame, whether in Europe or the Hollywood studio system, was the reward for his assertion of personal vision against corporate repression and vacuity.

François Truffaut's *Les Quatre cent coups* and Jean-Luc Godard's *À bout de souffle* were not just first films by new young filmmakers but an insistence that films be made and appreciated in a new way. While many of the early directors of silent film had gathered their inspiration from painting and theatre, and many later directors had submerged themselves in the enclosed world of studio production, the new generation found a sense of aesthetic freedom in their love of film itself and their commitment to its special nature, history, and traditions. Whatever their various commitments to the other arts, film was the prism through which they focused their vision, the newest art and thereby at least potentially the most inclusive.

Truffaut once remarked that the only similarity between the New Wave directors was that they all liked to play pinball machines. But a more substantial kinship was their interest in film criticism and theory, their commitment to a symbiosis between theory and practice, and their willingness to detail their views at length to any interested interviewer. More than their fellow directors in other countries, they felt a necessity to explain as much as to express. Because they believed that film both included and commented on the other arts, so they could define film criticism as not just another aesthetic outpost of the humanities but the crossroads of their coherence. In their concern with both film criticism and filmmaking, they remind me of Dryden, intent not only on creating individual works but also on establishing a vital tradition in which they could take their place, with criteria by which to judge who is the authentic and who the inauthentic artist, which the authentic and which the inauthentic work. By making their concern for the history and theory of film explicit, the New Wave therefore gathered to itself many less openly ruminative directors who yet included within their films the same self-consciousness: Ingmar Bergman, Federico Fellini, Michelangelo Antonioni, Roberto Rossellini, Akira Kurosawa, in particular.

The New Wave interest in theory came naturally, since most of the new directors of the late 1950s and early 1960s had either loose or specific connection with André Bazin's pioneering film magazine *Cahiers du Cinéma,* founded in 1951, which was dedicated both to an attack on any belief in a hierarchy of the arts and to praise of those films and filmmakers that French official culture either despised or ignored. To a great extent the dust has settled on many of these battles. The brave polemic gestures of the New Wave directors—such as substituting "un film de" for "réalisé par"—have like all rhetorics been appropriated by a later generation that has little idea of either the responsibility or the content implied by such an assertion. But our own appreciation of what of permanent value was accomplished in that exciting period has now been both defined and enhanced by Truffaut's new book *Les Films de ma vie,* an anthology of his criticism from 1954 to 1973, with special emphasis on the crucial years 1954 to 1958, many unpublished essays, and a long introduction of magisterial geniality, "À quoi rêvent les critiques?"

Of all the critics turned director, Truffaut may have been the most immersed in films. In his excellent essay on *Citizen Kane* and the reception of American films in France after the Second World War, he writes of his own growth as an autodidact, leaving school at fourteen to discover Shakespeare through Orson Welles, and Stravinsky through Bernard Herrmann. Yet it is Godard who has had the larger reputation as a critic and theorist, perhaps because Godard's most recent films have maintained a difficult experimentalism that demands close study, while Truffaut's have preserved a more beguiling and therefore seemingly more trivial surface. Godard, in May 1968, renounced all his previous work and launched himself into an explicitly political and theoretical form of filmmaking. His whole air of uncompromising self-analysis and criticism seems at odds with Truffaut's relaxed manner, even though Truffaut had himself heavily participated in the agitation to reopen the Cinémathèque and with Godard helped close down the 1968 Cannes Festival.

Perhaps the time has come to restore the balance. Truffaut in fact had at twenty-two written the most influential piece of polemical writing ever published in *Cahiers du Cinéma*—"Une certaine tendance du cinéma français"—which laid the groundwork for the *auteur* theory by attacking those filmmakers, such as Claude Autant-Lara, Jean Delannoy, René Clément, and Yves Allegret, who were controlled by the literary adaptations of their scriptwriters, and praising those such as Jean Renoir, Jacques Tati, Jacques Becker, and Jean Cocteau, who, by creating their own stories and writing their own dialogue, achieved a coherent personal vision. Godard's comparable work, written two years earlier, is "Défense et illustration du découpage classique,'' an argument defending montage construction against Bazin's view that film evolved toward the long shot and the least possible distortion of natural modes of vision.

Whereas Bazin's almost Auerbachian effort to establish a realist technology for film is attacked by Truffaut because it leaves out the director's decision to construct and manipulate reality within the scene itself, Godard concentrates on the definition and evaluation of particular stylistic methods. Godard is less interested in continuity than in reaction and discontinuity, less involved in story than in theory. Both Truffaut and Godard implicitly differ from Bazin's early insistence that the resources of film are fewer than those of the novel. But for Godard film is a world with its own separate standards, whereas for Truffaut it is only a special partner in the process of artistic interchange. Truffaut is too interested in the history of film to reject his own past work, no matter what he now thinks of it. His book on Hitchcock and his recent editing and compiling of Bazin's book on Renoir seem in fact to have prepared the way for *Les Films de ma vie,* the debts to the fathers now paid in full. New theory tries to break old forms; new history tries to include, absorb, and thereby dispense with the limits of the past. Godard in his criticism refers most often to Diderot, Truffaut to Balzac.

Auteur criticism has since been criticized severely and defended strenuously, but at the time Truffaut had achieved an important effect. Aiming to destroy ''the tradition of quality'' in French cinema, he had in fact undermined the moral evaluation of style that had characterized film criticism since the 1920s. Now any style, if coherently and thoroughly expressed, could single out a film and its director for at least interest and possibly greatness. Although the implication did not strike anyone at the time, Truffaut's emphasis on the director also undermined the most popular tenet of postwar criticism: the association of expressionist style with fascist belief and realistic style with democratic belief, and the subsequent devaluation of theatre, stylization, and genre in films as similar modes of audience manipulation.

Moved by love and passion, two words that come up frequently in his criticism and that of the other *Cahier* critics, Truffaut launched his campaign in *Cahiers, Art, Radio-Cinéma, Le Bulletin de Paris, La Parisienne,* and *Le Temps de Paris* under his own name and several pseudonyms. But in *Les Films de ma vie,* we find little of the sarcasm and ferocity that made Truffaut the terror of the French film industry; in two of his favorite words, the *éreinteur* has turned to *étreintes,* the critical savagery into an embrace. A shred of his intransigent pose appears once in a brief review of George Cukor's *It Should Happen to You:* we watch the film, writes Truffaut, ''parce que c'est lui et tout ce qu'il fait est très bien.'' But for the most part such a flat assertion of value rarely appears without some fruitful application of the kind of attention a personal commitment to the work of an individual director can bring.

Les Films de ma vie contains only about one-sixth of Truffaut's total output as a periodical and occasional film critic. Most of the reviews he includes are positive, not because he wants to present a rose-colored view of the period, but because the negative reviews tend to be limited and reactive, while the positive are much more exploratory. The article defining *auteur* theory is itself not included.

(Autant-Lara is represented by two admiring reviews and Clouzot, another villain, by a more mixed one.)

A more justifiable omission, but one that would be needed for a full picture of Truffaut's thought during the 1950s, is any portion of the numerous interviews he (and usually Jacques Rivette) conducted with directors as aesthetically disparate as Jacques Becker, Jean Renoir, Alfred Hitchcock, Howard Hawks, Jacques Tati, and Robert Aldrich. By carefully excluding the most polemically time-bound of his work, Truffaut has constructed a critical self in retrospect that can stand alongside his films instead of being a ragged forerunner.

The shadow of the missing interviews especially hangs over *Les Films de ma vie* because Truffaut's theory defines itself from the first as an extraction of principles from the best practitioners, whatever their aesthetic inclinations. Unlike Godard, whose aesthetic finally becomes one of the mind mulling over theory and practice—adjusting, disrupting, and disquieting his audience by denying their expectations—Truffaut retains an openness to new films, trying to expand audience appreciation by complicating their emotional reactions as much as their intellectual ones. There is no pure film, Truffaut insists. All films, he says, whether commercial or not, are at least *commerciables,* nonexistent without an audience, however small, and so a truly responsive criticism should be able to include the most successful popular works as well as the most obviously self-conscious, crafted, and mandarin works. The intellectually pretentious film, in other words, is as false as the emotionally exploitative film; both assume audience reaction instead of trying to evoke it.

Above all, Truffaut wants to learn from films how to watch them better, how to be more sensitive to what they have to offer. And such an openness does not allow for doctrinal rigidities or theoretical preformulations. It must at the same time be as able to meet the demands of the obviously great as the less unique. (At one point Truffaut apologizes because he is writing about a film he has seen only three times.) In the midst of an admiring review of Samuel Fuller's *Verboten,* he points out that while we stand in awe of the clearly grand work of such directors as Eisenstein and Welles, we learn more readily from the less grand work of such as Fuller and Howard Hawks. The great artist is necessarily inimitable, while the great professional has much to teach audience and fledgling filmmaker alike. The "ten greatest" theory of film criticism may help to convince those who believe every true art must have a canon of acknowledged classics. But it ignores the discontinuity classics force upon our understanding, their self-sufficiency and what Truffaut calls their "homogénéité d'intentions et d'exécutions," their tendency to aggrandize themselves at the expense of the form and the tradition that allowed them to come into being.

Truffaut's own urge is therefore to look for consistency rather than anomaly, to explain relation rather than difference. He is interested in both the complicated film that finally evades a total explanation and the simple film, the fairy tale, whose strength is in the unquenchable power of its fable. Instead of worrying about the difference in "quality" between the films of Renoir and a film like Joshua Logan's *Picnic,* he is more attuned to the way they can mutually illuminate each other as well as the one area in which Logan's film may be superior: unlike

Elena et les hommes, it doesn't have to be seen more than once. Instead of following the more formalist *auteurisme* of Godard to construct for his favorite directors an ideal film against which each real film is tested, Truffaut calls upon the unity of vision that underlies *auteur* theory to help him discover an intricately connected world of subject matter, visual style, acting, dialogue, and historical context that is potentially different for every film he sees.

It is in discussing the so-called simple films that Truffaut's methods may be most rewarding, since it is precisely these films that slip by the modernist criticism used to treating seriously only those works—whether *Ulysses* or *A Valediction Forbidding Mourning, Potemkin* or *Citizen Kane*—that announce their complexity as part of their program. The *Cahiers* critics, and Truffaut and Godard especially, most showed their involvement with the special aesthetics of film most clearly when they considered genre films—the westerns, the detective films, the musicals—in which realistic materials were used unrealistically in a structure dictated less by story than by myth. Once again, when Truffaut discusses Aldrich's *Kiss Me Deadly* or Nicholas Ray's *Johnny Guitar* or even *Citizen Kane,* he implicitly contradicts Bazin's assumption of a realist teleology in film history by celebrating the virtues of self-conscious stylization. In Godard's *À bout de souffle* and Truffaut's second film, *Tirez sur le pianiste,* this critical perception is carried still further as the motifs of the gangster film interplay with realistic "open" situations.

This method of interweaving the stylized and the "real" has since been debased into the now incessant round of genre parodies. But the power of these early films· of Truffaut and Godard resided in their ability not only to pay wry homage to a purely cinematic tradition of genre narrative and convention but also to express the way these fables had influenced and shaped what the audience considered reality to be.

Realism was an irrelevant criterion because there was always some interplay between the world of normally unorganized experience and the world of genre fairy tale, the paranoid hyperorganization of the world of art. If the New Wave directors were the first to display explicitly within their films their own history as lovers of films, their characters were also people whose personal natures and attitudes toward the world had been affected, usually for the worst, by the experience of going to the movies.

Michel, the Jean-Paul Belmondo character in *À bout de souffle,* admiring Bogart, living as he imagines Bogart would, dying because his girlfriend wanted to play Bogart as well, stands in contrast to Godard his creator, who in the film plays a bystander who recognizes Michel and turns him in to the police. Charlie Kohler in *Tirez sur le pianiste,* in flight from his celebrity as a concert pianist and what it has cost him personally, stands in contrast to his creator Truffaut, able to distance his own confusion about the virtues of fame and anonymity through this character. The invigorating paradox remained: films could be both a newly open world of potential connection and a closed malevolent world of lives warped by the limiting experience of film forms.

Les Films de ma vie therefore memorializes less a new departure in film understanding than a reweaving of old, previously incompatible, traditions with new

characters and a new directorial perspective. Truffaut repeatedly comes back to
the relation of director to audience, between whom the critic should stand as both
intermediary and complement. He is fascinated by the self-contained worlds of
fable that outsiders can only marvel at, but he feels more involved with those
films that the audience must help complete, where, as in Renoir and Bergman, we
have "l'impression d'assister au tournage, de voir le film en train de se faire et
même de le faire en collaboration avec le cinéaste."

Within a genre film, such a feeling of assistance is possible only through the
other important term in the film experience, the performer, especially those who,
like uncertain narratives, convey some mystery about their natures. So much has
been written about the New Wave assertion of the director that its fascination with
the actor and the actress has been almost lost. "Le cinéma est un art de la femme,
c'est-à-dire de l'actrice," Truffaut wrote in 1958, and in 1974 he refers to "le
thème majeur de la création artistique: l'identité."

Two essays published in this volume for the first time deal with Humphrey
Bogart and James Dean. The Bogart essay is well done and adequate. Its main
virtue is that, unlike most Bogart biographies, it tries to trace and credit the influence of Bogart's directors—Huston, Ray, and Hawks—in defining Bogart's screen
personality. But the Dean essay is one of the best in the book.

Truffaut places the essays at the end of a section entitled "Quelques outsiders"
and he associates them as creative spirits with the directors included there: Bergman, Buñuel, Norman MacLaren, Fellini, Rossellini, and Welles. But the creativity of Bogart and Dean does not appear in the construction and articulation of a
film; it lies instead in their ability to play against their images, to convey a complexity and mystery about character typically cinematic and opposed, for Truffaut,
to traditional psychological realism. Bogart is the actor who creates situations in
defiance of what is forced upon him: "Il joue *autre chose* que ce qu'il prononce,
il joue *à côté* de la scène, son regard ne suit pas sa conversation, il *décale*
l'expression et la chose exprimée comme, par sublime pudeur, un grand esprit
prononcera de fortes paroles sur un ton humble comme pour s'excuser d'avoir du
génie, pour ne pas en importuner autrui."

Décalage often carries a weight of approval for Truffaut, signifying a skewed
disposition, a nonparallelism, what might be called a montage of the self, in which
the audience enters the film through its empathy with the in-between places an
actor has carefully included in his nature, or a director in his narrative. As he says
with approval of Elia Kazan's *Baby Doll,* "les personnages pensent une chose, en
disent une autre et, par leur jeu, en expriment une troisième."

As these examples show, the heart of Truffaut's aesthetic derives in great part
from his response to the American films of the 1950s. When he was at his most
prolific as a critic, these were the films (plus those of Bergman) that startled and
provoked him to formulate his most challenging ideas. Intent at first to counter
the programmatic anti-Americanism of French culture after the Second World War,
Truffaut and many of his fellow critics began to see in American films of that
period a more complex and ambivalent view of American society and character
than was at all possible in the films turned out by the official French film industry.
The great figures of Renoir, Lang, Eisenstein, and Welles might be beacons for

the form and possibility of film art, but the less imposing and more intriguing American directors—Ray, Kazan, Fuller, Aldrich, and even Jerry Lewis—represented a way of mediating the demands of commercial product, personal vision, and professional craft.

Similarities between Truffaut's critical ideas and his moviemaking practice will occur to every reader and there is little need to detail them here, although it might be mentioned that the appearance of Truffaut as the exacting teacher in *L'Enfant sauvage* displays an ambivalence about the roles of teacher and student that appears in his criticism as a tension between the dictatorial *auteuriste* and the involved *cinéaste-cinéphile*. Luckily, however, it is the *cinéphile* who is uppermost in *Les Films de ma vie*. Truffaut's willingness to revise all previous dicta at the appearance of a new work that breaks the rules displays a vitality and flexibility that most film theory has since abandoned in its desire to be as rigid and hermetic as the older forms of aesthetic criticism. "Il faut sans cesse revoir les films et reviser nos jugements," wrote Truffaut in a 1957 review of Anthony Mann's *Men at War,* expressing an ideal definition of reviewing that would be good advice for the bulk of periodical reviewers, who seem to believe that a public critical identity requires more assertion and invulnerability than sensitivity and reflection.

Truffaut erred more often in his critical writings than is apparent from the careful selection here. But he usually erred from generosity rather than from either restraint or a constricted sense of values. Completely apart from any aesthetic judgment, he praises the ability of Cocteau to be open to every artist, of whatever ability, because he believed that "le plus médiocre artiste vaut le meilleur spectateur," not the audience "qui . . . jugent sans courir aucun risque," but those who by being critically aware share the artist's risks with him.

The riches of *Les Films de ma vie* should not therefore be limited by the usefulness of the book as a companion piece to either the recent history of international film, the New Wave, or Truffaut's own films. The essays on James Dean, *Citizen Kane,* Ernst Lubitsch, and Luis Buñuel deserve to become part of the small group of permanently valuable works of film criticism, and in other essays, especially the group on Rossellini, with whom Truffaut once worked, the desire to hear more is not satisfied. The concluding section, "Mes copains de la Nouvelle Vague," is definitely the weakest part of the book. It marks a kind of diminuendo in Truffaut's film-watching life when the films of other directors no longer interest him very much—"finie pour moi la générosité du cinéphile"—although he is inspired by Claude Berri to discuss films about children and attack the increasingly impersonal intellectual content of recent films.

But long before then the book has proved itself, not as a system and hardly as a history, but as the record of an acute and engaging sensibility for whom theory and practice, the experience of a single film and the experience of all films, are continuous. One might wish for some clearer chronology, so that the actual development of Truffaut's ideas could be more specifically traced. Bu the coherence is that of the man himself, and his decision to arrange his essays by directors rather than by chronology properly subordinates his responses to their practice.

When Godard makes his movie about a movie, it is called *Le Mépris (Contempt):* the villian is Jack Palance, a ruthless Hollywood producer, and the director is played by Fritz Lang: a great tradition has been sold out by the moneymen, the merchants of bodies and ideas. When Truffaut makes his movie about a movie, *La Nuit américaine (Day for Night),* he himself plays the director, a little deaf, a little withdrawn, and the center stage is left to the actors and the technicians and staff, who interweave their roles with their jobs and their lives until the film becomes a celebration of the possible microcosm of the film world, the reflective and renewing power of its magic. Godard wants to break down the frame like a good Brechtian to show the political and moral manipulations made possible by the form. But for Truffaut sincerity lies in accepting and thereby transcending the form, undercutting artifice by allowing it its appropriate place as yet another way of organizing the world.

I used to make a distinction between film critics and film reviewers, because I thought that no film reviewer could have any general ideas that would withstand the pressure of incessant repetition with different example. But Truffaut in *Les Films de ma vie* is the model of the critic–reviewer, attempting to respond to each film with a method that will correspond to its individual amalgam of subject matter and style. Only films are permanent, while film theory is in constant flux. At a time when films seem once again to be changing, when the first impact of the New Wave has begun to run thin, and when film theory, under the impact of semiological and structural analysis, is becoming more and more academic and rarefied, Truffaut reminds us by his interplay between the absolute and the individual, the historical and the momentary, the world of ideas and the world of feeling, that film first arrived to break down the old hierarchies of art so that we might resee and reexperience the world in more intense shapes. He reminds us that it is the best goal of film criticism not only to take its place among the humanities but to cleanse our vision of them as well.

[1975]

Hitchcock, Truffaut, and the Irresponsible Audience

In the beginning of his opulently mounted interview with Hitchcock,* François Truffaut writes that Hitchcock has always feared technicians who might "jeopardize the integrity of his work." But in this "definitive study" (to cite the dustjacket) Truffaut's own approach is so doggedly technical, so intent on style as opposed to meaning, that one wonders if the feared technicians haven't come in by a rear window after all. The interview is an anatomy of Hitchcock's work that shows little sense of what technical methods signify, or what stylistic devices express. Truffaut draws back from any exploration of the psychological depths of either Hitchcock himself or the movies Hitchcock has made. Hitchcock makes many leading remarks about his themes and methods that Truffaut glosses over. Hitchcock reveals fascinating shards of his psychological nightlife, but Truffaut only alludes to the dark area of voyeurism, exhibitionism, and fetishism that Hitchcock's films explore; he is too interested in showing his own knowledge of plot and technical details to go any further. And because of his lack of interest in the psychological dimensions of Hitchcock's films, Truffaut misses. how Hitchcock in his best films manipulates the deepest reactions of his audience.

Has Truffaut been hampered by the difficulties of a long interview (fifty hours spread over several days), complete with translator? If we cannot have the experience of two directors talking equally, let us have an incisive picture of one. But Truffaut gives us neither. Recent journalism has developed the interview into a vehicle of self-revelation. But what we learn about Hitchcock from *Hitchcock* is less due to Truffaut's insight than to his inclusiveness. There are 472 stills and full credits for all of Hitchcock's films. There is even a developing plot relation between two characters named "Hitchcock" and "Truffaut" which can be followed as a welcome counterpoint to the more obvious play of question and answer. But this plot reveals neither Truffaut nor Hitchcock; each tries to direct and each has cast the other in an uncongenial role. Truffaut's early impulse is to score points. He shows that his memory of *The Last Laugh* is better that Hitchcock's and he tries to make Hitchcock admit that his work was influenced by Fritz Lang.

*F. Truffaut, *Hitchcock*. (New York: Simon & Schuster, 1968).

Hitchcock responds with his usual mask of evasive humor: he can't remember *M,
The Spy,* or *The Testament of Dr. Mabuse,* but he will admit to changing a scene
in the first version of *The Man Who Knew Too Much* because he had noticed a
similar scene in Mervyn LeRoy's *I Am a Fugitive from a Chain Gang.* Underground arguments sometimes flare. While discussing *The Ring* Hitchcock mentions visual touches he thinks no one noticed; Truffaut nods but wants to talk
about what *he* noticed; Hitchcock replies that all the reviewers noticed *those* details. None of these conflicts is more than trivially illuminating. And it is difficult
not to find Truffaut at fault. Instead of facing Hitchcock with probing questions,
he plays the eager young man, ready to reel off complicated plots the master has
forgotten, adulatory and bumptiously arrogant at the same time. Instead of drawing Hitchcock out, Truffaut forces him back into his old masks.

Ideally, an interview can be a process of understanding. But Truffaut has certain set ideas about Hitchcock. His emphasis on Hitchcock's technique of suspense and "dramatic impact" shows traces of the same kind of condescension or
reverse snobbery that dubs Hitchcock "the world's foremost technician": however
great a director Truffaut believes Hitchcock to be, he may not expect him to be
interested in psychological themes as complex as those dealt with in *Jules and
Jim.* This bias leads naturally to Truffaut's concern with workmanship and technical detail. He calls *Notorious* "the very quintessence of Hitchcock," "a model
of scenario construction." Hitchcock calls the single-shot technique of *Rope* "quite
nonsensical," but Truffaut's questions follow the familiar litany: "What about the
problems with the color?" "What about the problems of a mobile camera?" "What
is truly remarkable is that all of this was done so silently that you were able to
make a direct sound track." Faced with Truffaut's almost programmatic bias,
Hitchcock finds he can respond only in Truffaut's terms, and in the latter part of
the interview he finally asserts—with Truffaut's approval—that he likes technical
tricks much more than subject matter or acting.

Hitchcock's seeming agreement with Truffaut rests actually on a very different
definition of technique that uses, however, much of the same language. Both
Truffaut and Hitchcock make oddly archaic statements about the way sound film
ended the great era of the cinema. Truffaut seems to have forgotten André Bazin's
attacks against "pure cinema" cultists (as in "The Virtues and Limitations of
Montage"), for he comes on like the young Raymond Spottiswoode. In line with
his interest in technical details and fragments of directorial style, he treats each
film as a "pure" object: a compound of techniques, or problems solved and un-
solved. But all of Hitchcock's "techniques" are aimed at destroying the separation between the film and its audience. When Truffaut talks about the emotional
effect of a film, he is speaking of a dramatic irony, surprise, and the shock of
realism. When Hitchcock talks about emotion, he is asserting the audience's involvement and implication in what is happening on the screen. In speaking of
Psycho, Hitchcock appears to follow the "pure" cinema line: "It wasn't a message that stirred the audience, nor was it a great performance or their enjoyment
of the novel. They were aroused by pure film." Truffaut answers, satisfied, "Yes,
that's true." But Hitchcock explains further what he means: "the construction of
the story and the way in which it was told caused audiences all over the world to

react and become emotional.'' Truffaut responds: ''Yes, emotional and even physical.'' Hitchcock snaps: ''Emotional.''

In the first half of the interview Hitchcock frequently drops hints of some larger issues, but Truffaut, bound in his own interests, plows on. Hitchcock suggests, for example, that his use of handcuffs has ''deeper implications'':

A.H. Being tied to something . . . it's somewhere in the area of fetishism, isn't it?

F.T. I don't know, but I have noticed that handcuffs have a way of recurring in your movies.

While Hitchcock vainly implies the emotional and psychological relevance of his details, Truffaut concentrates on an intellectualized appreciation of fine finish and professional gloss. He says of the death of Mr. Memory in *The Thirty-Nine Steps:* ''It's this kind of touch that gives so many of your pictures a quality that's extremely satisfying to the mind: a characterization is developed to the limit—until death itself.'' Truffaut therefore interprets the paranoia implied by the subjective camera in *The Thirty-Nine Steps* in technical terms as Hitchcock's effort ''to sacrifice plausibility in favor of pure emotion.'' He does not perceive the relation between Hitchcock's typical technical devices and his deepest thematic concerns.

Truffaut's analysis and questioning falls down therefore whenever he touches upon larger areas of structure and meaning in Hitchcock's films. Truffaut dispenses with plot in the name of ''pure'' cinema; Hitchcock cares little about the minor springs of plot—what he calls the ''MacGuffin,'' the gimmick—because he is dealing with more inclusive rhythms. ''To me, the narrator, they're of no importance.'' And this narrative sense, Hitchcock asserts, despite Truffaut's concern with technical virtuosity, is the most important part of his directorial method. Truffaut talks about technique, but Hitchcock talks about the audience and its psychology. He manipulates the audience for his own ends, and he wants them to leave his films with a narrative sense of what has occurred. Truffaut does not grasp this idea because each film is for him a pure aesthetic object. But for Hitchcock it is the medium for a relation between the director and the audience. Truffaut discusses camera movement in terms of ''dramatic impact,'' but Hitchcock continually expresses it as an element in establishing point of view.

Because of Truffaut's inability or unwillingness to explore Hitchcock's interest in point of view and his skirting of psychological themes and preoccupations, he is particularly blind to the central area of Hitchcock's work where technique and theme coincide in the study of voyeurism. Building on the interplay between directorial construction and audience understanding that is the basis of montage, Hitchcock develops certain themes that rely directly on the experience of watching a film itself. Even when Truffaut touches on the theme of voyeurism, he believes that the psychological interest is fortuitous:

F.T. Would you say that [James] Stewart [in *Rear Window*] was merely curious?

A.H. He's a real Peeping Tom. . . . Sure, he's a snooper, but aren't we all?

F.T. We're all voyeurs to some extent, if only when we see an intimate film. And James Stewart is exactly in the position of a spectator looking at a movie.

A.H. I'll bet you that nine out of ten people, if they see a woman across the courtyard undressing for bed, or even a man puttering around in his room, will stay and look;

no one turns away and says, "It's none of my business." They could pull down their blinds, but they never do; they stand there and look out.

F.T. My guess is that at the outset your interest in the picture was purely technical, but in working on the script, you began to attach more importance to the story itself. Intentionally or not, that back yard conveys an image of the world.

All through the interview Hitchcock has made remarks about "Peeping Tom audiences" and his efforts to manipulate them. But Truffaut never sees the larger thematic and structural implications of this interest.

Every movie is naturally voyeuristic, not only the most intimate ones, and that is a great part of their appeal—the sensuous immediacy that goes beyond the stylized realism of the fourth-wall theater. A feeling of occasion and artifice may separate us from a particular movie, as it usually separates us from even the most realistic play. But with the camera eye substituted for our own the potentiality for greater intimacy, mediated by "me, the narrator," is still there. The films of Hitchcock play in different ways with these psychological assumptions of the film form itself. Some are less successful and perhaps deserve the technically oriented analysis of Truffaut. But voyeurism is more than a metaphor for Hitchcock; he also emphasizes its moral dimension. In movies we can get away with observing without responsibility. André Bazin remarks in another context: "Incontestably, there is in the pleasure derived from cinema and novel a self-satisfaction, a concession to solitude, a sort of betrayal of action by a refusal of social responsibility." In some of his movies Hitchcock exploits this irresponsibility: "[In *Notorious*] the public was being given the great privilege of embracing Cary Grant and Ingrid Bergman together. It was a kind of temporary *ménage à trois*." In a basically comic film like *Notorious* the audience can remain irresponsible, but in his best films the irresponsible audience must go through the punishment of terror. And Truffaut's approach breaks down most clearly when he is faced with what may be Hitchcock's most perfect expression of the interdependence of his themes and techniques—*Psycho*. In *Psycho* Hitchcock brings the voyeuristic assumptions of film form to the surface and in the process brings his audience from the detachment of irresponsible spectators to the involvement of implicated participants.

Hitchcock's films frequently approach the problem of detachment and involvement through separate but complementary treatments that might almost be called "genres." In "comedies" like *The Lady Vanishes, North by Northwest,* or *Torn Curtain,* the central characters are a romantic couple with whom the audience automatically sympathizes. They serve as audience surrogates in a series of adventures that turn out happily. The axe is never far away from the neck in these comedies, but all conflict is finally dissipated by the end of the film, frequently by near fairy-tale or romance means. At the end of *North by Northwest* Cary Grant tries vainly to pull Eva Marie Saint to safety, while she dangles from the face of Mt. Rushmore. He can't do it. But then he can do it. The straining impossibility turns into fairy-tale ease. He pulls her up—into the top bunk of their Pullman, speeding away from the Dakotas.

Hitchcock's tragedies have no such romantic couple for ease of audience identification and sympathy; Truffaut remarks that there is no one in *Psycho* to identify with. We cast around without bearings, looking for conventional movie clues to tell us we have found the "right" character. But everyone is suspect. The first possible romantic couple in *Psycho*—Sam Loomis and Marion Crane (John Gavin and Janet Leigh)—have a melancholic relation in which sex and money are the prime topics of conversation. The later relation between Sam and Marion's sister Lila (Vera Miles), because it is founded on such dubious grounds, only emphasizes that *Psycho* is not the place to find a romantic couple. Solving a mystery may bring together Margaret Lockwood and Michael Redgrave in *The Lady Vanishes,* but it does not work in *Psycho.* Neither Sam, nor Marion, nor Lila, is particularly attractive. We can never give any of them our full sympathy, although we are often sympathetic to each. And Hitchcock manipulates our desire to sympathize and identify. He plays malevolently on the audience assumption that the character we sympathize with most, whose point of view we share, is the same character who is morally right in the story the movie tells. He gleefully defeats our expectation that our moral sympathies and our aesthetic sympathies remain fixed throughout the movie.

Hitchcock begins this manipulation at the very beginning of *Psycho.* He forces the audience, although we may not realize it immediately, to face the most sinister connotations of our audience role—our participation in the watching and observing that shades quickly into voyeurism. We see first a long view of a city and titles that read successively "Phoenix, Arizona, Friday December the eleventh. Two forty-three P.M." We sit back and turn on the "objective" vision we reserve for documentaries, the aesthetic equivalent of a detached contemplation of the truth. But we are forced instead to watch an intensely personal, even embarrassing, scene. The camera moves closer and closer to one of the buildings, until finally it ducks under a drawn shade and emerges in a hotel room where Marion, in bra and halfslip, and Sam, bare to the waist, are having a late lunch-hour tryst. Perhaps we can call on our documentary detachment to insulate us from this scene, and thereby resist Hitchcock manipulations. Truffaut insulates himself by an interest in plot dynamics: "The sex angle was raised so that later on the audience would think that Anthony Perkins is merely a voyeur." But throughout *Psycho* Hitchcock continually assaults our claims of objectivity and detachment in order to emphasize and illustrate our real implication.

Hitchcock successively involves us with Marion and then Norman Bates (Perkins) through the gradually increasing use of a subjective camera. In both involvements there is at first a residual doubt, a nagging compunction about the moral aspects of our aesthetic involvement. In terms of conventional movie morality, or what our second-guessing has provisionally told us about the morality of *Psycho,* Sam and Marion are wrong; she's even overstayed her lunch hour. Hitchcock plays on our desire to feel superior because we have figured out *Psycho*'s system of rewards and punishments: "You know that the public always likes to be one jump ahead of the story; they like to feel they know what's coming next. So you deliberately play upon this fact to control their thoughts." He invites us next to feel morally superior as well as aesthetically. We can make a few moral distinctions on the basis of this first conversation between Sam and Marion. They can't get married and can't even find a pleasant place to meet because Sam has no money, at least not enough both to get married and to pay off his ex-wife's alimony. The lecherous rancher in Marion's office confirms our acceptance of the Sam-Marion relationship. What poetic justice it would be if his sexually tainted money could be used to make the dreams of Sam and Marion come true! By this point we have gone beyond Marion. We wait impatiently as she moves about her bedroom, debating whether or not to take the money; through Hitchcock's manipulation of our moral responses, we have already decided.

Our identification with Marion becomes more directed as we drive away from Phoenix with her. We sit in the driver's seat and look out the window; when we look at Marion herself, we hear the voices in her head, fantasies about what everyone in Phoenix must be saying. Except for the single establishing shot in which we see the police car pull up near Marion's parked car (and after all, at this time she is asleep), we remain inside the car with her, limited within the world of her imaginings, accomplices with her—for a time—in what she has done. The state trooper appears as a figure of vague malevolence; his shades reinforce his blankness. When he waits across the street from the used car lot, we are apprehensive with Marion. When she drives away and an offscreen voice yells "Hey!" we know it's the trooper. But it's not and he really doesn't seem to be waiting for Marion at all. Through the subjective camera and the audience's belief in economy of means ("every character fits in somewhere"), Hitchcock has given us that guilty, almost paranoid, state of mind that converts all outside itself into images of potential evil.

This feeling of guilt begins to dissipate when we arrive at the motel owned by Norman Bates and his mother. Norman is a genial, shy young fellow, unassuming, pleasant. He's friendly, he makes jokes, he even invites nervous Marion to dinner. When his mother makes him withdraw the invitation, he talks to Marion feelingly about the traps life has put him in. Marion callously suggests that he should have his mother committed, "put someplace." We are beginning to turn against Marion. Norman is a sensitive boy and he loves his mother. Once again our conventional reactions come into play. We wonder if we have been wrong about Marion. Perhaps she did have some cause for the theft, but she has a bad streak. And that first image of sex in the afternoon may recur as proof. She invites Norman into her room, but he draws back. Was her sexuality a threat to Sam in the same way?

Hitchcock's gradual separation of our sympathies from Marion and attachment of them to Norman now becomes even more delicate. We follow Norman into the next room and watch as he moves aside a picture to reveal a peephole into Marion's cabin. He watches her undress and, in some important way, we feel the temptress is more guilty than the Peeping Tom. In the first scene of the movie Marion wore white bra and white halfslip. When she finally decided to take the money, while it lay on her bed as she packed, she wore a black bra and halfslip. She drove off in a black car and then traded it in for a light-colored model. But our conventional moral–aesthetic sense can't be fooled. Once again, as Norman peers through the peephole, we see the black bra and halfslip, and remember Marion's guilt, a guilt we do not want to share. This perhaps dubious pattern of dark and light only reinforces something more basic. Whether we realize it or not, we have had a Norman-like perspective from the beginning of the movie. We too were Peeping Toms when we looked through the window of the hotel room Sam and Marion rented. We shared the Peeping-Tom exposure of Marion when her boss noticed her (and us) staring at him through the car window. When we look through the peephole with Norman, we are doing something we have done before; this time, like the first time, we know we won't be caught. We tend to blame Marion and not Norman because we are fellow-voyeurs with him, and we do not want to blame ourselves.*

It is worthwhile to emphasize the way Hitchcock manages our shift from Marion to Norman, since many commentators on *Psycho* assume that Marion's murder is somehow justified because she is a thief. But ironically enough her talk with Norman has convinced her that she has done wrong and should return to Phoenix. Her last act before the fatal shower is to figure out how to cover from her own bank account the loss sustained in buying the car. But her bra and halfslip have already given her away to Norman, whose psychotic view of people admits no shade between black and white, no difference between a mildly flirtatious invitation and a blatant proposition. Hitchcock masterfully implies that we can't tell the difference either. Perhaps the murder may also sardonically mirror our beliefs about Hollywood: Janet Leigh was the star of the first half of the movie; Perkins murders her and becomes the star of the second half. Perhaps we're also being invited to remember that Janet Leigh had recently disported herself sexually in another motel in Welles's *Touch of Evil* (1958; *Psycho,* 1960). In any case, Norman had added her to his collection of dead birds; when he emerges from the bathroom after his "first" look at her, he knocks one of the bird pictures from the wall. Marion fits well into the collection because, after all, her last name is Crane and she comes from Phoenix. But she won't rise again. There's only one phoenix, and in this movie it's Norman's mother.

The sight of Norman cleaning up the bathroom after the murder reinforces our identification with him aesthetically and morally. Our hands hold the mop and swirl the towel around the floor; Hitchcock cryptically remarks to Truffaut about his own hypercleanliness. Norman cleans up so well because he is a dutiful son trying to protect his crazy mother. Once again, Hitchcock forces us into the security of conventional moral reactions in the face of an absurd situation. In many of his movies he begins with an excessively normal, even banal, situation and then proceeds to show the maniacal forces seething just below the surface. Norman's mop reverses the process; the bathroom is gleaming and conventional once more. We are relieved that the most characterless place on the American landscape has become characterless once again. We have become so identified with Norman's point of view that we feel a moment of apprehension when the car refuses to sink all the way into the black pool. But it finally goes down. We heave a sigh of relief with Norman; the insanity has been submerged once again. Our relief masks our progress from the acceptance of illicit sex to robbery, to murder, what Truffaut with his rage for precision calls a "scale of the abnormal." The memory of our pleasure in Marion's nudity, even while the murder was in pro-

---

*Because of the importance of the motif of observation, especially through windows, it's worth noting that we see Hitchcock through the window of Marion's office.

cess, our effort to see if that was a breast or only an arm we half-glimpsed, all become submerged, especially since, with Norman, we may have decided that she deserved it.

Our sympathy with Norman also controls our feeling about the detective, Arbogast (Martin Balsam). Arbogast upsets Norman with his questions, and we have little or no sympathy with him through the camera. When he walks upstairs in the house, we get only one short shot of his lower legs. Then all the shots are face on, as if we were at the top of the stairs with "Mother." When the murder begins we look straight into Arbogast's face as he staggers back down the stairs under the knife blows. We follow him along with "Mother," striking again and again. The conventional and self-protective operations of our aesthetic and moral sympathies have once again implicated us in something we were not ready for. Hitchcock plays to Truffaut's prejudices by saying that the high camera shot—the bird's-eye view—that begins the murder segment was used to avoid showing "Mother's" face. But when he returns to it at the end of the scene, as Perkins carries her down to the fruit cellar, Hitchcock checks off our complicity. We are no longer so terrified.

Sam and Lila arrive during the day, presaging the illumination of Norman's dark subconscious. Previously the dark brooding vertical shaft of the house had stood high in the shadows behind the banal well-lit horizontal of the motel. With light now striking them both, the house is potentially no longer so mysterious. Sam cannot go in to discover the secret. Like Marion and Arbogast, he had first visited the motel (in one of the few inept scenes) at night. But this is Lila's first visit; Sam delays Norman through conversation. His bad acting (on two levels) and accusations of Norman keep us sympathetic to Norman and divided from Sam. In the house Lila has begun to move through the rooms and examine the furniture of Norman's mind. She sees a movement behind her and turns to find a full-length mirror. Like the audience, she has rummaged around in someone else's inner darkness and discovers there, instead of unknown horrors, something akin to herself. With Norman's return she races toward the fruit cellar and the final secret is revealed—"the foul rag-and-bone shop of the heart."

Norman's psychosis is the MacGuffin of *Psycho;* its special nature is irrelevant. Hitchcock concentrates instead on problems of presentation and point of view, the uncertain line between the normal audience and the psychotic character, and the actually hazy areas of moral judgment. Throughout the movie we are placed in situations that challenge our conventionalized aesthetic and moral responses. Hitchcock's attack on the reflex use of conventional pieties is basically an attack on the desire of the audience to deny responsibility and assert complete detachment. The viewer who wants such placidity and irresponsibility is mocked by the psuedodocumentary beginning of the movie. If he chooses, he has another trapdoor available at the end—in the explanation of the psychologist.

Because Norman has murdered both his mother and her lover, we don't have the conventional out of psychiatric exoneration from guilt. But the psychologist does offer us a way to escape responsibility by even more acceptable means: he sets up a screen of jargon to "explain" Norman. For the viewer who has learned anything from *Psycho* he must be dismissed. The visual clues are all present: he is greasy and all-knowing; he lectures and gestures with false expansiveness. But it is his explanations that are really insufficient. And one wonders if any categories would be sufficient. Like the moral tags dispensed by the Chorus at the end of *Oedipus Tyrannos,* the bland wisdom of the psychologist bears little relation to the complex human reality that has been our experience in the rest of the movie. We understand Norman because we realize the continuum between his actions and our own. We leave the front office of "clear" explanation, while the psychologist is still talking, to enter Norman's cell. Through Hitchcock's manipulation of point of view and moral sympathy, we have entered the shell of his personality and discovered the rooted violence and perverse sexuality that may be in our own natures. Our desire to save Norman is a desire to save ourselves. But we have been walled off from the comfortable and reasonable and "technical" explanations of the psychologist. The impact that *Psycho* has upon us shows how deeply we've been implicated.

In 1955 Truffaut and Claude Chabrol had gone to interview Hitchcock on the location set of *To Catch a Thief* at Joinville. In their excitement they walked on the ice of a little pond in the center of a courtyard and fell in, tape recorder and all. Truffaut turns this into a charming anecdote: "It all began when we broke the ice." But he conducts the interview as if this first encounter were cautionary. It symbolizes his unwillingness to leave the surface and plunge, however uncertainly, into the dark and icy depths.

[1968]

◼

Maidstone: A Mystery by Norman Mailer

In the late fall of 1967 Norman Mailer spoke at Yale. The Law School auditorium was packed with a nervous audience, many of whom had never read a word Mailer had written, but all eagerly waited for a show, knowing that he always made a spectacle of himself. Mailer didn't let them down. Rocking back and forth towards the microphone as though unwilling to rest too close to or too far from his audience, he began a rambling series of good jokes and bad ones, sly attacks on Yale at the expense of Harvard, and casually slipped in obscenities.

Soon the audience began to feel that it wasn't getting its money's worth. (Admission was free.) Rolled-up wads of paper pelted the authorial presence. More pointed obscenities followed. The audience relaxed cheerfully. But then another stretch of rhetorical dead space brought forth another barrage of paper.

"The next person who hits me will be invited onto the stage for an existential confrontation," announced Mailer with the mock-heroic solemnity of Falstaff challenging an innkeeper. The challenge was quickly picked up, the challenger invited to the stage, insults were traded, and the challenger was finally forced to leave the auditorium in order to prove his assertion that Mailer wasn't worth listening to.

Then Mailer smiled again. "I've brought something I'd like to read." The audience breathed more easily. Something structured might come out of this mess after all. "It's from a piece I'm doing for *Harper's* on the Pentagon March."

In retrospect, of course, Mailer's choice is easy to predict. He read the "Ambassador Theater" section from *The Armies of the Night,* an account of a manipulation of chaos into esthetic order on a somewhat larger scale than the five-finger exercise of the Yale Law School auditorium. There was fair warning: what Mailer dubbed "an existential situation" turned out to be an affair of marionettes and puppet master.

The filming of *Maidstone,* whose background, script, and metaphysic take up Mailer's latest book, is similarly described as "the advanced course in existentialism." To make the third in his series of movies (after *Wild 90* and *Beyond the Law*), Mailer, in the early summer of 1968, took almost a hundred people out to a series of Long Island estates for five days and nights of filming during which they were to become "a bunch of enforced existentialists." The film was finally shown to mixed reviews in late October of this year, more than three years after it was filmed. *Maidstone: A Mystery* is the literary product of the experience.

This literary twin of *Maidstone* the movie is compounded of three different approaches to those five days on Long Island: first, a descriptive introduction to the scene of production woven from articles written at the time by J. Anthony Lukas *(New York Times)*, Sally Beauman *(New York* Magazine) and James Toback *(Esquire)*. Then comes the "script" itself, that is, a transcript of the final film with Mailer's Shavian stage directions and comments (there was no shooting script). Then finally there is "A Course in Filmmaking," Mailer's part-metaphysical, part-descriptive account of the process that led to the finished film. A cast list, technical credits, and stills fill out the book.

Like anything Mailer undertakes, the resulting melange of journalism, film, and speculation is fascinating, with a labyrinth of data and fancy presented in the tones of that whimsical didacticism Mailer has fashioned for his literary voice since *Advertisements for Myself.* Two ideas of filmmaking battle against each other in Mailer's theory: the desire to release the untapped "existential" potential in his (largely) unprofessional cast; and the belief that the film director is like a general, somehow coordinating a mass of conflicting desires and details into a successful campaign. To combat the director's tendency to extract meaning that he himself had already placed into a scene, Mailer allowed the actors to improvise their lines and set loose several camera crews to film scenes simultaneously so that his own presence would not be continually inhibiting.

But, as Mailer recounts it in "A Course in Filmmaking," the film he had hoped for never emerged from the 45 hours of film he shot. "A Course in Filmmaking" in fact has little of the originality and suggestiveness of an earlier essay on *Wild 90* Mailer published in *Esquire* in 1967. Its true interest lies much more in its account of the failures of Mailer's esthetic premeditation than its successes. Despite his interest in releasing "existential" potential in his actors, in fact his own personality, expressed either as Norman T. Kingsley, the movie director/ Presidential candidate (in the film), or Norman Mailer, the movie director/noted author (in the film as well), had manipulated them into what turned out to be often not very interesting postures. After a long section "On the Theory," Mailer must therefore throw away his theoretic ladder and proceed to "In the Practice," because a story has been revealed in the film that its maker never expected. One of the marionettes had in fact revolted. Appropriately enough, it was Rip Torn, the only professional actor in a main role, who finally hits Mailer several times over the head with a toylike but blood-drawing hammer. After watching the rushes for many hours, Mailer realizes that Torn's attack on him (which now ends the film) was the film's true conclusion and represented a more profound conception of what was going on in the film than he himself realized.

Torn's revolt in fact makes *Maidstone* one of the few films one ought to see at least twice, since the ending, with no indication of being a cheap reversal, makes the viewer immediately want to reevaluate what came before, so authentic is the emotion released.

Now, with the printed script, it is fascinating to see how the film inevitably, but also surprisingly, leads up to the attack. Kingsley/Mailer boxes with his sparring partner and tells him not to go for the head. Mailer/Kingsley pedagogically instructs his cast and crew about the levels of reality they are plumbing. Torn's hammer applied to Mailer's head does not complete the plot of the film so much as it completes the esthetic of the film, the odd balance between control and uncertainty that Mailer was searching for. One wonders if in the back of Torn's own head was Mailer's remark in *Advertisements for Myself* that the reader of James Baldwin felt a need "to take a hammer to his detachment, smash the perfumed dome of his ego."

In its esthetic play with the levels of reality, *Maidstone* is a marriage of the violent dislocations of Godard's *Weekend* with the playful theatricality of *A Midsummer-Night's Dream*. Once again, the theoretical aspect is less congenial than what finally emerged. At the end of "A Course in Filmmaking" Mailer concludes that in the search for reality "the ineluctable ore of the authentic is our only key to the lock," and too often in his essay the "authentic" seems to have something to do with the documentary. Mailer scorns *cinéma vérité* (although less cogently than in his earlier essay) because people do not do so well playing themselves. Yet the process of filmmaking he describes sounds very much in accord with *cinéma vérité* beliefs: Set up as many cameras as possible, and then with judicious editing, the "real" will appear. The form of *Maidstone: A Mystery* seems to repeat that formula: first the "objective" reportorial views of the filming, then the emergent script, and finally the director's meditation.

Mailer claims that his main impulse in making the film was to get away from the merciless collectivity and rigorous schedules of the Hollywood product. Yet he is uncertain about his own fixing of the line between spontaneity and control. Film may be an individual dream, in contrast to the social ritual of theater. But Mailer has also remarked that in his dreams every individual writes his own vast social novel, and so he alternately refers to his cast and crew as an army and as a party. Are they the army floundering into success in *The Naked and the Dead*? or the party proposed in *Advertisements for Myself*, which will be recounted by a dead man?

Coming between *The Armies of the Night* and *Miami and the Siege of Chicago* in Mailer's work, *Maidstone* (and *Maidstone: A Mystery*) continues that as yet incomplete process of dismantling that Mailer is performing on the public ego that has served him so well over the years; it is a prelude to the political uncertainty of *Miami and the Siege of Chicago* and the "loss of ego" that begins *Of a Fire on the Moon*, as well as the defense of his literary integrity and style in *The Prisoner of Sex*. I like the film *Maidstone* very much, its wit, its frequent visual beauty, and its unique infusion of emotion into what might have otherwise been dry Pirandellian exercises. *Maidstone: A Mystery* is more important for the light it casts on Mailer's other writings. It is a staging ground for later experiments with narrative method, for example, the emphasis on mood in *Of a Fire on the Moon*.

But what remains compelling about both film and book derives less from Mailer's theory than from his acute sense of deception and self-deception, in the characters of others and especially in his own, along with his willingness to change his preconceptions. At one point in the film Mailer as Kingsley the director is interviewing an actress and asks her to do some Shakespeare. She begins to speak, but his attention is distracted and he never quite hears or recognizes what she recites. It is, in fact, Titania's speech when she wakes and sees Bottom with his ass's head standing before her. At its best, *Maidstone: A Mystery* explores with charm and power one of Mailer's great themes, the potentialities of human character. Like the dream, it is an exploration that has no bottom.

[1971]

◻

Stargazer by Stephen Koch

If one person's name could be shorthand for whatever has happened to art in the last 10 years, the owner of that name is Andy Warhol, born Andrew Warhola, the son of Czechoslovakian immigrant parents, his father a Pittsburgh steelworker and coal miner, himself the signer of works that include Campbell soup cans, Brillo boxes, silk-screened portraits of Marilyn Monroe and Jacqueline Kennedy, and films such as *Sleep* (six hours of a man sleeping), *Empire* (eight hours of the Empire State Building as seen from the 44th floor of the old Time-Life Building), *The Chelsea Girls, Flesh,* and *Trash.* This description may sound circumstantial, but so is Warhol. He can be critically surrounded but not really specified. As Stephen Koch's new book makes clear, the essence of Warhol's work is evasiveness. Talented, creative in himself, Warhol may be more important as an absorber of forces from the atmosphere, a rotating mirror or radar screen.

Warhol is not a manipulator of situations, but a contextualizer, a setter of frames, who changes objects and people less than he changes our perceptions of them. All of Warhol's works enclose themselves even while they reflect the world around them in its most common and terrifying details from deadly car accidents to S & H Green Stamps. On opposite sides of Warhol's Moebius strip esthetic are two 1963 works, "Thirty Are Better Than One" (30 exactly similar photographs of the Mona Lisa) and "Ethel Scull 36 Times" (colored 4-for-25-cent snapshots): the unique but infinitely reproducible work of art and the unique but always changing individual; art taken out of the eternal and made commodity, individuality taken out of the everyday and made art.

According to Stephen Koch, a novelist *(Night Watch)* and writer for *World Magazine,* Warhol's works are obsessed with the presence that expresses itself as absence, the voyeur removed from the scene his removal has helped to create. Koch generally concentrates on Warhol's life and films, invoking the painting and sculpture only peripherally. His two critical dowsing rods for Warhol are Baudelaire and Duchamp, especially Baudelaire's attitude toward life style in his essay on the Dandy and the attack Duchamp's formal games made on the self-sufficient sanctity of the art object. Koch situates Warhol's special contribution in his gaze, "a major metaphor for art and life in our time," a starmaking stare that transforms everything "this tycoon of passivity" chooses to look upon.

Duchamp was an iconoclast, a destroyer of established forms. Warhol, for all his hermeticism, has also changed the way we see the world and made more of its variety accessible to us. Abstract Expressionism assumed a disbelief in the esthetic vitality of real objects, and retreated from the world to a more direct. expression of the artist's sensibility. But Warhol—along with Roy Lichtenstein, Claes Oldenburg, Robert Rauschenberg, Jasper Johns, Ed Kienholz, and all those representational artists whose personal publicity could never match Warhol's— returned us to both the energy and the multiplicity of common things.

Warhol is a highly visible creator whose role in his creations is both complex and obscure. Koch states much of what he has to say about Warhol in paradoxical terms like these, for paradox is the heart of Warhol's art: movement and stillness, attention and boredom, fame and anonymity, the eternal and the ephemeral. Warhol's gaze, coolness, mirrors, passivity, his debt to Duchamp (no happenstance Mona Lisa)—all have become part of the established critical vocabulary about Warhol's works. Koch enriches and elaborates these terms with his own intelligence and sensibility, even though he may cling to the paradoxes a bit too long and occasionally falls into the prophetic formalisms of those who criticize the avant-garde from the inside, speaking to the already initiated.

Koch does want to bring Warhol's work into a world of wider understanding. Yet his desire to explain falters oddly when he comes to discuss Warhol's collaboration with Paul Morrissey and the subsequent "decline" in the quality of Warhol's films. Koch believes the process of decline first shows itself in *My Hustler* (1965), made just after Morrissey joined Warhol's group at the Factory, and is consolidated by *Flesh* (1968), signed by Warhol but made entirely by Morrissey, because Warhol was in the hospital recovering from his near-fatal shooting by Valerie Solanas. With a few hedgings, Koch says that Morrissey's influence has destroyed the creativity that was evident in such early Warhol films as *Kiss, Sleep, Haircut,* and *Vinyl.* Morrissey thought people who liked films like *Empire* were snobs and so, argues Koch, he made Warhol commercial and narrative, helping to produce "pornographic indulgences" that illustrate "the collapse of a cinematic idea." Instead of continuing to "redefine the nature of film," Warhol concentrated on the "Super Stars," "deserted by his taste, his artistic intelligence, his touch."

Koch's book falls into two parts. He analyzes with accuracy and interest the formal qualities of Warhol's early films—the testing of limits, the games with the audience. Then, in the second half of the book, he discusses with sensitivity and insight the subject matter of the later films, the theme he calls "the characteristic and drastically alienated experience of inhabiting the male body" and the place of figures like the hustler and the transvestite in defining that theme. But Koch's critical prejudices seem to prevent him from seeing how the formal experiments and the subject matter are connected.

Subject matter is always a nemesis to the avant-garde (as opposed to the underground), since avant-garde artists and critics are almost invariably formalists, testing and teasing the givens of whatever art form they are engaged in. But the gap between form and subject matter is neither so apparent nor so necessary. Seen as a whole, Warhol's films move from an exploration of the thematic possibilities of method—films about themselves and about Film—to a theme of mixed narcissism and self-hate, in other words, a subject matter exactly equivalent to the formal self-reflectiveness of the early films.

Koch has sensitive and compelling remarks to make about both form and subject matter, but because, I take it, his esthetic is basically formalist, he does not see the critical connection between the two, and therefore considers the Warhol–Morrissey connection to be a degeneration rather than the continuation I would argue it really is. According to Koch, Morrissey's work lacks "an artistic algebra that is the critic's dream of simplicity." Perhaps it is the dream of the formalist critic. But when form becomes formula, it becomes too easy to decipher. And formula formalism is doomed to repeat itself in the same way that so many contemporary avant-garde films merely repeat the experiments of the 1920s and 1930s.

Koch builds solidly, and often brilliantly, on the foundation laid by John Coplans' lavishly illustrated *Andy Warhol* (New York Graphic Society), which is still the best introduction to Warhol's work. But Koch's book is finally more exploratory than definitive because he never pulls together the elusive fragments of his subject—artist, filmmaker, cultural symptom, high-fashion illustrator, Catholic Pittsburgh poor boy. If Koch had made more of an effort to dissolve the fashionable paradoxes about Warhol, *Stargazer* would have come closer to explaining Warhol's appeal as an artistic and cultural figure.

[1973]

The Double Detachment of
Ernst Lubitsch

. . . short of being an intriguer, if one wishes to devote one's
books to the true benefit of one's country, one must write
them abroad.

ROUSSEAU, *Confessions*

Thus Rousseau sets the format for the literary expatriate, who is so much the ideal
citizen of his own country that he opposes its entrenched establishments and can
express its genius only in the freedom of exile. Just so, for the expatriates of the
early twentieth century—Hemingway, Joyce, Stein, Picasso, Miller, et al.—one
went away in order to look back with a cleansed eye, to express the true faith in
languages sharpened by distance, if not detachment.

But for the film expatriate of the same period, the situation was very different.
Certainly the transition to another culture seemed to be an easy one for Ernst
Lubitsch and to play little part in his work. Along with many other bright lights
of the Ufa studio in the early 1920s, Lubitsch was brought over by a Hollywood
simultaneously trying to undercut the strong competition it was getting from a
revived German film industry and to enhance its own product as well. Already
hailed as "the Griffith of Europe" (an honorific that has little to do with his
present reputation), Lubitsch went from a highly successful European career as
actor and director to a similar one in Hollywood, even becoming head of production at Paramount in 1935 and still later directing classics like *Ninotchka* (for
MGM in 1939) and *To Be or Not To Be* (1942). Originally he had been hired by
Mary Pickford to supervise her transition from child to adult roles. (She was 30
and the film was *Rosita* in 1923). Unlike other European directors tapped by
Hollywood, Lubitsch was chosen not to give local color to a European story but
because he was, according to Pickford's publicity, one of the world's greatest
directors and, more relevantly, had been instrumental in creating the reputation of
Pola Negri.

So for Lubitsch at least the vexed self-consciousness of literary expatriatism
seemed hardly relevant. But in the silent period he could not be considered unique.
It was primarily to divert postwar German-hating that in 1920 the first German
film to be exhibited in the United States, Lubitsch's *Passion*, was advertised as
starring Pola Negri, the "famous Continental star," with no mention of either
Lubitsch or Emil Jannings, her costar. The pragmatic decision of the distributors
has an emblematic significance as well. In a sense, all filmmakers of the silent

period can be considered expatriates, or superpatriates, above and beyond the differences of nations that had caused World War I. Even though the lines dividing countries had hardened, silent films promised a new international culture of images that would transcend the babel of tongues and politics.

To a sympathetic eye, therefore, Lubitsch's easy transition from Germany to Hollywood casts him as the archetypal director of the silent period, whose art, because it is not tied down to a specific national language, is therefore beyond nation, national cultures, and national politics entirely—a truly international artist. Unlike those directors who migrated in the sound era, Lubitsch never had to face, until he was quite ready, the possibility that he might have a tin ear for his adopted language and an obliviousness to its verbal customs. His medium was sight, and both his powers of observation and his visual techniques were remarkably acute and powerful. In an artistic world whose language was images rather than words, John Ford, born into a family that periodically went back and forth from Maine to Ireland, could be considered as much of an expatriate as Ernst Lubitsch from Berlin.[1] Hollywood already was the mecca for a range of writers, artists, and entertainers who saw the new medium as a way out of old confines, a place (and Lubitsch explicitly appreciated this when he arrived) where a career could blossom overnight and identities might be created by one's own landscaping. No, perhaps the theme of expatriation is the Hollywood theme par excellence, so common that it is a normal undertone of any Hollywood life. The strange people in Hollywood to me aren't the expatriates. They're the natives, like Leo McCarey, born when the major LA industry was cattle-raising, and Frank Capra, who arrived not long after from Palermo, at the age of six.

But even among this group of outsiders from a variety of outsides, Lubitsch is an especially intriguing figure because of his enormous success in adapting to the Hollywood system. A usual element in the stories told of the great foreign directors in Hollywood, as in those of so many eastern or southern American writers, is the lament of co-optation—sell-out for some, or the inability to get "great material" filmed for others—because of the crassness of the studio bosses, "the system," etc. To all such stories Lubitsch seems to be the counterexample. Although he insisted on being identified as German (even when fan magazines and studio publicists wanted to turn him into an Austrian or a Pole), with the intriguing exception of *To Be or Not To Be,* he seems hardly to have artistically looked back to his German background at all. He didn't help Mary Pickford very much, even though some critics said he did succeed in making her appealing. But he did tremendously well after that with a new kind of sophisticated comedy exemplified in *The Marriage Circle* and *So This Is Paris.* As a silent director he was acclaimed for his mastery of the form and for his quickly imitated innovations in camera technique and in the direction of crowds. Then, when the coming of sound threatened a renationalizing through language, he succeeded again in showing how the new technology might enhance the movement and fluidity of film instead of becoming a sensational but leaden burden. He made some early sound musicals, especially *The Love Parade, Monte Carlo,* and *The Smiling Lieutenant,* that broke the early musical away from its footlights format and demonstrated how sound could complement and even replace sight, instead of merely tagging along in tandem. It is in this early sound period—after about thirty-four films in Germany, eleven silent films in America, and four sound films—that he directs *Trouble in Paradise,* the closest he gets in his films to a meditation on his own artistic motives.

Yet Lubitsch has not fared very well with critics who consider his success to be the mark of his evasion of the important social and political issues of the times. For them, his sophistication and his international cosmopolitanism are the hallmarks of his triviality. From the European Left, Lubitsch is usually seen as a kind of high-level Hollywood time-server—a "good servant" *(bon serviteur)* says Roger Boussinot—who satisfied the Hollywood taste for an upper-class dream world peopled by elegant men and women floating on glittering bubbles of wit. Siegfried Kracauer, writing in 1947 with World War II still closely in mind, is more severe. Lubitsch's historical films of the early 1920's—like *Passion and Deception*—were, he says, tailored for an audience disgusted with history. This accounts, he argues, for their great American success and the vogue that Lubitsch enjoyed: "Uneasy about the failure of Wilson's policy, the American people had obviously such a craving for history debunked that they were attracted by films which pictured great events as the work of unscrupulous wire-pullers." Lubitsch's film and those of his imitators, Kracauer says, "instinctively sabotaged any understanding of historic processes, any attempt to explore patterns of conduct in the past"—by which he means patterns of conduct that do not "persistently present . . . [all revolutionary events] as the outcome of psychological conflicts." Yet, typically, even Kracauer allows the trivializer of history his due as a stylist. Lubitsch's comedies, he argues, are as nihilistic as his historical dramas: "This tendency made it easy for him to drain great events of their seriousness and realize comical potentialities in trifles. Seasoned by him, such trifles become truffles." [2]

Similarly, a much more recent book by Andrew Bergman, *We're in the Money,* a chronicle of American films of the 1930s, quotes Kracauer approvingly and cites Lubitsch's "facile nihilism about personal relations." [3] This, from the man who was to direct *So Fine* (1980), with its straining after Lubitschean surrealism and effervescence, seems bad faith indeed. But it is typical of the reaction Lubitsch touches off. Even a Lubitsch appreciator like Gerald Mast, who can put the style together with the content, still concludes that Lubitsch "did not take his social realism or Marxism very seriously (as *Ninotchka* would show). Whereas Chaplin's *Verdoux* is acid and (eventually) specific about its social seriousness, *Trouble in Paradise* dances along the shiny comic surface without an apparently serious thought in its head." [4] Mast does allow the importance of what he calls "the film's essential moral contrast of is and seems," but his attitude bears clear affinities with the view that such an old "film as art" stalwart as Lewis Jacobs voiced almost forty years before: "Beginning with *Trouble in Paradise* (1932), a story about an intrigue among sophisticated jewel thieves, Lubitsch narrowed his range of expression to pantomime, *double entendre,* and suggestive continuity." [5] Jacobs allows Lubitsch to argue that he has developed such a technique to allow the audience to leap the gaps itself. But Jacobs still thinks it's only trickiness, not real art. After all, he says, there's no camera movement.

Thus the problem of Lubitsch as expatriate. All those characteristics that the critic normally takes as the due of the expatriate's heightened awareness become the grounds for dismissing Lubitsch as superficial. The mastery of visual form that allowed him to transfer his talents from Germany to the U.S. so effortlessly is considered either to be from the start, or to decline into, an empty style that tricks out trivial themes. Even among his admirers, like his virtual hagiographer Herman G. Weinberg, Lubitsch's greatness is explained as "the Lubitsch touch," which makes a moment or a scene memorable by a focus or a gesture that only he could have conceived. Once again, the emphasis in admirers and detractors alike is on the detachable motifs of Lubitsch's style. The difference being that, if you are unmoved, the "touch" is mere embroidery, while if you're an aficionado, it is, like Matthew Arnold's literary touchstone, the evidence of pure film poetry.

The question of Lubitsch's style is crucial to thinking about the role of an expatriate consciousness in filmmaking because style is precisely the most marketable and most portable evidence of talent or genius anyone in films has. Whether the expatriatism is voluntary, as it was in the 1920s (Hitchcock, Murnau, Seastrom, Stiller), or involuntary as it would be in the 1930s and 1940s (Lang, Renoir), or a bit of both, as it was in the 1960s (Forman, Malle, Antonioni, Passer), the displaced creator presents his style as his aesthetic passport. In such a situation, those creators whose style is primarily visual will translate better than those for whom words are just as important. Godard, with his developed international language, can conceive of making a film in America and did *(1 a.m.)*—not a good one. Truffaut cannot.

But I find it hard to believe that it is entirely possible to admire Lubitsch's style and condemn what he is saying in that style. Whatever "nihilism" implies, it is not sufficient to describe the way Lubitsch tells stories and the implications he wrings from them, far beyond but always through their immediate plots. Lubitsch is the master of style, because he has such an unerring sense of the object or gesture that will crystallize and morally comment on a situation without flattening it out into didacticism. To be such a master, he must understand the infinite visual and verbal systems that make up social intercourse and deploy them for his own use. And he also knows, as I'd like to argue, that the frank acknowledgement of such manipulation is itself part of the meaning of the film he creates.

Trouble in Paradise is an excellent case for a discussion of Lubitsch that takes this view because its hero, Gaston Monescu, himself makes his living by just such an awareness of the power of the interpreting outsider over social codes and those who use them. Monescu (Herbert Marshall) is the master of being well seen when he wants to, and invisible when he does not. And much of the comic motion and suspense of the film depends on whether or not Filibba (Edward Everett Horton) can remember Gaston's face. We ourselves first see Gaston as a shadow leaving an apartment. But, unlike a casual observer, we have also just seen the beginning of the film. There, in a justly celebrated scene, garbage is being collected. But, since this is Venice, the garbage is dumped into a gondola and the gondolier poles off, singing *O Sole Mio*. "Beginnings are always difficult," Gaston will say shortly. But the beginnings of *Trouble in Paradise* neatly situates Lubitsch, and us, in relation to Gaston. We are not tied to his point of view, as in a novel. But we are invited to see the world the way he does, to smile at the juxtaposition of gondola and garbage, even as we realize that it is socially and culturally logical, if romantically and sentimentally illogical, that Venetian garbage should be so collected. A further titillation for the knowing is that it is Enrico Caruso himself doing the singing—another play on the odd relation between what we hear and what we see, or what we see and what we expect to see.[6]

As a con man who manipulates social forms for his own ends, Gaston is the symbiotic twin of Lubitsch himself, the master of manners and social irony. In tracking the shadowy figure of the film's beginning, we have hung with Lubitsch outside the windows of the hotel, following Gaston from room to room, observing and reacting along with him, but at a discreet distance. As he escapes, the camera swoops through windows and around ledges following him. Similarly, later in the film, Gaston will use his binoculars to focus on details, in virtually an homage to the Lubitsch touch itself.[7]

From the start of *Trouble in Paradise* Lubitsch thus takes every opportunity to identify his own mastery with a kind of thievery, a simultaneous dependence on and disdain for the class he preys upon and in whose presence he spends most if not all of his time. In fact, it is a little misleading to call Lubitsch an expatriate in America, for in some very deep sense he was an expatriate in Germany as well, the son of Russian-Jewish parents, who left his father's clothing store to go into show business. After doing bit parts as an actor for Max Reinhart, he first achieved success when he played "Meyer" or "Moritz," a comic Jewish oaf in several short films that he later began to direct and help write. Insofar as I have been able to get some sense of the plots of these films, they were social and sometimes even aesthetic parodies, in which, for example, the inept young man, constantly falling all over himself and knocking everything down, finally marries the boss's daughter; or the foolish mountain-climber, whose garb ridicules the spiritual pretensions of the German preoccupation with mountains, finally triumphs over his mockers. Few critics comment extensively or much at all on the satiric side of these works, but they must have still been on the mind of the Nazi-oriented critic Oskar Kalbus, who in 1935 wrote that Lubitsch's early work had "a pertness entirely alien to our true being."[8]

With such a background in mind, we might look at Lubitsch's German films in a somewhat different way. In the early historical dramas, particularly, Lubitsch's characteristic detachment from the pieties of social order, might, from the perspective of a Kracauer, be said to serve a German nationalist desire to attack the possibility of revolutionary action by showing mobs incapable of any action more complicated than vengeance and bloodshed. On the other hand, as Herman Weinberg points out, these films were also praised as a subtle propagandistic attack against the decadent monarchies of England and France. To which Kracauer could easily reply that this was true nihilism—to attack both mob and bloody tyrant at once. But for Lubitsch, I would argue, there is no alternative. The eye of the director, as both Jew and moviemaker, is totally sceptical of all social order. In its jaundiced view of politics and nationalism, it is perhaps most akin to that of an antisocial idealist. Whereas the Jewish outsider to history, who is a member of neither the mob nor the court, considers both to be in their way ridiculous, the outsider to comedy is the key to its potentially subversive vision of the social order. In *Trouble in Paradise* Mme. Colet advertises the loss of a jeweled purse, and a Russian radical of some sort appears to denounce her for owning such an object to begin with. "Phooey," he says and "Phooey" again, until Gaston intervenes and speaks Russian to him. What can this mean? Does Gaston know Russian? Is he Russian? The question never comes up again, but the implication remains subversive. What are you doing in here? the man maybe saying, and Gaston may reply, doing the same thing you are but in different way.

In Lubitsch's directorial style, the actor's sense of "business," the way in which he uses the psychosocial valence of objects and gestures to build up a recognizable character, is turned into a device to signal irony and distance rather than one to induce empathy and connection. Here is the real importance of the Lubitsch touch, with its frequent Freudian overtone of revealing previously hidden motivations, the sexual story, by an adroit bit of business or a focus on a significant object. The Lubitsch touch signals to the audience that the old interpreter is at it again, letting us in on a privileged perspective, embracing the audience as a co-conspirator of interpretation, an accomplice in the director's and the camera's knowingness. Sometimes we may agree with a critic like Lewis Jacobs that the knowingness we are let in on is in substance not very interesting, even trivial. But *Trouble in Paradise,* a film whose main theme is the question of what one ought to do with one's great interpretive and imitative social skills, indicates the central importance for Lubitsch of that distance, that irony, that knowingness itself, as a necessary social characteristic. Unlike the significant objects in a more expressionistically inclined director like Lang, whose meaning seems almost always to point toward the God or fate in whose unyielding control the characters remain, Lubitsch's underlining or "touching" on his objects represents a possible ideal for the audience as well.

As a thief, Gaston is a cut and run type. But the plot of *Trouble in Paradise* forces him to choose what his whole life will be like and whether he will keep up the surface perpetually, never letting it down even at home. Lubitsch himself kept his own sense of role-playing keenly on the surface. Herman Weinberg reports how he enjoyed yelling ferociously at his actresses on the set when there were visitors around, to satisfy their sense of how a great director behaved. In fact, in the regular rehearsals and shooting, he was very calm and gentle.[9]

Lubitsch is not the Langian or even the Kubrickian overseer of the lives of puppets. He has instead the melancholic wit of the outsider contemplating a world in which he would like to succeed himself, or at least survive. He is attracted, for example, to operetta for the way the form itself light-heartedly inflates manners and passions into extremes that can be portrayed simultaneously at full tilt and with a genially mocking eye. In this way it is intriguing how many expatriate directors have a strong satiric streak in their works, no matter whether their formal inclination is toward realism, expressionism, or the kind of stylized story that attracts Lubitsch.[10] Directors otherwise as disparate as Schlesinger, Forman, Hitchcock, Lang, Sirk, and Kubrick thus have styles that embrace the light-hearted as well as the sinister. (Perhaps *Zabriskie Point* reads better as satire too.) As one of this band of expatriate satirists, Lubitsch also stands outside his creations, but without condescending to them. His love for the visible world includes a love as well for its frauds and its infinite details. As Gaston says, so Lubitsch implies: "I believe in doing things correctly." But his correctness, more than Gaston's (as Gaston learns for himself), delays the revelation that lies just under the surface.

At one point in the filming of *Rosita*, Pickford stormed off the set, complaining that Lubitsch didn't direct people, he directed doors. But doors and other objects play an important role in *Trouble in Paradise*'s vision of wealth and the way it seeks to run the world. Advertising, consuming, gorgeousness are the life-blood of the Colet company. Manners are the way it extracts tribute and asserts its importance. Gaston's own premeditatively acquired manners for the purpose of thieving are mirrored in M. Gorin's (C. Aubrey Smith) constant use of manners to put Gaston down and angle for his own interests. Manners of this sort are empty language, and a good deal of the fun in *Trouble in Paradise* flows from the first comic juxtaposition of sound and image in the garbage gondola into the innumerable misunderstandings of language at the center of which is Filibba. Words seem to connect, seem to imply something beneath the visual surface, but they in fact refer to nothing but themselves. Translation only confuses matters, as in the scene with the police inspector. Far better, it seems, to watch mouths move and eyebrows raise; that way we know what's happening humanly without the warping verbal confusion of social formulas. All the awareness of technique and perspective that the director willingly shares with the audience allows a stepping back, not so much that a particular moral assessment can be made, but so that the viewer may become equally detached from the illusion that society exists as anything more substantial than a collection of manners, gestures, and objects. This is an epistemological subversion in Lubitsch, a demonstration of the theater of behavior, that can hardly be accounted for by the complaints of Kracauer and others about his triviality. For Lubitsch is displaying the actual thinness of the social fabric, the ease with which it is learned, and the insubstantial claim to respect that those who manipulate its forms truly deserve. There is no call for revolution: the context is comic and the events farcical. But the mobs lie just outside the doors, sometimes bursting in, like the Russian, sometimes only murmuring. The glossy image does keep away the chaos outside. But we should *know* that it does. And the window to it Lubitsch opens is as quick and should be as piercing as Pope's glimpse of social tyranny in *The Rape of the Lock:* "Wretches hang that jurymen may dine."

By the affinity between the director and the character of Gaston, Lubitsch further dramatizes the self-conscious way social personality creates and presents itself to the world. Again unlike the more magisterial and Godlike directors, he has some sympathy with such characters and, further, those characters with whom he most sympathizes usually wind up doing well. As a young actor, he played a hunchback clown in a Reinhart production, who out of jealousy causes the dancer he loves to be inadvertently killed. The short play *(Sumurun)* ends with him returning to his booth at the fair because he still has to entertain people; it's his job. Several years after he played the part as an actor, Lubitsch decided to make a film of the play and play the part again (1920). It obviously had some hold on his imagination, and the ability to play the roles of both actor inside and director outside allowed him both to indulge and to step away from its compulsions. The psychological self-staging aspect of the story is intriguing. But here I would like to refer to it primarily for what it shows of Lubitsch's double loyalty, to the actor's perspective and to the director's. In *Trouble in Paradise,* as in many of Lubitsch's other films, the performer, the person who has a high level of social self-awareness and a high degree of social self-presentation, is at center stage. In *Trouble in Paradise* particularly (as opposed, say, to *To Be or Not To Be),* he is also in essence alone, an individual making his way through the world armed only with his self-confidence and his knowledge of how society works, its pretensions and its hypocrises. As Moll Flanders says of herself, Gaston is a kind of "artist," not the robber who steps out and demands payment or the bourgeois white-collar criminal, but a con man who through disguise and insinuation wins by style and guile what the other would take by force or bland deceptions. In one nicely hidden detail, Lubitsch is not only Gaston Monescu's co-conspirator but also Herbert Marshall's. For years I wondered why it is that Gaston climbs so many stairs in the film. Were these vast expressionist stairs that seemed so impossible to climb neatly mocked by Marshall's swift movements, or was it a pleasant, although not very interesting, metaphor of his social rise? Well, I now have one explanation, because a few years ago I ran across the information that Herbert Marshall had lost a leg in World War I. Looking at those scenes again, I can now see how the action has been speeded up. Lubitsch is propelling Gaston up those many stairs at a speed created not by life but by the camera's eye.

Yet the identification of Lubitsch with Gaston can never be complete and the crucial gap lies at the center of the meaning of *Trouble in Paradise,* where it offers some intriguing suggestions for what we might finally think of the expatriate-nurtured detachment that shapes Lubitsch's vision of society and history. Gaston may be a con man and the person to whose perspective the audience is most closely tied. But Lily (Miriam Hopkins) shares our sympathy. And the central conflict of the film is whether Gaston will stay with Mme Colet and run the company or rob her in company with Lily. Visually we know that the relation with Mme Colet is less than substantial. When they finally make love, in one of Lubitsch's most brilliant bits of business, they are first figures embracing, then reflections in a mirror, and then finally two shadows on a bed. We have watched Gaston progress in our eyes (and Lily's) from a shadowy thief to the suave man-about-town, and then to the complicated con man he really is. In this scene with Mme Colet, he regresses along the same visual route. Even though he is the hero, we can't be quite sure he won't fall to the blandishments of Mme Colet and become respectable in fact as well as in appearance. In movie terms, will Gaston join the front office? Finally he does not, even though he saves himself at almost the last minute. Somehow, the prospect of having a partner in social deception like Mme Colet is less attractive than having a partner in crime outside society like Lily. In this world of empty riches, the true privilege is perspective. As Gaston and Lily try to one-up each other with their trickeries in the final scene, we see a community of two now made from the separate voyaging individuals, with a social and emotional knowing that does not qualify their feelings or their fun. It's perfectly possible, given this ending, that their next step could be political engagement or more of the same free-lancing. But at least two separate individuals have become two together, and that's the largest subversive group that Lubitsch seems to allow. Although each one of us in the audience swells it the more.

Gaston doesn't join the front office. But Lubitsch a few years later becomes head of production at Paramount. We know little about his attitudes during this period, and no one that I know of has looked very deeply into the factual material that might give us some sense of how he did work, how he managed to supervise the films of others as well as his own, and in what directions his decisions tried to take the entire company. But that he was given such a position implies that the backers of the company believed that he would do as well for them as Gaston would for Mme Colet. In 1930 he and his wife had been divorced, with Helene Lubitsch charging that Ernst was "99 percent in love with his work and had no time for home." In 1932 his Paramount contract had expired among demands for more artistic freedom. But in February 1935 he and Henry Herzbrun were given joint control over Paramount, Herzbrun for financial and physical production, Lubitsch for creative production. A year later, he was out as production chief and taking charge of his own productions. In his year running Paramount, amid supervising a variety of films, he had signed King Vidor and Lewis Milestone, renewed Wesley Ruggles, hired Harold Lloyd, fired Joseph von Sternberg, and battled with Mae West over the script for *Klondike Annie*.[11] It is unclear whether the job disagreed with him or he with the Paramount executives. Or perhaps the Lubitsch–Herzbrun regime was merely a stopgap until a more permanent production head could be appointed.[12] But in any case Lubitsch did not continue in such an established position. Shortly after he left the Paramount job, he was quoted somewhat cryptically as saying that "I feel, after all, that if I am to be useful in the making of motion pictures, it must be as an individual."[13] New production deals and the great triumph of *Ninotchka* were to follow. But the conclusion of *Trouble in Paradise,* with its expatriate allegory of the individualist artist caught between the comforts of status and the energies of alienation, had prophetically caught up with its creator.

Could Lubitsch have conceived his whole enterprise in America to be so smilingly subversive as some of his films? His moviemaking sensibility was such that he was brilliantly able to combine a virtuoso use of the various technologies and possibilities of film with a sophistication, a sense of nuance, and an evasion that underlined that technology's limits. In this way, he helped define the comic tone of so many films in the American 1930s. But both his strength and his limits came from his ability to see the entire social world, from emotions to politics, as a set of costumes and manners. No wonder that the most heroic action of his later films—in *To Be or Not To Be*—is carried by a troupe of actors, which includes a Jewish stagehand who has always wanted to play Shylock. It is an insight that has great power still, particularly now, when sociology and anthropology, not to mention the daily newspaper, are filled with talk of the theater of public life. But it was an insight of its period and of Lubitsch's own nature that World Events were for a time putting quickly out of date. I wonder also what kind of films Lubitsch could possibly have made after World War II. After *To Be or Not To Be* (1942) and *Heaven Can Wait* (1943), the only film he was able to complete was the tepid *Cluny Brown* in 1946. In 1947, a month before his fifty-sixth birthday, he died from his sixth heart attack. It was the same year that the House Un-American Activities Committee came to Hollywood to subpoena, among others, another cigar-smoking, Berlin-nurtured expatriate with a wry anti-establishment sense of humor—a man six years younger than Lubitsch, whose difference in age may have allowed satire easier commerce with politics. I refer of course to Berthold Brecht.

[1983]

Notes

1. Compare Ford's 1928 plea for a greater internationalism in films, "the great mental marketplace of the world." Richard Koszarski; ed. *Hollywood Directors, 1914–1940* (New York: Oxford University Press, 1976), 198–204.

2. Siegfried Kracauer, *From Caligari to Hitler: A Psychological History of the German Film* (Princeton: Princeton University Press, 1947) 52, 49, 57.

3. Andrew Bergman, *We're in the Money: Depression America and Its Films* (New York: New York University Press, 1971), 57.

4. Gerald Mast, *The Comic Mind* (New York: Bobbs–Merill, 1973), 219.

5. Lewis Jacobs, *The Rise of the American Film* (New York: Harcourt, Brace, 1939); (New York: Columbia University Teachers College Press, 1968), 360.

6. According to Samson Raphaelson, Lubitsch used Caruso's famous recording here. Caruso had died in 1921.

7. Even in this fluid tracking of Gaston's stealth, Lubitsch calls attention to the camera's willful construction of the impression of reality by an obvious cut right in the midst of a movement that makes no change at all. Compare his use of speeded-up movement in the frequent shots of Gaston scooting up the stairs.

8. Quoted by Kracauer, 24. Several of these films have been recently restored and were shown at the Los Angeles County Museum.

9. Herman G. Weinberg, *The Lubitsch Touch* (New York: Dutton, 1968), 16.

10. An intriguing counterexample is of course Renoir, whose American films include efforts to delve into a folk realism *(Swamp Water, The Southerner)*, as well as more expressionistic works verging on social satire *(Diary of a Chambermaid)* and film noir *(Woman on the Beach)*.

11. Lubitsch's hardly veiled attacks against von Sternberg or at least against the von Sternberg style are the most intriguing of his pronouncements as studio chief: "There was a time when directors thought that by making silly camera angles and dissolves they were geniuses. They didn't know how to tell a story and they covered up with a pseudo-artistry. . . . They impressed for a short time, but their day is over. No man is a genius unless he can deliver honest entertainment." *(New York Times,* March 31, 1935 XI, 4:1). Most of the factual material I use above has been culled from many interviews and articles about Lubitsch appearing in the *Times* and *Variety* during this period.

12. Paramount had recently been financially reorganized as Paramount Pictures, Inc., after the previous company, Paramount Publix, had declared bankruptcy. According to Robert Carringer and Barry Sabath, "During Lubitsch's term in the post, production had lagged, costs had soared, and profits dwindled." William LeBaron replaced Lubitsch and stayed with Paramount until 1941. See Carringer and Sabath's excellent compendium of bibliographical and biographical material, *Ernst Lubitsch: A Guide to References and Resources* (Boston: G. K. Hall, 1978), 12–13.

13. *New York Times,* March 1, 1936, IX, 5:8.

III
BODY AND TEXT

Fanny Hill and Materialism

> . . . I felt every vessel in my frame dilate—The arteries beat
> all chearily together, and every power which sustained life
> performed it with so little friction, that 'twould have con-
> founded the most *physical precieuse* in France: with all her
> materialism, she could scarce have called me a machine——
> LAURENCE STERNE, *Sentimental Journey*

Fanny Hill presents an uncomfortable problem to both the theorist of pornography and the historian of literature; it has too broad a sense of social milieu and literary tradition for the writer interested in describing the "pure" elements of pornography as a literary genre, and it has too much erotic content for the literary historian to treat it with much seriousness. Its world is not so completely "hard core" as are the worlds of those nineteenth-century works that so obviously spring from it. The atmosphere of *Fanny Hill* is too exuberant and Fanny's character too vital for either to be part of that gray, repetitive world that Steven Marcus has named "pornotopia."

Now that *Fanny Hill* has been generally available for a few years and the first furor of its republication has died down, Cleland's work seems far more central to "above ground" trends in eighteenth-century literature and philosophy than could be previously appreciated. The particular aspect of *Fanny Hill* I would like to explore in this essay is the relation of the novel to the materialism that was part of the most advanced philosophical thought of Cleland's time—the philosophic naturalism more familiarly advocated by Helvétius, d'Holbach, and especially Julien Offray de la Mettrie in his *L'Homme machine*. I would like to entertain the hypothesis that there is some relation between the view of sexuality presented fictionally in *Fanny Hill* and the view of human nature presented in more discursive philosophical form by La Mettrie in *L'Homme machine*. *Fanny Hill* might then be interpreted not only as a polemical attack against Richardsonian ideals of moral and sexual nature, but also as a defense of the materialist view of human nature popularized by the publication of *L'Homme machine* only a little over a year before.[1]

L'Homme machine was published in Leyden late in 1747 and was quickly seized by the authorities. Although it was not immediately known that La Mettrie was the author, the secret came out rapidly and La Mettrie fled Holland in January of 1748, taking advantage of an invitation from Frederick the Great to come to Berlin. Meanwhile his publisher, Elie Luzac, despite a promise to the authorities to deliver all copies for destruction, succeeded in clandestinely putting out two more editions in 1748. In Europe the book's success was rapid and lasting. It reached England soon after its first appearance. A first translation appeared in 1749 and two more in 1750; the first erroneously ascribed *L'Homme machine* to the Marquis d'Argens, the second and third to La Mettrie.[2]

One difficulty in appreciating the importance of La Mettrie's work is our own lack of sympathy with the idea (or even the hypothesis) that man is essentially a machine. La Mettrie had no such problems. He believed the man–machine hypothesis could be humanistic, liberating, and a support for the uniqueness of the individual; and he says so in *L'Homme machine*. But between us and La Mettrie rises a barrier of interchangeable parts and assembly lines. Our natural response to the word "machine" or "mechanical" is negative. Our mind's eye is clouded with images ultimately derived form Karel Capek's *R.U.R.*, the endlessly identical marching soldiers in totalitarian war machines, or the image originating in eighteenth-century georgic of the machine despoiling the garden. The machine is the robot, and both are inhuman; they neither feel, nor procreate, nor err, nor change. Each is the same as every other machine.[3]

If the word "machine" summons up ideas contrary to our general beliefs about human nature, it is even more inimical to our ideas of the erotic, either in life or literature. Bad sex is "mechanical" or "clinical," that is, devoid of life and feeling and emotion. Pornography is bad because it stimulated "mechanistic" responses, that is, responses without the alloy of either mind or will. Many recent theorists of the erotic argue that if, in a post-Freudian world, we recognize the role of sexuality in defining the self, we must also recognize that the erotic impulse is directly opposed to a scientific and materialistic society that stifles and destroys the self.[4]

Such responses will not do for a proper understanding of either La Mettrie or Cleland. The machines La Mettrie invokes are not the repetitive machines of industrialism, but the machines of wonder, like the duck and flute-player of Jacques Vaucanson, or the young writer and organ player of Pierre Jacquet-Droz.[5] In order to appreciate how *Fanny Hill* may have emerged from a philosophical context in which the emphasis on the physiological and mechanical view of human nature was both liberating and individualizing, let us look for a moment at some of the topics discussed by La Mettrie in *L'Homme machine*.

La Mettrie begins his polemic by asserting that neither the Lockeans, nor the Leibnizians, nor the Cartesians have presented a compelling account of the nature of the soul. The true answers, he asserts, are to be found only in those writers who build their knowledge of man on a basis of physical fact; those who proceed from the metaphysical to the physical have caused all the trouble and confusion. The mind and the body, argues La Mettrie, are only different forms of the same substance. Their interconnections prove this. La Mettrie cites example after example of the dependence of the mental on the physical and the control that bodily events can have over the mind. He does not believe that the mental is reducible to the physical; but they are intimately interrelated and always proceed together: "Les divers Etats de l'âme sont donc toujours corrélatifs à ceux du corps" (p. 158). Despite the usually antipsychological implications of the assertion that man is a machine, the great majority of La Mettrie's observations are directed toward psychological explanation. He argues, for example, that an understanding of normal fear and confusion or abnormal hypochondria and hysteria is impossible if one holds to the Cartesian belief in two separate substances for mind and body, but more feasible if one believes that mind is a more highly organized form of body.[6] Even the ability to innovate in speech, which Descartes reserved for man, must in La Mettrie's hypothesis be an ability that at least in principle can be taught to apes. Language, which La Mettrie defines as the ability to manipulate symbols, is all that separates man from apes, and even that barrier is not insurmountable: "Qu'étoit l'homme, avant l'invention des Mots & la connoissance des Langues? qui avait beaucomp moins d'instinct naturel, que les autres" (p. 162).[7]

How, then, is La Mettrie using a word like "soul"? Writers since Descartes had tended to concentrate on the separate realms of extension and spirit, rather than on that which connected the realms—the soul, situated according to Descartes in the pineal gland. For this reason, there could be a double tradition of Cartesianism, in which both atheistic and orthodox natural scientists could equally proclaim their discipleship. But La Mettrie is not interested in defining the soul as a spiritual faculty that rules the lower being, or in assigning it to a specific place in the body. Instead, he considers the soul to be the principle of organization that unites body and mind. In *Histoire naturelle de l'âme* (1745), he had elaborated the meaning of soul along a more spiritual line. Within *L'Homme machine,* in accordance with his general argument, the concept has become more physicalized. Soul frequently seems coextensive with words like *"organisation," "ressort," "matrice,"* and *"imagination." "Organisation,"* of course, is a general word of connection. Along with *"ressort"* it invokes the Cartesian image of the body as a clock, with La Mettrie's special twist to the basic metaphor: "Le corps humain est une Machine qui monte elle-même ses ressorts; vivante image du mouvement perpétuel" (p. 154). God is not required either as watchmaker or winder: "l'Ame n'est qu'un principe de mouvement, ou une Partie matérielle sensible du Cerveau, qu'on peut, sans craindre l'erreur, regarder comme un ressort principal de toute la Machine" (p. 186).[8]

Imagination and *matrice* are more interesting synonyms for soul. La Mettrie frequently writes as if soul and mind were similar: "L'Ame n'est donc qu'un vain terme dont on n'a point d'idée, & dont un bon Esprit ne doit se servir que pour nommer la partie qui pense en nous" (p. 180). In what Aram Vartanian calls "the first radical rehabilitation of the imaginative faculty in his epoch," La Mettrie than associates thought with imagination. Imagination makes connections, and these connections define man's true knowledge: "Je me sers toujours du mot *imaginer,* parce que je crois que tout s'imagine, & que toutes les parties de l'Ame peuvent être justement réduites à la seule imagination, que les forme toutes" (p. 165).

But La Mettrie's originality does not stop here, for the most fascinating aspect of his use of imagination is its association with *matrice.* Previous metaphors of scientific discovery might invoke images of divine illumination or logical conclusion. La Mettrie's metaphors are most often sexual. Vartanian remarks on the fact that "scientific and erotic curiosity seem for him to function together in a sort of alliance, each serving to strengthen and stimulate the other" (p. 32). And La

Mettrie's metaphoric language is allied with his basic theme of the strong inter-connection between imagination and sexuality. His metaphor for scientific insight is sexual penetration; his metaphor for the development of ideas is human generation and birth. The imagination is the womb *(matrice)* of ideas, and he calls the mind "cette matrice de l'espirit." *Matrice* as womb and *matrice* as matrix (of ideas) is a double meaning that La Mettrie plays upon throughout *L'Homme machine*. In one section, for example, he argues that organization is the first merit of man, and then must come education:

> Il est aussi impossible de donner une seule idée à un Homme, privé de tous les sens, que de faire un Enfant à une Femme, à laquelle la Nature auroit poussé la distraction jusqu'à oublier de faire une Vulve, comme je l'ai vu dans une, qui n'avoit ni Fente, ni Vagin, ni Matrice, & qui pour cette raison fut démariée après dix ans de mariage   (p. 167).[9]

The association La Mettrie makes between sexuality and imagination, between sexual penetration and scientific insight, calls into question the traditional role to which sexuality had been assigned by philosophers. The earlier attitude emphasized the opposition between the cognitive operations of the mind and the distracting and trivial operations of the body. In more extreme though still familiar terms, sexual motives impelled the search for forbidden knowledge, the realm of evil and the devil. The body in general and sexuality in particular worked against man's effort to achieve wisdom and transcendence.[10]

La Mettrie uses sexual examples as well as sexual metaphors. Sexuality is so important in his language because it is central to his philosophy. If man has achieved so much more than animals because of his larger brain, he has concomitantly lost in instinct what he has gained in organization and understanding. Man must re-learn his instincts in order to live fully and most humanly. And the instincts that need the most relearning are the sexual instincts, because they are so closely allied to the force of imaginative coherence and the exuberance of both physical and mental creativity:

> c'est [l'imagination] encore qui ajoute à la tendresse d'un coeur amoureux, le piquant attrait de la volupté. Elle la fait germer dans le Cabinet du Philosophe, & du Pédant poudreux; elle forme enfin les Savans, comme les Orateurs & les Poetes.   (pp. 165–166).

> Mais si le cerveau est à la fois bien organisé & bien instruit, c'est une terre féconde parfaitement ensemencée, qui produit le centuple de ce qu'elle a reçu.   (p. 167)

La Mettrie's emphasis on sexuality and the idea of the body as machine is for him, as for many who followed his ideas, a liberation from theories of the inferiority of body to mind and from the neo-Cartesian orthodoxy that accepted the mechanical nature of the physical world but reserved final respect and adoration for the realm of spirit and soul. The true view of man, asserts La Mettrie, emphasizes both his physical and mental nature. Each man–machine is for him unique.

Once the machine hypothesis has restored to man his human nature, political or social tyranny based on man's "divine part" will vanish.

Cartesian dualism furnished a philosophical foundation for physiological research. But the postulate of the two separate substances of body and spirit allowed the same metaphysical distrust of the body that had always existed. La Mettrie's machine hypothesis allows the body a dignity to equal the mind's. Instead of man being a Hamlet crawling between heaven and earth or a Gulliver whose disgust with his "lower" self finally leads him to reject the human race, La Mettrie's man, his mind and body part of the same being, could now rise even higher. "Pourquoi faire double ce qui n'est évidemment qu'un?" Like human beings in sexual intercourse, the body and mind "se réunissent toutes suivant leur nature." "L'âme et le corps s'endorment ensemble," La Mettrie writes in another place. What more appropriate transition to *Fanny Hill?*

Much more factual information must be discovered about Cleland's life before any question of the direct influence of *L'Homme machine* on *Fanny Hill* can be resolved. Cleland's activities before the publication of *Fanny Hill* are vague at best. He was appointed a writer for the East India Company at Bombay on 10 February 1731 and took up official service there on 19 July 1731. He rose steadily in salary and rank, becoming Secretary for Portuguese Affairs, and later Secretary to the Bombay Council in January of 1739. He left Bombay sometime about 20 September 1740 and arrived back in England shortly before 26 March 1741, when he appeared before the East India Company Board of Directors. Why he left Bombay seems more obscure, although perhaps it was due to reports of the troubles of his father, William, who was a friend of Pope and died 21 September 1741. Cleland's activities until the publication of *Fanny Hill* are less certain. David Foxon reports that the first advertisements for *Fanny Hill* he has been able to find are in the *General Advertiser* for 21 November 1748 (volume one) and in the *London Evening Post* for 14–16 February 1749 (volume two). But according to the records of the Beggar's Benison Society of Anstruther, Scotland, a work called *Fanny Hill* was read at a gathering in 1737.[11]

The special relation I would argue between *Fanny Hill* and the views of La Mettrie (including the actual use of the phrase "man–machine") is strong proof against a fully conceived Fanny Hill in 1737.[12] At best, the earlier date, if not spurious, might mark the appearance of a primitive version of the novel's earlier parts. If I might speculate further, perhaps this early version was then laid aside until the appearance of *L'Homme machine* furnished a polemical framework for Cleland's earlier and fragmentary *jeu d'esprit*. The perfunctory structure of the work supports this contention. The novel is divided into two letters, both directed to a female correspondent, to whom Fanny is describing and explaining her life.[13] In the second letter most of what might be called direct references to La Mettrie's ideas appear, although there is not an abrupt shift in attitude from the first to second parts of the novel. The change, in fact, could be interpreted as part of Fanny's increased awareness.

Perhaps the most striking indication of Cleland's possible assimilation of the principles of philosophic naturalism is Fanny's constant use of the word "machine" to refer to the penis. As far as the OED and Eric Partridge can enlighten us, this usage seems to begin in English with Cleland, and he may also have been a precursor of its usage in French. One could argue that Cleland is only adapting a common military usage ("apparatus, appliance, instrument," reports the OED with a 1650 first reference) to his eighteenth-century version of the Renaissance topos of the siege of love.[14] But Cleland's image derives more directly from Descartes's characterization of the *bête–machine,* to cite the OED again, a being "without life, consciousness, or will." Cleland's usage again seems to be individual and unique, the two references cited in the OED being Robert Boyle's description of beasts (1692) and Alexander Hamilton's of soldiers (1770).[15]

Obviously, then, Cleland is implying something with his use of "machine" beyond Fanny's practice of elaborate euphemism and elegant variation. Fanny may actually be expressing a genuine wonder at the physiological reality of the human body and the philosophic celebration of this reality contained in mechanistic language.[16] In incidents reminiscent of La Mettrie's examples, Fanny realizes that the body can make demands on the mind that the mind cannot resist. When Charles, her first lover (with whom she will be reunited and married at the end of the novel), begins to caress her, "My fears, however, made me mechanically close my thighs; but the very touch of his hand insinuated between them, disclosed them and opened a way for the main attack" (p. 41). Sexual relations can be the perfect human instance of Cartesian *choc,* the direct collision between entities that defines the causal relations of the universe. But Cleland, like La Mettrie and unlike Descartes, continually emphasizes that, at least in sexual experience, human beings have as little consciousness or will as the *"bête-machine."* Mr. H——, one of Fanny's later lovers, is not so personally appealing as Charles. Yet the effect of intercourse is the same: "he soon gave nature such a powerful summons down to her favourite quarters that she could not longer refuse repairing thither; all my animal spirits then rush'd mechanically to that center of attraction, and presently, inly warmed, and stirred as I was beyond bearing, I lost all restraint" (p. 75).

In her narration, Fanny has an abundance of life and an acute sense of the world around her. She can make satiric comments about London society, briefly and effectively sketching someone she meets. But when sexual excitement begins, she seems to lose both will and self. Is Cleland therefore arguing against La Mettrie and asserting that sexuality is a threat to mind and personality?

In descriptive terms, Cleland does recognize that sexual indulgence invites a loss of self-consciousness and self-control. The body itself, defined in the sexual moment only by its physiological makeup, responds mechanically, like a mere machine. In an important scene in the second letter, Fanny goes along with her friend Louisa, who wants to lure "Good-natured Dick" into their rooms, to see if the half-witted delivery boy had been sexually oversupplied by nature for his mental shortchanging. Fanny, as she does so frequently, will only watch. But Louisa indulges fully, and the effect is more than she anticipated:

she went wholly out of her mind into that favourite part of her body, the whole intenseness of which was so fervously fill'd and employ'd; there she alone existed, all lost in those delirious transports, those extasies of the senses. . . . In short, she was now as mere a machine as much wrought on, and had her emotions as little at her own command as the natural himself.   (pp. 188–189)

If we take passages like this in purely descriptive terms, Cleland's view of sexuality is close to Richardson's. Both believe that the sexual instinct can be a threat to the control of the mind. For Pamela and Clarissa the loss of chastity threatens the loss of all morality and self-integrity. In this way, Cleland is must closer to Richardson than he is to Fielding, for whom sexuality is neither so momentous nor so problematic.

Cleland therefore proceeds from the same assumption about the importance of sexuality as Richardson. But his conclusions are quite different. Richardson seems to assert that sexuality is a dire threat against the "real" self. Cleland, on the other hand, uses the metaphor of military contest to express the engagement between man and woman rather than the despair of a riven self. Richardson further implies that sexuality is a looming horror from the primitive self that the needs of society and morality should have succeeded in repressing. Like La Mettrie, Cleland presents a more integrative view: instead of being a threat to the mind, the body, when its nature is properly understood, joins with the mind in the total human character. Fanny is fascinated by the physiology of sexual reactions not merely because Cleland wants to stimulate his readers but also because, in the development of her own character, she wants to know. Sexuality is a possible and much neglected way into knowledge of the self. Cleland emphasizes that it is not the only way: Fanny often loses her self-consciousness in the sexual act, but she uses the experience as part of a search for more consciousness. Louisa's transformation into a mere machine seems closely related to her previously expressed belief that her human nature may be thoroughly searched through masturbation: "Here I gave myself up to the old insipid privy shifts of my self-viewing, self-touching, self-enjoying, *in fine,* to all the means of *self-knowledge* I could devise, in search of the pleasure that fled before me, and tantalized with that unknown something that was out of my reach" (p. 125). Louisa's exclusive preoccupation with her sexuality therefore acts as a foil to Fanny's more comprehensive view.

Perhaps a whimsical answer to the questions "Why pornography in the eighteenth century?" and "Why Fanny Hill?" might involve the relation of the materialist viewpoint to the nature of pornography itself. Cleland may see pornography as another didactic form to stand beside both satire and the novel in the first half of the eighteenth century. Pornography is in fact a surer method. The stimulus of reading a scene in *Fanny Hill* makes in the reader's own nature the point made in the text. The reader may be moved to reconsider the merits of stoicism, reevaluate the powers of the mind to control the body, reread his Descartes, and think again of the dividing line between man and the *bête–machine*. By a species of imitative form, pornography enforces and answers the hypothetical question of La Mettrie:

N'est-ce pas machinalement qu'agissent tous les Sphincters de la Vessie, du *Rectum* & c.? que le Coeur a une contraction plus forte que tout autre muscle? que les muscles érecteurs font dresser La Verge dans l'Homme, comme dans les Animaux qui s'en battent le ventre; & même dans l'enfant, capable d'érection, pour peu que cette partie soit irritée?   (p. 183)

Despite the loss of self and mental control that Cleland describes, he, again like La Mettrie, does not consider the emphasis on the sexual side of human nature to be reductive. Both Cleland and La Mettrie seem to deny the moral and theological implications in Descartes's association of body and beast: the beast is a machine because it lacks a soul; man without a soul would be a mere beast. Instead they consider their emphasis on the body to be positive and humanizing. In order to understand human nature more fully, one must first understand the sexual and physiological side of it. In her own way Fanny is presenting a program of action to supplement the polemic of La Mettrie's first paragraphs: trust the writers who begin with the body and then move to metaphysics, not those who go the other way. Yet sexuality is only a beginning. Body without mind, in another favorite image from *Fanny Hill,* is like food without savor. In mind lust is transmuted into love, and, as Fanny says, love is "the Attic salt of enjoyment."

Nowhere in *Fanny Hill* is Cleland's commitment to both the man–machine view of human nature and to the dignity that it can restore to the individual more apparent than in the scene in which Fanny and Louisa experiment on "Good-natured Dick." Dick is "withal, pretty featur'd," although his clothes and general appearance are in "so ragged a plight, that he might have disputed points of shew with e'er a heathen philosopher of them all" (p. 184). Dick is "good-natured" and a "natural" in the sense of those words that most interested both La Mettrie and Cleland. Louisa invites him upstairs for his payment and he responds with confusion. Fanny flirts with him, and watches his cheeks begin to glow: "The emotion in short of animal pleasure glar'd distinctly in the simpleton's counte-nance" (p. 185). When Fanny leads him further, her language emphasizes the natural level at which she aims (and may even allude to La Mettrie's next work, *L'Homme plante,* published at Potsdam in 1748): "My fingers too had now got within reach of the true, the genuine sensitive plant, which instead of shrinking from the touch, joys to meet it, and swells and vegetates under it" (p. 185).[17] Dick's "plant" is no disappointment: "Nature, in short had done so much for him in those parts, that she perhaps held herself acquitted in doing so little for his head" (p. 186). When Louisa initiates further stages of the experiment, both the language and the the themes are once again strikingly reminiscent of La Mettrie in *L'Homme machine:*

> she presently determined to risk a trial of parts with the idiot, who was by this time nobly inflam'd for her purpose, by all the irritations we had used to put the principles of pleasure effectually in motion, and to wind up the springs of its organ to their supreme pitch; and it stood accordingly stiff and straining, ready to burst with the blood and spirits that swelled it . . . to a bulk!   (p. 186)

The "irritations" that Fanny speaks of are not those we commonly call irritations. They are, however, very close to the scientific definition of the principle of irritability that Vartanian asserts is "one of the most original and impressive features of *l'Homme machine*" (p. 20). As Vartanian explains, La Mettrie brilliantly proposed that irritability was "a general property of living substance," even though his examples dealt only with muscular contraction. "Contractility was, in his time, the only experimentally known phase of the irritable process." But La Mettrie's frequent use of erection as an example of mechanism does not seem wasted on Cleland.

A further reflection of La Mettrie's language in this short passage is the phrase, "to wind up the springs of its organ," which implies the metaphor of the body as a clock, held together by *"ressorts."* The final phrase (the ellipsis is Cleland's own) is so close to some lines of La Mettrie, that I am almost willing to drop my tentativeness and assert direct influence. La Mettrie is speaking of the interplay of the muscles and the imagination when the body reacts to the image of beauty, "qui en excite un autre, lequel étoit fort assoupi, quand l'imagination l'a éveillé: & comment cela, si ce n'est par le désordre & le tumulte du sang & des esprits, qui galopent avec une promptitude extraordinaire, & vont gonfler les corps caverneux?" (p. 183).[18]

The importance of this scene is not exhausted by the possible parallels that I have already mentioned. Louisa leads Dick to bed, "which he joyfully gave way to, under the incitations of instinct and palpably deliver'd up to the goad of desire" (p. 187). The two come together, and the great size of the "master-tool" of the "natural" causes Louisa to cry out in pain.

But it was too late: the storm was up and force was on her to give way to it; for now the man-machine, strongly work'd upon by the sensual passion, felt so manfully his advantages and superiority, felt withal the sting of pleasure so intolerable, that maddening with it, his joys began to assume a character of furiousness which made me tremble for the too tender Louisa. (p. 187)

As she has before, Fanny thinks for a moment that the man might be too much for the woman, but Fanny also observes how the awakening of sexual feeling can be ennobling, even for one perhaps too deficient in mind to take advantage of it:

He seemed, at this juncture, greater than himself; his countenance, before so void of meaning, or expression, now grew big with the importance of the act he was upon. In short, it was not now that he was to be play'd the fool with. But, what is pleasant enough, I myself was aw'd into a sort of respect for him, by the comely terrors his motions dressed him in: his eyes shooting sparks of fire; his face glowing with ardours that gave another life to it; his teeth churning, his whole frame agitated with a raging ungovernable impetuosity: all sensibly betraying the formidable fierceness with which the genial instinct acted upon him (p. 187).[19]

In this passage and the descriptions that follow, Cleland adroitly keeps in solution two views of human nature that more frequently separate. Like La Mettrie, he is calling a truce between mechanism and vitalism, almost before the battle has really begun. Dick is the creature solely of his body, "instinct-ridden as he was" (p. 188), and Louisa too under the second onslaught of the "brute–machine" be-

comes "as mere a machine." The reference to brute–machine seemingly reinforces the reductive aspect of the sexuality. But Fanny has observed also the
transfiguration of the half-wit in the grip of sexual passion; he is discovering an
essential part of his human nature. There is a vitality and warmth in true sexuality
that can liberate human nature, even when neither mind nor reason, soul nor
spirit, is sufficient.

Both Fanny and Cleland believe that in the ideal sexual relationship the mind
and body have equal share. Fanny's last lover before she is reunited with Charles,
her first, is a "rational pleasurist":

> he it was, who first taught me to be sensible that the pleasures of the mind were
> superior to those of the body; at the same time, that they were so far from obnoxious
> to, or incompatible with each other, that besides the sweetness in the variety and
> transition, the one serv'd to exalt and perfect the taste of the other to a degree that the
> sense alone can never arrive at. (pp. 199–200)

Fanny has viewed her own adventures retrospectively through this union of body
and mind that allows each its full role. She enjoys sex for its own sake, but her
most pleasurable encounters mix body with mind:

> what an immense difference did I feel between this impression of a pleasure merely
> animal, and struck out of the collision of the sexes by a passive bodily effect from
> that sweet fury, that rage of active delights which crowns the enjoyments of a mutual
> love-passion, where two hearts, tenderly and truly united, club to exalt the joy, and
> give it spirit and soul that bids defiance to that end which mere momentary desires
> generally terminate in, when they die of a surfeit of satisfaction. (p. 75)

Such speculations are common for Fanny, "whose natural philosophy all resided
in the favourite center of sense," although not for her lover, Mr. H——, "whom
no distinctions of that sort seemed to disturb," The "active delights" raise the
"passive bodily effect" to full realization in the same way that Fanny's meditation
and explanation make sense of her sexual adventures. And, as experience alone is
nothing for her without an interpretation of that experience, so it is only in love
that the physical and the mental are truly combined. Fanny's love for Charles is
"a passion in which soul and body were concentre'd, and left me no room for
any other relish of life but love" (p. 62). Her ability to experience as well as to
meditate gives a vitality and exuberance to her character that affirms the rehuman-
izing program behind Cleland's sexual emphasis.

Fanny Hill is therefore much more than a piece of pornography whose only
intent is mercenary.[20] In many ways it appears to be a detailed polemic in support
of some of the most advanced philosophic ideas of its time. If one test of a major
novel is the extent to which it experiments with and changes the received assumptions of novelistic form, *Fanny Hill* surely qualifies for consideration. Cleland
recognizes the unique relationship possible in erotic literature between the reader
and the work. In *Fanny Hill* he raises this relationship to the level of artistic
consciousness by making it not only a criticism of the Richardsonian epistolary

method, but also an exploration of the forces of mind and body in human character. The erotic scenes in *Fanny Hill,* instead of being only stimulating, are both stimulating and an essential part of "the soft laboratory of love" in which Fanny herself mingles the correlative impulses of body and mind. Our view of what Cleland has achieved has become unfortunately clouded, less by the censorship of *Fanny Hill* than by the way in which Cleland has become the victim of his imitators, who repeat scene, motif, and style with no understanding that, when Cleland used them, they were something more than a cabinet of stylized gestures.

Fanny's world is larger than the merely sexual, as she herself is the first to point out. The natural freedom of sexuality also implies a natural world of social relations, which is behind Fanny's jibes at upper-class London life. Cleland here again resembles Richardson in his emphasis on the egalitarian possibilities of sexuality. But, as before, Richardson and Cleland come to opposite conclusions. Egalitarian sexuality is a threat in *Pamela* because it threatens the class lines of society and the social order itself. Like the medieval antifeminists, Richardson considers the sexual impulse to be primarily reductive, with its origin in the devil. In Richardson's terms, however, the devil is an aristocrat, and the licentious aristocracy is forfeiting its natural right to rule by allowing a lust that cuts across the barriers of class and upsets the rules of morality. Pamela's marriage to Mr. B. breaks the class divisions in the name of morality, although with the socially subversive implication that morally all human beings are equal.

In Cleland's world of class, it is sexuality that makes all men and women equal. The naked body implies the naked heart. Fanny comments derisively on "the false, ridiculous, refinements of the great," so inferior to the natural and unalloyed joys that can be found with people of lesser rank. Here are the first articulated beginnings of the sexual and moral primitivism that is so much more elaborately developed later in the century. Mr. H——'s servant Will gives Fanny more real pleasure (physical and mental) than Mr. H——'s "loftier qualifications of birth, fortune and sense" (p. 94). La Mettrie may retain his masculine point of view even while praising the exuberant sexual nature that had previously been associated primarily with women. But Cleland through Fanny is transmuted into the first feminist. Fanny may bear a love for Charles so great that she yearns for him in what seems to be a fairly submissive way. But when she discovers him bereft of status and fortune, she likes him even better, "broken down to his naked personal merit" (p. 206).

Since sexuality in Cleland is so invariably part of the natural, one might entertain the idea that a major figure behind the growth of eighteenth-century erotic literature both in England and France is John Locke. In addition to the mechanical metaphor, the most frequent descriptive image in *Fanny Hill* is the *paysage érotisé* or, perhaps more accurately, the *corps paysager*. The natural world of the body is an unspoiled Eden. The girls whom Fanny admires have healthy country looks. Sexuality at Mrs. Cole's establishment is edenic and countrified. Her clients "would at any time leave a sallow, washy-painted duchess on her hands, for a ruddy, healthy, firm flesh'd country maid" (p. 110). "The authors and supporters of this secret institution would, in the height of their humours, style themselves the restorers of the golden age and its simplicity of pleasures, before their innocence became so injustly branded with the names of guilt and shame" (p. 108). The language of mechanism and the invocation of nature are therefore total complements in *Fanny Hill,* although later pornographic works, in which great machines penetrate mossy grots, have undoubtedly lost this kind of understanding. In line with his attack against the Cartesian assumption that the *bête–machine* was without feeling and his support of La Mettrie's belief in the soul of the man–machine, Cleland seems to reflect Lockean ideas about the purity of natural impulses in the state of nature, and his egalitarian motif also may have Lockean roots. Bolingbroke argued against the Lockean state of nature because natural equality undercut the idea of a hierarchical society. Cleland's natural world of sexuality obviously has similarities to the "pornotopia" that Steven Marcus discovered in nineteenth-century pornography. But Cleland's sexuality is related to a vital social and cultural context, however ideal it may be, whereas "pornotopia" remains hermetic and self-justifying. "Pornotopia" may be defined, in fact, as the innovations of *Fanny Hill* forced by censorship and by familiarity into dull repetition, the unique machine now turned out by assembly lines.

Cleland invokes the natural body and the natural landscape in a deliberately natural use of language. Fanny is conscious of language as a problem, excuses herself "for having, perhaps, too much affected the figurative style," and apologizes to her correspondent:

> I imagined, indeed, that you would have been cloy'd and tired with uniformity of adventures and expressions, inseparable from a subject of this sort, whose bottom, or groundwork being, in the nature of things, eternally one and the same, whatever variety of forms and modes the situations are susceptible of, there is no escaping a repetition of near the same images, the same figures, the same expressions.   (p. 105)

To remedy this cloying, Fanny calls upon the "imagination and sensibility" of her correspondent to supplement her work, in a manner very similar to Fielding's demands in *Tom Jones* that the reader fill in his own idea of feminine beauty when Fielding mentions Sophia Western. The inability of words to express the sexual experience either fully or adequately is most apparent when the subject is closest to nature: "No! Nothing in nature could be of a beautifuller cut; then, the dark umbrage of the downy spring-moss that over-arched it bestowed, on the luxury of the landscape, a touching warmth, a tender finishing, beyond the expression of words, or even the paint of thought" (p. 133). Cleland contrasts the vitality of nature with the corrupt sophistications of society and the spurious niceties of art. Phoebe's labia, Fanny remarks, "vermilioning inwards exprest a small rubid line in sweet miniature, such as *Guido's* touch of colouring could never attain to the life or delicacy of" (p. 37). In the same way Charles's parts are

> surely superior to those nudities furnish'd by the painters, statuaries, or any art, which are purchas'd at immenses prices; whilst the sight of them in actual life is scarce sovereignly tasted by any but the few whom nature has endowed with a fire of imagination, warmly pointed by a truth of judgement to the springhead, the originals of beauty, of nature's unequall'd composition, above all imitation of art, or the reach of wealth to pay their price.   (p. 54)

Penises are compared to ivory columns and breasts to marble so that their actual superiority to these things of art may be clear: "a well-formed fulness of bosom, that had such an effect on the eye as to seem flesh hardening into marble, of which it emulated the polished gloss, and far surpassed even the whitest, in the life and lustre of its colours, white veined with blue" (p. 136). Once again, a phrase of La Mettrie's in *L'Homme machine* seems apposite, another of La Mettrie's paeans to the imagination: "Par elle, par son pinceau flatteur, le froid squélette de la Raison prend des chairs vives & vermeilles; par elle les Sciences fleurissent, les Arts s'embellissent, les Bois parlent, les Echos soupirent, les Rouchers pleurent, le Marbre respire, tout prend vie parmi les corps inanimés" (p. 165).

Many of the themes that I have found in *Fanny Hill* sound much like those usually associated with sentimentalism: the truth of feelings and instincts, the natural as the basic part of human nature, the superiority of nature to art, the inadequacy of language, and social egalitarianism. This is no error. *Fanny Hill* is a storehouse of sentimental themes that achieve full expression and circulation only in the 1760s and 1770s. Cleland looks forward to Sterne, the Smollett of *Humphrey Clinker,* and the Diderot of *Le Rêve de d'Alembert* much more than he looks back to Defoe, Richardson, and Fielding. But unlike the self-conscious sentimentality of Sterne or the less self-aware sentimentality of Henry Mackenzie, sentiment in Cleland's *Fanny Hill* moves comfortably in complement to sexuality. La Mettrie's integration of sexuality and imagination and Cleland's of sexuality and sentiment are beautifully articulated accounts of previously inarticulate forces in the human personality. But the balance, at least in English literature, does not seem to last very long. Part of the melancholy in *Tristram Shandy* and the fun in *Sentimental Journey* is the association of Toby's sentiment with his impotence and Yorick's sentiment with his prurience.

As true first-generation philosophees, Cleland and Le Mettrie share an optimism about man's ability to deal with his sexual nature once he has recognized it. Sterne deals with the same themes of imagination, sexuality, and sentiment. But for him they have become much more problematic. Toby retreats from his own body and feelings into the artifice of history, the reconstructed Battle of Namur, while Yorick refuses to acknowledge the frequently salacious impulse beneath his sentimental sightseeing. Yorick constantly digs at the materialists. He has emotions that "could not be accounted for from any combination of matter and motion." He is positive that he has a soul despite what the materialists say. But all his philosophy, like that of the misanthropic Matthew Bramble in the first parts of *Humphry Clinker,* seems the projection of his inability to understand the nature of his own body and how it affects his mind and feelings. Mackenzie's *The Man of Feeling* (1771) carries this divorce of "feeling" from physicality even further. Sterne makes the difficult relation between emotions and bodily feeling part of his theme. But Mackenzie indicates that the highest form of feeling has no physical dimension whatsoever. The purity of the emotional relationship between Harley, his hero, and Miss Walton, is ratified by their lack of physical contact, and Harley's death occurs at just the moment when they might finally be married.[21] Somewhere between the exuberant blend of sensation and sentiment celebrated by La Mettrie and Cleland has fallen the shadow of this eighteenth-century version of Petrarchan love. Sexuality has once again become a force that reduces human nature. In the late 1740s, *L'Homme machine* and *Fanny Hill* detailed a liberating combination of human imagination and bodily feeling that turned its face against centuries of philosophical subordination of body to mind. By the 1700s this potentially revolutionary force had become a secular religion of mere gesture, in which the only approved response of the body to a situation that involved human feeling was an interminable downpouring of tears.

[1970]

Notes

1. The difficult problem of the seventeenth- and eighteenth-century origins of pornography, as distinguished from bawdy or erotic literature in general, has been broached by David Foxon in *Libertine Literature in England, 1660–1745* (New Hyde Park, N.Y., 1965). Foxon's book also includes a detailed account of the publication and prosecution of *Fanny Hill*.

2. Aram Vartanian, *La Mettrie's L'Homme machine: A Study in the Origins of an Idea* (Princeton, 1960), pp. 6–8, 137–38. My debt to Vartanian's thorough and subtle work will be apparent in the following pages. Further references to it will be included in the text.

3. In *Culture and Society, 1780–1950* (New York, 1960), Raymond Williams comments frequently on the changing meaning of words as an index to the quality of change between eras. See especially "A Note on 'Organic,' " pp. 281–82, in which Williams dates the distinction between "organic" and "mechanical" from Burke and Coleridge.

4. Susan Sontag in "The Pornographic Imagination," *Partisan Review*, 2 (1967), 195–96, follows French theorists in tracing the connection between machinery and pornographic eroticism to Sade: "Sade's ideas—of the person as a "thing" or an "object," of the body as a machine and of the orgy as an inventory of the hopefully indefinite possibilities of several machines in collaboration with each other—seems mainly designed to make possible an endless, non-culminating kind of ultimately affectless activity." Georges Bataille, whom Miss Sontag frequently cites, images the contrast in the picture of a naked girl on a bicycle: "le spectacle irritant, théoriquement sale, d'un corps nu et chaussé sur la machine" *(Histoire de l'oeil, Paris, 1967)*, p. 37.

5. For photographs of these "automata" and a history of machines that concentrates more on wonder than on uniformity, see K. G. Pontus Hultén. *The Machine as Seen at the End of the Mechanical Age* (New York, 1968), pp. 20–21.

6. It is intriguing that a century usually characterized by its desire to reduce mystery to intelligibility could contain among its greatest empiricists men so interested in the diseases of mind and the vagaries of imagination. One example of this fascination may be the growing importance of doctors in the English novel, not as satiric butts for their use of jargon (as in Fielding), but as abettors of a pervasive hypochondria (as in Sterne and Smollett). Within a more clinical context Michel Foucault in *Madness and Civilization* (New York, 1965) argues that madness in the eighteenth century served to identify the outsider (and by implication the "normal" society) in much the same way that leprosy had done in the Middle Ages. For his discussion of hysteria and hypochondria, two subjects frequently referred to by La Mettrie, see chapters 4 and 5, "Aspects of Madness" and "Doctors and Patients." See also *Minds and Machines,* ed. Alan Ross Anderson (Englewood Cliffs, N. J., 1964).

7. Another parallel between the materialist and the pornographic perspectives is their common preoccupation with the problem of language. La Mettrie's views are discussed by Keith Gunderson in "Descartes, La Mettrie, Language, and Machines," *Philosophy*, 39 (1964), 193–222. See also Noam Chomsky, *Cartesian Linguistics: A Chapter in the History of Rationalist Thought* (New York, 1966). Cleland was also interested in the origins of language, first publishing a pamphlet entitled *The Way to Things by Words, and to Words by Things* (1766), and in 1768, *Specimen of an Etimological Vocabulary, or, Essay by Means of the Analitic Method, to Retrieve the Antient Celtic.*

8. Compare the language used by Louis Racine, one of the last defenders of Cartesian animal automatism, in a poem written prior to 1719: "Je ne puis rapporter cet étonnant savoir / Qu'à de secrets ressorts que le sang fait mouvoir." Cited by Leonora Cohen Rosenfield, *From Beast–Machine to Man–Machine* (New York, 1940), p. 58.

9. It is difficult for the English or American reader to appreciate this aspect of La Mettrie's thought, since the only available translation of La Mettrie into English since 1750 (according to Vartanian's bibliography) has been that of Gertrude C. Bussey, published by Open Court and reprinted several times since 1912. The Preface remarks that the translation is based on Miss Bussey's Wellesley dissertation, corrected by M. W. Calkins with the help of M. Carret and George Santayana. But there is no way for the reader to find out, except by comparing the French and English texts, that a total of almost five pages—in words, phrases, and entire paragraphs—have been omitted from the English translation, their departure marked only by dots. I should say "bowdlerized" rather than "omitted," for the passages removed almost without exception refer to sexual matters. I have compared the Open Court edition with Miss Bussey's original, and her "correctors" have been even more scrupulous than she was, omitting passages that seem to contain sexual reference, although one or two actually do not. (Miss Bussey is at least consistent and also ellipsizes the corresponding French passages.) Stylistically, the Open Court translation also leaves much to be desired. *Matrice,* for example, is almost invariably rendered as "matrix," even when "womb" is the primary meaning.

10. Although La Mettrie's argument serves to enhance the stature of sexuality in general, his own prejudices are still male-oriented. In the great controversy between the ovists and the spermatists over the origins of generation, La Mettrie leans to the spermatist position: "Il me paroît que c'est le Mâle qui fait tout, dans une femme qui dort, comme dans la plus lubrique" (p. 194). One intriguing indication of the way in which later pornography becomes fixated in eighteenth-century beliefs about physiology is the prevalence of the idea that both men and women ejaculate with orgasm. This belief, sanctioned by Hippocrates and Galen, was also supported by Descartes, who based his theory of generation on a "mélange des deux liqueurs." Maupertuis had revived the idea in *Venus physique* (1745) and Buffon later held similar beliefs. La Mettrie takes a measured view: "Il est si rare que les deux semences se rencontrent dans le Congrès, que je serois tenté de croire que la semence de la femme est inutile à la génération" (p. 194). See the discussion by Vartanian, footnotes 114 and 119, pp. 247–49.

11. The DNB account of Cleland's foreign activities seems retrospectively colored by the notoriety of *Fanny Hill*. The statement that he was consul in Smyrna may be based on a long footnote in John Nichols's *Literary Anecdotes of the Eighteenth Century* (6 vols., London, 1812) that calls Smyrna the place "where, perhaps, he first imbibed those loose principles which, in a subsequent publication, too infamous to be particularized, tarnished his reputation as an author" (II, 458). A search of the relevant Public Record Office documents shows no reference to Cleland at Smyrna in 1734, the date cited by the DNB. His honorable and successful career in Bombay was documented at the India Office Library, where I was helped very much by all the staff, especially Mr. Ian A. Baxter. The fact that Cleland was in India from 1731 to 1740 makes the so-called earlier performance of *Fanny Hill* at the Beggar's Benison even more suspect. The Beggar's Benison is described by Louis Clark Jones in *The Clubs of the Georgian Rakes* (New York, 1942), p. 230. G. Legman refers to the possible performance in *The Horn Book: Studies in Erotic Folklore and Bibliography* (New Hyde Park, N.Y., 1964), pp. 76–77, 250. It is supposed that the work was read by a relative of Cleland's named Robert Cleland, a charter member of the Beggar's Benison. The notes themselves were published privately in 1892, although the years 1733–38 are represented by a resumé based on fuller notes that were destroyed. The exact reference is to 30 November 1737: "Fanny Hill was read." Another possibility, of course, is that the work in question has been lost, and Cleland has whimsically named his own work after it.

12. What seems to be an early allusion to *Pamela* also makes the 1737 date difficult to support: "she told me, after her manner and style," as how several maids out of the country had made themselves and all their kin for ever: that by preserving their VIRTUE, some had taken so with their masters, that they had married them, and kept them coaches, and lived vastly grand and happy; and some, may-hap, came to be Duchesses; luck was all, and why not I, as well as another?"; with other almanacs to this purpose." *Fanny Hill* (New York, 1963), pp. 5–6.

13. Cleland's concept of the epistolary method can certainly bear comparison to Richardson's. In

place of Richardson's effort to preserve immediacy and present the epistolary form as a virtually transparent medium for experience and emotion, Cleland explores its confessional and meditative possibilities.

14. One immediately calls to mind the changes worked on this image by Corporal Trim and Uncle Toby, who, Tristram remarks, wanted to see his bowling-green battlefield with a desire like that of a lover for his mistress *(Tristram Shandy,* II, v).

15. For an account of *bête–machine* references in English literature that does not, however, include Cleland, see Wallace Shugg, "The Cartesian Beast–Machine in English Literature (1663–1750)," *JHI* 29 (1968), 279–92.

16. Cleland, of course, may be trying to express a subjective element in Fanny's perceptions by these exaggerations. Pamela's dislike for snakes and fear of the bull (that turns out to be a cow) may come to mind. Compare also the account in La Mettrie's philosophical pastoral *L'Art de jouir* (1751) of the *"berger"* and the *"bergère"* examining each other's parts for the first time, and the young girl's upset at her first sight of an erection. *L'Homme machine suivi de l' Art de jouir,* intro. Maurice Solovine (Paris, 1921), p. 155.

17. Who knows whether Shelley was aware of this earlier "sensitive plant"? In any case, Cleland seems to be the primary reference for anyone who wishes to trace an eroticized nature from Spenser and Milton to the Romantics. The natural and the sexual unite in *Fanny Hill* in a way that Thomson and other eighteenth-century poets of nature never explore so thoroughly. Similarly, conceptions of an idyllic and edenic sexuality appear in Cleland to presage Keats.

18. There are other elements in *Fanny Hill* of what might be called a "scientific" language. Here is a particularly notable example: "Chiming then to me, with exquisite consent, his oily balsamic injection, mixing deliciously with the sluices in flow from me, sheath'd and blunted all the stings of pleasure, it flung us into an ecstacy that extended us fainting, breathless, entranced" (p. 97). "Chiming" may refer to "harmonizing like two bells." A more suggestive possibility in this context may be that Cleland is referring to "chyme" or "chyle," the milky, fluid mass in which food moves from the stomach to the intestine: "Le corps n'est qu'une horloge, dont le nouveau chyle est l'horloger. Le premier soin de la Nature, quand il entre dans le sang, c'est d'y exciter une sorte de fièvre, que les Chymistes qui ne revent que fourneaux, ont dû prendre pour une fermentation" (p. 186).

19. Compare the effect on Harriet: "In the mean time, we could plainly mark the prodigious effect the progressions of this delightful energy wrought in this delicious girl, gradually heightening her beauty as they heightened her pleasure. Her countenance and whole frame grew more animated: the faint blush of her cheeks, gaining ground on the white, deepened into a florid vivid vermilion glow, her naturally brilliant eyes now sparkled with ten-fold lustre; her languour was vanish'd, and she appeared, quick spirited, and alive all over" (p. 134).

20. Cleland actually received only £20 for *Fanny Hill* (Foxon, *Libertine Literature,* p. viii).

21. This motif has already been presaged in *Memoirs of an Oxford Scholar* (1756), ascribed without warrant to Cleland in a recent paperback edition. (This ascription may have occurred because the copy used by the publisher was that in the Beinecke Library at Yale, a copy that has "Cleland's Oxford Scholar" on the spine. I have seen two other copies, neither marked in this way.) In the *Oxford Scholar* the narrator alternates between erotic adventures and periods of extreme sentiment in which he laments his inability to marry the girl of his dreams, Chloe, because of family and financial reasons. At the end of the novel, when the obstacles have been cleared away in appropriate romance fashion, he and Chloe indulge sexually, whereupon, in about two pages, she dies. The epigraph is from Pope's *Eloisa to Abelard.*

Zola on Film:
The Ambiguities of Naturalism

Since the beginning of the cinema, sixty or more films have been adapted, extracted, or plagiarized from the works of Emile Zola.[1] Most of Zola's important novels and many minor ones have gone one, two, and even more times before the cameras. Why should Zola provide such a fertile field for directors and scriptwriters in search of material? The answer lies in the nature of naturalism itself. Zola explores in his novels the ways in which social and individual reality can be most appropriately and most accurately represented. This exploration, although perhaps only one of many possible roads for the novel, is essential to the film medium. It throws into bold relief questions about the role of physical detail in defining a scene, and it attempts to deal with the nagging problem of observation itself—the vexed relation of observer and object. In the cinematic versions of Zola, we can see more clearly than in the novels the actual ambiguities that existed in his attitude toward naturalism. Throughout his career, while his strongest theoretical statements—such as the polemical preface to the second edition of *Thérèse Raquin*—outline the "scientific" nature of his fictional method, at the same time his novels themselves frequently include subversive parodies of both the scientific point of view and the logical command of facts.

In the preface to *Thérèse Raquin* Zola argues that the novelist who wants to use the methods of "scientific analysis" should treat his characters as collections of nerves, fibers, blood, and bones—objects in "a physiological study" of their actions and their milieu. The novelist must imitate "scientific" detachment in his observations because only through detachment can his observations be validated.

Yet within *Thérèse Raquin* itself Zola includes partial observers whose presence implies that something more than mere observation is required to find the truth. In the preface we find the example of the detached painter, who can paint nudes without either sexual excitement or emotional involvement. In the novel Zola presents Laurent, the painter who can paint neither nudes nor portraits without his obsession with the face of the murdered Camille dictating both his choice and his treatment of the subject. The possibility that the detachment Zola praises in the preface may not be so aesthetically relevant arises when one of Laurent's friends remarks that (since the death of Camille) Laurent has become a much better painter. Similar epitomes of the "scientific" author are the lunchtime strollers who come to the morgue for a diverting free show. Does Zola, too, only pretend detachment, while he actually stands gaping and fascinated by the sexuality, violence, and death in the lives of his characters? He describes Laurent's visits to the morgue: "He then became a mere sightseer, and found a strange pleasure in looking violent death in the face, with its lugubriously bizarre and grotesque postures. The show entertained him, especially when there were women displaying their bare breasts." The detached scientific observation threatens to change abruptly into voyeuristic sensationalism. Turning to look at Zola rather than Laurent, one thinks of the frequency with which he describes Thérèse and Laurent as already dead.

Thérèse's and Laurent's feelings of paranoia and guilt after the murder seem in part to be related to a sense that the narrator is watching them through the microscope of his "physiological" method. Although they begin as watchers, Thérèse peering for hours out her window and Laurent wandering the streets in search of subjects, they become instead pathologically afraid of being watched—by François the cat, by the woman who sells artificial jewelry, and by the paralyzed Mme. Raquin. Gradually, they lose their fear of Mme. Raquin. And it is she, sitting immovably between the two murderers, unable to do anything to punish them, forced to watch their arguments and violence, who becomes the novel's image of the author himself, whose scientific detachment prevents him from acting to change conditions; or an image of the voyeuristic reader, who has decided that he can enter this world of horror with neither obligation nor responsibility. Mme. Raquin sees, understands, but cannot act. Grivet, on the other hand, sees, can act, but cannot interpret properly. Like an observing scientist, he believes he can extrapolate everything from the details of Mme. Raquin's slightest movement. "But every time Grivet deceived himself." Grivet and Mme. Raquin, by their inability to understand or their inability to act, cast severe doubt on the pureness of the theoretical position enunciated in the preface, and they imply similar reservations about the role of the disengaged reader, who contemplates the minute accuracies of naturalism for his own purposes of sensation, entertainment, or, at best, sociological antiquarianism. The basic question of aesthetics and epistemology that the novel raises is whether the author and the reader are either as obtuse as Grivet or, more likely, as paralyzed as Mme. Raquin "who was just alive enough to be a spectator of life without taking any part in it." Mme. Raquin is the most attractively presented character in the novel, the one the reader should be expected to identify with, and Zola has placed her in a situation that mirrors both the reader's helpless voyeurism and the author's scientific detachment. As she watches Thérèse and Laurent destroy themselves, "she finally understood that the facts didn't need her help." At the end of the novel she sits and watches them lying dead on the floor for twelve hours.[2]

Such motifs continue through Zola's novels. More than a mere transformation of the theatrical convention of eavesdropping into the novel, these passive and even paralyzed observers, who watch actions through windows, around doorjambs, and through the cracks in doors, are attempts to formulate a moral problem that arises directly from the method of naturalism: if the scene is so accurate, if the observations are so true, if the problems are so obvious, then what should be the appropriate action?

In *La Bête humaine,* after Zola had formulated and reformulated the problem for more than twenty years, he affirms in the character of Denizet, the examining magistrate, the possible objections to the scientific method, with its logic and order, as an appropriate means to understand human beings. Denizet's methods are exact and scientific, but his conclusions are invariably wrong. He is not an amiable fool like Grivet, but a serious and intelligent man. Yet in his approach to the murder of Grandmorin he becomes almost a caricature of a bad naturalistic novelist, or even Zola himself. Cabuche, he believes, is obviously the killer, both because of the "facts" and Cabuche's "deplorable ancestors." [3] Denizet's method of investigation is reminiscent of one of the subgenres created by naturalism—the police procedural novel, with its fatalistic accumulation of facts. But he thinks of his role in more exalted terms that recall the preface to *Thérèse Raquin:* "a sort of moral anatomist, gifted with second sight, extremely witty and intelligent." Denizet is specifically undone by his overly systematic explanation, the deductive theory into which he has absorbed all the facts: "holding fast to his rigid theory of the crime, the judge lost his footing, through too much professional ingenuity, complicating, going beyond the simple truth." Zola is here not so assured as he was in *Le Roman expérimental* that the roles of the objective observer and the goal-oriented experimentalist can be easily combined in the novelist. He had remarked there that "the experimentalist is the examining magistrate of nature." The examining magistrate Denizet makes this analogy less optimistic than it first appeared.

Denizet gets another chance when Jacques Lantier murders Séverine Roubaud, but he is wrong again. He prosecutes Roubaud for paying Cabuche to commit the murder. According to himself and all his associates, he had made an ironclad construction of the facts: "It was a masterpiece of ingenious analysis, they said, a logical reconstruction of the truth, a real creative work"—almost a naturalistic novel. To complete the ironic picture, Zola refers also to Denizet's "profound knowledge of criminal psychology, that everyone admired so much." When Roubaud confesses the truth about the previous murder, Denizet refuses to believe it. As Roubaud says later, "why tell the truth, since only lies were logical?"

Along with the observer of facts and the eavesdropper, another figure who bodies forth Zola's uneasiness with naturalistic method is the wanderer, who comes inadvertently upon some strange situation, Jacques Lantier witnessing the murder of Grandmorin through the train window, or Old Fouan coming upon Lise and Buteau murdering Françoise by accident in *La Terre.* Still another such character is the passive member of a triangle relation, who observes and in his way manipulates the other two in life and death. Whether the complaisant or dead husband (e.g., *La Bête humaine and Thérèse Raquin*) or the watchful child *(Une page d'amour),* this character is an implicated yet passive observer who can represent the moral complicity of the author and the reader in their attempt to mediate detachment and empathy. With the recognition of this kind of problem, pure naturalism becomes a difficult task. The fear that irresponsible voyeurism or sensationalistic observation become ends in themselves—as facts become ends in them-

selves for lesser naturalistic writers—rises to demonstrate the antagonism between
an assertion of the "truth" of factual detail and its actual source in the observations and prejudices of the author. The happenstance nature of voyeurism, the
discovery of a privileged position from which to observe, persuades the viewer
that he is privy to a truth more profound than that available through any other
method. But the observer becomes actually more deluded than he was before,
because he believes he is more perceptive. The more one uncritically assumes
that facts and logic and scientific detachment supply the whole truth in human relations and character, the more likely one is to reason falsely and reach false conclusions.

Guy Gauthier in a recent article argues that Zola's growing interest in photography in the 1890s influenced the type of description he used in his later works.
In terms of the themes I have explored above, one might also argue that Zola's
distrust of certain aspects of naturalistic method also spring from his new hobby.
Photography might represent a new way to search out the relevance of detail and
siphon off the "scientific" urge to make detail count for so much in the novels.
Zola retouched nothing, used no fancy props, and photographed either daily life
or his own family, plus a few still lifes. More than 6,000 of his photographs and
negatives are preserved in the collection of Pathé-Frères at Vincennes.[4] Zola once
remarked to an interviewer: "In my opinion, you cannot say you have thoroughly
seen anything until you have a photograph of it, revealing a lot of points which
otherwise would be unnoticed, and which in most cases could not be distinguished." Zola, the physiologist might remember at this point, suffered from my-
opia.

But Zola's interest in the problems of observation long predates and probably
spawns his interest in photography. His photographs remain things in themselves,
related to his novels only in complement or analogy, not as sources or correctives.
Whatever he photographs, Zola composes within the frame an arrangement, even
a stylization. In many of his photographs of street life and crowds, he delicately
chooses the exact angle from which to capture mutability—in human beings, in
fashions, in surroundings—through the frozen moment of photographic time,
demonstrating an acute sense of what will pass and what remain. He prepared
elaborately to take his pictures. (Much of his equipment still exists.) And he maintained two fully equipped darkrooms, one at his Paris home in the rue de Brux-
elles and one in the country at Médan. An anonymous picture reproduced in Michel
Braive's The Era of the Photograph: A Social History conveys a sense of Zola's
minute preparations. Zola sits, hunched hugely over his camera in the backyard
of a house. Less than a foot away sits the subject of his camera: a small doll on
a chair. In the final photograph nothing will remain of the photographer and his
elaborate equipment. But for this meta-photograph the image that remains is Zola
himself, in an attitude reminiscent of Thackeray's drawings of the author and his
puppets for Vanity Fair, overpowering by his presence the puny doll that he nominally wishes to immortalize.

❑ ❑ ❑

Zola's awareness of the ambiguities of the naturalistic method makes them into strengths rather than weaknesses in his novels. But the early movie adaptors of his novels show little awareness or understanding of the problems. The novels of Zola were the most appropriate subjects for the new medium because they emphasized the accurate recording of physical reality. Most critics agree that the embryonic French film industry was nourished by both the example of Zola's practice and the injunctions of his theory. Many of the early filmmakers were associated with André Antoine's "Théâtre Libre" group, which had specialized in the naturalistic presentation of plays adapted from Zola's novels. When they came to make films, they emphasized an urge for naturalistic detail an authenticity of location that would exploit the ability of film to be a recorder of contemporary reality. Ferdinand Zecca and Lucien Nonguet sought natural locations for the two films they made from *Germinal: La Grève* (1903) and *Au pays noirs* (1905). To make his version of *Germinal, Au pays des ténèbres* (1912), Victorin Jasset took his crew to the north of France where, as Georges Sadoul remarks, "the galleries had been reconstructed above the mines themselves, out of actual blocks of coal." In 1919 Henri Pouctal got permission to use the Creusot factories to shoot *Travail,* and in 1921 André Antoine went on location in Beauce for *La Terre*. The movies, with their ability to present a fully detailed physical reality, seemed to many of these directors to have been invented and perfected at precisely the right time to translate the precepts of *Le Roman expérimental* and *Le Naturalisme au théâtre* into their purest practice.

Although the enthusiastic rush to coal mines, factories, and the countryside may have liberated the early cinema from a dependence on studio sets, it also confined the filmmakers in a net of facts and crude naturalist theory from which they could rarely free themselves. Georges Sadoul remarks that they made the same mistakes as the bad naturalistic novelists: "a minute description or the reconstruction of dress and authentic settings aren't enough to achieve the kind of truth that was the mark of Zola's work." In the films made from Zola's novels that are of any interest—those that attempt to deal with Zola beyond the mere transposition of plot or its fragments—there can be discerned two basic trends: one seeks to accumulate details, while the other cuts more deeply into the problem of observation itself, and those ambiguities of involvement and detachment that are a special part of the nature of the films.

The most prevalent kind of film concentrates on naturalistic reconstruction. In its early career it searches out natural setting and treats the accumulation of detail as the direct way to evoke the reality of a milieu. In its later career it becomes more self-indulgent; the wider French idea of décor turns into the American idea of decoration. Two Zola films worked on by Christian Jaque illustrate this transformation. In 1929 he was the set decorator for Julien Duvivier's *Au bonheur des dames*. Duvivier's camera moves caressingly over the array of objects in the department store as Denise Baudu first sees them, counters and counters of all sorts of clothing, tall piles of glasses and cups, innumerable brightly shining appliances. But this accumulation of things is reined strictly to the establishment of milieu. It never becomes self-indulgent. The multiplicity of the front of the store is matched by the details of the store's behind-the-scenes life. Despite the expressionist dream of the ending, Duvivier's film is a fascinating adaptation of a Zola novel that itself concentrates more on an exuberance in detail than on an awareness of its limitation.[5]

But by the time Christian Jaque has come around to make his own Zola film, *Nana* in 1955, starring his then wife Martine Carol, decoration as an end in itself has taken over. The purple titles on a red velvet background announce that it is to be a decorator's movie, rather than a director's or a novelist's. The movie is good in its spots of decoration. Martine Carol swings her long red hair and banters with a comic hardness that owes more to American films of the 1930s and 1940s than it does to Zola. The scenes in the different milieus are also pleasant: Napoleon III's court, the backstage of the theatre, the milk dairy in the Bois, and the race track. But the final effect remains one of decoration only, the lure of details the audience is either previously unaware of or whose opulence they must admire. The story itself becomes obscure and then disappears under the weight of the decoration. Nana plans to run off with Vandeuvres after the racetrack coup. But he has been found out and commits suicide in the stable. (The novel is toned down here. Vandeuvres shoots himself first; the fire is accidental; and he manages to open the doors and free the horses before he dies.) Nana is packing to leave when Muffat (Charles Boyer) rushes in to stop her. He never mentions the death of Vandeuvres and he may not even know; Nana behaves as if Vandeuvres is still alive. She tells Muffat her decision to leave is irrevocable. Apocalyptically muttering "ordure, mon amour," Muffat catches Nana on a stair landing as she is leaving and strangles her. He leaves. The camera pulls up and back from Nana, lying on the red carpet of the stairs, prettily posed and dead.

This kind of treatment is especially unsuitable for *Nana*. Through its theatrical setting *Nana* brings together themes of voyeurism, acting, and the relation between the author, his audience, and his characters. *Nana* is in a sense Zola's fictional version of *Le Naturalisme au théâtre*. It begins with a crowded audience watching Nana on stage, almost naked, in front of the stage light that elsewhere "seemed like a giant yellow eye." Then the novel proceeds to present us with the drama of her life, again almost completely naked. When the crowds are gone, minor characters like Satin and Zoë stand off to the side of the action, but continually watching. Nana loves to undress in front of her mirror. The appropriate complement to her exhibitionism is the voyeuristic observation of the author and his audience.

A remarkable and rarely shown film that almost perfectly catches the nuances of Zola's approach, while it preserves most of his plot and characters, is Jean Renoir's excellent 1926 version of *Nana,* starring Catherine Hessling, with Werner Kraus as Muffat.[6] From the start of the film Renoir makes an important distinction between stylized and naturalistic methods of acting that corresponds to a contrast in the moral natures of the two main characters. Nana is the consummate stage actress in her basic nature. For most of the film she is covered with obvious makeup. This makeup seems appropriate in the early scenes that deal with the play. But Nana continues to wear her makeup backstage and beyond. When Muffat appears looking perfectly natural, the contrast becomes obvious. Renoir also uses the exaggerated conventional gestures of the silent-screen acting style to make a comment about Nana and her world. Although Renoir has already used close-ups and partial shots before, in the scene in which Muffat first confesses his love for Nana, the camera is placed center stage and back to simulate the photographed plays that provided much of the early history of cinema. While Muffat goes through some fairly natural-looking anguish, Nana continues her broad gestures and mugging beneath a pasty mask of makeup. The set itself is very stagey: a table in the center, two chairs on either side, a window at back, and a door on the left. The clash in styles becomes part of Renoir's basic themes: he has made real life into a stage set and placed within it a man who is trying to act in accordance with his emotions and a woman for whom the stylizations of the stage have replaced emotions. Nana remains stylized and isolated in her lack of emotion, while the men who surge about her are in touch even in their self-destruction with a kind of natural energy. Of course, in the same way that Renoir the movie director is fascinated by the stage version of reality, Muffat is fascinated by Nana's stylization and lack of emotion. When she finally gets emotional with him, in the cabaret after the suicide of Georges Hugon, Muffat leaves her. Perhaps he has been disillusioned by the human nature under her makeup.

The importance of the motif of observation to *Nana* is underlined by Renoir all through the film. In the same way that the camera itself moves about, picking up the details of stage life, characters in the film itself are continually observing. While Muffat is meeting Nana for the first time, Bordenave looks through a peephole in the curtain to observe the Comtesse Muffat and Faucher talking together in the empty theatre. This is an oddly gratuitous scene, since the Faucher–Comtesse Muffat subplot has otherwise been dropped from the film. But its narrative gratuitousness may indicate that Renoir, even after the intrigue between Faucher and the Comtesse had been omitted, wanted to preserve the image of Bordenave furtively peeping. In the novel the scene in which Muffat watches the silhouettes of Faucher and the Comtesse flit across the windows of Faucher's apartment brings together the motif of observation with Muffat's own position as the voyeuristic observer who becomes entrapped by what he sees. Since the subplot has been dropped, Renoir cannot use this scene. But he instead invents another similar scene that makes an even more inclusive point. Nana walks slowly down a backstage corridor approaching her dressing room. Her slowness emphasizes the importance of what comes next. On the windows of her dressing room door she sees a male and a female shadow, and she watches them for a few moments until the door opens to reveal Muffat—and the charwoman. Once again, the scene does little to advance the plot beyond its suggestion that Nana may be slightly jealous of Muffat. But, in its epistemological implication that Nana too is one among a whole cast of observers and observed, it touches something essential in Zola's novel.

The theme of observation is also developed in many smaller ways. Nana picks up Muffat's monocle to peer at him after he has persuaded Bordenave and Faucher to give her the lead role in Faucher's new play. Muffat peers with his binoculars at Nana and the exposure of Vandeuvres at the racetrack. Nana looks into a mirror only to see herself as reflected in a second mirror. Renoir also frequently begins a scene by a close shot of a significant detail: Nana's broken shoe heel in the scene in which she competes with Rose Mignon for the role of the little duchess by trying to behave like a lady of distinction; an eggcup to begin the scene in which Muffat makes his plea to Bordenave and Fauchery that she get the part. Renoir's cinematic naturalism, he implies, concentrates on the relevant detail rather than on incessant accumulation. Not only does his film include the theatre by gradually passing from the stage to the dressing rooms to the outside world, it also includes small tableaus reminiscent of the paintings of Auguste Renoir, no doubt partly in homage, but also to place their stasis against the film's movement. In one scene reminiscent of Auguste Renoir's *Le Moulin de la Galette* (1876), Jean Renoir has Nana join the cancan dancers for an absolute frenzy of motion that winds up with her kicking the hats out of the hands of men all around the room. By scenes like this, Renoir implies that the resources of the film, if properly understood, can easily help it to supersede both the stage and painting as explorations of visual reality. In another self-conscious use of what is more usually an unconscious convention of the silent screen, he frequently ends scenes that emphasize observation with the familiar closing iris, while other scenes merely dissolve to black. Perhaps he remembers the old brothel cat in *La Terre,* "the mute dreamer, witnessing all that is going on, watching through the narrow pupils of his gold-encircled eyes!" *Le Muet Rêveur*—not a bad title for a history of silent movies.

In Zola's novels, then, there lies a potentiality for adaptation to the screen greater than that in the works of many authors, specifically because Zola is so obsessed with the nature of observation and the conflicting impulses of detachment and involvement. But most filmmakers do not go beyond a surface evocation of milieu and social character. In the early years of the cinema *Germinal* and *L'Assommoir* were favorite sources, while *Nana* was a slower starter that gradually gained more popularity. In D. W. Griffith's *A Drunkard's Reformation* a young man is cured of drinking by seeing a stage adaptation of *L'Assommoir.* Although two-thirds of the film adaptations of Zola were made during the silent era, many important contemporary filmmakers still consider his novels to be good prospects for scripts. Different directors in different eras respond to Zola in different ways. In Marcel Carné's 1953 version of *Thérèse Raquin,* Thérèse and Laurent (Simone Signoret and Raf Vallone) become existential heroes fighting an absurd universe of inexorable fate, courtesy of a leather-jacketed motorcyclist who appears to have ridden into the lives of Zola's characters fresh from a Cocteau film. Fritz Lang based *Human Desire* (1954) not directly on *La Bête humaine,* but on Jean Renoir's 1938 film version of the novel. The period interiors of René Clément's *Gervaise* (1956) continued the best part of the tradition of naturalistic detail, while Roger Vadim's *La Curée* (1965), starring Jane Fonda, wallowed in opulent decor. It has recently been announced that Joseph Strick, the director of *Ulysses,* is working on a script of *La Terre.*[7]

But for most filmmakers it is still the realistic setting or, more recently, the steamy mixture of sex and violence, that make Zola's novels perfect sources for films. Only in the work of a great director like Renoir is there an appreciation of the ambiguities in Zola's naturalism. But when Marcel l'Herbier has a character in his film of *L'Argent* go blind in punishment for some venality, this is surely an un-Zolalike retribution. In Zola's novels the problems of seeing are too important to be so easily avoided. Zola's early novels have been criticized for their "journalistic, unparticipating approach to life." Georg Lukács has commented: "Zola . . . was by nature a man of action, but his epoch turned him into a mere observer and when at last he answered the call of life, it came too late for his development as a writer." In this view, the commitment to action with the Dreyfus Affair supposedly rescues Zola from detachment. But from his first experiments with the novel Zola seems aware of the problems inherent in his method. His interest in photography and his involvement in the Dreyfus Affair grow directly from a tension that energizes all his best novels. Etienne Lantier in *Germinal* is Zola's most sustained attempt to mediate in one character the conflicting demands of detached observation and involved action. Early in the novel he stands on a hill above Montsou with a total perspective of the entire countryside: "with wandering eyes he strove to pierce the darkness, tormented by a desire to see and yet a fear of seeing." The similarity between Etienne and the typical member of a movie audience, observing yet uncertain about the outcome of the observation, indicates why Zola's novels and the movies that were derived from them are not only an important part of the history of film, but also a key to its essential aesthetic and epistemological nature.

[1969]

Filmography

This list is based on an unpublished list supplied to me by the Museum of Modern Art and compiled by Alex Viany, a short list contained in the article by René Jeanne (see Bibliography), and the Filmographie compiled by Guy Gauthier (see Bibliography). All of these lists contain errors. I have tried to correct all I could discover and have supplemented their lists by references in other articles and in histories of various national cinemas.

L'Argent
   Penge. Carl Mantizius. 1919. Denmark.
   L'Argent. Savoia. 1914. Italy.
   L'Argent. Marcel l'Herbier. 1928. France.
   L'Argent. Pierre Billon. 1936. France.
"L'Attaque du moulin" from *Les Soirées de Médan*.
   Attack on the Mill. No Director listed. 1910. USA.
L'Assommoir
   Les Victimes de l'alcoolisme. Ferdinand Zecca. 1902. France.
   L'Assommoir. Albert Capellani. 1909. France.
   A Drunkard's Reformation. D. W. Griffith. 1909. USA.
   Les Victimes de l'alcool. Gérard Bourgeois. 1911. France.
   Le Poison de l'humanité. Emile Chautard. 1911. France.
   Drink. No director listed. 1917. England.

L'Assommoir. Charles Maudru and Maurice de Mersan. 1921. France.

L'Assommoir. Gaston Roudès. 1933. France.

Gervaise. René Clément. 1956. France.

Au bonheur des dames.

Au ravissement des dames. No director listed. 1913. France.

Des Paradies der Damen. Lupu-Pick. 1922. Germany.

Au bonheur des dames. Julien Duvivier. 1929. France.

Au bonheur des dames. Andre Cayatte. 1943. France.

La Bête humaine.

La Bête humaine. Leopoldo Carducci. 1916. Italy.

La Bête humaine. Jean Renoir. 1938. France.

Human Desire. Fritz Lang. 1954. USA.

La Bestia humana. Daniel Tinayre. 1956. Argentina.

La Curée

La Curée. Baldassarre Negroni. 1917. Italy.

La Curée. Roger Vadim. 1965. France.

La Débâcle

Gransfolken. Mauritz Stiller. 1913. Sweden.

Fécondité

Fécondité. N. Evreinoff and Henry Etievant. 1929. France.

Germinal

La Grève. Ferdinand Zecca. 1903. France.

Au pays noir. Lucien Nonguet. 1905. France.

Au pays des ténèbres. Victorin Jasset. 1912. France.

Germinal. Albert Capellani. 1914. France.

Germinal. No director listed. 1920. France.

Germinal. Yves Allégret. 1963. France-Italy-Hungary.

Lourdes

Miraklet. Victor Sjöström. 1913. Sweden.

Madeleine Ferat

Maddalena Ferat. No director listed. 1920. Italy.

Naïs Micoulin

Naïs. Raymond Leboursier. 1945. France.

Nana

Nana. Knud Lumbye. 1910. Denmark.

Nana. Camille de Riso. 1914. Italy.

Nana. Nino Martoglio. 1916. Italy.

Nana. Jean Renoir. 1926. France.

Nana. Dorothy Arzner. 1934. USA.

Nana. Celestine Gorostiza. 1943. Mexico.

Nana. Christian Jaque. 1955. France.

Nantas

A Man and the Woman. Alice Blaché. 1917. USA.

Nantas. Donatien. 1921. France.

Pot-Bouille

Pot-Bouille. Julien Duvivier. 1957. France.

Pour une nuit d'amour

Per una Notte d'Amore. No director listed. 1914. Italy.

Pour une nuit d'amour. Iakov Protozanoff. 1921. France.

Pour une nuit d'amour. Edmond Gréville. 1947. France.

Le Rêve
　Le Rêve. Jacques de Baroncelli. 1920. France.
　Le Rêve. Jacques de Baroncelli. 1931. France.
　(Completely different cast.)
La Terre
　La Terre. Victorin Jasset. 1912. France.
　La Terre. André Antoine. 1921. France.
Thérèse Raquin
　Thérèse Raquin. Einar Zangenberg. 1911. Denmark.
　Thérèse Raquin. Nino Martoglio. 1915. Italy.
　Thérèse Raquin. Jacques Feyder. 1926. France. (USA title: *Shadows of Fear.*)
　Thérèse Raquin. Marcel Carné. 1953. France. (USA title: *The Adulteress.*)
Travail
　Travail. Henri Pouctal. 1919. France.
Une page d'amour
　Une page d'amour. Pina Menichelli. 1924. France.

Bibliography

Zola as Photographer:

Anonymous. "Zola's New Hobby." *The Photo-Miniature,* 21 (December 1900), 396.
————. "Zola reporter." *Arts et loisirs,* 57 (26 octobre-1er novembre 1966), 30–31.
Harmant, Pierre G. "Emile Zola, chasseur d'images." *Le Photographe,* 52 (1962), 532–40.
Loize, Jean. "Emile Zola photographe." *Arts et métiers graphiques,* 45 (1935), 31–35.

Zola on Film:

Anonymous. "Pourquoi ce retour de Zola?" *Arts et loisirs,* 57 (26 octobre–1er novembre 1966), pp. 28–30.
Bouissounouse, Janine. "La vie d'Emile Zola au cinéma." *Europe,* 83–84 (1952), pp. 155–58.
Gauthier, Guy. "Filmographie [de Zola]." *Europe,* 468–69 (1968), pp. 416–24.
Jeanne, René. "Emile Zola et le cineéma." *Présence de Zola,* pp. 204–13. Paris, 1953.
Sadoul, Georges. "Zola et le cinéma français (1900–1920)." *Europe,* 83–84 (1952), pp. 158–70.

Notes

1. For a list of these films see the filmography that follows this article. I would like to thank at this time those people who helped me locate and see as many of these films as I could: Charles Powell of Columbia Pictures, Garry Carey of The Museum of Modern Art, Ernest Callenbach of *Film Quarterly,* and especially Beaumont Newhall, James Card, and George Pratt of the George Eastman House in Rochester, who extended to me all possible courtesy when I came there to see the Zola films in the

Eastman Collection. Mr. Pratt also helped me to add to my filmography through his wide knowledge of the American silent film.

2. I saw a Zola movie long before I read a Zola novel. By the same token, towards the end of my researches I was directed to John C. Lapp's suggestive comments on observation in "The Watcher Betrayed and the Fatal Woman: Some Recurring Patterns in Zola," *PMLA*, 74 (1959), 276–84; and *Zola before the Rougon-Macquart* (Toronto, 1964). A fuller and more incisive account that interestingly summarizes various motifs of observation is Roger Ripoli's "Fascination et fatalité: le regard dans l'oeuvre de Zola," *Les Cahiers Naturalistes*, 32 (1966), 104–16. Both Lapp and Ripoli tend to emphasize the narrowly psychosexual elements in voyeurism and give only brief attention to the aesthetic.

3. Another interesting parody of the theory of heredity within a novel is Fauchery's article on Nana, "La Mouche d'or." Nana herself is also observed reading a novel about the life of a courtesan, and several men are overheard discussing new criminological theories that claim there is no more responsibility for crime, only sick people. This self-conscious and even satiric aspect of Zola's novels deserves more exploration.

4. Le Cercle du Livre Précieux is currently bringing out an edition of Zola that uses his photographs and other contemporary sketches and pictures for illustration. [An album of Zola's photographs, *Zola: Photographer,* comp. François Emile-Zola and Massin, tr. Liliane Emery Tuck, appeared in 1988.]

5. Another important example of this kind of approach occurs in Marcel l'Herbier's *L'Argent* (1928). A rapid montage shows the variety of activity in the Bourse: trading, typing, chalking quotations, orders going through pneumatic tubes. But l'Herbier betrays his chances with a fabricated love story and a camera that is supposed to imitate an airplane swooping over the Bourse floor.

6. Renoir has remarked about his silent period: "I made only one real film, *Nana:* the rest were for fun or money." In a recent letter Renoir writes that he is attracted to Zola because "his novels are rich and poetic. I like films or books which give me the feeling of a frame too narrow for the content. By poetic I do not mean so much the description of nature but the sincere emotion of Zola when he describes a young woman or a child."

7. An interesting film that is more a commentary on Zola than an actual adaptation is Jean-Luc Godard's *Vivre sa vie* (1962) with Anna Karina as the modern-day prostitute Nana Kleinfrankenheim.

Lexicography and Biography
in the *Preface* to
Johnson's *Dictionary*

The biographer of Johnson and the historian of dictionary-making dismantle his *Preface* in accordance with their special concerns. Although both may recognize that Johnson has fused the scholarly and the personal elements with extraordinary power, neither is very concerned with exploring the importance of this fusion for Johnson's ideas. James. H. Sledd and Gwin J. Kolb, for example, assert that the *Preface* "is one of the finest things Johnson ever wrote, a moving personal document and an excellent statement of the aims, methods, and difficulties of one kind of eighteenth-century lexicography." Yet they caution that it should not be read outside of its historical context, "for the basis of its merit is not originality." [1] Later in their book, in fact, they agree with Noah Webster that the *Preface* contains "less sense than sentiment." [2] Boswell, appropriately enough, considers the *Preface* primarily for the biographical insight it may yield. Praising its style, he says that "there are few prose compositions in the English Language that are read with more delight." After hazarding a few short remarks that treat the lexicographic concerns of the *Preface,* Boswell then proceeds to speculate about Johnson's state of mind while writing. He cites especially the last paragraph: "we must ascribe its gloom to that miserable dejection of spirits to which he was constitutionally subject, and which was aggravated by the death of his wife two years before." [3]

The final paragraphs of the *Preface* possess, however, a power that is the result of a complex and close relation, built up through the entire essay, between procedural problems in the making of the *Dictionary* and personal problems in Johnson's own life. The nature of such a relation is, I think, first suggested by two paragraphs in the *Plan of an English Dictionary* (1747). After detailing how he wishes to bring order into the study of the English language, Johnson sums up his proposals:

> Thus, my lord, will our language be laid down, distinct in its minutest subdivisions, and resolved into its elemental principles. And who upon this survey can forbear to wish, that these fundamental atoms of our speech might obtain the firmness and immutability of the primogenial and constituent particles of matter, that they might retain

their substance while they alter their appearance, and be varied and compounded, yet
not destroyed.[4]

Such is Johnson's hope for his undertaking. Yet already he feels the impossibility
of ever achieving his ideal, not merely because of the failures of the French and
the Italian academies to "fix" their respective languages, but also because of the
inescapable presence of mortality that is associated with man and his works. Johnson's next paragraph therefore qualifies his hope of establishing the permanence
of words:

> But this is a privilege which words are scarcely to expect; for, like their author, when
> they are not gaining strength, they are generally losing it. Though art may sometime
> prolong their duration, it will rarely give them perpetuity; and their changes will be
> almost always informing us, that language is the work of man, of a being from whom
> permanence and stability cannot be derived.   (p. 171)

In the *Plan* Johnson appears conscious of a disparity between the perfection he
seeks to achieve in the *Dictionary* and the human tools with which he must achieve
it. The eight years consumed in the making of the *Dictionary,* with their poverty,
disappointments, and personal tragedies, must have made the apprehension of this
disparity bulk even larger in Johnson's thought. But Johnson's dedication to his
ideal of perfection does not cease through these years. As the *Preface* shows more
explicitly than the *Plan,* he considered the pursuit of perfection to be a means
through which fallible man could for a time escape the plaguing consciousness of
mortality.
    Johnson once remarked to Sir Joshua Reynolds:

> There are two things which I am confident I can do very well; one is an introduction
> to any literary work, stating what it is to contain, and how it should be executed in
> the most perfect manner; the other is a conclusion, showing from various causes why
> the execution has not been equal to what the author promised to himself and to the
> publick.[5]

Boswell considers the *Preface* to be an admirable example of what he calls this
"double talent" of Johnson. But Johnson is not merely indulging in the most
congenial method of literary construction. The tension in the *Preface* between the
two parts of his "double talent" mirrors a tension that pervades the whole work,
and his whole life. By the time of the writing of the *Preface,* Johnson considers
the attempt to achieve perfection and the knowledge of human fallibility to have
almost equal importance. Although he continues to strive toward perfection—the
perfection of the *Dictionary* and the fixing of the English language—in the *Preface* he expresses more strongly than before his feeling that language like human
life is something inherently incapable of perfection: "Language is only the instrument of science, and words are but the signs of ideas: I wish, however, that the
instrument might be less apt to decay, and that signs might be permanent, like the
things which they denote" (p. 185). Throughout the essay Johnson emphasizes
his attempts to fix the language as well as his realization that there are some parts

of language that cannot be fixed, which change with each new fad and discovery. Through his elimination of many technical "terms of art" and ephemeral "cant," Johnson attempts to define the unchanging core of the language. He has given up his goal of complete perfection. But in order at least to make linguistic change more difficult, he appeals to the authority of past writers, rooting usage in tradition: "every quotation contributes to the stability and enlargement of the language" (p. 198). Although his hopes of fixing the language have been severely qualified since the *Plan,* "even when the enterprize is above the strength that undertakes it" (p. 199), Johnson believes that it is necessary to continue striving toward the goal of perfection.

The association that Johnson makes between the inability of language to achieve permanence and the demands of human nature becomes more explicit towards the middle of the *Preface:*

> When we see men grow old an die at a certain time one after another, from century to century, we laugh at the elixir that promises to prolong life to a thousand years; and with equal justice may the lexicographer be derided, who, being able to produce no example of a nation that has preserved their words and phrases from mutability, shall imagine that his dictionary shall embalm his language, and secure it from corruption and decay, that it is in his power to change sublunary nature, and clear the world at once from folly, vanity, and affection. (p. 202)

Johnson shows that changes that occur in language are directly related to changes in the affairs of men. He points out that as a people becomes more civilized the language of that people must change more and more. Even the process of thinking itself inevitably forces changes in language. The state of language—growing, maturing, decaying, and dying—is an image of the state of man. In *Idler* 103 Johnson asserts that every ending we experience necessarily must remind us of our own deaths. "This secret horror of the last is inseparable from a thinking being, whose life is limited, and to whom death is dreadful."[6] In the *Preface* he similarly desires to fix the English language at least partly because its decay, the death of individual words, evokes the same spectre of human mortality. Johnson, therefore, can with absolute propriety bring his personal problems into the *Preface* because for him they are intimately related to his ideals for the *Dictionary:* they are the human limitations that thwart and qualify his striving toward perfection.

The final pages of the *Preface* are concerned primarily with the possible inaccuracies of the *Dictionary.* Far from being merely a sly method of disarming possible critics, this exercise of the other part of the "double talent" continues the concern with ideal stability and inevitable transience that we have seen earlier in the essay. Johnson points out that there must be some measure of inaccuracy, for the compiler is human and therefore fallible. The only necessity in such an undertaking, he says, is that one "endeavour well." We should not "acquiese with silence" to necessary imperfection. "It remains that we retard what we cannot repel, that we palliate what we cannot cure. Life may be lengthened with care, though death cannot be ultimately defeated" (p. 205).

The scholarly concerns and the personal references in Johnson's *Preface* are tightly bound together. We do not have to delve into biography in order to justify the powerful concluding paragraphs. They have had their way amply prepared by what has gone before them in the essay. The consciousness of human mortality that pervades the end of the *Preface* comes directly from Johnson's sharp sense of man's inability to achieve permanence, stability, or perfection in any of his works. And it is his work on the monumental *Dictionary* that has clarified this insight: "the *English Dictionary* was written with little assistance of the learned, and without any patronage of the great; not in the soft obscurities of retirement, or under the shelter of academick bowers, but amidst inconvenience and distraction, in sickness and in sorrow" (pp. 206–7).

Lexicographers may accuse Johnson of "linguistic authoritarianism" because of their hostility to his attempt to fix the language.[7] Yet Johnson's adherence to such principles of procedure has much deeper importance to him than the mere establishment of linguistic criteria. These principles were part of his life-long struggle against disease, decay, and death. He saw in language a medium as fallible and as weak as his own body, but one that might, through the mediation of his mind and will, be capable of permanence and power. At the same time, by the end of his work on the *Dictionary,* as that process is mirrored in the *Preface,* he has found that his achievement is meaningless without a human context for its appreciation: "I have protracted my work till most of those I wished to please have sunk into the grave, and success and miscarriage are empty sounds. I therefore dismiss it with frigid tranquility, having little to fear or hope from censure or from praise" (p. 207).

[1970]

Notes

1. *Dr. Johnson's Dictionary* (Chicago, 1955), 19.

2. *Dr. Johnson's Dictionary,* 199. See also Gertrude E. Noyes, "The Critical Reception of Johnson's *Dictionary* in the Latter Eighteenth Century," *Modern Philology,* 52 (1954–55), 175–91.

3. *Boswell's Life of Johnson,* ed. G. B. Hill, rev. L. F. Powell (Oxford, 1934), 1:291, 298.

4. I have used the 1816 edition of *Works with His Life by James Boswell, Esq.* as the source for both the *Plan* and the *Preface.* This particular quotation appears on 1:171. Subsequent citations will be included in the text. For the bibliographic history of the *Preface* see W. R. Keast, "The Preface to *A Dictionary of the English Language:* Johnson's Revision and the Establishment of the Text," *Studies in Bibliography.,* 5 (1952–53), 129–56.

5. *Boswell's Life,* 1:292.

6. *Works,* 5:286.

7. See, for example, the unpublished dissertation (University of Michigan, 1941) by Harold B. Allen, "Samuel Johnson and the Authoritarian Principle in Linguistic Criticism."

Daniel Defoe and the
Anxieties of Autobiography

From Apuleius to Norman Mailer writers have written about characters bearing their own names and left the reader with the problem of distinguishing between the two, or at least with the nagging feeling that such a distinction could add to the fuller understanding of their work. Daniel Defoe did no such thing. Although the first-person singular was his favorite literary pose—he used it in fiction and nonfiction alike—he rarely spoke as Daniel Defoe, the private person. Two voices sound through his work: the public person of his nonfiction, detailing and explaining his opinions about the issues of the day; and the private impersonation, the first-person voice that gives life to the characters who are the most enduring part of Defoe's legacy as a writer: Robinson Crusoe, Captain Singleton, Moll Flanders, Colonel Jacque, and Roxana.

When critics speak about the psychological side of Defoe's novels, they often complain that his characters never "develop." But I would like to consider Defoe's first-person novels (a term less cumbersome than "pseudoautobiographies") as the record of his exploration of what constitutes human individuality and how to write about it. Many of the great literary changes of the eighteenth century— the new importance of the novel, the disappearance of satire, the fascination with sentiment and sensibility, the exploration of extreme states of feeling—seem to me to be related to an anguish and uncertainty about human character. The question is not "what is human nature?" (too broad and timeless), but "what separates one individual from another?" and "what is personal identity?" After a lifetime of writing what was largely expository nonfiction, Defoe at 59 began the series of first-person novels for which he is most famous, from *Robinson Crusoe* (1719) to *Roxana* (1724). The power of these novels comes from Defoe's energetic awakening to the implications of speaking in his own voice or masquerading in the voice of another, and within the novels he grapples with the problem of individuality and identity with an energy bordering on obsessiveness. Older forms of autobiography and new possibilities rest side by side in the hollow of Defoe's novels, bound together by his acute sense of the mystery of human separateness, that point beyond which someone, real or imagined, can no longer be "explained."

Although Defoe's works frequently sport didactic aims and exhortations to the reader, their inconclusive endings and elusive tone announce their preoccupation with uncertainty. The heart of Defoe's originality is to introduce uncertainty into autobiography. Few early autobiographies are *about* uncertainty in the same way that Defoe's first-person novels are; in few early autobiographies does the question of whether or not the narrator deserves our trust ever arise. Whatever the differences, say, between *The Golden Ass* of Apuleius and Augustine's *Confessions,* they both deal with false certainty that is transformed into true certainty, abruptly in the first and gradually in the second. *The Golden Ass* requires the active participation of an intelligent reader to make its meaning clear; Augustine more explicitly makes his path a route every man and every woman can follow. But both works assume a continuation and limitation of their precepts in the life of the reader. Modern confessional autobiography—one of the most important descendants of Defoe's work—has little of that kind of didacticism or edification. It seeks to give meaning to a seemingly meaningless life by casting that life in literary form. It seizes upon the uncertainty of the meaning of life as its true subject, and it supplies meaning not by analogy to some supervening spiritual order, but through the self-conscious act of literary self-preoccupation.

Whatever credit is usually given to Defoe in the history of the novel, Richardson tends to be awarded the title of "father" of the psychological novel. He has been taken at his own valuation as the writer without a past or a tradition, untainted by insincerity and "art," who for the first time in literature looks directly at human beings. Defoe, on the other hand, has been denied the ability to create "real" characters because he draws on past autobiographical and biographical traditions. The most common study of Richardson concentrates on characterization; the most typical study of Defoe discusses either what works lie behind his own or what works he actually ransacked to create his own. This kind of critical emphasis disintegrates Defoe's works into what has influenced them and diverts attention from Defoe to the mass of seventeenth- and early eighteenth-century biographies and autobiographies, whether criminal, political, military, or spiritual. By implication it characterizes Defoe as merely a much more skilled and successful practitioner of the old forms, and tells us little about what Defoe has personally accomplished or the historical moment that helped create the enormous difference in emotional and aesthetic intensity between Defoe's work and what preceded it.[1]

Before Defoe, works that dealt with an individual life usually did not see character as a problem because their intentions were openly didactic. In the spiritual autobiography the writer was in great part offering a model for the individual reader to imitate; in the criminal autobiography the reader was offered a model to abhor. Anything excessively particularizing in the character of the model could possibly debar the reader from the vicarious participation that was essential to the success of the form. Whether they were exemplary or cautionary, the idea of the self in these works is a settled question. Even though the writing of a spiritual autobiography may have been a unique and individual attempt to discover the shape of one's life, the *form* of the work was a purgation of the demons of individuality, and conversion a reacceptance into the fold of general religious truth. In the same way, the final repentance and submission of the criminal made up for the sins of his individualism, so that the reader could enjoy surrogate straying while he was assured of a final security. Whether such "lives" took the form of "do what I do" or "I'll do it so that you don't have to," the presentation of the subject's character was done with as little real individuality as possible. The lives of criminals and saints, military men and whores, followed a preset pattern.[2]

Defoe's first-person novels may make us uneasy because the formula of didactic sameness coexists with definite personalization. Despite Defoe's own later efforts in *Serious Reflections of Robinson Crusoe* (1720) to make Crusoe into a paradigm and the book an allegory of Defoe's own life as well as the life of everyman, when we read the novel, we feel with great power Crusoe's individual problems, his craziness and his idiosyncrasies. And at the same time we sense Defoe's struggles with the problem of creating a truly separate character in fiction, a character who draws his energies not from the canons of spiritual autobiography (or economic individualism), but from some core sense of uniqueness, even a uniqueness with pathological overtones, that he shares with his creator.

Instead of taking *Crusoe* as a model by which to judge the other works, I would characterize it as Defoe's first and last attempt to align his exploration of the possibilities of autobiography with a settled and traditional paradigm of human life and behavior.[3] Within it there is an already apparent fascination with the efforts of the individual to define himself in accordance with some preexisting spiritual, social, cultural, or literary pattern. Until the eighteenth century, history-writing, like biography and autobiography, sought primarily to discover the sameness of history, the repetition of patterns. Defoe's novels engage the uniqueness of human identity outside the rhythmic repetitions of public history and the causal control of a verifiable past. Time is basically irrelevant to him, and his heroes and heroines in general have little to do with the cycles of weeks, months, and years, or the events of public history, unless, like the plague of 1666 in *A Journal of the Plague Year* or the 1715 Jacobite Rebellion in *Colonel Jacque,* such events are important less for themselves than because they play a role in the lives of his narrators. After *Crusoe* the pressure of genealogy on Defoe's characters also almost vanishes, unless it is genealogy like Colonel Jacque's belief that his origins were "gentlemanly," a self-generated belief again more important than any external reality. Defoe discovers within autobiography its central paradox of eccentricity laid down with universality: the unique self making himself and his ideas palatable for a large audience. Even in *Crusoe* he rejects the solution of spiritual autobiography that egotism should be channeled into a religious paradigm that asserts the basic similarity of everyone's problems and solutions. In *Crusoe* and more markedly in his later novels, he explores the actual anxieties of personal identity and the inability of earlier autobiographical forms to offer sufficient solace.

❏ ❏ ❏

Defoe developed his first-person style largely as a vehicle for his journalism and nonfiction, and much of the basic solidity of his novels comes from the unhurried power of a matter-of-fact tone that helps enforce belief. Defoe chose the first person to convey an impression of clarity and nonpartisan interest in the plain truth of whatever he was discussing—a reasonable and friendly voice that when it talked about politics or discussed the intricacies of some contemporary economic issue could be believed. The first person is so obviously a conscious style in Defoe's works that it is difficult to believe that it was chosen only for moral reasons, to contrast with the rhetorical flourishes of a more blatantly self-conscious style. Defoe made many statements about fiction that seem to align him with Bunyan in a "Puritan" hostility to artistry in literature.[4] But a solider motivation for his "plain" style seems to be a distrust of the ability of language to convey with any accuracy the nuances of personality. The straightforward first person has its definite limits: it is fine for conveying the specifiable. The first-person of De- foe's nonfiction yields the objective, recording side of the novels: the lists of Crusoe, Moll, and Colonel Jacque; the descriptions and statistics of *A Journal of the Plague Year;* the military events of *Colonel Jacque* or *Memoirs of a Cavalier* or *Captain Carleton.* The disengaged and detached narrator can successfully con- vey some fragment of public history to the reader because he is not a public man himself and has no partisan jawbone to swing. But when the focus is on the narrator himself, when the point is not explanation and description of the outside world but self-explanation and self-description, when the list is less a reflection of what is objectively true than a symptom of distress sent up by a confused sense of self, then the plain style becomes a mask as deceptive as any other. In late works like *Conjugal Lewdness* (1727), Defoe often talks more about the difficul- ties of finding the proper words for his delicate subject than he does about the subject itself. The speakers in his novels manipulate the plain style to disguise and dissemble; all of them tend to speak in the same accents on their separate occasions of supposed self-revelation. Unlike many later novelists (who are much easier to discuss critically), Defoe does not use style as a mode of characteriza- tion. Behind a seemingly transparent screen of plain talk, his narrators conduct their elaborate evasions.

The energies that brought forth Defoe's novels do not seem rooted in any desire to justify the orders of history, society, or religion, nor do they seem to be merely another expression of the previous clarities of Defoe's first-person method. The power of the novels and their ability to move us even now spring from some darker potentialities in Defoe's earlier works. He senses within the autobiograph- ical form a way to explore eccentricity and uniqueness rather than a way to in- clude the individual within orders larger and more comprehensive than his own understanding. In Defoe's novels the didactic autobiography that deindividualizes its subject gradually gives way to a type of autobiography that searches out the *once* of a human life. Defoe's novels reflect a (frequently inconclusive) search for identity within the confines of the self, and they draw upon such general orders as providential explanation in much the same way that contemporary authors use Freud or that Milton played with Copernican and Ptolemaic theories of the uni- verse—explanations to be tested as much for their literary usefulness as for their truth.

Defoe's characters are not characters the way we usually understand the term, with an inner life so rich and complex that we expect them to leap off the page and onto the psychiatrist's couch. They are more like characters in films, with whom we may share the most intimate moments and who may tell us everything about themselves, but whose essential natures remain elusive because they necessarily are seen and heard only from without. Our sense of their individual reality comes from mystery not complexity, even while they profess to be revealing all.

Many of Defoe's characters, like Moll or Singleton, are in actual flight from legal authority, and therefore have practical reasons for remaining evasive and disguised. But other, less threatened, narrators, like Crusoe and Colonel Jacque, express the same paradoxical mixture of reticence and revelation, self-protection and self-exposure. Play with identity, through disguise and name change, has a specific plot function in many of Defoe's novels. Yet it appears so often that it begins to take on a larger significance. Defoe's narrators combine personal evasion and literary self-assertion to preserve personal identities that often seem precariously defined. Their stories are told under the shadow of a world that threatens their sense of self, less from legal punishment than from the implacable pressure of family, society, or the providential order of the universe. Most of Defoe's narrators are in flight from such a priori definitions of themselves, in much the same way that the new form of his first-person narratives may be attempting to break away from earlier autobiographical forms. Through daring and uncertainty, Defoe's characters try to restore to themselves a sense of personal identity and worth that is constantly in doubt, because of birth as an orphan, or the dehumanizing effects of anonymous poverty, or the uncertainty of a place of final security (or a neatly tied-up last paragraph). After rejecting a frame of traditional values that pinch and push the personality into acceptable shape, Defoe's heroes and heroines seek unlimited possibility for self-definition. Faced with such terrifying freedom, the individual must establish an identity to deal with it, simultaneously mediating potential and repression. Part of Defoe's insight about the character in search of security about his identity is his discovery of the similar anxieties of confinement and freedom.

Robinson Crusoe is the main counterexample to the argument I have sketched above. Crusoe, say many critics, revolts against his father and therefore against the entire divine order (taking all authority to be equivalent). Crusoe, they then go on to argue, finally adopts a providential interpretation of history that underlies his reconciliation, repentance, and "conversion." But in fact Crusoe never does return to his father and family, and becomes rich more by the accretions of time than by his own abilities. Essentially Crusoe is as much a wanderer at the end of his memoirs, whether the *Adventures* or the *Farther Adventures,* as he was when he began, "inur'd to a wandering life," hardly even wondering, as Captain Singleton does, whether there is anything beyond "this roving, cruising life." I suppose that it could be argued that Crusoe can continue his wanderings after "conversion" because now he is more errant than erring, his desire for new places now securely stabilized by the rudder of Providence. At the end of *Farther Adventures of Robinson Crusoe* Crusoe anticipates another journey, this time to heaven: "And here [in England] resolving to harass myself no more, I am preparing for a longer journey than all these, having lived seventy-two years a life of infinite variety, and learnt sufficiently to know the value of retirement, and the blessing of ending our days in peace." [5]

But Crusoe still sees this final adventure like his other ones, a chance for more movement. Few of Defoe's characters seem happy at rest, and the relative ease with which Crusoe accepts his final retreat seems belied by the inconclusiveness of *Captain Singleton, Moll Flanders,* and *Roxana.* All of them may one time or another talk about themselves in terms of money; as Moll says, "Money's virtue, gold is fate." [6] But money satisfies only society's demand for identity. Movement more keenly satisfies the self. Even H. F., the narrator of *A Journal of the Plague Year,* confined by choice in London, tells the utopian story of the three men who escaped, and considers it his duty to be constantly on the go, checking every rumor, while throughout the novel appear images of being buried alive, quarantined, and shut up in locked houses. [7]

"A life of infinite variety" says Crusoe at the end of the *Farther Adventures,* and the phrase is echoed frequently in Defoe's later novels until it even appears in the extended title of *Roxana, The Fortunate Mistress or, a History of the Life and Vast Variety of Fortunes of Mademoisells de Beleau, afterwards called the Countess de Wintselsheim in Germany, Being the Person known by the Name of the Lady Roxana in the time of Charles II.* But the variety that Defoe's narrators use as a touchstone of value has little to do with the *Bildungsroman* variety of experience through which we watch the narrator grow in character. Once again, our usual ideas of character must be put aside to see clearly the value Crusoe or Moll or Roxana place on variety. Variety and movement complement one another; Defoe's characters achieve authenticity not through learning and development (our usual criteria for judging the "fullness" of a literary character), but some basic sense of *being.* Variety and movement enhance this sense of being because they are the means by which Defoe's characters can change identity, become other people, disguise themselves, and hoodwink others. Defoe does not define his characters through a gradual revelation of their basic natures; his understanding of character is not that settled. He seems instead to view identity as combat, either against the secure identities of others or against definitions of character inherited from tradition and ideology. By their manipulation of many identities, his narrators attempt to solidify the one mysterious identity that belongs to each.

John Richetti has emphasized Defoe's "ability to suggest a world of controlling circumstances, which we can recognize as real, in which at the same time extravagant fantasies of success and conquest can take place." [8] But after *Crusoe,* I would argue, the forces of control have had their exposition, and Defoe begins to explore more fully the individual resistance to control. The decrease in providential language in *Captain Singleton* (1720) is remarkable after the importance of providential language in *Crusoe,* and it implies as well the irrelevance of spiritual biography to Defoe's later explorations of character. [9] *The Life, Adventures, and Piracies of the Famous Captain Singleton* effectively contradicts any complacencies about the ability to understand character that may have been set up by *Robinson Crusoe.* At the end of the novel, in one of the most surrealistic scenes in all "realistic" literature, Singleton sets up his conditions for retirement to England after a life of piracy: (1) his friend William, the Quaker with whom he has carried on most of his adventures, will not reveal himself to any relative (although Singleton later marries William's sister); (2) neither William nor Singleton will remove the Greek beards and the Greek clothes they assumed in Istanbul to pass as merchants; (3) neither will ever speak English in public; and (4) they will live together and pass as brothers. This does not recall the serene "retirement" at the end of *Farther Adventures,* with its Horatian echoes, in which the self takes ease after long toil. Instead of being satisfied by the repentance for a life of piracy that Singleton asserts, we are horrified and fascinated with this vision of perpetual disguise in what is nominally Singleton's native land. Revelation of character isn't a problem in spiritual autobiography because all is ultimately to the glory of God, even what would otherwise be hardly bearable outbursts of egotism. But the final vision of *Captain Singleton* shows the potential clash between the purposeful revelations of spiritual autobiography and the damage to the tender self that may result when revelation goes too far. At one point, William warns Singleton that he should be careful lest he reveal himself accidentally while talking in his sleep. This motif of involuntary self-disclosure appears again in *Moll Flanders.* But in *Singleton,* Defoe seems not yet clear about where he will go. The form of the novel itself changes oddly: it begins as a pirate "biography" and ends as a familiar letter to a friend. Singleton's revelations withdraw from the public stage of writer and audience to a more intimate kind of connection. *Crusoe* barely hinted at the possibility that frankness about oneself held any problems, whether psychological or literary. Its preoccupation with Providence may have been the expression of an actual providential anxiety, a desperate need to assert that God had not left the world behind, even though the orders of society and culture seemed to possess none of their old authority or effectiveness. By *Singleton,* the literal and metaphysical cannibals who come to rob Crusoe of his body and soul have become more intriguing subjects for Defoe than any analysis of the inadequacy of older forms.

In flight from pressures that threaten to distort their sense of identity and faced with a possibly malevolent freedom, Defoe's characters protect themselves principally by disguise. Disguise appears so often in Defoe's novels that it finally occupies some shadowland between symbol and metaphysic. Through disguise Defoe and his characters can simultaneously escape the world of facts, lists, and documentary realism, and manipulate it at a distance. By changing names, they assert that finally there is something unspecifiable about human nature, a fact that cannot be pinned down.

Defoe's own life provides many intriguing instances of the pitfalls and benefits of disguise and assumed identity. In 1702 he was arrested, pilloried, fined, and given an indefinite prison term for too successfully imitating a High Church point of view in *The Shortest Way with the Dissenters.* Biographers of Defoe, like James Sutherland, do not speak of any attempt at recantation or explanation, as if Defoe were willing to take the consequences of either the inability of his plain-listening audience to understand his ironies or his own inability to project it. Three of his anti-Jacobite pamphlets in 1712–13 tried the ironic approach by setting forth an exaggerated pro-Jacobite case.[10] In the early 1700s, Defoe traveled about the countryside, acting as a kind of political spy for Robert Harley, and later went to Scotland to report on the political climate preceding the Act of Union in 1707. From 1704 to 1713 he published the *Review,* professing an independent political

point of view, although in fact he conferred with Harley regularly and was paid
with government secret-service money "rather irregularly." [11] From 1715 to 1724,
after the Hanoverian Succession had brought the Whigs into power and Harley
and Bolingbroke were out, Defoe made some kind of deal with the Whig government by which he would write most of *Dormer's News-Letter* and later *Mist's
Weekly Journal* as if they were continuing their previously pro-Tory point of view,
when in fact he was supporting Whig policies. James Sutherland has noted: "The
extension of Defoe's habit of playing a part in real life to playing one in such
ironical pamphlets as *The Shortest Way with the Disenters* is sufficiently obvious.
But deception and make-believe are also prominent features in the stuff of his
fiction." [12] One may argue, as Sutherland has, that Defoe's main interest was the
support of the Protestant Succession and that he had the ability to write as he
wanted to, trimming his Whig or Tory sails to suit himself when the issue was
particularly important to him. But the second- and third-guessing involved in such
long-term projects as *Dormer's* and *Mist's,* the political spying, and the attempts
at plain-speaking irony could not help but breed many minds in Defoe. Conscious
deception may be in part a restitution for being previously misunderstood. Typically in Defoe's novels we find characters who are simultaneously trying to explain themselves and conceal themselves. Perhaps through his experience in political deception, Defoe was able to strike a common chord in an anxiety about
identity more general than he knew.

    Defoe's own experiences with disguise seem to permeate his characters, and in
the light of his sometimes unsuccessful experiments with irony, it is appropriate
that his characters tend to consider disguise a liberation from more confining conceptions of their identities. Ironically enough, Defoe may have gotten the cue to
draw upon this shifting side of his literary personality when Charles Gildon attacked *Robinson Crusoe* as an impersonation in which Defoe was actually talking
about himself in the fantastical guise of Crusoe and Friday. [13] In *Serious Reflections of Robinson Crusoe,* Defoe picks up and elaborates the allegorical suggestion
beyond anything Gildon anticipated. He was obviously intrigued by it and, better
than Gildon, perceived that it was a way of vindicating himself from charges of
entertainment by showing the more metaphysical uses of *Crusoe.* But Defoe also
turned another of Gildon's charges to his benefit, less obviously than the moral
allegory. Gildon began his attack by calling Defoe a "Proteus" for his constant
changes of political allegiance and writing voice, for his disguises of himself under the name and nature of others. It is difficult to say that Defoe immediately
saw the validity and importance of this attack; but in *Singleton* and the novels that
follow, disguise assumes an importance far greater than it had in *Crusoe,* and the
relation between providential order and personal identity becomes correspondingly
less important. Moll Flanders first describes a theft she made without special disguise and then continues, "but generally I took up new figures, and contriv'd to
appear in new shapes every time I went abroad" (p. 229). Colonel Jacque may
complain that his second wife "was a mere posture mistress in love, and could
put herself into what shapes she pleased" and call her a "chameleon," but he
himself changes names and disguises with frequency, at one point living in Can-

terbury and passing among the English as a Frenchman and among the French as
an Englishman, with the alternate names of Mr. Charnock and Monsieur Charnot.

Being able to impose on others through disguise brings a joy and elation to
Defoe's characters far beyond any pragmatic gains the disguise may bring; it seems
to assure them that they are real. Such situations might be compared with Defoe's
description to Harley of his travels in Scotland before the Act of Union:

> I Converse with Presbyterian, Episcopall-Dissenter, papist and Non Juror, and I hope
> with Equall Circumspection. I flatter my Self you will have no Complaints of my
> Conduct. I have faithfull Emissaries in Every Company and I Talk to Everybody in
> Their Own way. To the Merchants I am about to Settle here in Trade, Building ships
> &c. With the Lawyers I want to purchase a House and Land to bring my family and
> live Upon it (God knows where the Money is to pay for it). To day I am Goeing into
> Partnership with a Membr of parliamt in a Glass house, to morrow with Another in a
> Salt work. With the Glasgow Mutineers I am to be a Fish Merchant, with the Aber-
> deen men a woollen and with the Perth and western men a Linen Manufacturer, and
> still at the End of all Discourse the Union is the Essentiall and I am all to Every one
> that I may Gain some.[14]

Sutherland wonders why Defoe had to tell so many lies, since a sceptical Scot
could always collate the stories. But Defoe seems to exult in the ability to change,
assuming and discarding identity. "Converse" and "Union" define the poles of
his identity. Defoe in Scotland resembles Colonel Jacque, with his two names and
two nationalities within the narrow confines of Canterbury, or Moll Flanders, who
steals a watch from a woman after pretending to be a friend of the family and
then toys with the idea of getting into the woman's coach after the theft is noticed
to help catch the thief; all three manipulate disguise on the edge of exposure and
even move closer to exposure in order to savor the preserved self more keenly.

As part of their natural progress through the world, Defoe's narrators take on
new names and shed old ones, and another indication of the distance between
Crusoe and the later novels is the way Crusoe is solaced by the parrot who continually calls him by name, a recognition characters like Moll, Jack, and Roxana
often live in fear of. *Memoirs of a Cavalier,* written between *Crusoe* (1719) and
Singleton (1720), spends most of its time presenting the main character within the
framework of military engagements and public history. But it begins with a taste
of the kind of mystification about names that will become more prevalent in the
later novels:

> It may suffice the Reader, without being very inquisitive after my Name, that I was
> born in the County of SALOP, in the year 1608; under the Government of what Star
> I was never Astrologer enough to examine; but the Consequences of my Life may
> allow me to suppose some extraordinary Influence affected my Birth.[15]

Whatever Defoe's motives at this point in his novel-writing career, this introduction contains the same combination of revelation and reticence that he exploits

more elaborately in other works: specificity about date, vagueness about name, and assurance about self-importance.

A name you are born with can relate you to a past history, especially to a genealogy; a name you choose yourself can help you to disengage yourself from your past and family. Even in *Crusoe,* the novel most preoccupied with the pressure of authority and the past on the individual, one of the first things we learn about Robinson Crusoe is that his last name is really Kreutznaer, "but by the usual corruption of words in England, we are now called, nay, we call our selves, and write our name *Crusoe,* and so my companions always call'd me." Names connect an individual to a world of verifiable facts: baptismal records, prison records, newspapers, rate rolls—all of the legal ways Locke defines personal identity as a social term. But Defoe's characters slip their moorings to this world of human facts and steer carefully between it and total anonymity. Both Singleton and Moll, for example, are presented as widely known figures now finally telling their own stories: *The Life, Adventures, and Piracies of the Famous Captain Singleton; The Fortunes and Misfortunes of the Famous Moll Flanders*. Yet their "fame" contrasts strangely with the elusiveness of their "real" selves. Singleton gets the name "Captain Bob" only when he asserts and separates himself from the anonymous crowd of pirates: "Before I go any farther, I must hint to the Reader, that from this time forward I began to enter a little more seriously into the Circumstances I was in, and concern'd my self more in the Conduct of our Affairs." [16] Both he and Crusoe brag that they have been in places no other man has ever ventured into before. (I'll forego any speculation about Singleton's name.) But at the end of *Singleton,* he and William are sworn to disguise and anonymity. Moll too is "famous," yet changes her name and guise with the speed and opportunism of the Proteus Gildon accused Defoe of being. She is called "Betty" early in the novel and takes the name "Mrs. Flanders" while living in the Mint; "Here, however, I conceal'd my self, and tho' my new acquaintance knew nothing of me, yet I soon got a good deal of company about me." (p. 57). When she is called "Moll Flanders" later, she is puzzled:

> it was no more of affinity with my real name, or with any of the names I had ever gone by, than black is kin to white, except that once, as before, I call'd my self Mrs. Flanders, when I sheltered my self in the Mint; but that these rogues [other thieves who were jealous because she was so rarely caught] never knew, nor could I ever learn how they came to give me the name, or what the occasion of it was.   (p. 186)

Later she gives the name "Mary Flanders" when she is arrested for something she did not do, and at one point is even disguised as a man, named Gabriel Spencer, the name of one of the actors in Shakespeare's Globe company—although how strongly Defoe meant us to feel the force of this allusion, a type of rhetoric he rarely uses, is questionable. Moll preserves her name from her companions in the same way that she preserves her money; no matter how open with them she may be, no matter how much she trusts and loves them, there is always something withheld, some mystery to keep for herself. By a quick switch of her apron she changes disguise and disappears. But the most remarkable part of this mystification is that it does not stop at her companions in crime. The reader is told when she holds back money, but we never learn her true name. The freedom to establish a new identity in America may make her less apprehensive about this final revelation, and we do learn that she sends goods "consign'd to my real name in Virginia" (p. 272). But the phrase is ambiguous, and in any case we never hear what this "real name" is.

Colonel Jacque changes disguise with as much glee as Moll; I have already mentioned the way he passes as a Frenchman among the English and an Englishman among the French. In some basic way he does not feel comfortable among his native society, and he uses the possibilities of freedom in America and stylization in France to purge the anxieties of being born poor and English. Like Moll, Colonel Jacque considers that money and name are inextricably bound in the validation of identity. At the beginning of the novel, he is only one of three orphan boys named Jack who live among the ashes at the glassworks. There seems to be little reason to have the other Jacks around—they hardly play any part in his later adventures—except to heighten the way he emerges as the most important Jack, who can easily change himself into a Jacque when necessary, even to the extent of being "Colonel Jacque" in the book's title. Jack believes that his mother "by oral tradition" was a gentlewoman and his father a man of quality; his actions in life are predicated on that belief. When he assumes the clothes of a gentlemen, he becomes what he has been innately all along. Like Roxana, he uses French culture as a means of assuming and changing identity. Roxana's own name is given her at a fancy dress ball because she is wearing a Turkish costume; the ability to change clothes is directly related to the ability to change identity. Roxana's daughter pursues her in order to verify that this older woman is the same who appeared in Turkish clothes at that ball long ago. Amy, Roxana's maid and alter-ego, kills Roxana's daughter because she threatens to link the various identities in Roxana's life; she presents little threat to Roxana beyond the fact that she is *someone who knows.* The hasty ending of *Roxana,* in which the final sentence hurriedly hints of some "Blast of Heaven" that many years later seems to punish her and Amy for their crime, preserves the ambiguous status of the murder, part mortal sin and part psychological necessity. Unlike the titles of the earlier novels, which detailed adventures *(Robinson Crusoe, Singleton, Colonel Jacque)* or social roles *(Moll Flanders), Roxana* speaks of its subject in terms of her many names, "Mademoiselle de Beleau, afterwards called the Countess de Wintselsheim in Germany, Being the Person known by the Name of the Lady Roxana in the time of Charles II." And once again the reader is never quite told what her real name is. For people writing about themselves, Singleton, Moll, Jack, and Roxana seem singularly hostile to the idea that anyone might want to meet them in person; no matter how much she may reveal, Roxana does not drop the final veil, even for the reader.

❏ ❏ ❏

Defoe therefore seems to define personal identity simultaneously as a structuring and merchandising of the self in a public form (your talent sold to politicians, your adventures to sensation-hungry readers), and a final reticence about the depths of the private self. Balanced between seventeenth-century and earlier "patterned" autobiographies and the idiosyncratic confessions of the later eighteenth century, his characters use disguise to preserve the final secret. In the world of Defoe's characters everything that preexists the individual—family, society, culture, and Providence—threatens his or her identity. These orders can be accepted, if at all (e.g., *Crusoe*), after the individual has become secure in his sense of self. Throughout his first-person novels, Defoe searches for the source of self-knowledge and self-realization, through the constant movement of Singleton, Moll, and Roxana, or the stasis of H.F. in London and Crusoe on the island. In some cases, his main characters spawn partners, so that the problem of individuality might be studied in more detail: Crusoe has Friday, Singleton has William, Moll has the "governess," Roxana has Amy. These "doubles" emphasize the inner complexity of human character in opposition to any unitary view, which believes evil, for example, to come from the outside. Friday allows Crusoe to discover things about himself he never knew before; and the pairing of the philosophical William with the adventuring Singleton, or the pragmatic Amy with the romantic Roxana, makes their individual stories larger comments on human personality in general.

Defoe's characters use disguise to facilitate the search outside themselves for ways of proving their separate being. Moll's "governess" joins Friday, William, and Amy as part of a new "family of the self" that Moll, Crusoe, Singleton, and Roxana seek to create. But the most important means of self-definition and self-justification for Defoe's narrators is the act of telling their own stories. Throughout the novels there are points when each narrator decides the limits of his or her story. They use the formula "that's another story" to define what their story is and what their world contains to the exclusion of anyone else's. By this literary formula each establishes his own uniqueness, his separability from others. Moll separates her story from those of her many husbands, and Jack even more explicitly separates his from the stories of the two other boys named Jack who lived with him in the glasshouse ashes. Within each narrator's story, there are other stories that further enhance the separate importance of his own: Singleton tells about Captain Knox; H. F. tells of the biscuit baker, the sailmaker, and the joiner; and when Colonel Jacque meets his second wife again in Virginia, she won't tell him her story in full because "it would take a great many days to give me a history of it" (p. 290). The book, or the story, instead of being an external form to which the self subordinates its uniqueness for the edification of an audience in search of general truths, becomes a vehicle for a kind of guarded self-expression, in which the reader may explore his own changing self-definition.

Defoe's narrators gradually realize that the creation of a book can be a source of identity for themselves, as well as a self-justification before the world. In proving to a buyer that one's self is worth something, one proves it to oneself. In July 1711 Defoe proposed to Harley a plan to colonize Patagonia and southern Chile; it was shelved. But, as James Sutherland points out, Defoe did not rest there. In 1724 he includes such a venture, successful but fictional, in *A New Voyage round the World*.[17] The reality of the book can restore some failed reality in life. In *Moll*

Flanders the life of "infinite variety" and the book of "infinite variety" are already identified. H. F. writes *A Journal of the Plague Year* because he believes that he has been spared from the plague specifically to bear witness. By *Roxana* the identification between narrator and book has been made explicit: "The History of this *Beautiful Lady,* is to speak for itself: If it is not as beautiful as the Lady herself is reported to be . . . the *Relator says,* it must be from the Defect of his Performance; dressing up the Story in worse Cloaths than the *Lady,* whose Words he speaks, prepar'd it for the World." [18] We remember here how important Roxana's clothes are for the definition of her identity (and recall the similar importance of clothes in *Colonel Jacque*), at the same time that we note that Roxana hides behind a "Relator," who doesn't even say he has ever seen her, her beauty being only "reported" to him. Without arguing influence, one could say that Defoe brings Montaigne's identification of book and self into English literature. But, unlike Montaigne, Defoe also concentrates on the partiality of that sense of self the book preserves, because its inner nature remains inaccessible.

Diane Trilling once wrote of Norman Mailer: "Where the novelist of an earlier day helped us to understand and master a mysterious or recalcitrant environment, the present-day novelist undertakes only to help us to define the self in relation to the world that surrounds and threatens to overwhelm it." [19] Diana Trilling is here obviously defining Mailer against the earlier novelists of society. But it is fascinating to see how easily Defoe can sit beside Mailer in her definition. Society in Defoe is never an object of exploration. It is a threatening world of others, a world not to be understood but to be gotten through with the least damage to skin or psyche, as Moll Flanders or Colonel Jacque or Roxana speed through the labyrinth of London streets. Defoe's first-person novels move further and further away from older definitions of human character, based so much on the position of an individual soul in the providential order. His works deal basically with the difficulty of knowing and being yourself, amid the bankruptcy of previous psychological and autobiographical forms. Defoe is fascinated by the rigid order to which human beings so often appeal when they try to explain themselves, and he sees the potential of such orders—genealogy, society, Providence—to help avoid explanation. The form of autobiography, which his narrators manipulate to expose and hide themselves, is another such form. But it is self-created, through an isolation and retrospect that becomes an important part of its meaning. Through the isolation of his characters, Defoe examines the epistemological and ontological basis of his own detached narrative voice and discovers its inadequacies. In a narrator like H. F., in *A Journal of the Plague Year,* we sense Defoe's engagement with the wellsprings of such detachment: the fear of others, and the implication that sociability automatically means sickness and death. Such a fear is constant in Defoe's narrators, even if they are not on a desert island or in the middle of a plague-stricken city. It is basically a fear of discovery, not the discovery of something tangible, but the discovery and therefore the violation of a sense of personal identity, a sense of self.

Defoe, therefore, has no real answer to the anxieties of self-definition he explores with such power. The closest he comes to one lies in his exploration of the possibilities of retreat, a concept from which the inadequacies of detachment have been distilled. One fascinating characteristic shared by many of Defoe's narrators is a sympathy with Catholicism; Charles Gildon even called Defoe pro-French and propapist. But I think that the real lure of Catholicism for Defoe was in the combination of society and refuge encompassed by the concept of "retreat." In *The Memoirs of an English Officer* (1728), the narrator, Captain Carleton, visits a monastery in Spain. He envies the lives of the monks, the mingling of nature and art in their work, and the unique beauty of each cell, with its individual rill from a common spring. This is not the cave in which the fearful Crusoe finds a sick goat, but an image of fruitful isolation, the "most happy and comfortable retreat, though it was a kind of an exile," in which Colonel Jacque tells us he wrote his memoirs. Money is an anchor for the identity of those who wish to stay within society, manipulating disguises and names so that the core of self is never revealed. But "retreat" has no need of money, and Defoe's final ideal seems to be an introspection without society, a replenishing of human insides that, although it takes its image from a religious situation, is basically pastoral and pagan in impulse. Through their compelling delineation of the mystery at the heart of human personality, Defoe's first-person novels change the basic nature of autobiography and announce one of the most important preoccupations of eighteenth-century literature.

[1973]

Notes

1. In his excellent study *Popular Fiction before Richardson: Narrative Patterns, 1700–1739* (Oxford, 1969), John Richetti aptly asks why, if these early authentic and fictional life-histories really laid the foundation for the novel, did it take so long for the house of fiction to be raised (p. 23).

2. Paul Delany in *British Autobiography in the Seventeenth Century* (London: Routledge & Kegan Paul, 1969) has carefully shown the frequency with which the seventeenth-century autobiographer tried to make his life exemplary "rather than trying to assert the value or singularity of his individual personality" (p. 67).

3. If the making of an allegory of human life were in fact Defoe's primary goal, why did he continue to write first-person novels after *Crusoe*? G. A. Starr, in *Defoe and Spiritual Autobiography* (Princeton: Princeton University Press 1965), is somewhat annoyed to discover that the links between Defoe's novels and the earlier works from which they undeniably spring weaken as Defoe continues to write. He goes so far as to say that Defoe "injudiciously elected to make Roxana her own commentator" (p. 164).

4. For a good account of Defoe's views, see Maximilian E. Novak, "Defoe's Theory of Fiction," *Studies in Philology*, 61 (1964), pp. 650–68.

5. *Romances and Narratives by Daniel Defoe*, ed. George A. Aitken (London, 1895), 2:319.

6. *Moll Flanders*, ed. James Sutherland (Cambridge, Mass., 1959), p. 69.

7. H. F. is himself antiquarantine and, although he supports the efforts of the city government to contain the plague, he specifically refuses to be a "closer" of the homes of the plague-stricken and buys his way out of the job when appointed to it.

8. *Popular Fiction before Richardson*, p. 89.

9. After *Crusoe*, providential language is taken most seriously in *A Journal of the Plague Year*. But the elaborate discriminations of H. F. about the role of Providence in the plague are at once more problematic (since they deal in great part with public events) and more intellectualized than anything attempted by Crusoe.

10. See James Sutherland, *Daniel Defoe; A Critical Study* (Cambridge, Mass., 1971), pp. 12–13.

11. Ibid., p. 11.

12. Ibid., p. 15.

13. *A Dialogue betwixt D . . . . . F . . . e, Robinson Crusoe, and His Man Friday* [1719], ed. Paul Dottin (London, 1923).

14. *The Letters of Daniel Defoe,* ed. George Harris Healey (Oxford, 1955), pp. 158–59; quoted in part by Sutherland, p. 15.

15. Daniel Defoe, *Memoirs of a Cavalier,* ed. and intro. James T. Boulton (Oxford, 1972), p. 7.

16. Ed. James Sutherland (London, 1963), p. 66.

17. Sutherland, *Daniel Defoe,* pp. 153–57.

18. Ed. Jane Jack (New York 1964), p. 1.

19. "The Radical Moralism of Norman Mailer," *Claremont Essays* (New York: Harcourt, Brace and World, 1964), p. 178.

A Genealogy of Mind
Under the Sign of Saturn by Susan Sontag

"The highest criticism," said Oscar Wilde, is "the record of one's own soul.
. . . It is the only civilized form of autobiography." Susan Sontag, at the center
of her new collection of essays, finds a similar truth revealed in the work of the
cultural critic Walter Benjamin, who "projected himself, his temperament, into
all his major subjects, and his temperament determined what he chose to write
about." Like Wilde's, Sontag's invitation seems clear enough, for the varieties of
her own cultural career since the middle 1960s (five collections of essays, three
films, two novels, and a collection of short stories) entice us as well to wonder
what beyond a voice of impersonal but passionate authority binds it together and
where her self resides within the work.

Trying to assess *Under the Sign of Saturn* therefore crucially requires a coherent
definition of Sontag's cultural presence over the last 15 years, not least because
she now seems to be wondering the same thing about herself. Each essay treats
someone whose accomplishment might be a model or a cautionary example for
what Sontag, in speaking of Elias Canetti, calls the "itinerant intellectual," the
cultural commentator and theoretician who supports himself through the personal
entrepreneurship of books, articles, grants, and the occasional teaching position—
without any permanent academic post and therefore without any corporate alle-
giances to local or neighborhood humanisms.

The master image of this self-assemblage is in the first paragraph, and it is
characteristically expressed as a purification. There Sontag depicts herself sitting
down to write an essay on Paul Goodman, who has just died. She is in a sparsely
or spartanly furnished room in Paris—which she describes in some detail—stripped
down, she says, "while finding a new space inside my head . . . to make a new
start with as little capital as possible to fall back on."

In fact, although the essay on Goodman and those that follow (on Artaud, Leni
Riefenstahl, Walter Benjamin, Hans-Jürgen Syberberg's film *Our Hitler,* Roland
Barthes, and Canetti) appeared in print between 1972 and 1980, in this collection
they form an almost inevitable suite on the theme of the critic/artist in search of
an audience that by its understanding will bring him being.

Since her first essays began appearing in the mid-1960s, all of Sontag's critical writing has focused on the question of intellectual connection: what is the central tradition of Western thought in the twentieth century and which writers have contributed most to its creation? In the midst of the conflict and collapse of nations, she implies, the reestablishment of a clear genealogy of mind could overlay and make coherent the disruptions and fragmentations of individual careers and beshrewed lives. The mediations of the critical perspective would create a "new sensibility" (as she called it in *Against Interpretation*) hospitable to what was best regardless of preexisting cultural prejudice (her examples are Jasper Johns, Jean-Luc Godard, and the Beatles), reconnecting the broken fragments of tradition.

In *Under the Sign of Saturn* Sontag is at work again reshaping the canon of modern European literature. Her particular polemic—a strong element in the general thrust of postwar New York literary criticism—is to celebrate the leopards in the temple of literature, not those cool and calm consciousnesses (like the Sophocles and Shakespeare of Matthew Arnold) who abided all questions and saw life whole, but those whose own derangement allowed them to explode the lies of order so that better forms might be discovered. In her criticism she labors to turn even the most self-isolating, uncompromising, and personally outrageous of such figures (I think here especially of Artaud) into humane teachers, whose flame, all the brighter for being trimmed, she will pass on to future generations.

In the 1960s such a critical project was both exuberant and expansive. But as Sontag wrote further and became part of the critical establishment herself, her tone became more sober and somber, until in *Saturn* she finds a moral and emotional benchmark in the melancholic temperament (specifically Benjamin's), with its "self-conscious and unforgivable relation to the self, which can never be taken for granted," born under "the star of the slowest revolution, the planet of detours and delays." Sontag's heroes are, therefore, those writers whose acute sense of the difficulties of using language properly allows them, paradoxically, to pierce its veil and see into the heart of things. Without being system-builders, they search for the core of a newly whole reality that gives due respect to the fragmentations of twentieth-century knowledge and perception. Descending, like T. S. Eliot, from the late nineteenth-century French symbolist poets, this "heroic avant-garde" of critic/artists constitutes a next generation of self-awareness. But their work (or antiwork) makes Eliot's ruminations on the way words lose meaning seem like optimism—if only because he could express such sentiments poetically and thereby for the moment divert their destructive potential.

Part of the heroism of these writers comes from their struggle to create a Total Work—modernism's version of the Bible—whose virtuoso arrangement and articulation of the fragments embodies a bold and decisive synthesis. But they feel (much more cripplingly than did, say, Eliot or Pound or Joyce) the futility of such an effort, even if it could be accomplished. Here then is the other side of avant-garde heroism: the willful incompleteness and fragmentation of the artist's own work. In the array of modernist masters, Sontag is more attracted to the noble failures than to the proud successes, for they understand that questioning never ends and that artistic language has no special status when language itself is on trial.

In *On Photography* Sontag remarks that "all possibility of understanding is

rooted in the ability to say no,'' that is, to resist the versions of reality others
press upon us. The heroism of the rampant artist in search of the Total Work may
seem to define that protest. Yet the twentieth century has also taught us that the
Total Work—authoritative, self-sufficient, and infinitely interpretable—can easily
verge at one extreme into a fascistic blurring of distinctions and at the other into
a formless multiplication of objects and gestures. By attacking such extremes,
Sontag hopes to preserve the integrity of the original vision. In *Saturn* it is the
monolithic aestheticizing of experience that gets the brunt of her wrath. Some of
her early essays explored film, camp culture, and science fiction in part to undermine the tradition of high seriousness in literary and cultural criticism. But in
Saturn she finds the aesthetic pose to be colored with self-indulgence and edged
with fascism. In *On Photography,* by contrast, her main target is the democratic
aesthetic of prepackaged life, the trivializing repetition of the image that smothers
true value in a myriad of titillating inessentials. In *Illness as Metaphor* she con-
demns the way we have used metaphoric language to obscure and mystify the
physical and material world, turning diseases into imagery, metamorphosing the
final reality of bodily decay and death into the shrouded fantasies of moral pollu-
tion and staining sin. Like the mute, deceptive images in the photographs she
scorns in *On Photography,* the metaphoric uses to which cancer and tuberculosis
have been put screens our minds from—Sontag, unlike Nabokov, doesn't want to
put the word into quotation marks—reality.

Reality is a crucial term for Sontag, not least because, for all her appreciation
of movies, she is specifically hostile to what she calls nominalism, the view that
there are no absolute concepts or ideas, only words that are socially accepted ways
of communicating. Of course, the philosophical realist need not live entirely in a
world of Platonic ideas and the nominalist is hardly happy only when he contemplates fragments and ruins. But Sontag's sympathies are clear. Her goal is an
understanding of what is essential and what is real, and those she most admires
retain a Platonic sensitivity to the disorder of the world and a Platonic faith in the
ability of mind to penetrate that disorder and find truth.

To celebrate such a project, even or especially in the works of those for whom
the failure to achieve is a vital part of the meaning of the quest, requires the
honing presence of villains. In *Saturn* they are Leni Riefenstahl and Adolf Hitler,
who embody the evil that results when a falsely coherent artistic perspective is
applied to the world. Because the critic/artists Sontag admires and explicates in
Saturn wear their marginality like a banner, she particularly resents Riefenstahl's
efforts to characterize herself as ''the beautiful outcast,'' as if Hitler's patronage
never happened. Intriguingly enough, the false artist Riefenstahl is also the only
woman depicted in a gallery of heroic critic/artists whose frequent misogyny or
lack of feminist consciousness Sontag sometimes fleetingly notes. But Riefenstahl,
whatever her status as Sontag's personal antitype in *Saturn,* explicitly embodies
the artist totally coopted and compromised in great part because of her success in
putting her aesthetic ideas into political practice. Sontag never implies that, if
Artaud and Benjamin or others in her pantheon were in power, the results would
be beneficent or even predictable. Their influence is less on action than on other

minds, and it is in the sufficiency of mind, its continuous critical presence, that Sontag rests her ultimate value. Mind, that is, primarily as expressed in books; mind as opposed to body; mind that cures the fallible individual of the frailties of body and the sliverings of vision by its rigor, clarity, and spirit.

To pursue the life of the mind and maintain its vitality in the face of both the dehumanizing horrors of twentieth-century war and the more subtle dehumanizations of technological advance and aesthetic democratization, implies Sontag, requires the self-questioning detachment of the melancholic critic/artist, whose essentially passive objectivity her own style seems to imitate. Ever since the Renaissance, melancholy has been the mark of the artist whose work or aspiration made claims on the philosophic and eternal. Sometimes the melancholic artist, separated from ordinary men by his link to what is permanent, could be a satirist as easily as a high-stalking dreamer of the divine. (Dürer keeps his edge; Swift turns away from transcendence almost entirely.) Sontag's essays are in fact filled with traditional satiric themes—the incoherence of public sources of information, the corrupt emptiness of theatrical versions of reality, the pressure that time and bodily decay put on human aspirations—even though she never writes satire as such (unless you count, as I tend to, *Oh Photography*). Instead, she is fascinated with the effort, through writing and sometimes film, of creative individuals to be Romantic eccentrics in a time of mass societies. The strategies of such an assertion obviously have changed since the days of Wordsworth, Byron, and Napoleon. But Sontag adds her own emphasis on the importance of the melancholic's corrosive self-awareness. In the view that she derives primarily from Benjamin, twentieth-century history has forced the critic/artist to take up a custodial relation to the world—collecting, deciphering, rearranging what is discovered into patterns that in their turn must be criticized. Enter, then, the interpreter of such writers, who deciphers *their* references and fragments not by the piecemeal process of ascertaining the meaning of each but by enlightening us about the cultural significance of such fragmented referentiality.

Such a role suited Sontag well in her earlier incarnation as a questioner of critical and cultural clichés, when her special status as an émigré by adoption allowed her to champion many artists and thinkers whose moral purpose was often less clear than her own. But in our climate of confusion over what political, aesthetic, or spiritual leadership might be, *Under the Sign of Saturn* raises more questions than its ideals can satisfy. Where Sontag once strode the marches in search of outlandish but crucial sensibilities to bring back struggling and vital to the general reader, her trophies now have the slightly greenish tinge of the coterie or the salon. The fault lies more in her net than in her quarry.

In essence, I think it is difficult for Sontag to maintain an argument that attacks one side of Romantic individualism (that leads to political megalomania) in order to accept another (that leads to artistic self-aggrandizement). I hardly want to equate the two myself: strutting artists do much less harm than strutting dictators. But the paradox of the grandly assertive work of art that attacks the grandly assertive gesture in the public world of politics is a delicate one indeed, and Sontag is unconvincing about the terms of the competition, perhaps because she is so caught up in it herself. Syberberg's *Our Hitler* is Sontag's set piece here—"probably the most ambitious Symbolist work of this century''—and *Saturn's* structure very carefully poises it against Riefenstahl's *Triumph of the Will*. In this implicit contrast Syberberg is the modernist virtuoso of fragments, playing in the spray of twentieth-century images, constantly aware of the lie and deceit of all visual insignia, while Riefenstahl is the monolithic God's-eye director, soaring over the world like her subject, reducing all to pattern, sentimentally invoking the coercive abstractions of leader, nation, and body, and leaving her film unetched by any nuance of individual life and doubt.

In this contest the palm is clearly to Syberberg (or to Sontag's account of him). But from the competition seeps a corruption of means and terminology. Sontag devotes some telling comments to Syberberg's ambivalent relation to Wagner (who plays second fiddle to Hitler in the film), but scants the extent to which Syberberg, with his seven-hour film, administers an aesthetic dictatorship to his audience in order to purge the political dictatorship whose paraphernalia he portrays. Movies especially raise the question of how to draw the line between aesthetic and political control. Welles may satirize Citizen Kane, but Welles also becomes Kane (and to our loss seems to have stayed that way). Must the artist counter the sins of political absolutism by an absolute gesture of his own?

Sontag no doubt thinks that melancholic self-questioning can keep the true artist and critic from such indulgences. But the coolness of her own style belies her prescriptions for self-awareness. Melancholia, as every Elizabethan knew, is as much a means of drawing attention to oneself as it is a psychic communion with higher values. Sontag remarks on the fact that many of the exemplary thinkers she treats—from the modernist monk Artaud to the goliard intellectual Goodman— were riven by the worry that they hadn't been appreciated, hadn't become famous enough.

Such an inquiry is especially appropriate for Sontag, who burst forth in the early 1960s, when the fashionable world was ripe to take note of a critical talent that a few years before would have been much less widely celebrated because her direct sphere of influence would have been much smaller. But in the wake of the Kennedy years critics and thinkers and creative artists were starting to be news and a photograph of Sontag and her son appeared in a fashion magazine.

For the secular writer and artist, musing on the face of death and the failure of the body and mind, the question of fame is crucial. If *On Photography* is Sontag's belated neoplatonist turning away from that image of the critic in vogue, then *Under the Sign of Saturn* is her effort to reassess the public aspect of her pursuit of a career that has been defined historically by its distaste for public life and display. Searching for the shape of other careers, she implicitly meditates on her own: what am I to make of this pile of books that in some way is me? The question is all too modern. At the end of the Middle Ages Chaucer's *House of Fame* described statues of the great writers of antiquity, each holding up his greatest work. By the eighteenth century, in Pope's rewriting of Chaucer, *The Temple of Fame,* they are standing on top of their books. Sontag similarly first dons the costumes of her various heroes and villains and then packs each neatly away in the cultural closet. As always, her intelligence makes her essays refreshing, even though we may often learn less about her subjects than about what she thinks of them and how their ideas affected her. In pursuit of new connections she has fashioned a rhetoric of subordination that puts her forward as the humble lightning rod of culture. This is my tradition, she seems to say, these are my boys, and thus the Romantic project of finding the heart of a culture in its eccentrics winds up recommending instead the eccentricity of its own quest.

[1980]

Adulation and Revenge

It's wonderful to be someone before you're old.
JACKIE COOGAN

The first American President to be assassinated was killed by an unsuccessful actor during a theater performance. But John Wilkes Booth had at least professed political motives. At our own moment in the history of the competition between performers and politicians, it takes no complicated cultural sensitivity to realize that the election of a former actor to the Presidency presented us with the first Presidential assassin whose motivations were wrapped up in his adulation of an actress. John Hinckley, it is said, never met Jodie Foster. But she occupied a place in his heart like the icon of a saint or (in the imagery of *Taxi Driver*) like a magdalen. No doubt he had photos or even posters of her in his room. He went to New Haven not, it seems, to meet her, but to slip notes under her door and to brag in bars that she was his girlfriend. Meeting her would have dissolved the feeling he had for her; she would have become too tangible—taller or shorter, fatter or thinner, more real than he had imagined.

Instead of making her real, he had to make himself unreal, to raise himself to her rarefied and untouchable stature by becoming an assassin. Buying a gun and shooting a famous person is a much easier way to fame these days than virtually anything else people do. The Son of Sam in New York was so deluded as to murder people who weren't famous, and therefore had to write letters to the newspapers warning them of his crimes and his craziness.

John Hinckley had no time for such lengthy self-promotion. If killing a public person assures one of fame, then killing a public person who is both performer and politician makes the act definitive. That the full brunt of Hinckley's determination fell on the President's press secretary only intensifies the imagery of the moment. The face and name of Reagan clearly loomed large in Hinckley's family. He was the grander father who would repurify family and country with his direct answers, easy affability, and incandescent grin.

The world of images is so much better than real life. The famous live in a world of their own, to which we can only aspire. One story had it that Hinckley decided to attack Reagan because he heard that Reagan had snubbed Jodie Foster. Unlike Hinckley, so goes the implication, Reagan had met Foster and didn't want to talk to her, even though they both inhabited the same glittering world. It was like one saint snubbing another, a heresy for which Foster's champion would mete out the appropriate revenge.

Murder domesticates the great and heroicizes the banal and the everyday. So at least is the opinion of murderers, particularly those murderers who rise up out of anonymity to make the assertion that confirms their sense of their own nothing-ness: making nothing of another. The attempt to murder a public person is an effort to seize control of history and force it to revolve around oneself. Overshad-owed by Reagan's image in his home, Hinckley sallied forth to counter it, wearing on his sleeve the corrupt innocence embodied in Jodie Foster's screen image.

With John Hinckley, we have at least emblematically made the transition from being a nation of voters to being a nation of fans. In one way or another we are all fans, and we seek out and honor those who move us by their public appear-ances, their images, the echo of their voices inside our heads. Political assassina-tion assumes that the public figure is the linchpin of an organized power that will fall apart once he is removed. But American assassinations are increasingly psy-chological and spiritual. They are committed by people caught in a psychic com-petition with those they attempt to murder. Like the fan, the assassin nominates himself as both celebrator and executioner. Murder reduces the distance between the fan and the star. Now both are famous and they will go down in history together.

Guns let such things happen. But those who use guns share attitudes with others who never let their lives be ruled so totally by the ache to be pure. Some psyches are more tender than others and public people who are successful often draw to themselves the tender who look for sustenance and certainty.

Adulation turns into revenge because stars enhance fans by robbing them of some essential part of their identities. If the goal is recognition, then, up until the second trigger is pulled, there is a chance the assassin could become the lover again—if only he is recognized. Mark Chapman was so taken over by John Len-non's public image that from the time he was sixteen he virtually became Lennon. But, oddly enough, when he approached Lennon with an album to be auto-graphed, Lennon didn't sign it to Chapman's satisfaction—with the kind of rec-ognition he knew he deserved. Murder would balance that terrible asymmetry. Perhaps John Hinckley, well-brought up boy that he was, merely wanted Reagan to introduce him to Jodie Foster, so that he too could be at home in the world of the famous.

Assassinations and assassination attempts of this sort, the American sort, have by now almost completely removed themselves from any political sphere. Instead, they have become revenges on the world for crushing the murderer's fragile shell of being. The more that public persons are honored for their powers of spiritual uplift—their gifts as performers rather than as makers or thinkers—the more they will be the potential victims of fans whose own temperaments confuse worship with sacrifice. Mark Chapman idolized John Lennon until he realized that John Lennon neither knew him nor was like him. John Hinckley could present to Jodie Foster nothing more handsome than the death of Ronald Reagan, the hero of the entire Hinckley family.

Fame for such people is equivalent to sainthood for the religious. It promises entrance to realms beyond confusion, chaos, and the divisions of normal life, where people are always what they ought to be, never what they are. But in a world where Christian ministers preach humbleness on television, psychic assassinations like that of John Lennon and the attempted one on Ronald Reagan can only become more prevalent. Surely we would all be better off with more stringent gun control. All of us, that is, but the public performers whose purified personalities gather up and sustain for a time the gaps and lonelinesses in the hearts of their audience. Interviewed during the intermission of Jodie Foster's student play at Yale, one fifteen-year-old New Haven boy said he had come to see her because he had never seen anyone famous before.

[1984]

IV
FICTIONS OF FEELING

Providence, Paranoia, and the Novel

I became particularly attached to the playhouse, conversed with the actors behind the scenes, got acquainted with a body of Templars, and in short time commenced a professed wit and critic. Indeed, I may say without vanity that I was much better qualified than any of my companions, who were, generally speaking, of all the creatures I ever conversed with, the most ignorant and assuming. By means of these avocations, I got the better of care, and learned to separate my ideas in such a manner that whenever I was attacked by a gloomy reflection I could shove it aside and call in some agreeable reverie to my assistance.

TOBIAS SMOLETT, *Roderick Random*

"You've conceived somewhere the notion that I am intimate with the details of a conspiracy. In a world such as you inhabit, Mr. Stencil, any cluster of phenomena can be a conspiracy. So no doubt your suspicion is correct. But why consult me? Why not the Encyclopaedia Britannica? It knows more than I about any phenomena you should ever have interest in."

THOMAS PYNCHON, *V.*

Providence, it was called, the all-pervasive order that held the world together, subordinating and arraying everything by the immanence from within and the eminence from without. But between the seventeenth and the eighteenth centuries its powerful ability to explain the coherence of things was in the process of becoming yet another interpretive fiction, secularized and often parochial, no longer even the exclusive belief of the religious. A basic assumption about the divine force that linked visible and the invisible world had somehow been transformed into only another way of looking at things, another lens, no more or less authoritative than any other.

In the more familiar aspects of the story, the sufficiency of a spiritual cosmol-

First versions of parts of this essay were included in papers delivered at the VIIth International Conference on the Enlightenment (New Haven, 1975) and at the English Institute (Cambridge, 1976). A few sentences from it have appeared, with quite a different turn, in "Realists, Naturalists, and Novelists of Manners," a chapter I wrote for *The Harvard Guide to Contemporary American Writing*, ed. Daniel Hoffman (Cambridge: Harvard University Press, 1980).

ogy had been undermined by the rise of empiricism and scientific rationalism. What Descartes, like Milton, had attempted to hold in suspension stood on the verge of schizophrenic separation into polarities and opposites. Newton, towards the end of the century, could still be as attracted to explaining the parallels between sacred and profane history as he was to quantifying the connective forces of the physical universe, and Robert Boyle alternated his writing between works that laid the foundations of modern chemistry and theological treatises like *Some Motives and Incentives to the Love of God.* In such willfully separated compartments, divine pattern and human understanding might coexist for one individual's lifetime. But for thinkers like Hobbes and Locke, focused on the structure of society, cosmological order was primarily a highflown justification for the existence of the state. Of course they each had their own conception of what kind of state that was. But both agreed that cosmological order was tied to political order, and political order was more worthy of explication. By the eighteenth century, the goal of the philosophes would similarly be to show that many other total systems might exist, many other coherent explanations. Absolute belief in a Designer God played little part in the new epistemology. Gibbon and Voltaire made as much fun of heresy as they did of justification by faith.

Providence may not always have been very helpful on the details, but at least it allowed you to assume that Someone had put them all together. When it was replaced by a group of competing coherency theories, the assumption could easily be made that no one held them together: each was an individual, original product. The explanatory force of providence, the desire to see the universe as a whole in which one participated, was taken over in one realm by the explorers of science and material progress and in another by the newly professional practitioners of verbal and aesthetic order. Pascal had paved the way for literary criticism by postulating a God who appreciated the ability to make intellectual distinctions more than he appreciated belief itself, a God who didn't mind if you believed primarily in order to hedge your bets. But no longer could religion solely aggrandize the kingdoms of the spirit. As such disparate phenomena as the gothic novel and the rise of Methodism indicate, the spiritual became associated instead with the emotional, the affective, even the sexual—that is, the realm of nonpublic, nonscientific language. Through the medium of the novel particularly, providential causality was giving way to psychological causality. To speak properly of providence and its fortunes, therefore, it is necessary to talk as well of narrative and language, the new sense of structure and its new building blocks.

With the loss of belief in providential explanation, and with an increasing number of things in the world, the stage is temptingly set for either socially approved fictions or personal paranoias to fill the aching gap of ignorance. Enter, then, narrative, perhaps under the sponsorship of Titus Oates, *A True Narrative of the Horrid Plot*—narrative, that is, as the discovery of conspiracy. What is incompatible to the logician or scientist can be vitally ambivalent, dialectic, and richly tense to the explorer of narrative. The English Civil Wars mark the end of a period when anyone could reasonably or sensibly assert the possible congruity of language and nature. Despite the efforts of such as Bishop Sprat and John Wilkins to tighten the correspondence of words and meanings, the next hundred or so years pioneered the possibilities of different uses of fictional language, not to resolve propositions so much as to contain and express ambivalence. Hobbes had explained that language was really invented to facilitate social order by repressing the nonsocial self. Thus, the use of language became a profession, competing as Wycherley, Dryden, and a hundred lesser satirists clearly saw, with law, medicine, and the priesthood. Prose through the seventeenth century had maintained many of the functions of oratorical assertion and argumentation, while poetry was reserved for the more lyric and aspiring modes. Into this separation interloped the possibility of prose fiction, something between objective assertion and poetic implication. Milton's poetic narrative in *Paradise Lost* preserves a sense of transition. Its first six books return us to its chronological beginning, constantly recirculating the fatality of the fall. But the last six books open endlessly outward in narrative line: the story keeps happening. The contrast between the stasis of the first six books and the movement of the last six of *Paradise Lost* is mirrored as well in that between the fatal message of *Pilgrim's Progress* (its concentric frontispiece) and its narrative movement. One aspect looks back to a world of order, providential hierarchy, and divine control, while another glimpses the possibility of both individual authorship and a continuous narrative, not necessarily progressive or evolutionary or even (in the language of the time) "rising"—but ongoing and changing.

The novel is a form without a past that tries to supplant the past, and its basic impulse has always been to replace a pattern received from authority with a pattern newly conceived by the novelist. The implied hostility to a religious framework that is contained in the early novel is thus a hostility less to God than to an imposed cosmological order that restricts individual nature. Poets of ambition like Pope remain divided between the urge to codify objectively and the urge to make some direct statement of their personal view of the world. But, in the eyes of the novelists, the Designer God must give way to a more personal God who can support the authority of the first-person.

Without providence, the longing for order can be satisfied either with progress or with paranoia. Thus the main motive forces in the novel from the eighteenth century on have been the attitudes towards history, society, and the outside world of others on the one hand, and the sense of injured or unappreciated merit on the other. The way out of this bind, the third term, has always been the creation of the work itself to stand between the isolated, unappreciated self and the distant, uncaring world. As the order of God loses explanatory force, there arises a longing for other orders. To embody that longing the late eighteenth century and early nineteenth century summon up a parade of world-historical hero—villains, no longer the enemies of God who populated Jacobean drama but a group of men willing to focus on the limited and therefore controllable group of others who now defined the secular world. Less theological tyrants than social ones, they remain dark possibilities, still subordinate to their literary creators. Bunyan's Christian reached a celestial city to which his creator could only aspire. But M. G. Lewis both indulges and stands apart from the satanic excesses of his monk Ambrosio. By the late eighteenth century the novelist has become free to take over and reimagine history. Within the pattern, then, the protagonist, the author's other self, can indulge his sense of injured merit, thus expressing a psychic paradox common since the Romantics: simultaneously feeling tremendous and all-encompassing, but unappreciated and sour. James Joyce and Stephen Daedalus have their ancestors in Victor Frankenstein and his monster.

Richardson versus Fielding, Tolstoy versus Dostoevsky—the single combats staged by literary criticism reflect an impulse in the works themselves to assert the sufficiency of their particular view of the coherence of the world against all comers. The loss of providence is the loss of God's foresight. Competition for literary fame will then compensate for the cursed otherness of the world. Before the Renaissance, God was the only creator. With the eighteenth century, he became one among many. Like Blake, the writers of early industrialism all sensed the need to create a system in order not to be taken over and absorbed by someone else's. Like Pamela, the novelist attempts to convince others that the written form he has given experience (even *theirs*) is not only shapely but also true.

Although Defoe, Richardson, and even Fielding share pieces of this isolated perspective, it is really Tobias Smollett's *Roderick Random* that best exemplifies the way the early novel defines itself as a revenge against a society that has no place for any sensibility resembling the author's. Twenty-five years later, Adam Smith argues that the random behavior of individuals is guided by God to a socioeconomic coherence. But Roderick Random believes that the world is constantly elbowing him out of the way and that therefore he, like Milton's Satan, must create his own plot to compete with it. Smollett's novels are not only about competition in a world of work; they are also competitive themselves. In the midst of uncontrollable forces, revenge can create a personal meaning, and paranoia becomes its aesthetic twin. As a sense of injured merit might be compensated through a magisterial view of history, so paranoid order and personal revenge seek each other out for survival and self-definition. Literary narrative is not necessarily clinically paranoid. But, just as paranoia has much in common with the aesthetic completeness of narrative order, so narrative may gather coherence and strength from a paranoid vision.

For the moment let me now leap over the more optimistic fictional orders of the nineteenth century into our own period and there examine the legacy of the novel's early years and upbringing, specifically the mixture of American and European traditions that begins after World War I and is consolidated after World War II.

Ulysses and *USA*: to pair the titles suggests the way modernist fiction was assimilated into the American novel, Joyce's sweep of history translated into the breadth of an American landscape. America is the appetite for space, said Martha Graham. *Ulysses* heated up the essential competition between the novel and society by taking the dissociations and discontinuities of modern life as a cue to pierce beneath the inane immediacies to discover the mythic continuity, the timeless relationships that strum beneath the sludge. But the American naturalists like Dos Passos looked to create history, through plan or people fashioning a personal mosaic of scheme and luxuriance. In Europe the past overhangs, demanding its due. But America, like the novel, was born without a past. Each new vision must here justify itself by its total power, as a rival to history, even as history, according to Cervantes, was the rival of time. Modernist European fiction has few characters. But American fiction floats in barges of refugees, as the author tries to encompass and to include, to masquerade as and to impersonate, every dissonant voice, face, and landscape in the American symphony. And, if all else fails, at least on the dust jacket bio the American novelist from Jack London to Jack Kerouac will list the jobs—shortorder cook in Texas, logger in Oregon, surfer in California, English teacher in New York—that furnish his synoptic credentials. The modernist is thus an outsider, cherishing his expatriate and mandarin status. The naturalist is a chauvinist, submerging himself in the varieties of national life. The modernist uses language self-consciously and referentially, to invoke the already completed forms outside the chaotic present. The naturalist searches the energies of the inarticulate and the popular, intent on making his own synthesis of the looming world before it overwhelms him.

After the experimentation of the interwar period, World War II definitively coalesced the growing feeling of the twentieth century that there was too much to pay attention to, let alone hold together with any degree of grace or geniality. Writers and readers alike stood before the awesome mass of contemporary facts and contemplated the frightening possibility of submission, whether personal, aesthetic, or both. The orders that the modernist or the naturalist had part-created and part-discovered rarely had threatened to grow larger than the work itself. But, with World War II, History came to America, sweeping along individuals, shaking them into categories that suited its needs, not theirs. Europe and its fatalities could no longer be ignored. Hawthorne had complained that America had no luscious dark past, no intricate history. Now, quite suddenly, there was too much. In Fortress America everything was counted. If you did not fit in, you might be thrown out. If, as Irving Howe implies, the Jews of the *shtetl* believed that history was gentile, World War II made everyone Jewish. In the midnineteenth century Hawthorne described in *The House of the Seven Gables* how time had stopped for Judge Pyncheon. In the same moment, he implied, progress with its speeding, sparkling technologies had begun, and the drumroll dread of myths and ancestral curses was drowned out by the clatter of gleaming rails. But World War II effectively ended for a good time to come any residual optimism in the easy relationship between material advance and human progress. Despite Hitler's defeat, the Hitlerian myths achieved a kind of structural legitimacy. A handy devil had been done away with. The Jews really didn't run the world. But the total experience of the War buried deep in the popular mind the feeling that Somebody or Something did.

In the terms of the eighteenth century, we had all become Uncle Toby, wounded and perhaps unmanned by History. The American promise of the unconditioned place seemed over. The Harburg-Saidy-Lane musical comedy *Finian's Rainbow* (1947), with its postwar dream of community, was outfaced by a world whose nature would be brilliantly summarized in Thomas Pynchon's *Gravity's Rainbow*

(1973) with its wartime nightmare of organization. The cold-war period took the World-at-War omniorganization of World War II and projected it into the skies of political science fiction. Paranoia became no longer a mental aberration or a modernist cowering before the modern world, but an articulated national policy. We–They delusions, as Pynchon might call them, became the common coin of official communications in the 1950s; only individuals seemed anomalous. Cold-war America—like cold-war Russia or cold-war Europe—had the same sense of coherent purpose, but without the moral *telos* of the war. Paranoia had become a providence without eschatology. The less clear the villain, the more clear the pattern. The German cultural development from *Caligari* to Hitler had implied that fearing something could make it come true. In the 1950s the incessant allegorization of the US–Soviet conflict conditioned the country to the immanent possibility of destruction by its opposite, whether it came from outer space or from over the Arctic. One classic set piece of popular journalism in the 1950s was the Russian rewriting of history—poking fun at their claims that they invented the car, the ocarina, or the bandsaw. But underneath was the possibility that each of us could be similarly disinvented if we were not good citizens—a lesson American schoolchildren, crouching under their desks for airraid drills, took to heart. In a paradigmatic plot of later 1940s films, the hero returns from the war to discover that his identity, his job, his wife, his children had been taken over by ''the man with my face,'' And so the cold war elaborated brilliantly on fears bred by World War II over the absolute gap between apocalypse and domesticity, self-justifying glory and annihilating anonymity.[1]

Against the monoliths that threatened to absorb the individual stood the possibility of the family as a refuge against the pressures from without and within. The family with a weak, well-meaning father, like that in the film *Rebel without a Cause* (1956), could breed only aimless violence—another incessantly analogous paste-up of the basic political conflict. With the loss of FDR, the last benevolent father figure in American life, the 1950s plunged American public imagery into the most oedipal period of our recent national life. Appropriately enough, the oedipal relationship was founded in revenge. Communists worked, the *Reader's Digest* told us, by setting families against each other, with good children turning in erring parents (the Soviet drama of the pure future), while in American cold-war films, the parents tended to turn in the children. *Hamlet* was everyone's favorite Shakespeare play, to be replaced in the early 1960s by *Lear*, the epic of nihilism and unnaming, parental weakness and children's ungratefulness. In a thousand courses undergraduates read about the Big Brother of Orwell and the Big Father of Kafka, and discussed Kierkegaard's *A Sickness unto Death*, in which Abraham's willingness to sacrifice Isaac is only at the last second considered by the highest Father to be an unnecessary literalization of the injunction to obey.[2]

Faced with an increasingly complex and competitive society, the eighteenth-century novel had evolved the narrative strategy of the individualist observer, making his way with élan and irony through a world he shaped by his art. In the wake of the war, a new stage of national economic, political, and social organization had been achieved, and the themes and methods of novelists like Smollett took on a renewed vitality. In Smollett's world, the world was not out to get you; it just looked that way. By the 1950s the paranoid interpretation had become more direct and more personal, and every wife-avenger stalking the films of the 1950s recapitulated the novelist's effort to create a personal pattern of meaning that could absorb, explain, and transcendently settle accounts for his loss. Paranoia solved your life; it was a kind of health. Your sense of yourself was created by the world's hostility to your nature: better to be attacked then ignored. As a character in Joseph Heller's *Catch-22* (1961) says, echoing one in Norman Mailer's *The Naked and the Dead* (1948): "Someone out there is trying to kill me."

In postwar American culture, the only way to evade the plot against your identity, to escape destruction by the organization that works without you, was to establish a position, literally or literarily, in the middle. Like Mike Hammer or Lionel Trilling, the lone wolf detective or the adversary critic, the individualism of the 1950s appealed to the ideals of the past, simultaneously condemning all systems and proclaiming its ability to mediate between them. Such figures tried to preserve a precarious innocence in the face of a cynical world. But it was a difficult position to maintain, and Alfred Hitchcock—in films like *I Confess* (1952), *Rear Window* (1954), and *North by Northwest* (1959)—delighted in displaying the not-so-innocent bystander sucked into a web of intrigue through his pride in his own detachment.

To a great extent, this individualist security of the self-professed middle man was itself an emblem of the project of fiction. Like the astronomer in *Rasselas*, who would not leave his telescope for fear the stars would fall if he didn't keep watching them, both the modernist and the naturalist created structures by remaining separate from them. The difference was that the American naturalist had generally chosen withdrawal over revenge. But, after World War II, he could no longer remain so pure. Even Augie March wished for a cause larger than himself. In the early 1950s Richard Nixon wrote in a *Saturday Review* comment on Whittaker Chambers's *Witness:* "America is a political reading of the Bible."[3] The new goal of the American novelist would be not to disagree but only to offer another textual analogy by which to order the American conglomeration. The tone of the times was to want things to be simpler than they were. The encyclopedic wanderer of the nineteenth century had crossed with the modernist virtuoso to produce the paranoid naturalist. Better off than those poor characters, in fiction and in film, who didn't have the good luck to be writers, the novelists could use the tradition of narrative simultaneously to order the world and assure their own places in literary history. Instead of attacking or retreating from the entrapping history, the novelist could absorb it or substitute for it. In the popular novels of the 1940s and 1950s—by Frank Yerby, Kathleen Windsor, Taylor Caldwell, Kenneth Roberts, and others—the past was a retreat, an idyll, in which individuals were freer, sexier, and more able to accomplish heroic action. But in the historical novels of more assertion and ambition—*The Naked and the Dead, The Manchurian Candidate, Catch-22, The Sotweed Factor, Little Big Man, V., An Infinity of Mirrors, The Armies of the Night, Julian, Gravity's Rainbow, Burr*—to name only some of the most prominent—the individual was generally lost in history or trying

desperately to survive it. Instead of being a refuge for passion and jollity or a
primitivist playground of purer political values, the past, like the present, had
become a Joycean nightmare.

One important mode of survival was the observing, amassing, and articulation
of facts—a process equally celebrated in the characters of scientists, detectives,
and novelists—those archetypal modern heroes. But, as movies from their beginnings have shown, an excessive focus on objects and facts may blind one to the
invisible order that connects them. The complex array should lead us to search for
an arrayer; the watch implies the watchmaker. In a welter of watchmakers, novels
sought more and more obviously to imply that they were made and that it was the
reader's job to explicate the mechanism.

A nineteenth-century novel like *Adam Bede* is clearly offered more in analogy
to the world than as a substitute for it. Dinah, the Methodist preacher in *Adam
Bede,* speaks to a God present in the trees and the implication is that her sensitivity to the God in the trees should be matched by ours to George Eliot in the text,
benevolently permeating the world, informing and signifying its beings and objects. Similarly, Defoe in *Robinson Crusoe* had tacitly weaned himself away from
the externally assured providential narratives that furnished his inspiration, while
Fielding had cheerfully introduced himself as the creator of his own novel. All
three participate in a progressive effort to arm the reader against all forms that
pretend to be innate. For George Eliot, the act of novelistic good faith is contained
in the seventeenth chapter, where she moves ahead in "time" to tell the reader of
a recent discussion she had had with Adam Bede, long after the events of the
novel. Thus she brings Adam out of the story, making him less totally defined by
the frame of the plot, even while she also recalls to us her own role in the creation
and articulation of the novel's elements, not as Mary Ann Evans but as "George
Eliot," the novelist. Adam is thus allowed a detachment about his own earlier life
akin to that with which the reader looks at the book, wondering to what extent it
is historically true and to what extent it is a projection of the fiction-making ability
of those we call authors.

The creation of a convincing story often involves an assertion of verisimilitude
like George Eliot's, in which the ordering goal is denied, but not the ordering
power. The novelist therefore constantly faces the problem of where the responsibility for coherence resides: is History causative or are the links only in the
sensibility and perspective of the author? Are the orders of narrative fiction truly
alternative, or are they always in fief to an order perceived in the world? For the
most part, the nineteenth-century novel phrased such issues with assurance. But
in the modern period novels came to resemble machines more than trees. They
were less likely to grow than to run down, or elaborate into endless intricacy. The
blithe creative self-consciousness of a Fielding or a George Eliot seemed hardly
open to the writers in the third century of the novel.

Let me draw then the tightrope of this period of paranoid surrealism or modernist
naturalism from *The Naked and the Dead* to *Gravity's Rainbow,* 1948 to 1973. In
these twenty-five or so years the novel responds to the baroque efflorescence of

the outside world by relying more and more on the coherence of the author's style, spawning a generation of history's standup comedians, one-line determinists who use parody as defensiveness, puns as entrapment, and language to punish rather than absolve. Mailer's war in the Pacific is matched a generation later by Pynchon's war in Europe, Mailer's personal experience by Pynchon's phantasmagoric reconstruction of a world he was too young to know, in which his collage of discovered and invented detail overwhelms him with despair at his own patterns.

The contrast is appropriate. In sitting down to write *The Naked and the Dead*, Mailer believed he was engaged in a literary battle for the prize of head man of American fiction. Disheartened by the postwar expansion of the business of literary celebrity, Pynchon seems to believe he can avoid the inevitable competition of the novel by becoming the vanishing American writer, the adversary who is not there, except as a voice who, in *Gravity's Rainbow,* constantly pokes the reader in the chest and says "you." For Mailer literary style is identified with a personal response to the specificities of a project, a newly minted variety of order and control. After *The Naked and the Dead,* he never again writes in such an omniscient third-person voice. But Pynchon, because he inherits the modernist assertion that language is the best history and the author at best an invisible mediator, fashions a style that asserts itself as the essential structure of the universe. There is no place to stand, no solacing glimpse beyond the text. To exist, a rainbow requires sun, atmospheric moisture, and an observer. If any one of these is lacking, there is no rainbow. The observer arrays the world, but where stands the observer who can see beyond *Gravity's Rainbow?*[4]

The different approaches of Mailer and Pynchon to the problem of narrative coherence are mirrored in their different conception of the novelist's cultural role. George Eliot again may presage the issues. The choice of the name "George Eliot" may be a strategy to defuse the reader's assumptions about the differences between male and female perspectives on the world. But it also serves to distinguish between the person and the novelist, Mary Ann Evans and George Eliot. In *Adam Bede,* George Eliot furnishes an escape-hatch from her plot for her main character, who is allowed to grow beyond pain and melodrama. By calling herself "George Eliot," Mary Ann Evans, along with Currer Bell, Mark Twain, and other nineteenth-century pseudonymous fiction-makers (both male and female), also prepares an escape-hatch for herself, the all-seeing, plot-ridden novelist.

In their own versions of the same escape, Mailer becomes the naturalist self-exposer and Pynchon the modernist *deus absconditus,* the one creating a manipulable public mask, the other vanishing into silence until, it is said, even his college records have disappeared. Two myths are here, one of visibility, one of invisibility, and each brings in its revenges. Mailer's doubling appears like that of Clark Kent and Superman, the mild private self and the powerful public self, while Pynchon's resembles Sherlock Holmes and Dr. Moriarty, the brilliant clue-assembling detective and the monstrous man of genius who sits at the center of the invisible web. Unlike Mailer, who plays between his various selves, brandishing their shifting possibilities, Pynchon does not create a famous presence to distract us from the coherence of his creation. Like the scientist–novelist he is, he wants the reader to assume that the facts will lead to the malevolent deity who connects them—himself. In seeking to disappear so that his creation will be more real and all-consuming, he makes his novels the way-stations between history and paranoia, public pattern and private obsession, while Mailer's creations, even the first broad canvas of *The Naked and the Dead,* remain less committed to interpretive absolutes of any sort. When Mailer experiments with the proffering of a second self, he thus provides a place both for the observer of the rainbow and for the ambiguity of his observation—allowing more clearly than does Pynchon the mediation of pattern by psyche.

Mailer the war novelist embodies the paradox of the postwar period: able to create history but unable to make it; a virtuoso of detail, milieu, and connection, but an impotent actor, deluded, defrauded, self-deceived. Like so many novels set in World War II, *The Naked and the Dead* implies that only sexuality offers any way out of the maze. In its momentary intimacy might be found a refuge from the depersonalizing orders of war. But the consolation is marginal. Like the pastoral scenes on the shield of Achilles, all of Mailer's erotic scenes are retrospective, contained in the little idylls of personal power he calls the Time Machine. In the war effort sexuality is as malleable as anything else. Major Dalleson's great idea at the end of the novel is to put a photograph of Betty Grable in a bathing suit under the coordinate grid system to "jazz up the map-reading class." By *Gravity's Rainbow,* sexuality has become the key to all connection, particularly the inhuman and impersonal. Tyrone Slothrop's conditioned penis, with its intimate connection to the bombing sites of V-2 rockets, shows that sex is no respite from war or technology, only a more intense involvement. Still hoping that desire had something to do with will, Mailer in *Of a Fire on the Moon* had said, "obviously a theory of sexual mechanics could never be based on gravity." Pynchon's rejoinder in *Gravity's Rainbow* seems to be that "the real and only fucking is done on paper." [5]

John Berger in *G.* (1972) remarks that sex is opposed to generalization. But Berger may here voice a sixties or a Reichian optimism about personal relations. The evidence of the American novel, on the other hand, is increasingly that sexuality is the final booby prize, the difference that cements us still further to a world in which will has no place at all. In the course of his novels, Pynchon's searchers for meaning become more and more passive; Hubert Stencil *(V.)* and Oedipa Maas *(The Crying of Lot 49)* are trying to figure something out; but Tyrone Slothrop is merely the object of everyone's tracings—the Rosebud that solves nothing except the requirements of form. In *Tristram Shandy* the creation of the work itself, a printed novel, constitutes a personal order that can restore sexuality and help the individual fight against the warpings of body and spirit caused by the patterns of mind—not so that mind be excluded but so that it might be used more flexibly. But the sexuality of Tyrone Slothrop—Tristram's acronymic twin, our priapic Lanny Budd—is harnessed to one of the most destructive products of modern technology, the V-2 rockets. Instead of breaking forms, Tyrone's sexuality portends total destruction. In a kind of Freudian cultural determinism, it is the one constant term in Pynchon's incessantly revolving fatal scenarios.

Pynchon's absence therefore affirms his watertight pattern, whereas Mailer's presence makes us not so sure. The modernist expatriate, alienated from his person and society, sees every detail as part of a guidebook iconography, signifying a fabric of reality and order that he can only guess at. Each detail becomes as significant as any other; each implies the supervening backdrop; and each turns readily into something else, never remaining itself for long. Benny Profane in *V.* thinks of life as an endless series of whistle-stops: the buildings and settings are different, but underneath everything is the same—because he never gets off the train. So too *Gravity's Rainbow,* for all its delight in the happenstance beauty of necessary forces, remains a novel that engages intelligence rather than perception. Thoroughly interesting and absorbing while we read it, if we but look up for a second, close it because of a hunger pang of other call of nature, we can hardly remember what was happening, until we decide to resubmerge. Its ambition, its scope, its good writing, finally even its comic self-awareness never escape the enclosure of its form. Pynchon's heroes are groups like the Hereros or the Gauchos, who are victims of History. But how could it be otherwise when the novelist himself, a revenger on the inside, is an intellectual who undermines our ability to act by saying everything is predetermined? Even Milton's God insisted that his foreknowledge, his Providence, in no way impeded human will.

In *Gravity's Rainbow* the absent author has escaped to tell the tale of how we cannot escape. But Pynchon never allows the curtain of History to be twitched aside to reveal Oz and his levers behind the scene. Chaucer simultaneously creates the work and presents himself as the most imposed upon, the silliest, person within it. Tristram Shandy becomes Sterne's spokesman about the categories, orders, and warpings of nature forced down upon him. But where are such personal voices, such awareness of the problematic relation between author and form in *Gravity's Rainbow*? Is Tyrone Slothrop's stuttering—never mentioned explicitly, only mimed— a key to Pynchon's own, the author's identification with his prime victim? Most of Pynchon's characters remain amalgams of details, facts, fragments of culture, pieces of clothing—creatures of History and therefore subject to its forces. The pattern is total and inescapable. As Pynchon is the first to say, the paranoid isn't innately paranoid; he places himself in paranoid situations—like reading *Gravity's Rainbow*. The only purgation possible is intellectual, that 1950s existentialist shrug over the absurdity of the universe. Pynchon's anonymity, with its effort to evade the media entrapment of the novelist, therefore also avoids the novelist's possible moral stature as well. Split between the roles of creator and victim, he moves to where the power is.

How does this happen? Is it a necessity of the novel's history that it finally collapse under the paradox of the personal assertion of overall form? One way to approach the problematic interplay of creator and creation is to search the analogy of the movies. *Gravity's Rainbow* not only contains references to films. It also constantly invokes the view of reality defined by the German expressionist films of the 1920s, with their mad geniuses, paranoid plots, and enclosed visual worlds of darkness and shadows so ready to impose themselves on the passive film audience. Mailer, especially in *The Deer Park* (1955), and Pynchon throughout his novels portray the role of the movies in the personal conditioning of Americans. A character in *The Deer Park* describes America as "a political system which reminded him of nothing so much as the studio for which he worked," and, amid a host of invocations of Orson Welles, Fritz Lang, G. W. Pabst, and others, Pynchon refers as well to "the guardian and potent Studio."[6]

The evil genius of both of these novels resembles Charles Foster Kane, Citizen Kane, the tycoon through whom radiates the power and pattern of America. But Kane has, I think, other significance for the novelistic attitudes of Mailer and Pynchon. In the 1941 film, Kane is both played and directed by Orson Welles— Welles the victim–character and Welles the God–director. Thus in the nexus of Kane/Welles we can see an emblematic statement of the mixed public and private role of the narrative artist. Similarly, the novelist becomes both superior to his text as the creator and trapped within it as the protagonist, buried in his own plot—corpse, gravedigger, and eulogizer all in one. Two possibilities of escape represent themselves: Mailer's publicity, the distancing of the public self through ironic brandishing and role-playing, and Pynchon's withdrawal from possible vulnerability. Mailer follows a more eighteenth-century practice of emphasizing the creation of a work by an author who also acts within it. Pynchon, in contrast, follows a late nineteenth-century line of novelists who identify their stories with fate and thereby write about characters, much like themselves, who yet have no chance and must finally be defeated primarily because they do not have the distance to be authors: Wharton and Lily Bart, Hardy and Jude, perhaps even Joyce and Stephen Daedalus. The loss is in our sense of the character's substance and will. To the extent that the reporter/detective/scientist/novelist stands outside his work, he will see the world not as events and people, but as plots, for creating plots is one sure way to escape them. Throughout nineteenth-century fiction, characters aspire to be authors. In our own time performers seek to become directors or politicians. As Houdini in E. L. Doctorow's *Ragtime* concludes after contemplating the career of Admiral Peary, "the real-world act was what got into the history books."[7]

Both the formal self-consciousness of twentieth-century art and the rise of the artist as a special brand of public person lie behind the paradoxes of theme and method I have been discussing. At all levels, the ideal is to enter history, conquer it by fame, and thereby escape it. But, as readers and teachers of reading, we should not assume that our recognition of the paranoia made possible by language and the German-Jewish-Puritan fealty to the word and the book that Pynchon invokes, guarantees any escape from its tyranny. The kind of novelist I have been describing may be defined as someone who takes notes on everything, tries to make it all fit together by putting it in a book, and then decides to call the book America, or at least the great American novel. Like Hubert Stencil in *V.*, he traces himself on the world. As Pynchon writes, "There may be no gods, but there is a pattern: names by themselves may have no magic, but the *act* of naming, the physical utterance, obeys the pattern."[8] As teachers and critics, although we are not especailly noted for telling good stories or sustaining fictions, we are certainly committed to interpretation, founded in a text, and spawning ideas that must be verified with a kind of proof–demonstration method similar to that of science. Roderick Random may think that critical detachment can salve psychic wounds. But Oedipa Maas in *The Crying of Lot 49* (1966) attributes her belief in paranoid explanation to her schooling in the textual criticism of the 1950s. Going one step beyond Hubert Stencil, we trace ourselves and our theories and ideas not on the world but on the writer, on his works, and on his life, and on the past that contains him, each in our gleeful turn. Analysis reoutfits and retailors an author into simpler colors (although often stronger and brighter) and thereby the diffusion of detail, the nuance and suggestion, become hard, impermeable, and necessary. By interpretation we try to insure that the undetermined must nevertheless recur, and the paranoid novelist may find the interpreting critic a willing collaborator in the creation of a world more self-sufficient than even he expected or wanted. Paranoia thus stands in relation to narrative as critical theory stands to reading. It is the faith of a victim who believes that understanding is power. To think that the world is separate from us in order to be contemplated already assumes the despair that in fact it has nothing to do with us at all.

The last stand of a victim's integrity is his narcissism, and so the world of paranoid fiction has plot but no connection, demonstrativeness without sympathy, and the copulativity of grammarians rather than people. Pynchon may indeed be the great university novelist because he dramatizes and expands on (not to say satirizes and mocks) that excessive respect for and interest in the Word that university English departments have so ably and elaborately spawned. He exemplifies with peculiar brilliance a virtuosity with language that shunts all emotion aside by swiftly interposing some sort of verbal play or allusion. It is an evasion of feeling with the pretense of involvement, reminiscent of Samuel Johnson, who faces the end of *King Lear* only when he can edit it. The self-protectiveness of all systems is the source of their power, and what is paranoid to one view is consoling to another. But the imperialism of language over experience, rather than its sociability or its companionship, has become the hallmark of our period. In the eighteenth century the metamorphosis of the cosmological God into the numinous God spawned a longing for order that could be satisfied either with progress or paranoia. In our own time we seem to have formulated an amalgam of the two, unwilling to give up the quantitative progress of science or the comforting fatality of political and social conspiracy.

The danger lies in the possibility that the comfort of pattern, however vile, will absolve us of responsibility, and our professional and aesthetic pleasure in style will render us its prisoners. Such a passivity before history, the self-defining paranoia that annihilates will, seems to be the invariable telos of competition and revenge. Charles Foster Kane, Pierce Inverarity, Barney Oswald Kelly, Howard Hughes—the imagination of apocalypse produces the paranoia of the authoritarian victim. Like the tycoon with his money, the novelist with his words wreaks his own revenge on society for the loss of self society has imposed, the message that he and we are personally incomplete. As teachers, as critics, as readers, it may now be our role to see the point at which this exploration becomes more self-involved than expansive, when the necessary narcissism of the novelist becomes an effort to deny the will of his characters and thereby to undermine and deny our own, and where our own fiction-making ability begins to frighten us by its fruitless rigidity.

Perhaps then the self-destructive quality of *Gravity's Rainbow* announces that we have come full circle. Perhaps paranoid fiction, as Richard Poirier has suggested about literary modernism, may finally be an indictment of its own nature, a warning about the word, guised in a paean to its sufficiency.[9] If so, it is a fiction so tied to what it seeks to dynamite that it must necessarily be attacked by the consciousness it wishes to create, before the order of the world can again become provisional and playful. In so many novels about the modern world, connection is in bureaucracies, not individuals. Perhaps it may be true that, as Mailer in *An American Dream* (1965) implies, failure in personal relations leads to a paranoid overdetermination of the relationships between politics and history. Could *Gravity's Rainbow,* with its urge to package, purge, and solve the past be therefore like the first six books of *Paradise Lost,* with their eternal round of primordial competitions? If so, we might remember the next step, in which the inspired Bard relinquishes his omniscient perception to look upon the human story, "standing on earth, not rapt above the poles." Only love finally reconciles Roderick Random to society, and at the end of the novel he is married to the well-named Narcissa and expecting his first child, perhaps *Roderick Random* itself. He begins as "a solitary being, no ways comprehended within the scheme or protection of Providence," and he ends as a happy husband—and an author, telling his own story.[10] As Michelet remarks in *The History of France,* "J'ai passé à côté du monde, et j'ai pris l'histoire pour la vie," or, in the words of Ira Gershwin, "Who cares how history rates me,/So long as your kiss intoxicates me?"

[1981]

Notes

1. In "Paranoia" (*Harper's Magazine,* June 1974, pp. 51–60), Hendrik Hertzberg and David C. K. McClelland date the term to the midnineteenth century and then go on to make some intriguing points about its contemporary character, drawing particularly on the works of Pynchon and the bureaucracy of military "contingency planning."

2. Kafka is often cited as a shaper of modern paranoia. Perhaps so in atmosphere, but not in style. Unlike Pynchon, Kafka drains his worlds of detail and the mysterious forces behind them work through a patterned repetitiveness reminiscent of Bauhaus aesthetics or Art Deco. The naturalist paranoia I discuss here luxuriates in disparate detail. The more disparate the detail, the more assertive the pattern. It is a paranoia of plenitude.

3. Richard M. Nixon, "The Plea for an Anti-Communist Faith," *Saturday Review* (May 24, 1952), pp. 12–13.

4. Like John Barth, who contributes an admiring afterword to the Signet edition of *Roderick Random,* Pynchon is attracted to Wittgenstein's materialist dictum that "the world is everything that is the case." See, for example, *V.* (Philadelphia: Lippincott, 1963), pp. 258–59, in which it appears coded in German ("DIEWELTISTALLESWASDERFALLIST") just after Kurt Mondaugen experiences a "rare Achphenomenon: the discovery that his voyeurism had been determined purely by events seen, and not by any deliberate choice, or preexisting set of personal psychic needs."

5. *Of a Fire on the Moon* (Boston: Little, Brown, 1970), p. 223; *Gravity's Rainbow* (New York: Viking, 1973), p. 616.

6. *The Deer Park* (New York: Putnam, 1955), pp. 36–37; *Gravity's Rainbow,* p. 437. Gore Vidal gives this image of the totalitarian Studio a comic turn in the direction of individual will in *Myron* (1974), where Myra Breckenridge believes that she can change the whole future course of American politics and culture by several careful interventions in the 1948 Maria Montez film *Siren of Babylon.*

7. *Ragtime* (New York: Random House, 1975), p. 82.

8. *Gravity's Rainbow*, p. 322.

9. Richard Poirier, "The Difficulties of Modernism and the Modernism of Difficulty," *Humanities and Society* (Fall 1980).

10. *Roderick Random*, afterword by John Barth. (New York: New American Library, 1964), p. 46.

Penetration and Impenetrability
in *Clarissa*

That was the devilish part of her—this coldness, this wood-
enness, something very profound in her, which he had felt
again this morning talking to her; an impenetrability.
                    VIRGINIA WOOLF, *Mrs. Dalloway*

"Say what strange Motive, Goddess! cou'd compel/A well-bred *Lord* t'assault a
gentle *Belle*?" The questions posed by *Clarissa* and *The Rape of the Lock* are
remarkably similar. What cultural changes could have occurred in the thirty-odd
years between their first publications such that a situation, which in one major
work is the object of Olympian poetic satire, could in the second major work be
the subject of tragic fictional involvement? What could turn Pope's savage depiction of the social repression of natural sexual instincts (symbolized in the Cave of
Spleen) into the praise of the necessary repression of sexuality that characterizes
Clarissa? What connection is there between the barren Baron and the loveless
Lovelace, between the social imperatives of the poem and the personal imperatives of the novel?

To a certain extent, *Clarissa* continues *The Rape of the Lock* (as *The Rape of
the Lock* may continue *The Country Wife*), and Pope seems presciently aware that
his poem could not include a solution to the problem he posed in it. No matter
how brilliantly the poem might strive to laugh the real-life participants together
(and the Baron was already dead from smallpox the year before it was published),
in the more severe world of the poem itself, the conflict is not resolved. The battle
stops in midgesture, resolvable perhaps in the artifice of the couplet but not on
any social or psychological level that the reader might recognize as valid and
possible. "Trust the Muse," says Pope, and the ringing in of that Horatian topos,
have-faith-in-the-poem-to-transfigure-the-story-it-tells, marks the point where Pope's
genius gives up in its search for a form that might more fully express his new
subject matter. *The Rape of the Lock* is aware of the forces of a newly emerging
definition of the inner life that threatens to change Belinda's world of social banter
into the more terrifying conflicts of the world of Clarissa. But Pope is writing
poetry, not prose, and part of his greatness arises from the collision between his

This essay is based on a paper originally presented at a meeting of the English Institute held in
Cambridge, 1973.

François Truffaut directing Charles Aznavour and Marie Dubois in *Shoot the Piano Player*.

François Truffaut playing the director in *Day for Night*, which Truffaut also directed.

Norman Bates (Anthony Perkins) makes sure the trunk of his car is dark enough to hide the remains of Marion Crane (Janet Leigh) in *Psycho*.

The perfection of the mechanical body: front and back views of Pierre Jacquet-Droz's automaton "The Young Writer," constructed circa 1770 and capable of writing a full page, with appropriate gestures.

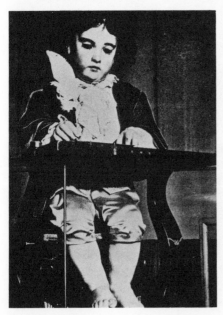

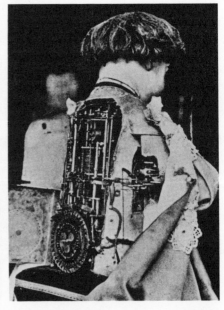

In Jean Renoir's *Nana,* Bordenave (Pierre Lestringuez), the theater manager, peeks through a backstage keyhole, while his star Nana (Catherine Hessling) charms Baron Muffat (Werner Krauss) and Georges Hugon (Raymond Guerin-Catelain).

In Zola's novel *La Bête Humaine,* the murder of Grandmorin is seen by Jacques Lantier through a train window, while in Jean Renoir's film version it is the audience that watches through the window.

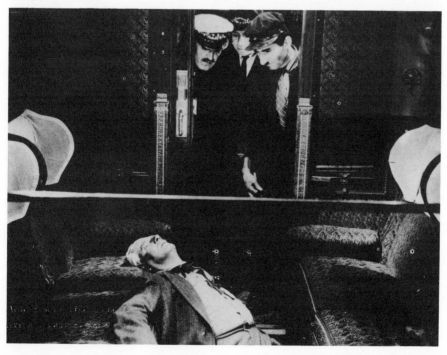

PAPER X.

LEAD me, where my own thoughts themſelves may loſe me;
  Where I may doze out what I've left of Life,
Forget myſelf, and that day's guilt!——
Cruel Remembrance!——how ſhall I appeaſe thee?

——Oh! you have done an act
That blots the face and bluſh of modeſty;
    Takes off the roſe
From the fair forehead of an innocent Love,
And makes a bliſter there !——

    Then down I laid my head,
Down on cold earth, and for a while was dead;
And my freed Soul to a ſtrange Somewhere fled!
    Ah! ſottiſh Soul! ſaid I,
When back to its cage again I ſaw it fly,
    Fool! to reſume her broken chain,
    And row the galley here again!
    Fool! to that Body to return,
Where it condemn'd and deſtin'd is to *mourn.*

O my Miſs Howe! if thou haſt friendſhip, help me,
And ſpeak the words of peace to my divided Soul,
    That wars within me,
And raiſes ev'ry ſenſe to my confuſion.
    I'm tott'ring on the brink
Of peace ; and thou art all the hold I've left!
Aſſiſt me——in the pangs of my affliction!

When Honour's loſt, 'tis a relief to die:
Death's but a ſure retreat from infamy.

    Then farewel, Youth,
    And all the joys that dwell
    With Youth and Life!
    And Life itſelf, farewel!

    For Life can never be ſincerely bleſt.
    Heav'n puniſhes the *Bad,* and proves the *Beſt.*

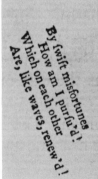

Death only can be dreadful to the Bad:
To Innocence 'tis like a bugbear dreſs'd
To frighten children. Pull but off the maſk,
And he'll appear a friend.

I could a Tale unfold——
Would harrow up thy ſoul!

By ſwift misfortunes
How am I purſu'd!
Which on each other
Are, like waves, renew'd!

The page and the self: disheveled typography to indicate the emotional turmoil of Clarissa after her rape by Lovelace.

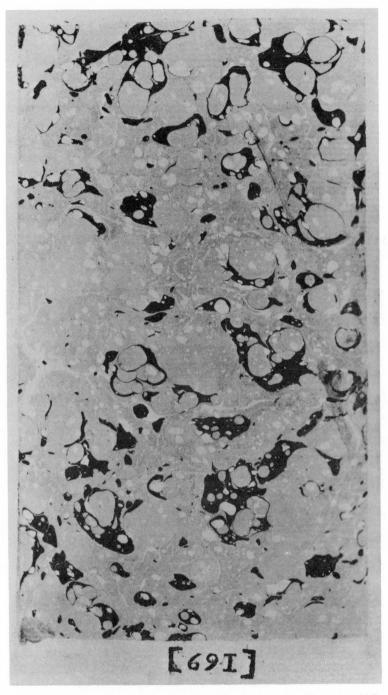

[691]

The uniquely reproduced object: a marbled piece of paper tipped into the middle
of the third volume of *Tristram Shandy*.

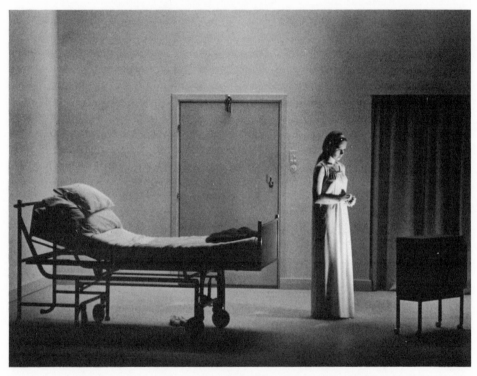

In Ingmar Bergman's *Persona,* Elisabet (Liv Ullmann), the now mute actress, hospitalized for a nervous breakdown, watches a monk immolate himself on television.

Elisabet frames the audience in her own camera eye.

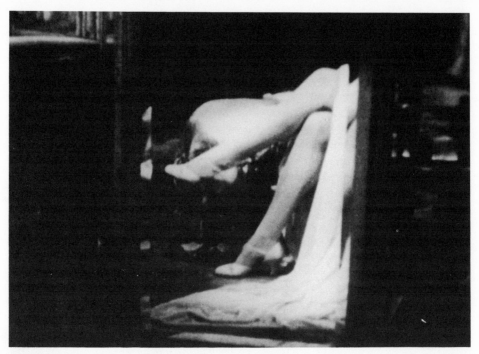

The camera as voyeur: Una Merkel's legs reflected in a mirror during the opening sequence of *42nd Street*.

Actress versus role: the honors of impersonation in the guise of credits for *42nd Street*.

The camera celebrates itself by including theater. Jordan Marsh rehearses the kid from the chorus (Ruby Keeler) in *42nd Street*.

Under the shadows of giant ancestors: in *Pennies from Heaven* Steve Martin and Bernadette Peters imitate a Fred Astaire and Ginger Rogers dance sequence.

Who really represents America? Steve Martin and Bernadette Peters in *Pennies from Heaven*, impersonating Edward Hopper's painting *Nighthawks*.

Rituals of Battle: Holy Communion celebrated amid the attack helicopters in *Apocalypse Now*.

Media sainthood: Rupert Pupkin (Robert DeNiro) helps Jerry Langford (Jerry Lewis) escape from frenzied fans in *The King of Comedy*.

Power over Objects: Telekinetic Carrie (Sissy Spacek) wreaks havoc at the high school prom after her prank baptism in pig's blood in *Carrie*.

The Director and his Double: Martin Scorsese as a murderous passenger eggs Travis Bickle (Robert DeNiro) on to his own maniacal breakdown in *Taxi Driver*.

The Mirror of the Ear: Gene Hackman, portraying a professional eavesdropper and observer, watches two girls applying makeup in the two-way-mirror windows of his truck in
The Conversation.

Acting as History: A different image for every phase of his frontier life and for Jack Crabb
(Dustin Hoffman) in *Little Big Man.*

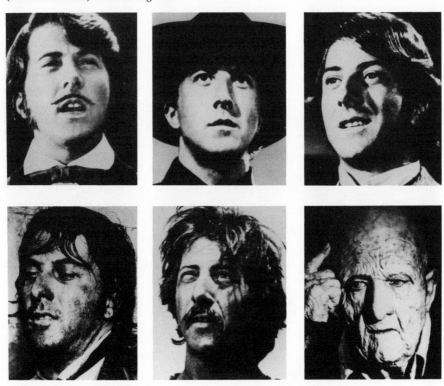

Narcissism, phallic and otherwise: Marlon Brando and Maria Schneider in *Last Tango in Paris*.

Male generational conflicts and conflicting acting styles: the climactic fight between Tom Dunson (John Wayne) and Matthew Garth (Montgomery Clift) halted by the offscreen gun of Joanne Dru (Tess Millay) in *Red River*.

new themes and his old forms. He understands the inadequacy of this kind of poetry to express and develop to the full the ideas about character that fascinate him; in the *Moral Essays* and *Arbuthnot* he takes his insight even further, moved in part perhaps by his immersion in Donne's lyric energies to personalize his own more public form. Like Swift in the creation of Gulliver, Pope in *The Moral Essays* and *Arbuthnot* seems posed between a satiric and a fictional view of character, between character viewed from the outside, in analogy to painting, with the goal of caricature and simplication; and character expressed from within through an essentially nonvisual exploration of the potentials of inconsistency and uncertainty.

The perception of cultural change often outruns the formal means at the writer's disposal to express that change. The creation of fictional character seems to arise from a feeling that earlier attitudes toward character are deficient psychologically, and therefore rhetorically, to face the newly perceived problems of self-definition. Seventeenth-century character, with its varied hagiographic, theophrastan, and satiric strands, is essentially character constructed by rhetoric and viewed externally. When such characters are placed on a stage, in the context of others, their rhetorical balance gives an impression of psychological self-containment. We may be asked to laugh at the self-containment (Jonson's Morose) or with it (Wycherley's Horner). But even in the triumph of such a character, there is a necessary human loss that is one of the main themes of Restoration comedy. "The satirist satirized" expresses in rhetorical terms the psychological truth embodied in Horner's final rejection of the affection of Margery Pinchwife in order to preserve the myth of his impotence. Style and language become an end in themselves, and the desire to feed one's ego by the control of others unavoidably leads to personal isolation and despair.

Thus, within traditional literary forms, the entrapped satirist or the entrapped satiric character is as far as the author can go. Wycherley's insight is presented with the traditional impersonality of the dramatist. Pope's use of poetry, with its traditions, precedents, and forms, its natural desire to bring the new into the frame of preexisting order, similarly leads him to the "solution" of detachment and distance, character viewed once again from the outside. "Trust the Muse," forget the terror beneath, remember instead "the moving toyshop of the heart." In *The Dunciad* Pope returns to the definition of the poet that he seemed to have left behind in *The Rape of the Lock:* the Olympian detached voice, contemplating with measured gaze both intricacy and grandeur, beauty and foulness, triviality and apocalypse. Strange that a poet who considered himself to be the latest in line of great poets stretching back to Homer should spend so much of his last years casting and recasting a more complex and elaborate version of *MacFlecknoe*. By turning Pope into MacDryden, *The Dunciad* implicitly announces the failure of detached poetic Olympianism, failed perhaps because it never distinguished clearly enough between the vices and virtues of the personal voice in literature, its mixed portion of fragmentation, empathy, and energy. When Pope attacks more and more people by name (at a stage in his career when one might expect Horatian detachment), he is stating quite distinctly that the problem is not action or institutions, not faulty generalizations or immoral principles. The problem is in individuals, in their weak sense of themselves and in that necessary corollary, the weakness of the written, self-justifying word.[1]

Personal identity is just as vexed a problem in seventeenth- and eighteenth-century philosophy as it is in literature. But the terms of the problem are generally less complex because conflict is not the philosophers' immediate concern. Descartes's elaboration of medieval distinctions between mind and body was a necessary prelude to his theories of perception and knowledge. Hobbes, Locke, and Hume, in their own ways, similarly recognize that the problem of personal identity cannot be separated from general questions of knowledge, memory, and bodily continuity. But their arguments about individuals all aim toward conclusions about what each considers to be larger matters. They ask "what is identity in general?" and "how do we understand the term identity when it appears in other contexts?" They wonder "what is a person?" and "how is one person not another person?"

Hobbes and Locke, for example, are especially interested in personal identity within society. Hobbes wants to define the limits of individuals so that no man encroaches too much on the next, and he therefore seeks to dispense with the unquantifiable and uncontrollable in human nature. His model for the state is a mechanical being, and his model for human nature is a completely socialized being. Unsocialized thoughts, like unsocialized behavior, must be either brought into the frame of society or expunged:

> The secret thoughts of a man run over all things, holy, prophane, clean, obscene, grave, and light, without shame, or blame; which verball discourse cannot do, farther than the Judgement shall approve of the Time, Place, and Persons. An Anatomist, or a Physitian may speak, or write his judgement of unclean things; because it is not to please, but profit: but for another man to write his extravagant, and pleasant fancies of the same, is as if a man, from being tumbled into the dirt, should come and present himselfe before good company.[2]

Locke is similarly interested in the social extensions of the self and defines consciousness in such a way that he can answer the later questions "what is a person in law?" and "how do we determine responsibility for action?" He calls the question of personal identity a "forensic" one and discusses such problems as the difference between a person drunk and a person sober, a person sleeping and a person waking.[3] Hobbes and Locke would basically like to purify the definition of personal identity by connecting it only with one's personal responsibility for action within society: any antisocial or nonsocial component of personal identity is thereby an aberration. Even though, for example, at one point Locke seems to anticipate the use of psychiatric testimony in courts of law, he also assumes that it will not serve to exonerate or explain but to assign reward and punishment with more precision.

Since Hume is more sensitive to the phenomenology of everyday life than Hobbes and Locke, he does not demand the same fixity of personal identity. He basically attacks any belief in a substantial self that remains unchanging through life and experience. Personal identity, he says, is a "grammatical" fiction that serves to connect the "republic" or "commonwealth" of one's impressions and ideas. Memory is insufficient to provide total continuity because it "does not so much produce as discover personal identity, by shewing us the relation of cause and effect among our different perceptions."[4] Hume finds no difficulty in asserting that our perceptions are always our own, never anyone else's; and that we are always ourselves, whether conscious or not, whether we remember or forget. One might expect that Hume would then argue for bodily continuity as the main criterion of personal identity. But he does not take that step explicitly. Hume's attack is better than his explorations. His pages on personal identity tend to refer more to mind than to body, and more to identity than to person. In one of his first references to personal identity in the *Treatise,* Hume remarks, " 'Tis certain that there is no question in philosophy more abstruse than that concerning identity, and the nature of the uniting principle, which constitutes a person." But in the Appendix to Book I of the *Treatise,* after saying that consciousness seems to come from "reflecting on past perceptions," Hume can go no further: "[A]ll my hopes vanish, when I come to explain the principles, that unite our successive perceptions in our thought or consciousness. I cannot discover any theory, which gives me satisfaction on this head."[5]

The final pun indicates Humes' real interest. When the first book of the *Treatise* is rewritten as *An Enquiry Concerning Human Understanding,* the discussion of personal identity is essentially dropped. Despite his attack on a static concept of the self, Hume does not want to pursue the discussion of personal identity any further into, say, a definition that might combine process with bodily continuity. Like the other philosophers, whatever range of definitions they offer, Hume finally also seems to consider personal identity a point of vantage from which to view the world outside.

By comparison with the philosophers, who consider personal identity as an epistemological vantage point, the novelists deal instead with a recurrent anxiety over being able to be (and speak) at all. With Defoe's first-person narratives or Richardson's epistles (which, unlike Pope's, separate correspondents rather than link them), the pressure of self-definition, the pressure on the working out of problems *now,* intensifies both formally and thematically. There can be no invocation of the traditional topoi of superior poetic insight, no turning aside to more pressing philosophical problems, to be asserted as saving solutions. Fiction identifies the mind and the page, making the creation of a book into an act of self-justification; self-expression becomes inextricably linked to personal identity. It is within the novel, as defined by Defoe and Richardson, that a new sense of human separateness begins to be analyzed and explored—all our basic attitudes towards ourselves, our minds, and our bodies, and our relationships with other people, especially male–female relationships. In the uncertainties of prose fiction, with its uncertain grasp on the expository and ordered, all the questions have to be asked again and again, formulated and reformulated; they cannot be provisionally locked into some traditional aesthetic form. Neither muse nor machinery nor philosophic system can be trusted to provide a safe literary refuge. Everyone, author and character alike, must tell his own story. As Anna Howe reports to us after Clarissa's death, "it was always a matter of surprise to her that the sex are generally

so averse as they are to writing; since the pen, next to the needle, of all employ-
ments, is the most proper, and best suited to their geniuses; and this as well for
improvement as amusement."[6]

Pen and penetration. Richardson is not usually considered to be a writer who
uses figurative language. He is a plain writer: steeped in common speech, un-
poetic, unsoaring. But within *Clarissa* repetitions of certain words and their cog-
nates build patterns that contain a force larger than any immediate context. One
such word is *penetration,* as used to characterize the wit and understanding of
both Clarissa and Lovelace. Another is *impenetrable,* used to describe the barriers
put up by both Clarissa and Lovelace. Still another is *prepossession,* frequently
used by the Harlowes to characterize what they believe is Clarissa's predilection
for Lovelace. Add to these the varieties of will, legal and personal: *good will, ill
will,* and *willful. Character,* of course, is yet another, not only the social nature
Pope speaks of in *To a Lady,* but the elements of writing as well, the cryptograph-
ical form Lovelace uses for his secret letters, his "cursed algebra." All these
words have many interrelations. Here I would like to concentrate on *penetration*
and *impenetrable,* with an implicit nod at the others, because the poles of penetration and impenetrability express most clearly what I take to be Richardson's
main theme: the efforts of individuals to discover and define themselves by their
efforts to penetrate, control, and even destroy others, while they remain impenetrable themselves.

Almost everything that happens to Clarissa she perceives to be a diminishment
of her freedom. In *Pamela,* the urge toward marriage and children implies a sense
of continuity, a commitment to society, an effort to bring Pamela's values to bear
upon a corrupt social world and hopefully reform it. In *Clarissa* society has become the real enemy, and the battleground is inside the self. Clarissa enters the
novel believing that there are timeless social relations that insure her personal
security. She quickly finds that her assumptions are untrue and in the process
becomes aware of what she had unconsciously assumed. Her own desires, she
finds, will be sacrificed to the desires of her father and brother to aggrandize the
family wealth and perpetuate the family name. The family good is superior to her
own. The first threat to the self comes therefore from what had seemed to be the
most secure part of Clarissa's life. She had discovered that familial roles and
relations will not bear the moral weight she had placed upon them. She first tries
to convince her family that she is not subversive. But she is unsuccessful. They
lose their legitimacy for her as keepers of value not because they do not understand her position but because they understand too well the point where family
and individual values fatally clash. On this issue Mrs. Harlowe is as much Clarissa's opponent as Mr. Harlowe, or James, or Arabella.

But Clarissa's basic value is singleness, as defined by the relations between
both men and women and between parents and children. The novel therefore details the process of Clarissa's disappointment with the traditional ways identity
had been defined outside the self. Rationality had failed; legal and religious institutions have failed; and finally the family has failed. What then does "I" mean
in a world without these traditional contexts of institutional and intellectual order?
Clarissa will finally found her personal continuity and substantiality solely upon

the purity of her principles—and in such self-definition deny her less certain past selves, her treacherous heart and body, and her fallible need for other people.

Clarissa's primary fear about marriage, and her objection to Solmes, the suitor her family forces upon her, is the loss of identity it entails:

> *Marriage* is a very solemn engagement, enough to make a young creature's heart ache, with the *best* prospects, when she thinks seriously of it! To be given up to a strange man; to be ingrafted into a strange family; to give up her very name, as a mark of her becoming his absolute and dependent property; to be obliged to prefer this strange man, to father, mother—to everybody; and his humours to all her own—or to contend perhaps, in breach of a vowed duty, for every innocent instance of free-will. To go no-whither: to make acquaintance: to give up acquaintance: to renounce even the strictest friendships perhaps; all at his pleasure, whether she thinks it reasonable to do so or not: surely, sir, a young creature ought not to be obliged to make all these sacrifices but for such a man as she can love. If she be, how sad must be the case! How miserable the life, if to be called *life*![7]

In other words, in order to survive, you must distrust society and the world around you, even your own family and the one you love. They all want to steal your self away, to penetrate your ideas, to prepossess your feelings, to bend your will to their own. The only answer is to trust the principles you find within: "Principles that *are* in my mind; that I *found* there; implanted, no doubt, by the first gracious Planter: which therefore *impel* me, as I may say, to act up to them, that thereby I may, to the best of my judgment, be enabled to comport myself worthily in both states (the single and the married), let others act as they will by *me*" (2:306). But how is that *me* to be defined?

For Clarissa, as for Lovelace in his own way, the true self is everything that everyone else is not. Self-definition excludes the rest of the world, and, when it does find its values, finds them either in the innate principles of "the first gracious Planter" or in the values of the past. Fred Weinstein and Gerald Platt, in *The Wish to Be Free,* have argued that generalized cultural insecurity arises from an attack on contemporary systems of value and the concomitant fear of building a new system of values solely from within. The revolutionary then seeks the sanction of older forms to legitimize his rebellion.[8] As Robespierre reintroduced many feudal and patriarchal values and practices, so Clarissa, whose radical idealism rejects even such primitive social forms, will gradually define herself as an example, an antiphysical saint. And so she is accepted by her admirers, notably Belford, her prime disciple, who writes to Lovelace:

> I have conceived such a profound reverence for her sense and judgment, that, far from thinking the man excusable who should treat her basely, I am ready to regret such an angel of a woman should even marry. She is in my eye all mind: and were she to meet with a man all mind likewise, why should the charming qualities she is mistress of be endangered? Why should such an angel be plunged so low into the vulgar offices of domestic life? Were she mine, I should hardly wish to see her a mother, unless there were a kind of moral certainty that minds like hers could be propagated. For why, in short, should not the work of bodies be left to *mere* bodies? (2:243–44)

Clarissa explores and helps define the cultural moment when the self-willed isolation of the individual that insures a security against the world becomes first an opposition between self and society and finally a mutually exclusive definition of the images of male and female. Weinstein and Platt have further argued that, with the Industrial Revolution, the formerly undifferentiated roles of husband and wife—both controlling and both nurturing—separated into the controlling father and the nurturing mother, the one who comes home only to command and the other who stays home, without commanding and with only ameliorative power. This division is already present in Mr. and Mrs. Harlowe: the unapproachable Godlike tyrant and the wheedling, sympathetic, and subordinated mother. None of Clarissa's experience in the novel does anything to contradict this definition of male and female roles. In fact, she expands and institutionalizes it—as Belford's remarks indicate—into a general denial of sexuality. Like Richardson when he writes the novel, Clarissa separates herself into masculine and feminine parts and defines them against each other into even greater purity. In search of the antimasculine self Clarissa desires, Richardson has taken a crucial step towards the concept of "the opposite sex" and the rigidification of male and female roles that would be the heritage of the nineteenth century and our own.

Pen, penetration, prepossession, impenetrable. Obviously the sexual nuance is there in the abstract language. But, without undervaluing sexuality, I think that its function in *Clarissa* should be seen in a larger context. The fear of sexuality in *Clarissa* constitutes only the most obvious expression of a general fear of relationship and vulnerability that characterizes both Clarissa and Lovelace.[9] Here are two passages, both from the third volume of the novel, and both remarks by Lovelace. In the first, to Belford, Lovelace describes an incident during which he had grabbed Clarissa's hand and implored her to accept him as a lover: "And I snatched her hand, and more than kissed it; I was ready to devour it. There was, I believe, a kind of frenzy in my manner which threw her into a panic like that of Semele perhaps, when the Thunderer, in all his majesty, surrounded with ten thousand celestial burning-glasses, was about to scorch her into a cinder" (2:98).

The unbowdlerized story, of course, is that Semele desired Zeus to come upon her in all his godhead, undisguised, and that the intercourse itself destroyed her, except for the fertilized germ that would become Dionysus. Whose coyness then is the ten thousand celestial burning-glasses, Richardson's or Lovelace's? It certainly suits with Lovelace's character, for, in its avoidance of the actual myth, it expresses Lovelace's simultaneous desire to assert sexual power and to shrink from that power's destructive potential. His own remark in this situation, as Clarissa has reported it to Anna Howe a few pages earlier, is much more passive: "take me, take me to yourself; mould me as you please, I am wax in your hands; give me your own impression, and seal me for ever yours" (2:80). How precarious is that self-assertion by which Lovelace defines himself! Precarious in the same way as Clarissa's, for both fear the weakness and vulnerability that they blame on their sexuality. To compensate for his weakness, Lovelace makes his sexuality into a weapon, and Clarissa's refusal of sexuality is the shield she fashions from the same impulses. Because of his disguises, Clarissa calls Lovelace the "perfect Proteus" and insists to Anna Howe that she is not being contradictory herself, but only reporting Lovelace's self-contradictions. Yet Lovelace's uncertainties awaken a "divided soul" in Clarissa as well, and to his changeability she gradually opposes her self-purification. Clarissa becomes clarissima.

Far from being the expression of an abstract, semiallegorical opposition between flesh and spirit, the relationship between Clarissa and Lovelace develops into a set of polarized self-images, because the characters believe those responses are increasingly appropriate to the situations in which they find themselves.[10] Clarissa and Lovelace further elaborate the balance-sheet self that so preoccupied Robinson Crusoe and Pamela, in which goods and evils, benefits and demerits, were entered in parallel columns. But identity in *Clarissa* can no longer be the combination or even the choice of one or the other side of the equation. One must choose absolutely; there is no third term. Using Lovelace to define herself (as he uses her), Clarissa believes that she is a totally interior being, while he is totally exterior. The true self, as she defines it, is a purging of the external world—the theatrical, role-playing definition of identity Lovelace embodies—as well as the divisions he excites within her, her "divided soul." In order to achieve true singularity, there can be no ambivalence, no vacillations. Each step along the way to Clarissa's self-willed death is a sloughing away of the snakeskin of some past self. In Richardson's profound paradox of personal identity, Clarissa believes that her justification will come through the opinion of others about her inner worth, and she becomes pure to justify the exemplary view of her others hold. Like so many Enlightenment figures, torn between the desire for autonomy and the anxiety over rejecting traditional standards, Clarissa seeks her justification in the future, from those who will learn from her story and her example.[11] Samual Johnson tried to purge some of his own anxiety about self-assertion by coming as a grown man to bare his head in the public square of Uttoxeter, there to expiate a childhood disobedience of his father. But Clarissa turns her will inward and expresses her self-sufficiency by destroying the self that dared assert itself.

Since physicality is the most obvious barrier to that self-definition, Clarissa turns more and more against her own body. The body, she decides, is the weak barricade before the mind, the will, and ultimately the soul. The eye first allows the breach in that barricade: another's eye, which attempts first to possess one visually, then physically, and finally psychically; or your own eye, which must necessarily be deluded by the specious beauty of external form. As Anna Howe writes to Clarissa, "The eye, my dear, the wicked eye, has such a strict alliance with the heart, and both have such enmity to the understanding! What an unequal union, the mind and body! All the senses, like the family at Harlowe Place, in a confederacy against that which would animate, and give honour to the whole, were it allowed its proper precedence" (2:116–17). That which would animate is, of course, the anima, the soul. Anna Howe's parallel invokes neither Locke's legal definition of identity, self as the name for the individual acting in society, nor Hume's conglomerate identity, self as the name for all that is you. It implies instead a need to purge oneself of the senses, as Clarissa must purge herself of her family, to gain true self-identity. Passion, Clarissa writes to Anna Howe, is the same in both sexes: "Those passions in our sex which we take no pains to subdue, may have one and the same source with those infinitely blacker passions which we used so often to condemn in the violent and headstrong of the other sex; and which may be only heightened in *them* by *custom,* and their *freer education.* Let us both, my dear, ponder well this thought; look into ourselves, and fear'' (2:236).

Lovelace, too, is preoccupied with the threat to his eyes. He claims that his antagonism toward women, the revenge he seeks, dates from a youthful jilt. But in a more violent passage, he gives a clue to the depths beneath his attack: "How usual a thing is it for women as well as men, without the least remorse, to ensnare, to cage, and torment, and even with burning knitting-needles to put out the eyes of the poor feathered songster . . . which, however, in proportion to its bulk, has more life than themselves (for a bird is all soul), and of consequence has as much feeling as the human creature!'' (2:247). I could here detail the many analogies in *Clarissa* between caged birds and caged human beings or recall Clarissa's remark about the suitability of the pen and needle to the talents of women. But it is enough to note the importance that both Clarissa and Lovelace give to the eyes.[12] Richardson has in effect transformed a Renaissance trope into a psychological compulsion. Lovelace may owe his existence in part to the precedent of Wycherley's Horner. But this time lives and not just maidenheads are at stake. Visibility is not a metaphor for sexuality, just as sexuality is not a metaphor for identity. They are interlocked concepts for Richardson, and the general rejection of metaphor by the eighteenth-century novel underlines its search for what might be called a rhetoric of essences rather than surfaces. Clarissa's refusal of physicality parallels the almost nonvisual world of Richardson's novel. Were Adam and Eve blind in Eden? Clarissa supposes her story to show first of all that "the eye is a traitor'' (2:313), indicting the treasonous nature of the visual world, that world of otherness, that the frail eye opens us to. The division between mind and body that Descartes developed as an epistemological assumption has in *Clarissa* become an ontological imperative.[13]

What feminine roles are available to Clarissa in her relationship with Lovelace? Possible models are her mother's relation to her father and Anna Howe's to Hickman, the former an abdication to masculine authority and tyranny and the latter a genial subordination in which the woman has the actual control. There is no continuum of relationship between men and women like that which can exist between persons of the same sex.[14] Especially for the woman who wants to exercise her will morally and personally, there seem to be no real alternatives, only either a total acceptance of the myth of male–female relations or a split between mind and body, in which the body is defined as male and therefore rejected. When Clarissa decides to die after she has been raped by Lovelace, he does not understand. Since Clarissa had been drugged and her mind is therefore inviolate, why should his physical violation of her be so important? (Anna Howe makes the same point in 4:18.) But Clarrisa knows the truth of her frailty: *weakness comes from within.* It is not a diabolical imposition from the outside. The mind is its own place—and the body as well. Against Lovelace she defines her will as a totally mental and spiritual entity, not only separate from desire but opposed to it as well. In the process of her self-definition she rejects both memory, the psychological criterion for the continuous self, and body, the physical criterion. She holds to herself only the timeless assertion of spirit and will. Once again Richardson has psychologized rhetoric. This is no longer the Renaissance topos of the battle of the sexes, the military images of love poetry, but a definite statement about the incompatibility of the masculine and feminine egos, the warfare between their essential self-definitions. Lovelace believes that the mind and body are separate. But Clarissa believes they are connected as well to the death of the soul, if the taint of the physical goes too far.[15]

With little sense of the historical background or the way their researches had been foreseen by Richardson among many other writers, R. D. Laing and A. Esterson have systematized and thereby made familiar the pattern of family relationships so clearly portrayed in *Clarissa*. Clarissa first seeks to preserve her will inviolate when her family tries to force her to deny her grandfather's bequest. The social and economic pressures felt by the Harlowes are translated into a pressure upon the one member of the family they believe to be the weakest and most tractable, like Cordelia and Cinderella, each a youngest daughter. The bond of the Harlowes is their anger against a world they believe is about to attack them. By isolating one person's actions or refusal to act, the rest of the family is saved from insecurity and conflict. Through the example of the Harlowes we can see how the structure of the modern nuclear family may have been insensibly created as a response to otherwise intolerable social and economic realities. Clarissa responds by setting her mind against her body, becoming the spiritual ancestor of the young girls Laing and Esterson describe in *Sanity, Madness, and the Family*. But one aspect of Clarissa's character prevents her from being a case: her assertion of will and freedom, the step outside the garden gate, ends in her death. What is schizophrenia in the younger daughters of weak will described by Laing and Esterson appears in Richardson, thanks to the strength of Clarissa's will, as a psychic ideology. Richardson in *Clarissa* could perhaps justifiably consider Clarissa's response to be necessary and appropriate in a new and increasingly anonymous world. In our own time it has become one of the main elements in a self-limiting, self-destructive response to the world around us.[16]

Clarissa's desire to purify her sense of self bears many similarities to Gulliver's. Compressed between the demands of her family on one side, Lovelace on another, and the injunctions and coaxings of Anna Howe on still a third, Clarissa seeks to define herself to the exclusion of all others: purity of self shall become an example to all around her. Here is the point where satiric simplicity and saintly purity can intersect, in the belief that the truest vision of human nature involves a successive shedding of complexity and ambivalence, so that character may be defined by exclusion rather than inclusion. Faced with the hostile world around her, Clarissa adopts Gulliver's method, separating her personal identity from the contamination of body in search of a definition of character based on inner principles and order. Both consider the body to be a weak defense against the necessary incursions of the world. Gulliver defines the threat in terms of his fancied reputation for cleanliness. In Book I of *Gulliver's Travels* he attempts to "vindicate" himself against hypothetical attacks on his excesses, both sexual and scatological. In the context of Swift's work his overreaction is absurd. But underneath is a dark dilemma about the nature of the self that parallels Clarissa's desire to see herself solely as a being of mind and spirit. Look within and fear; look outside and fear as well. The mingled impression of caricature and characterization we receive from *Gulliver's Travels* conveys the way Gulliver stands between the comic concerns of Restoration drama and the psychological dilemmas of the novel.[17] I use Gulliver here as a foil to Clarissa because I do not want to consider Clarissa's situation to be totally that of a woman in a male world. It is also a human situation, and that is the source of its power.

Lovelace reflects Gulliver's worries over reputation even more directly. Servants, Clarissa says at one point, are bad nowadays because they imitate stage servants (4:164). That remark is a minor version of the difficulty of Lovelace, who models his character on the stage libertine—Don Juan, Horner, Dorimant—even though his personal nature does not really fit the role. Lovelace is less the descendant of these stage figures than their victim. Like Clarissa, Lovelace puts a great weight on his own consistency. She attempts to define and regulate her sense of personal identity by what she believes to be innate principles of virtue. He attempts to rule his life in accordance with preexisting literary and theatrical stereotypes—the "rakish annals" he so frequently invokes. Lovelace therefore represents a type of character and a type of human being very important to the history of the novel—the person warped or ruined by his experience of art.[18]

In the history of literature, the novel marks a transition from theatrical and satiric definition of character—character apprehended from without—to fictional character—character apprehended from within. When critics believe that Clarissa is superior to Lovelace because he seeks external approval while she cultivates the inner life, they accept the attack Richardson's fiction seems to make on the role-playing self and embrace the assumption that hidden things are necessarily superior to visible ones. But Clarissa is as enslaved to the moral attitudes of others in her desire to become an example as Lovelace is enslaved to older forms of literary character. In fact both Lovelace and Clarissa act out of fear that they will themselves disintegrate, if they do not first annihilate or by dying obviate the existence of others. In their search for wholeness neither will admit the need for others. The myths of survival that animate Robinson Crusoe, Moll Flanders, Gulliver, Lovelace, and Clarissa assert that the only acceptable self is a self-sufficient one. The only way to avoid the control of others is to control yourself. The response therefore to the threat of penetration, whether physical, mental, or spiritual, is to become impenetrable, to become independent by making others dependent upon you.

What ever the symbiosis of Clarissa and Lovelace, the novel is still Clarissa's. In the early novel, men tend to be the main characters when vocation and society are the main theme. The issue in such novels is often "what place in society is suitable to his merits?" In novels that have a woman for the central character, the basic question is usually "how is the self to be realized, whether society exists or not?"[19] We first can learn about the relations between men and women in a particular era from direct statements about masculine and feminine behavior, the legal situation, and other factual sources. But more important, more pervasive, and more elusive, is the symbolic situation of men and women: how do masculine and feminine stand for different aspects of a total individual, whether that individual is actually a man or a woman? how do new myths emerge from old? what other cultural forces accompany their creation?

Clarissa marks the definite reversal of the classical and medieval psychomachia of temperate man and emotional woman, for Clarissa's psychic independence and sense of personal identity are linked directly with her denial of a physical being that has responded too precipitately to the lure of a man. Belford reports to Lovelace: "The lady has been giving orders, with great presence of mind, about her body" (4:340). And, in the elaborate will she writes toward the end of the novel, Clarissa declares, "I am nobody's," affirming the interpenetrating relationship of self-possession and self-denial: "In the first place, I desire that my body may lie unburied three days after my decease, or till the pleasure of my father be known concerning it. But the occasion of my death not admitting of doubt, I will not, on any account, that it be opened; and it is my desire that it shall not be touched but by those of my own sex" (4:416).

The action of *Clarissa* lasts a year, but the yearly cycle is unrenewed. Without physicality, without sexuality, there are no bodies, no children, and no continuity. Clarissa's world is a dead end, and the only thing to do is quickly get out of it. Clarissa has triumphed by reducing her individual human nature to a purified personal identity. As Lovelace says to Belford shortly before her death, "I admire her more than ever; and . . . my love for her is less *personal,* as I may say, more *intellectual,* than ever I thought it could be to a woman" (4:262). Or, as Belford describes the deathbed of Mrs. Sinclair, with the prostitutes surrounding it: "as much as I admire, and next to adore, a truly virtuous and elegant woman: for to me it is evident, that as a neat and clean woman must be an angel of a creature, so a sluttish one is the impurest animal in nature" (4:381). Need I mention that Belford has referred to Swift's Yahoos in the previous sentence? The gulliverian hatred of the body and its messes has Clarissa as its ideologue and Belford as her acolyte. Sydney Shoemaker in *Self-Knowledge and Self-Identity* notes Descartes's argument that "since he could doubt the existence of bodies, but could not doubt the existence of himself, he could not be a body."[20] The bodily continuity that Hume implied was part of the definition of a person is summarily rejected in Clarissa's idea of herself. She has domesticated Descartes (although Richardson would have been upset at the suggestion) to create a self that exists without conflict or change, bound neither to time nor to society, expressing in her own way what Locke called "the sameness of a rational being."[21] The parameters within which Richardson's characters seek for a firm sense of identity have much to do with the ways in which the English novel subsequently explores characters as well as with the narrative structures that guide that exploration. Novelistic attitudes toward character both reflect and lead the way people think about themselves and their world. When literature on all levels of sophistication becomes the primary link between people, the main bridge between individuals and society, then self-images will be greatly controlled by literary images. Until the advent of film, it is the word that structures the self. Any discussion of penetration and impenetrability in character must necessarily lead finally to a discussion of the act of writing itself.

The will that Clarissa writes toward the end of the novel makes clear that it is not will alone which controls one's identity and relation to others, but will as embodied in writing. Once again, Clarissa bears comparison to Gulliver: both parallel their search for personal purity with a search for linguistic purity; Clarissa as immediate letter writer stands next to Gulliver as plain-speaking voyager. The work of recent literature most alluded to in *Clarissa* is not actually *Gulliver*, but Swift's *A Tale of a Tub,* and *A Tale of a Tub* not as a religious tract, but as a work about writing.

Language helps one to possess the potentially fragmented self and keep it whole. Pamela itched to write and hid her writings by sewing them into her petticoats to swathe her virginity from Mr. B———. Clarissa not only protects herself, she also objectifies and distances herself by writing. Throughout the early parts of the novel she worries about the pride involved in being an example. But, as the novel moves on, she gradually accepts her exemplary status, in great part because of the self-objectification created by her own writings. The woman with the pen confronts the man with the penis. Clarissa changes not so much by Lovelace's attacks on her as she does by the sense of self-sufficiency and self-enclosure that writing has helped to give her. Whereas Lovelace uses writing as a disguise, Clarissa uses it as an inward stay—another reenactment of the competition between the belief that the self is enriched through role-playing and stylization and the belief that the truly strong self is purified and sincere. Once again, Clarissa and Lovelace are similar in their sensitivities, if not in their final positions. In volumes one and two of the novel, they have both been established as adroit and polished users of words. Often admired, they are also often attacked by other characters who complain that they use language as wit, to penetrate, even while they remain personally impenetrable. Like Fielding's ideal in *Joseph Andrews,* they cannot be looked into like a simple book, even for a few pages.[22]

What happens when the two impenetrable penetrators meet? In the early pages of the novel they are both optimistic about their ability to use words for their own best ends. They seem to preserve a Hobbesian belief in the humanness of language and its suitability as a medium for explanation and correspondence. Unlike the word labyrinth of *A Tale of a Tub, Clarissa* does seem to imply that language can work: letters can be ways to communicate and justify. Swift calls on the violence of satiric language to renovate and revitalize the dead language around him, trying to prevent it from slipping further into nonmeaning. Richardson, in his commitment to plainness and clarity, shows a self-consciousness about language that never quite questions its basic nature. At the point where self-justification and communication finally conflict, Richardson chooses to explore while Swift is content to mock. The disappointed political propagandist seems to see little in language beyond manipulation, while the prosperous printer maintains his belief in its currency and solidity.

The problem of linguistic definition and clarification (to found a true science, to establish a workable society, to express basic religious truths) is therefore necessarily tied to the problem of personal identity. The existence of language may imply the existence of society. But it also implies the existence of self-conscious persons. The fears about linguistic fragmentation that plague writers like Swift

stand kin to the fears of psychic fragmentation and loss of identity that characterize the speaker of *A Tale of a Tub.* Pope's optimism in the 1730s about the poet's
ability to reform language parallels his optimism about the new possibilities for
human character. Clarissa in her turn implies that prose is the only medium possible for spiritual meaning and promulgates an antiphysical mysticism based not
on ineffability but on language. Clarissa's will assigns destinies and meanings to
all; and she designs her coffin as well, imposing her own meaning on her life:

> The principal devise, neatly etched on a plate of white metal, is a crowned serpent,
> with its tail in its mouth, forming a ring, the emblem of eternity; and in the circle
> made by it is this inscription:
>
> CLARISSA HARLOWE
> April x
> [Then the year]
> AETAT. XIX.
>
> For ornaments: at top, an hour-glass winged. At bottom, an urn.   (4:257)

The snake with its tail in its mouth is an emblem of eternity, but it is also an
emblem of Clarissa's "reptile pride," the unchanging mind, the necessity for
impenetrability and self-sufficiency, the rejection of inconsistency and division.
As Belford rails shortly afterward, "what wretched creatures are there in the world!
What strangely mixed characters! So sensible and so silly at the same time! What
a *various,* what a *foolish* creature is man!"   (4:299). The "infinite variety" so
prized by Moll Flanders has become the single-mindedness of Clarissa. Purified
language will make up for the fragmented self. The self-sufficiency through writing that Swift mocks in *A Tale of a Tub* becomes Clarissa's mainstay against the
fear of self-annihilation. Through the pen the deepest self is both realized and
corrected. As Clarissa writes to Anna Howe early in the novel, "I am almost
afraid to beg of you, and yet I repeatedly *do,* to give way to that charming spirit
whenever it rises to your pen, which smiles, yet goes to the quick of my fault.
What patient shall be afraid of a probe in so delicate a hand?" (1:345).

Richardson in *Clarissa* therefore finally rejects the possibilities of psychological
"inconsistency" and change that Pope explored so brilliantly in the *Moral Essays*
and *Arbuthnot.* Pope had firm roots in a literary past and had achieved economic
self-sufficiency with his translations of the *Iliad* and the *Odyssey.* Even as he saw
the shape of culture changing around him, he could explore and criticize those
changes as a kind of secure outsider in his society. Richardson was an insecure
insider, a figure of the new world, part aesthete and part businessman. In a period
of rapid social and economic change, he perceived the sympathy his audience
would feel for characters who needed to maintain a strict hold on the essentials of
self, to deny vulnerability, to become impenetrable, at the same time that they
insured their self-sufficiency by penetrating and hopefully puncturing everyone
who came near enough to threaten the fragile sense of personal identity that lay
within them. Self-sufficiency and self-creation is the general message of the novel,
and Richardson spoke to a world ready for that message. Clarissa's desire for self-
containment closely resembles the personal rigidity of Samuel Johnson, his fear

of sloth, his need to purge himself of fault, and his works of personality. To speak a *Rambler,* as Mrs. Thrale tells us Johnson could do on request, reflects the same subordination of self to work that Sterne worries in another way, by exploiting rather than fighting against the changing shape of the written self. Through Clarissa's rejection of the body, the devil within, and society, the devils without, Richardson articulated better than any writer of his time a group of attitudes toward personal identity and relations with other people that still influence us. Perhaps in our time we can finally cease to believe in those devils and continue Pope's exploration of the values of inconsistency and ambivalence. After all, as we can now see, Freud did not begin a new age. He was the prelude to the end of the old one—an age that the genius of Richardson helps us to define in all its literary fruitfulness and its psychic barrenness.

[1974]

Notes

1. In *Samuel Richardson and the Eighteenth-Century Puritan Character* (Hamden, Conn., 1972), Cynthia Griffin Wolff attempts to relate Richardson's ideas to still another aspect of seventeenth-century attitudes toward personal identity, the Puritan conception of the self. But she glosses over the difficulty, pointed out by Sacvan Bercovitch, that "precisely because spiritual autobiography highlighted the solitary confrontation between man and his Maker it came to form a powerful countercurrent to Renaissance individualism." Unlike Clarissa, the Puritans desire to escape the willful self: "self-consciousness functions in these writings to erode individuality." (In a review of *The Puritan Experience: Studies in Spiritual Autobiography* by Owen C. Watkins, *Seventeenth-Century News,* Spring 1973, p. 1.)

2. *Leviathan,* ed. C. B. Macpherson (Harmondsworth, 1968), p. 137. Hobbes later compares madness with drunkenness as similar effects of excessive (antisocial) passion: "For, (I believe) the most sober men, when they walk alone without care and employment of the mind, would be unwilling the vanity and Extravagance of their thoughts at that time should be publiquely seen: which is a confession, that Passions unguided, are for the most part meere Madnesse" (p. 142). We might look forward here to Gulliver, Roderick Random, Doctor Slop, and the many other medical men who populate the eighteenth-century novel.

3. *An Essay Concerning Human Understanding,* ed. John W. Yolton (London, 1965), 1:287–90. Hobbes says dreams "are caused by the distemper of some of the inward parts of the body" (p. 91), and are therefore connected to other unsocializable behavior. Perhaps the same assumption from a different point of view animates the form of *Pilgrim's Progress,* "delivered under the Similitude of a DREAM."

4. *A Treatise of Human Nature,* ed. L. A. Selby-Bigge (Oxford, 1888), pp. 261, 262. Derek Parfit has recently argued that Hume's concept of personal identity could accommodate schizophrenia, brainwashing, and identity crisis, because he seems to allow for discontinuous selves within the same body. "Personal Identity," *Philosophical Review,* vol. 80, no. 1 (January 1971), pp. 3–27. See also in the same issue the responses by Terence Penelhum and Fraser Crowley, with a rejoinder by Parfit.

5. *Treatise,* pp. 189, 635–36. Perhaps Hume does not pursue the issue because he is unwilling to take the time necessary for a full attack on the Cartesian assumption of the dependence of body on mind: "j'avais déjà connu en moi très clairement que la nature intelligente est distincte de la corporelle, considérant que toute composition témoigne de la dépendance, et que la dépendance est manifestement un défaut" (*Discours de la méthode,* ed. Geneviève Rodis-Lewis [Paris, 1966], p. 62).

6. Samuel Richardson, *Clarissa,* introd. John Butt (London, 1932), 4:495. Further citations will be included in the text. For a more extended discussion of nontraditional relations between form and

narrator, see Braudy, "The Form of the Sentimental Novel," *Novel,* vol. 7, no. 1 (Fall 1973), pp. 5–13. The use of the word "self-justification" brings to mind the printing use of "justify," that is, to bring out to the edge of the page. The *OED* records such a usage in 1683 and Richardson the printer would certainly have known it. Wolff, in *Samuel Richardson of the Eighteenth-Century Puritan Character,* has an interesting discussion of the passage from diary to autobiography in terms of self-presentation. See especially chapter 2, "Richardson's Sources." Diderot, in his *Eloge de Richardson* (1761), remarks that when he meets a friend who has been to England, he always asks first if he saw Richardson and then if he saw Hume, perhaps creating an emblem of his own effort to combine the two.

7. 1:152–53, the copy of a letter from Clarissa to her Uncle John Harlowe that she sends to Anna Howe. Compare Gibbon on Blackstone: "The matrimonial union is so intimate according to our laws; that the very legal existence of the wife is lost in that of the husband, with whom in general she composes but one person. . . . She is however sometimes considered as a separate but inferior being" (*The English Essays of Edward Gibbon,* ed. Patricia B. Craddock [Oxford, 1972], pp. 83, 84). See also Christopher Hill's classic article on the social and economic situation, "Clarissa Harlowe and Her Times," reprinted many times, perhaps most handily in *Samuel Richardson,* ed. John Carroll (Englewood Cliffs, N.J., 1969), pp. 102–23. Clarissa's metaphorical use of "ingrafted" bears strong resemblance to her invocation of "the first gracious Planter" in the next quotation.

8. *The Wish to Be Free: Society, Psyche, and Value Change* (Berkeley and Los Angeles, 1969), pp. 108–36.

9. Ian Watt, for example, emphasizes sexuality more exclusively and makes a dichotomy between Clarissa and Lovelace without discussing their similarities. See *The Rise of the Novel* (Berkeley and Los Angeles, 1957), pp. 230–38. On p. 232, Watts says, "Even so, Clarissa dies; sexual intercourse, apparently, means death for the woman." Here Watt glosses over both Clarissa's will and Lovelace's fears.

10. Compare, for example, Alan Wendt's statement that Lovelace is the "appeal of the flesh" to Clarissa, while Clarissa is the "appeal of the spirit" to Lovelace; in "Clarissa's Coffin," *Philological Quarterly,* 39 (1960), 485. But Lovelace's fear of sexuality is strong—"How does this damned love unman me!" (2:526)—and he generally avoids any real consummation (4:297). See also Gregory Bateson's discussion of "double bind," especially the way two people in a relationship will begin to caricature themselves each in opposition to the other, in *Steps to an Ecology of Mind* (New York, 1972), especially Part 3, "Form and Pathology in Relationship."

11. R. D. Laing in *Self and Others* (Harmondsworth, 1971) remarks: "To live in the past or in the future may be less satisfying than to live in the present, but it can never be as disillusioning" (p. 48).

12. One could, of course, also bring to bear Sandor Ferenczi's demonstration of the parallels between blinding and castration, the eye and the testicle. See "On Eye Symbolism," *Sex in Psychoanalysis* (New York, 1956), pp. 228–33.

13. It is no mistake then that Belford twice identifies Clarissa with Socrates, and, I would say, Socrates as opposed to Christ. The belief in the resurrection of the body constituted the most important difference between Christianity and the neoplatonism it sought to reject and replace. But even an idealized body is not sufficient for Clarissa. Socrates exemplifies a sense of self that considers its highest end to be a sublimation up the ladder of being to become . . . perhaps a bird, that being made almost entirely of soul that Lovelace aspires to as well. For further discussion of resurrection as a problem in Christian thought, see Terence Penelhum, *Survival and Disembodied Existence* (New York, 1970).

14. To make himself known to Belinda, the Baron must act in such a way that he totally alienates her. Does the creation of Thalestris require the creation of Sir Plume to do her bidding?

15. Both Clarissa and Lovelace are considered to have a "reptile pride," making the usual identification of Lovelace and Satan a little too facile. Satanhood is not an objective symbolization for the literary reader to make, but a psychological observation of impenetrability and recalcitrance. Such similar phrases and images break down the seeming polarities of Clarissa and Lovelace. Watt, for example, makes much of the Lovelace-spider, Clarissa-fly, formula. But Lovelace also characterizes himself as a fly (2:140). The satanic possibilities of both their prides may be the most recurrent example of this tendency in the novel.

16. R. D. Laing and A. Esterson, *Sanity, Madness, and the Family* (Harmondsworth, 1970).

17. Gulliver's worry about reputation is also paralleled by Clarissa's fear of crowds (3:436). Defoe gives a realistic dimension to the solitary's fear of others in *A Journal of the Plague Year*.

18. In later works, however, it is more often women than men who are supposedly affected. Richardson considered Lovelace to be an original creation: "I intend in him a new Character, not confined to usual Rules." Quoted by T. C. Duncan Eaves and Ben D. Kimpel, in *Samuel Richardson* (Oxford, 1971), p. 211.

19. This distinction reflects that made by Pope, in *To a Lady*, between the private nature of women and the public nature of men.

20. *Self-Knowledge and Self-Identity* (Ithaca, N.Y., 1963), p. 17.

21. *Essay*, 1:281.

22. Clarissa and Lovelace therefore both share Satan's powers of language. But while Lovelace revels in being Proteus, Clarissa tries to repress such changes. Yet in the process they are both consummate users of language, and, again like Satan, they use their language to enclose themselves still further.

The Form of the Sentimental Novel

Most discussions of sentimental literature, taking their lead from Goldsmith's "Comparison between Laughing and Sentimental Comedy," center on matters of content and atmosphere—especially the prevalence of tears, whether those of the characters or the audience. But sentiment on stage is not equivalent to sentiment in the novel, nor can the most striking formal characteristics of the fiction being written in the 1760s and 1770s be illuminated by invocations of such philosophic doctrines as Shaftesbury's benevolism. Through a discussion of the form of sentimental fiction, I would like to suggest that such works as *Tristram Shandy, The Man of Feeling,* and *The Sorrows of Young Werther* were neither the resurgence of a cultural stream that had somehow gone underground for almost half a century, nor part of an essentially discontinuous novelistic tradition. They show instead both a structural and a thematic continuity with earlier eighteenth-century novelists, and with the work of Pope and Swift, that is more central to the best of sentimental literature than any continuity with the themes, plot turns, and moral atmosphere of late seventeenth- and early eighteenth-century drama.

A convenient foil to my view is the frequent assertion that the form of the novel had become so established in the little more than twenty-five years between *Pamela* and *Tristram Shandy* that Sterne could already freely experiment with all the givens of the "well-made" novel, including its typographical conventions. In this literary–historical commonplace, formal balance and circumstantial realism are the assumed standards; sentiment, gothicism, and Sterne are the deviations, to be explained more by reference to the history of ideas than the history of the novel. At best the change is explained as a "revolt against realism": the critic defines subgenres and asks us to sit back and wait for Jane Austen. But I would like to argue that Sterne, among others, is not upending but extending the essential self-definition of the novel in England, and I would like to show how a literary form whose first appearance trailed banners of fidelity to real life and moral correctness could metamorphose into Sterne's elaborate formal games and the "discovered" manuscripts of Walpole and Mackenzie.

Structure in the sentimental novel strives to imitate feeling rather than intellect, and to embody direct experience rather than artistic premeditation; this basic imperative of the novel from Defoe on is made only a little more apparent in the works of Sterne, Mackenzie, and others. The form of the sentimental novel, the gothic novel, and eighteenth-century fiction in general never seriously imitates such nonliterary fictions as the order of providence, philosophic system, or social hierarchy, no matter how it may comment on them or include their patterns within its own. Ultimately the sentimental novel asserts the superiority of the inarticulate language of the heart to the artifice of literary and social forms, the articulate mind and the fluent pen. Like the novel in general, it rejects the older shapes of intellectual self-consciousness as well as any formal literary sophistications authenticated by tradition—in the same way that it often attacks intelligent and socially powerful women in favor of those with the less public charms of family devotion and spiritual profundity. The form of the novel must come from within, through a first-person narrator (or variants that include epistolary narration and Fielding's idiosyncratic voice), because the novel in the eighteenth century addresses itself to the problem of presenting and explicating character, whether that of the narrator or one of his underlings, in a literary mode that rejects or subsumes the methods of the past. Such a novel implies that the fictional shaping of a congruence between self and story is the best way to examine more closely those dim and submerged aspects of human character that earlier literary forms tend to obscure. In aspiring to a literary open-endedness that will express its thematic ideal of open-endedness for the personality, it searches for the most effective way to mime sincerity and to achieve thereby a form that is innate and individual, unbeholding to the preexisting orders of society, culture, and history.

How does one write a novel that makes some commitment to the values of nonliterary, even inarticulate, expression? The device most frequently introduced to keep the inarticulate and the articulate in their proper spheres is the narrative frame. *The Man of Feeling* begins with the rescue of a fragmentary manuscript from a bird-hunting curate, who has been using it for wadding in his gun. In the "manuscript," which is the body of the novel, the reader indistinctly sees the hero, Harley, through a series of screening narrators, some sympathetic, some unsympathetic, but all at a distance, relieving Harley of the excessively literary burden of having to tell his own story. These narrators resemble the poet in Gray's *Elegy,* who writes about the "mute inglorious Milton"; all are literary evils, perhaps necessary to bring the story of the seemingly insignificant, the totally private man, to the attention of the world, but otherwise inferior to "th'unletter'd muse" with his "uncouth rhymes." The discovered manuscript is fragmentary because any evidence of artistic completeness would undermine the emotional impact of the story. The frame implies that no one wrote all of *The Man of Feeling:* no total act of creation distorts its raw and real experience; no sophisticated "author" mediates between the reader and the work. The most admirable person in Mackenzie's hierarchy is the most inarticulate. But, since neither Mackenzie nor Gray can themselves be that inarticulate, they try to celebrate those virtues in as unassuming and anonymous a way as possible. As Mackenzie has the first narrator of *The Man of Feeling* ironically remark about the manuscript:

I was a good deal affected with some very trifling passages in it; and had the name of a Marmontel, or a Richardson, been on the title-page—'tis odds that I should have wept: But

One is ashamed to be pleased with the works of one knows not whom.   (London: Oxford University Press, 1967, p. 5)

The framing narration can therefore liberate an author to experiment with new forms that arise from the story itself. The myth of the discovered manuscript in *The Man of Feeling* or *The Castle of Otranto* parallels Chatterton's "discovery" of Rowley and Macpherson's of Ossian—all attempt to create a literature of emotional intensity that rejects official literary style. The "fraud" the eighteenth century perceived in Chatterton and Macpherson we perceive as a variety of fiction in Mackenzie and Walpole. Yet all are attempts to release sincerity through chicanery and to embody innocence and feeling *literarily*, without the premeditated symmetries of literary order. Goethe's *Werther* must be finished by Werther's friend William after Werther's suicide. *The Man of Feeling* and *A Sentimental Journey* are fragmentary works that include even more fragmentary tales. *Rasselas* seeks certainty through a group of inconclusive episodes until the search itself ends inconclusively. The bare conventional frame allows such works to achieve a new definition of form as well as to contain an argument for dispensing with older structural methods. The sophisticated Werther joyfully describes how he can find no words adequate to describe the tenderness of a peasant courting a widow. One of the narrators in *The Man of Feeling* pauses to mock the reader's desire for a more complex story: "to such as may have expected the intricacies of a novel, a few incidents in a life undistinguished, except by some features of the heart, cannot have afforded much entertainment" (p. 125). And Walpole in *The Castle of Otranto* presages Fuseli's distinction between the details of horror and the ineffability of terror: "The passions that ensued must be conceived; they cannot be painted" (London: Penguin, 1968, p. 91). All these works display the belief of their authors that uncompleted form and a suspicion about the expressive possibilities of language are necessary statements of literary good faith. Refusing to impose any traditional shape on their works and shying away from analogies to the larger schemes of philosophy and art, they assert that their novels find their most appropriate shapes when they become vessels of the consciousness that created them.

In part, Sterne, Goethe, Mackenzie, and others are turning away from the traditional problems of writing a literary work and toward the newer problem of being a literary man from whom a work will spring. At the very least, there is some blurring of the distinction. Even though Goethe revised *Werther,* Werther himself says that an author should write his work out directly and never revise, for revision distorts the immediate apprehension the novel seeks to embody. Formal aesthetic creation stifles the world of feeling and emotion that form ought to help express, just a society crushes the heart, or daylight banishes the terrors of night. The narrative frame of the gothic novel allows the reader to hold the two in balance by creating a bridge between his more ordered world and the emotions within; so *Wuthering Heights* is retold by Nelly Dean to the vacationing Lock-wood, and an array of journals, letters, and news clippings conveys to the reader the nightmare world of *Dracula*. The induction through the daylit public world to the private world of darkness and emotion beyond is the legacy of the sentimental novel to the gothic—the pathway to a world whose shape depends on neither society nor providence. In both sentimental and gothic works the author seems to separate in himself the desire for form—waylaid by such devices as the frame or the first-person narration—and the desire to explore those aspects of human nature that resist all the forms that literary tradition can furnish. Each of these novels is in some way an experiment with the novel, that form that announces itself to be without precedent, and in each the author strives to let the subject create the form, as the inner self creates the character by which one is known to the world.

It is therefore no explanation at all to call the gothic or the sentimental novel a "sport" or a kind of popular fiction, in which the more complex surface of "serious" fiction has been replaced by a thin-skinned orchestration of emotions and sensationalisms. The eighteenth-century novel in general, and the sentimental novel in particular, offer an answer to an argument about literary language and literary form that is expressed in the works of Pope and Swift. Tone is a crucial indicator: the general feeling of hope one gets from even Pope's most bitter poems (like *The Epilogue to the Satires*) and the despair that never leaves Swift. Pope's poetry allies itself with the fully meaning language of the past, or, in *Arbuthnot,* the family of the great poets of previous generations, with whom Pope can identify, o'erleaping his own degenerate times. In *To Augustus* Pope is confident enough to redefine the poet as a potential intermediary between public and private life, able to bring, in the manner of the domestic epic of *Paradise Lost,* the standards of private morality and insight, if not quite patience and heroic martyrdom, to a bankrupt political society. Pope seems to believe that there is still a possibility of renovating society, or at least that such a possibility is still a viable poetic theme. Despite the attack in the *Dunciad* against nonsense and no-meaning, the attack is carried on in poetry, whose form and meaning are created by Pope to combat the chaos outside. Pope may be embattled, but poetry and poetic form are still alive and vital, and the continuity of good poetry and good poets reaching into the past gives Pope heart and form for his fight. For Swift, however, any attempt to revitalize the role of the writer is a dead end. The possibility of good writing tends to be only implicit in Swift's work, when it exists at all; much more of his creative energy is poured into the miming of bad writing. In the same way, the only ideal of a stable society in Swift's work must be deduced by opposition to the partial and degenerate forms he does show us. Pope can confidently create Pope the poet because he believes that the type of the poet is a potential model to stabilize the slipping world around him. But Swift creates no positive character, only a series of grotesque maskings. Writing itself is basically a masquerade for Swift, not an enhancing masquerade, but one that feeds on all the worst potentials in himself and others, inextricably bound with and qualifying whatever elusive shreds exist of the best.

The basic difference between Pope and Swift flows from the fact that one wrote poetry and the other wrote prose. I am not minimizing Swift's poetry, but merely implying that it follows the same dictates as his prose, showing little if any interest in creating a "consistent" personal voice, considering himself and the rest of the world to be objects equally available for savage and impersonal description. Because he is a poet, Pope considers the relationship between form and content to be a much more settled issue than does Swift. "Settled" does not mean concluded, only that the parameters of possible relationship are less questioned than stylishly varied. Imitative form for Pope, in the manner of *An Essay on Criticism,* for example, is obviously the act of a virtuoso, enforcing an even tighter connection between sound and sense, or sight and significance. But imitative form in Swift—the hiatuses in the "manuscript" of *The Battle of the Books,* the incessant prefatory material to *A Tale of a Tub,* the maps and made-up language in *Gulliver's Travels*—has the primary purpose of authenticating the work through its incompleteness, its extension into a more complete world outside the literary text. Swift uses fraud and imitation on the largest scale, not in the small-scale technical tricks of Pope, but in the determination of the form of work by the psychology of its narrator and by an imitation of fragmentation and unfinished form that for Swift often parallels the psychic disintegration of his main characters. Whatever Pope's preoccupation in his later poetry with the "uncreating word," he seeks essentially to reestablish tradition with new vitality and content. But Swift transmits to the eighteenth-century novel the definition of prose evolved through Dante, Rabelais, Montaigne, Cervantes, and Descartes: a self-sufficient work, uncaused by, even though it may refer to, a preexisting past or tradition, and making its claims upon the reader by the sincerity, directness, and informality of its presentation. This is the tradition of the nontraditional work—and to it Swift adds his own obsession with the immanent destruction of language itself. Pope never expresses the same fears about basic nonmeaning—words don't work—that Swift does; for Pope there are mainly bad practitioners. But Swift believes the fault may be inherent in language itself, and his work is the first clear contradiction of Hobbes's idea that both language and society can be rationally clarified and ordered. Swift implies that any attempt to clarify only leads us even further into the trap. In the *Dunciad,* footnotes mock the pedants and then bring us back to an enriched poem. But footnotes in *A Tale of a Tub* become just another part of the never-ending work of misled interpretation, as we take our place with William Wooton, Sir Walter Scott, Louis Landa, and all the annotators who follow in their tracks. Pope uses the poetic form to express and by implication solve the doubts about language, self, and culture that are contained in his works. Swift uses prose to imitate the problems, but he is less interested in solving them than in ferociously lamenting their existence. In Pope the reader is allied with the poet against the forces of darkness: in Swift he is trapped with the rest of the blind.[1]

In *A Tale of a Tub* Swift attempts to convince us of the emptiness of one person's story when it is not told against a background of timeless value. In contrast, Defoe launches *Robinson Crusoe* and the eighteenth-century novel by asserting the importance of one person's story, whatever the objective or traditional truth to it. Swift perceives the evil and inadequacy of partial meaning; Defoe asserts the possibilities and energy of partial meaning and what is unsaid. *Robinson Crusoe* (as *Serious Reflections of Robinson Crusoe* makes clear) is still in thrall to the Bunyanesque need to justify one's story by saying it is everyone's story. But in effect *Robinson Crusoe* is also in flight from preexisting forms, whether the spiritual autobiographies against which it plays, or the providential order it invokes in analogy to Crusoe's creation of his world and work. Through its many prefaces, *A Tale of a Tub* embodies the fear of starting to write, the blankness of forced creation. But Defoe in his first-person novels tries again and again to recapture the energy of writing for the first time and searching for a form that can best explain your life to yourself and to others. Like Godwin in *Caleb Williams,* Defoe creates narrators who bring themselves out of isolation by telling their own stories in print, with a conviction and a form they could never achieve in person. Bunyan apologizes for his allegorical form, but Crusoe makes no apologies. He himself is form enough, and the individual shape he gives his story is more relevant than any eternal scheme. The early use of the journal in *Crusoe* is quickly dispensed with; even the meditations on providence become less important for their truth than for Crusoe's preoccupation with them. Bunyan completes his form with the arrival in Heaven, and Christiana's journey is only another version of her husband's. But Swift in *A Tale of a Tub* never ends, nor does Gulliver, feverishly writing prefaces even after his journey is over. And Crusoe too must have that strange experience with the bears while crossing the Pyrenees with Friday (not to mention the *Further Adventures*), because the final judge of form is the teller's sense of where to end, rather than the achievement of any end validated by philosophy, theology, or literary tradition.

In Defoe's first-person novels, the identification of self and work is clear enough. But the self-consciousness of writing a book also runs through *Clarissa* as well. As much as Moll Flanders, Roxana, or Colonel Jacque, Clarissa writes to justify herself, to present a living testament, in written, but not literary, form, for future generations. At the end she would rather no men saw her dead body or her living book; since the book is a direct expression of the self, it should be able to replace the self. Like Defoe, Richardson is fascinated by the ability of prose to explore new states of mind that he believes are inaccessible to the traditional means of poetry, epic, and drama. Like Swift, Richardson experiments with imitative form. After the rape, for example, Clarissa sends a group of letters to Anna Howe. Letter X is written in an especially distraught frame of mind, and the distraction is shown in two ways, by the effort to write melancholic poetry about her state, and by the scattering of sentences about the page, skewed in the margins. From such tentative seeds spring Sterne's more elaborate formal disruptions in *Tristram Shandy;* and both are efforts to create a fictional form that grows out of, instead of being imposed upon, what it contains. Defoe and Richardson and Fielding all treat the novel as a place where they can spend enough time to present contemporary human nature without the undue pressure of past ways of looking at people. Their methods are various: Defoe's inconclusive endings, Richardson's elaborations and refinements of feeling, Fielding's mockery of the reader's claims to certain judgment. But all in some way treat the page as a vision of the mind that creates it, whether author, narrator, or character, and all tend to consider the earlier forms of art an unnatural order from which they must escape.

The novel thus develops in response to the need to create a valuable and relevant fiction in the face of fears about the degeneracy of language and the chaos of traditional institutions. It does not totally reject all tradition, but always retains some for backdrop, because the novel—like the sentiment and emotion it so often contains—is always in danger of becoming excessive. It keeps its momentary but constant poise by slim hawsers to the familiar, and it enhances its themes by never allowing its readers to be totally sure about its essential commitments. Defoe, Richardson, and Fielding trust language in a way that Swift does not, first, because they do not care as deeply about the authority of the past, and second, because their own search for the best way to tell a story leads them to consider the uncertainties of language to be a breeding ground for fruitful ambiguities rather than Swift's all-absorbing bog.

Any discussion of the form and language of the eighteenth-century novel must finally come to *Tristram Shandy*. I have argued that Defoe and Richardson do not worry about words in the way Swift does. But the problem of words bulks as largely in Sterne's works as it does in Swift's—yet with almost reverse significance. One could even say that *Tristram Shandy* formally demonstrates exactly the opposite attitude to language and literary composition illustrated by *A Tale of a Tub*. What was terror to Swift—the slippage and incoherence of language without a spiritual center—becomes for Sterne a source of energy and exuberance. Digressions, instead of being both "modern" diversions from the simple truth and the literary evidence of a diseased psyche, are actually the lifeblood of literature, the marks of a truly creative imagination. The progression from *A Tale of a Tub* to *Tristram Shandy* is the progression from a writer trapped by subjectivity to a writer freed by it. Because Sterne places the self prior to the work, he can then explore the possibilities of seemingly uncontrolled literary form. Words, he implies, exist as expressions of the self at a particular moment in time; they cannot be used as counters for any external truth about the universe or human character because they can never be totally separated from the sensibility of the person who uses them. The best end of writing therefore is to develop a total awareness of the problems of writing, the lies brought about by either an excessive commitment to the sufficiency of words or an excessive belief in their inability to achieve true meaning. Swift's narrators are always flirting with potential insanity, their logic and clarity having carried them to look over the edge of rational experience. But Sterne flirts more vitally with the possible chaos at the verge of no-meaning. At one point Moll Flanders briefly considers getting into a coach with someone she has just robbed to pretend to help catch the thief. Like her, Sterne seeks a source of creative energy, for life or literature, in standing as close as possible to the brink. By Sterne's time clinical insanity has become for many a mark of sincerity, undistorted by the forms of public character. Swift's fear of madness, turned inside out, becomes the benevolent trips to the madhouses in *The Man of Feeling* and the attempt to use madness as subject matter in the poems of Cowper and Smart. Unlike Swift, Sterne makes digressions—the inability to control form— and puns—the inability to control meaning—into potentials that the writer must pursue for his health, rather than indicators of a linguistic and psychological chaos before which melancholia is the only appropriate response.

In general, the sentimental novel opposes intuition to rationality; disjuncture, episode, and effusion to continuity and plot; artlessness and sincerity to art and literary calculation; and emotional to verbal communication. Instead of being a foolish or perverse attack on literature itself, the exploitation of fragmented or incomplete form in the sentimental novel parallels the experiments of poets such as Collins and Chatterton, while its emphasis on the interaction between the work and the process of creation derives as well from some clear characteristics of the earlier eighteenth-century novel. These characteristics did not always have center stage. Even though *Clarissa* takes its form from an assemblage of points of view rather than the refilling of a preexistent form, Richardson is still involved in the problem of telling a complete story. At one level he wants the reader to be sure how all the characters wind up, even while at another his novel announces a new standard of completeness through its insistence upon Clarissa's ability to create herself through writing. In *Tristram Shandy* Sterne makes Defoe's structural in-conclusiveness a virtue: the self conditions the form of the fiction rather than the other way around. Fielding's careful coordination of *Tom Jones* implies, I have argued elsewhere, that the form of the novel is imposed by its narrator, who draws on other forms only to the extent that they are useful to his self-created fiction. In *Amelia* Fielding withdraws his narrator even further and, like Defoe, allows many of his characters to tell long stories about themselves. Sterne in *Tristram Shandy* answers that stories can never be completed, except as constellations of relation-ships, reconciliations of digression and progression, of conscious artist and unself-conscious experiencer, through the medium of imaginative form. The coherence exists between the storyteller's eye and the reader's sympathy—perhaps one rea-son why Sterne rarely uses metaphors.

When the effort to go beyond limit becomes a limit in itself, and the attack on the rigidities of an older form of self-consciousness leads to new orthodoxies, the writer may become trapped in paradoxes of his own making. The experimentation with incomplete form in many sentimental novels often extends on the level of plot to a refusal of sexual consummation, which is treated as a literalization of completion and the end of ideals and aspirations. Neither words nor bodies must limit the sentimental writer. All he aspires to must never be achieved, or it would be lost forever. No one in the Shandy family was "well-hung," remarks Tristram about the threatening window-sash; and the Yorick of *A Sentimental Journey* is a tease who refuses consummation at every point, especially after strenuously court-ing its possibility. Yorick is the prurient equivalent of Mackenzie's Harley or the philosophic Rasselas—all shying away, personally and literarily, from the loom-ing threat of an ending, for the essence of the form that gives them life is its tentativeness and its groping response to the nuances of feeling, rather than any embrace of the general truths of self or universe.[2]

The antiliterary pose of the sentimental novel is therefore neither naïve nor hypocritical nor some elaborate game designed to gull the reader. It is an essential part of the attack the novel in general makes in the name of private experience against the traditional modes of literary style and artistic self-importance. The older forms, no matter how well they had been used, seemed to the novelists of the eighteenth century to be insufficient to deal with themes of psychology and character that were more interesting to them and much more pressing. The difficulties of dealing with such themes may be observed in the varying attitudes of Pope and Swift. But the future really lay in developing a kind of narrative that could preserve both formal elasticity and a constant relation between what was being told and the act of telling. Pope tries to disentangle himself from the "trust the Muse" pose of *Rape of the Lock,* but is finally too willing to distance his material in the interests of creating a poetic self; Swift, in *A Tale of a Tub* at least, too completely submerges himself in what he most fears.

Thus the early eighteenth-century novel reflects much of pre-Romantic poetry in its efforts to free literature from traditional literary methods by showing that new problems might have new forms created for them. The unfinished form, the focus on the emotions, the emphasis on the immediacy of creation, and the shift of interest from work to writer—all are developments of the first self-definitions sketched in the novels of Defoe, Richardson, and Fielding, and the new way of looking at people they brought into English literature. The "serious" eighteenth-century novel holds within it the sentimental novel's typical assertion of antiliterary values. The separation of literary values from the knowledge of literary tradition presages the celebration of the primitive, the sublimely ineffable, and the inarticulate.

The true heir of the eighteenth-century novel, and its sentimental and gothic offspring, is not the nineteenth-century English novel but that great stepchild—the American novel. Jane Austen brings the novel into society in a way that the eighteenth-century novelists—even Smollett—were never interested in pursuing. *Emma,* for example, is as preoccupied with the weakness and insubstantiality of words as *Tristram Shandy.* But Jane Austen's fascination with social forms and the intricacies of their repressions moves her to encapsulate these themes within an ordered and symmetric form—perhaps another reason to read the marriage of Emma and Knightley with as much irony as possible. Jane Austen's detached narrative voice reveals to us an enclosed world, filled with the terror of the outside, self-willed and self-defined in its choice of the safe and understandable limits of boredom and familiarity. In the literary dialectic, holding at a distance has once again become a formal virtue and a source of insight. But the form vindicated by imagination rather than by tradition or control has already developed a tradition of its own, until, in the throes ourselves of facing new psychic and emotional changes, we try to analyze its appeal and discover its power once again.

[1973]

Notes

1. An interesting emblematic difference between Pope and Swift is their attitude toward Dryden. Pope considers him the great poet of the last age, a type of the literary man who can be material for Pope's self-definition, another link in the line stretching back to Spenser, Chaucer, Vergil, and ultimately, Homer. But Swift sees Dryden as just another trimmer, the man who said Swift's poetry was

no good—in short, a mere individual like himself, no part of a living tradition that has any worth or any potential to revitalize the present.

2. Since *Fanny Hill* attacks "unnatural" sexual behavior at the same time that it employs a high-flown rhetoric to describe sexuality, it too is sentimental in the sense I have described. In fact, Cleland's novel shares many other characteristics with later sentimental novels, except the value they place on nonconsummation, an extension of the commitment to open form that Cleland seems not to have anticipated.

Edward Gibbon and
"The Privilege of Fiction"

"The bards and the monks," says Gibbon, in the course of discussing the origins of the Scots, are "two orders of men who equally abused the privilege of fiction" (*Decline and Fall*, III, xxv, 42).[1] An eye for abuse implies a standard of use. But most of the critical commentary on Gibbon's great work assumes that his own willingness to indulge this "privilege" was rare indeed. David Jordan, who has astutely traced Gibbon's debts to previous antiquarians and historians, insists (therefore?) that Gibbon "made a rigid distinction between fact and fiction."[2] And Paul Fussell reflects many other readers and critics of the *Decline and Fall* when he places Gibbon with Swift, Pope, Johnson, Reynolds, and Burke in "the rhetorical world of Augustan humanism," where "ethics and expression are closely allied" and "man's relation to literature and art is primarily moral and only secondarily aesthetic"—assumptions that would seem to rule out any indulgence in the subjectivity and personal patterning that "fiction" usually implies.[3]

Yet Gibbon's remark that Voltaire had no narrative art indicates that his view of fiction was at least more hospitable than that of the author of *A Tale of a Tub* (the only on Fussell's list who spent some time perpetrating prose fictions).[4] In what follows I would like to explore how Gibbon's themes, methods, and even his conception of himself as a historian are conditioned less by the philosophe style of Bayle, Montesquieu, and Voltaire, or the methods of previous antiquarians, or the ethical assumptions of "Augustan humanism," than by a tradition of English fiction fascinated by the relation between "facts" and the patterns in which they find meaning. I have already pressed a version of this point in *Narrative Form in History and Fiction*.[5] But here I would like to emphasize even more the English side of Gibbon's literary genealogy, in those novelists attempting to mediate the conflicting demands of the providential and the social intepretations of history. With the *Decline and Fall*, I shall argue, Gibbon takes a central

This essay is adapted from a lecture given on the occasion of the bicentennial of the publication of the first volumes of *The Decline and Fall of the Roman Empire*, University of Wisconsin, Milwaukee, 1976.

place in eighteenth-century experiments with the uses of fiction and fiction-making in creating an interpretive and imaginative format for prose.

The lines of development, however, are gradual. Explicit statements of Gibbon's hostility to fiction are usually cited from the earlier sections of the *Decline and Fall*. In this way David Jordan's acute comments on what I would prefer to call Gibbon's *early* uneasiness with fiction are supported by references culled exclusively from the first half of the *Decline and Fall*, while Fussell's enlightening documentation of Gibbon's use of traditional humanist tropes and motifs derives from the *Memoirs* and chapters 1–16 of the *Decline and Fall*, with hardly a foray beyond. The area of quotation is in fact crucial, for Gibbon is the only member of Fussell's jolly crew to have written a truly long work, in which the demands of polemic and its armory of rhetorical weapons must give way to the gradually unfolding and the unforeseen discoveries of narrative itself. In the composition of the *Decline and Fall* Gibbon moves away from those often-cited moments in which he chastises past historians—even his favorite, Ammianus Marcellinus—for letting their style distort their facts. As he becomes more assured of his own ability to shape his mass of materials, fiction rejected as emotional or rhetorical distortion gives way to fiction accepted as narrative enhancement and personal perspective. So too Gibbon's growing imaginative security allows him to separate himself and his work from the traditional humanist topoi—corruption, luxury, fanaticism, the uniformity of human nature, and even the image of decline and fall itself—to respond more directly to the situations and individuals he discovers in the enormous body of information he has available to him.

In essence, Gibbon the orator, with his collection of set humanist themes and postures, has turned into Gibbon the narrator, with his delicate sense of time and its often arbitrary connections: "the order of time, and the division of chapters."

The early hostility to the distortions of fiction has engendered an inner revaluation of the appropriate uses of fiction; the criticism of the metaphors of others has established a style in itself, akin to an English plain style, not the fustian of a pleading lawyer but the clarity and personal involvement of a genial judge. Pleading and narrating are contrasted in Gibbon's work from the beginning, the distinction between them foreshadowed as early as the *Essai sur l'Étude de la Littérature* and the *Observations on the Sixth Book of the Aeneid*. But whatever the theoretical self-consciousness of a writer, traditional modes of narration die hard: repetition and variation come easier than invention or discovery, especially when one is faced with so much to digest and array. It would be some time further along in the writing of the *Decline and Fall* before Gibbon could himself absorb and implement his observations on the time of Valens:

> The simple circumstantial narrative (did such a narrative exist) of the ruin of a single town, of the misfortunes of a single family, might exhibit an interesting and instructive picture of human manners; but the tedious repetition of vague and declamatory complaints would fatigue the attention of the most patient reader. The same censure may be applied, though not perhaps in an equal degree, to the profane and the ecclesiastical writers of this unhappy period; that their minds were flamed by popular and religious animosity; and that the true size and colour of every object is falsified by the exaggeration of their corrupt eloquence. (III, xxvi, 116)

The image likens language to painting. But while painting conveys a personal and artistic truth, the distortions worked by language in the service of polemic undermine the testimony of sense and experience. Rhetorical persuasion invoked the specters of Gibbon's youth, when the doctrine of transubstantiation beckoned him out of the Protestant fold and into Catholicism. In retrospect Gibbon considered arguments for transubstantiation a double jeopardy, in which language was bent to persuade the faithful that matter itself had changed character. His reconversion then sets the stage for his subsequent decision that language cannot change the nature of things, although it might explain or create the relations between them. So in his *Memoirs* he juxtaposes his observation that it seemed "incredible" that he ever "believed in transubstantiation" with an attack on Bossuet's *Exposition of the Catholic Doctrine:* "a specious apology [in which] the orator assumes, with consummate art, the tone of candour and simplicity; and the ten-horned monster is transformed, at his magic touch, into the milk-white hind, who must be loved as soon as she is seen."[6]

If rhetoric is bad, how can fiction be good? Already by the beginning of the seventeenth century, the pejorative view that fiction was equivalent to deception was beginning to shade into the possibility that fiction might also be a feigning, an article of faith, or a belief with which one need not agree, but that for the occasion one was willing to entertain. Bacon uses the word this way in *The Advancement of Learning*. This newer meaning of fiction, in which moral judgment is for the moment suspended, emphasizes the root sense of *making,* fiction in its association with art, and, embryonically (the particular usage unfixed until the late eighteenth century), fiction as a separate literary form—the prose narrative. Yet all seems potential already in 1607, when a character in Beaumont and Fletcher's *Knight of the Burning Pestle* remarks " 'Tis a pretty fiction, i'Faith."[7]

Gibbon uses the word fiction in a typically mixed way, and his methods for separating fiction from history invite further distinctions. He is always on the lookout to discern some glint of historical ore in even the darkest fable, and he chastises Voltaire for being too quick to dismiss popular myths (VII, lxv, 60, n. 53). Gibbon's sensitivity to his own audience requires him to pay attention to such stories, while his critical and euhemerist method supplies the tools to refine their meaning. The line between the fictional and the factual is never absolute, especially when a greater writer is treating the materials of the past. Euripides, for example, in *Iphigenia in Aulis* has created scenes that "serve to represent a historical truth" by "embellishing with exquisite art the tales of antiquity" (I, x, 322). The impulse to create fictions is itself a historical detail that can lead to further insight, especially when the subject is not an event but an individual. The story that Majorian disguised himself to visit the Vandal Genseric in Carthage "is a fiction which would not have been imagined, unless in the life of a hero" (IV, xxxvi, 22–23), while in hagiography we find "the fiction, without the genius, of poetry" (IV, xxxvii, 75).

Quotations like these to one side, however, Gibbon's statements about fiction in the first three volumes of the *Decline and Fall* tend to emphasize how the storytelling of the past has impeded the truth-seeking of the present. As I have argued before, the gap of time between those volumes of the *Decline and Fall* published in 1776 and 1781 and those published in 1788 marks a striking change in Gibbon's sense of both himself (as historian and public figure) and of his audience. At the end of the third volume he wondered whether his audience would ask him to continue his work. The success of these early volumes gave him his answer. The "suffrage of antiquity' may have preserved the best works of the ancients, but it is the suffrage of the present that has approved the work of Gibbon himself, thereby allowing him a freedom of narrative and interpretive control only hinted at before. Two sides of this new relation to his audience deserve comment. I shall speak of its commercial aspects in a moment, but first I should like to examine how it changes Gibbon's conception of fiction.

If I had to specify only one influence on the new freedom with which Gibbon extends his own shaping ability and therefore the new favor with which he views fiction, I would point to Thomas Warton's *History of English Poetry* (1774–81), with its innovative discovery of the roots of poetic truth in the romances of the middle ages. First referred to in the notes to chapter 38 (IV, xxxviii, 152, n. 148), Warton's *History*, along with his earlier work, *Observations on the Faerie Queene of Spenser* (1754), both appear in Keynes's catalogue of Gibbon's library. "Fiction" in the sense of "a fiction" may be a modern usage, sanctified primarily by literary criticism. But Warton's appreciation for romance and fable may also have connected in Gibbon's mind with a related usage familiar to him at least as far back as his 1765 study of Blackstone, a usage that the OED traces back to 1590, the enabling and utilitarian fiction marked by the phrase "fiction of law."

The first three books of the *Decline and Fall* remain ambivalent about the place of romance and fable in a work of history. But by the fourth volume Gibbon seems to have regained the courage of his earlier views, like those, for example, in *Observations on the Sixth Book of Vergil's Aeneid*, where he says that "it is in the interest of every man of taste to acquiesce in THEIR POETICAL FICTIONS."[8] Urged by his distaste for the rhetoric of his sources, Gibbon in the early volumes of the *Decline and Fall* puts aside this positive view of "poetical fictions" in order to pursue problems of causality and "objective" analysis. But with public acceptance of him as "the historian of the Roman empire" he is freer to applaud "the sportive play of fancy and learning" (VII, lxvi, 130, n. 120) and to appreciate history as authentic romance.

Unlike Samuel Johnson, but much like Henry Fielding and other novelists, Gibbon could accept fiction as a mode of interpretive coherence superior to religious explanation, because it maintained a constant interplay with the phenomena it set out to contain and a constant willingness to let is own shape be modified by them. His mockery of Christian sectarians and schismatics subsides when he considers the religion of Mohammed. Islam, he says, is "compounded of an eternal truth, and a necessary fiction. THAT THERE IS ONLY ONE GOD, AND THAT MAHOMET IS THE APOSTLE OF GOD" (V, 1, 337), while "the Koran is a glorious testimony to the unity of God" (V, 1, 339). By obvious analogy, the *Decline and Fall* itself has become a testimony to the coherence of Gibbon's view of the past. In the later chapters he invites the reader to move back and forth through its pages, to check observations against each other, to refresh his memory, to expand his understanding of a particular point, and even to observe Gibbon correcting himself.[9] Fiction, Gibbon has discovered, is not a lie or deception but a mode or organization inherent in the act of writing a book. As the history of the eighteenth-century novel demonstrates, this discovery of the power and flexibility of fiction follows directly from the rejection of providential order. Many commentators on Gibbon have supposed that his refusal to adopt the explanatory models of Christian history necessitated a search for secondary, "scientific" causes. That may partly suffice as a way of understanding how Gibbon explains events. But how those otherwise separate events and personalities fit into an ongoing past called *The Decline and Fall of the Roman Empire* rests on Gibbon's new awareness of the possibilities of interweaving narrative order with historical fact, his willingness to replace one fiction with many.

Throughout the first three volumes of the *Decline and Fall*, Gibbon aims to abridge a multitude of events into "a clear and unbroken thread of narration" (I, x, 237), because the repetition of similar incidents would only "serve to oppress the memory and perplex the attention of the reader" (I, x, 254). But Gibbon's solicitude for the reader is inspired not only by an overwhelming quantity of historical material. As the later volumes make clear, the uniformities of the interpretive patterns of classical historiography can also oppress the historian as much as do the certitudes of the Christian view of history: "the impatience of the reader would be exhausted by the repetition of the same hostilities, undertaken without cause, prosecuted without glory, and terminated without effect" (V, xlvi, 39). Some new pattern must be created that can mediate causality and variety. Both humanist and Christian assumptions about historical pattern must give way to the search for an order that is both more humane and more explanatory, allowing the past its special nature as well as its relevance to the present. In the later *Decline and Fall*, as Gibbon moves away from the moral imperatives of enlightenment historiography and closer to the individualist perspective of the Romantics, "singular" and "particular" become favorite words.

Gibbon's study of Blackstone and his admiration for Hume might have suggested the growth of law as a model of historical coherence unwarped by the deductive pressures of religious or moral system: "The laws of a nation form the most instructive portion of its history" (IV, xliv, 492).[10] But, unlike earlier historians, Gibbon adds to the imagery of legal accretion the figure of the magistrate, who properly administers the legacy of the past, just as the historian's personal voice properly collects and arrays the materials of his narrative. What Gibbon says of Justinian's faults may therefore be a clue to how Gibbon defined his own ideals: "Instead of a statue cast in a simple mould by the hand of an artist, the works of Justinian represent a tessellated pavement of antique and costly, but too often incoherent materials" (IV, xliv, 463). Whether or not one agrees with Gibbon's preference for Republican sculpture over Imperial mosaic, the point of his image is clear enough, especially since he refers to "materials," the same word he uses to describe what he has mined from Tillemont, Muratori, and so many others to create his own work, not as rearrangement but as recasting. So in the course of the *Decline and Fall* Gibbon's master may be less Thucydides than Herodotus, his goal less an interpretive pattern than a plenitude constantly mediated by the demands of historical material and personal interest: "Nor will this scope of narrative, the riches and variety of these materials, be incompatible with the unity of design and composition" (V, xlviii, 171).

"This historian of the Roman empire" brings Thucydides into concert with Herodotus, absorbs plot into story, domesticates eternal pattern by individual voice, and abandons linear causality for an ever-branching system of association. Historians who try to place Gibbon in the history of historiography, like Owen Chadwick, therefore oversimplify when they argue that Gibbon's great innovation is his abandoning of annalistic arrangement for thematic: "this advanced perception of continuity" that "replaced the shackle of time with the freedom of theme." [11] But theme, which may conceptually organize much of Gibbon's material in the first half of the *Decline and Fall*, has by the second half become a shackle itself, a species of humanist topic-making that Gibbon increasingly ignores to make his own way through his text, discovering a shape as he goes along. In the first half of the *Decline and Fall*, we might say, thematic choices imply narrative shape; in the second half, narrative choice shapes themes.

"We sometimes detect a Romance by the easy, though wonderful annihilation of time and space," notes Gibbon in his marginalia to Herodotus, and the later volumes of the *Decline and Fall* are characterized by a mastery of time and space reminiscent of the free and easy sweep of Fielding's narrative voice in *Joseph Andrews* and *Tom Jones*.[12] But Gibbon's new willingness to experiment with his growing text is also presided over by two oddly but appropriately assorted forerunners: Vergil and Samuel Richardson. In what Sheffield titles "An Enquiry, whether a Catalogue of the Armies sent into the Field is an essential Part of an Epic Poem," Gibbon points out that Vergil had a general outline for his poem, whose specifics he worked out along the way: "Cette méthode de travailler n'a-t-elle pas ses avantages? On a donné des applaudissements à celle de Richardson, qui n'en est que l'imitation." [13] Such a style, says Gibbon, has more *vérité* and *hardiesse* than the preplanned. It also demands an admixture of personal nature that plot and other forms of deductive order usually rule out. Once again we have come upon the explicit importance for Gibbon of the personal element in his style and the force with which it shapes his historical themes and his narrative forms. But how is this personal element defined? It is surely more complex than merely an increasing number of first person singulars, which Gibbon in the *Vindication* called "the vainest and most disgusting of pronouns." [14] Yet it also avoids the other extreme of magisterial generalization, by which a writer like Samuel Johnson makes his escape from the "disgusting" first person. Gibbon may frequently join the ranks of those English authors like Milton and Hobbes and even Johnson, who distrust oratory because it does not distinguish between pleas for party and pleas for truth. But this distrust in his work is conjoined not with a desire to deny or to obscure authorship but to assert it. "Bigot" and "prejudice" are ambivalent terms for Gibbon. They do not necessarily imply a hermetic and partisan point of view; they may in fact also refer to an admirable personal energy. In order therefore to offer some precedent for Gibbon's developing method and thereby to place it within a history of modes of fictional narration, I briefly turn to another narrative of an individual trying to make sense and order to history—Daniel Defoe's *A Journal of the Plague Year*.

❑ ❑ ❑

I am not particularly interested in arguing that there is a direct influence of Defoe's work on Gibbon's, although a copy of it, under the title "The History of the Great Plague of London" (1754 edition) was in Gibbon's library, as well as such other works by Defoe as *The Four Years Voyage of Capt. George Roberts* (1726), *The History of the Union between England and Scotland* (1786), and *The History of the Wars of Charles XII of Sweden* (1720) on the more historical side; and *Captain Carleton* (1743), *The Memoirs of a Cavalier* (1784), and *Robinson Crusoe* (1785) on the more fictional. It is intriguing both that Gibbon turns to Defoe's first great work of pseudoautobiographical fiction in the period after he has written the first three volumes of the *Decline and Fall,* and that Defoe's two great works with a woman for narrator—*Moll Flanders* and *Roxana*—make no appearance in Geoffrey Keynes's researches into Gibbon's library.[15] In any case, I shall use *A Journal of the Plague Year* as a forerunner rather than an influence, exploring Defoe's effort and perhaps even his instructive failure to achieve what Gibbon did later in the *Decline and Fall*.

H.F., the narrator of *A Journal of the Plague Year,* tells us at the start that he has been chosen by God to stay behind in London during the plague of 1665 in order to be a witness both to the material nature of the plague and to the moral and religious lesson it is meant to teach. To reveal that lesson more clearly, H.F. promises to collect details, facts, anecdotes, make observations, verify stories and rumours, and generally establish a solid circumstantial basis for what we are quickly assured is the essentially providential nature of the plague, which has been sent by God to scourge the English for their immorality.

Thus H.F.'s declared literary and interpretive program. But he soon runs into two particular difficulties that forestall any expectations we may have had of reading a coherent and thoroughly explanatory narrative. The first is an issue Gibbon will polemically banish from the very onset of his own writing: the problematic relation of divine and natural causes. But H.F. is ideologically committed to a belief in their interplay and, as *A Journal* goes on, he finds himself more and more unable to bring together the secondary causes he has made it his duty to observe and the primary causes he believes it is his duty to affirm. Instead of being a material expression of the invisible causes of events, the facts—his description of the plague, its physical symptoms, and its social ramifications—become a variegated diversion from the simplicity of providential causality. He discovers, for example, that others use the same facts to justify totally different explanations, while many with providential beliefs similar to his own come up with quite different factual and practical conclusions. The providential pattern and the material facts no longer seem innately allied, and in the struggle between them it is H.F.'s providential premediations that first begin to weaken.

H.F.'s second difficulty may be the reason for his first. In his effort to be a pure witness and erect a factual superstructure on a providential foundation, he tries to become totally objective. But even so distanced, he must continually deal

with his own erupting point of view. At one point he tells of some blaspheming
drunks at a tavern who cursed him for his providential fulminations against them
and later died of the plague. Was he enraged at them, he wonders, because they
cursed God or because they cursed him? Along with such explicit questions H.F.
also implicitly reveals much of his personal nature. Why, we wonder, although
he does not, is he always drawn to stories of suffocation and enclosure, refusing,
for example, to help close down the plague houses (even while he approves of
those who do) and arguing against the practice of quarantine (even while he recognizes its effectiveness)?

Because H.F. has tried to obliterate himself in order to assert the greater glory
of God through his analysis of a historical event, he never develops either a mediating point of view or a more than wobbling commitment to objectivity. All he
rescues from his experience is more uncertainty about his beliefs and, of course,
his own skin. The immorality of the court of Charles II that supposedly brought
on the plague (along with other evidences of corruption) returns after the plague
disappears with hardly the cast of shame in its face, let alone disease, since the
court sat out the plague in Oxford. In fact, it is more often the God-fearing Lon-
doners who die, the extreme determinists, the Turkish predestinarians, as H.F.
calls them, whose belief in Providence makes them passive. H.F. begins the book
by describing the Biblical sortilege that directed him to stay. He concludes by
admitting that the best advice he could give after his experience is to tell everyone
to leave immediately. His preliminary decision in favor of passivity and stasis
therefore has evolved in a conclusion that prefers action and movement. His early
dedication to being an exemplary witness of God's will now has been transformed
into a moral diffidence, so that he wants to avoid the impression of "preaching a
sermon instead of writing a history—making myself a teacher instead of giving
my observations of things." [16] In a sense, all he is sure about is his own existence,
in that double sense of *character* so favored by Defoe, Richardson, and many
other eighteenth-century novelists—the characters of written language that shape
the character of being. For all his effort to efface himself before either the awe-
someness of providence or the materiality of facts, this is how H.F. ends his
account:

> I can go no farther here. I should be counted censorious, and perhaps unjust, if I
> should enter into the unpleasing work of reflecting, whatever cause there was for it,
> upon the unthankfulness and return of all manner of wickedness among us, which I
> was so much an eye-witness of myself. I shall conclude the account of this calamitous
> year therefore with a coarse but sincere stanza of my own, which I placed at the end
> of my ordinary memorandums the same year they were written:—
>
> > A dreadful plague in London was
> >   In the year sixty-five,
> > Which swept an hundred thousand souls
> >   Away; yet I alive!   H.F. [17]

"So much an eye-witness of myself" is H.F. that his effort to mediate the city
of God with the city of man can be ended only with the "coarse but sincere"

doggerel that presents him not as historian or theological moralist or even as autobiographer, but as *a writer living in his work*. If Gibbon's self-creation as "the historian of the Roman empire" is the standard, H.F. might be called protoself-conscious, struggling towards a synthesis of personal witness and historical pattern that he never quite achieves.

A Journal of the Plague Year is published in 1722. As I have argued in *Narrative Form*, by the time Gibbon embarks on the *Decline and Fall*, he can also take advantage of the experiments of Hume, Voltaire, and Robertson in historical narrative and Fielding and Richardson in fictional narrative. But the enabling perception that allows him to step beyond his predecessors occurs only after he has written almost the entire first half of the *Decline and Fall*. In the first three volumes, although, unlike H.F., he has refused to consider the operations of primary causes, Gibbon's narrative of the relation of national vice and national ruin is clearly reminiscent of the sectarian theology of *A Journal of the Plague Year*, even when he attacks its excesses.[18] In the later volumes his growing appreciation for his own narrative control and his own shaping fictions becomes a stronger influence on his thematic preoccupations and even his moral perspective. In the 1776 and 1781 volumes, for example, Gibbon favours absolute monarchy and hereditary succession as forces of political stability, while he scorns the tainting ambition of the lower-class person who rises to political power. But later he begins to value more highly the ruler who has come from a private position for combining in his nature both private and public virtue: "He who is born to the purple is seldom worthy to reign; but the elevation of a private man, of a peasant, perhaps, or a slave, affords a good presumption of his courage and capacity" (IV, lii, 539). Although Oliver Cromwell may be the most recent example available to Gibbon, and, while Theodora, Leo the Isaurian, Olga, Tancred, Tamerlane, and Cola di Rienzi share the characteristics, the most prominent such hero in the later *Decline and Fall* is Mohammed: "the base and plebeian origin is an unskillful calumny of the Christians, who exalt instead of degrading the merit of their adversary" (IV, l, 336).[19] Like Gibbon himself, these figures have risen above the circumstances of their background, transmuting their original private prejudices and passions into the public good and demonstrating, as Gibbon demonstrates in the *Decline and Fall*, the ability of mind to reshape individual background and even personal nature. That human nature which, according to the humanists and perhaps the early Gibbon, was uniform and categorizable has now become celebrated for its protean adaptability.

Synthesis, transmutation, reconciliation, reshaping: whatever the usefulness of any of these words to describe what Gibbon accomplishes in the *Decline and Fall*, none carries with it the vitally provisional quality of *fiction*. As the entrepreneur of a coherence that mediates abstract history and individual perspective, Gibbon places himself in the position of Adam Smith's laissez-faire God who invisibly reconciles all the individual wills of the free market economy. But instead of evolving into greater and greater purity and invisibility, Gibbon both experiments more freely with personal reference and becomes more sympathetic to the virtues of personal energy. Like Samuel Johnson, Gibbon was fully aware of the need to write not just to contribute to literature but also to make a living. But whereas

Johnson created "Dr. Johnson," who magisterially hovered above the Sam Johnson who said that only blockheads wrote except for money, Gibbon becomes more
and more sensitive both to himself and to his audience as determinants of his craft
and co-conspirators of his artistry. Therefore when I speak of Gibbon's awareness
of himself as the creator of the *Decline and Fall* and his invitation to the reader
to appreciate the shaping hand that has brought about its most important moments,
I do not mean to cast Gibbon as a writer whose work is about writing. Such self-
involved aesthetic "purity" is far from the impure and inconclusive contemplation
that the *Decline and Fall* becomes. Gibbon values his self-consciousness about
both his subject matter and his way of presenting it because such self-consciousness is useful, a cue to action and entertainment, a satisfying demand for the
suffrage of the present. In an age of empiricism Gibbon and Johnson represent
different solutions to the problem of literary and moral authority. For all Johnson's
praise of biography, he sublimes his earthly nature from his works to create the
image of pure mind. To a certain extent Gibbon imitates the Johnsonian method
in the first volumes of the *Decline and Fall*. But in the later volumes Johnson's
pedagogical condescension gives way to the playful authority of a Fielding. Perhaps Johnson's death in 1784 has some part in the change. As his *Memoirs* and
Autobiography show, Gibbon was always very susceptible to the influence of moralizing father figures and his few brief appearances in Boswell's *Life of Johnson*
highlight his nervous peripherality to Johnson's circle. It is certainly true that his
references to Johnson in the 1788 volumes of the *Decline and Fall* are invariably
sour and often caustic. I have argued that Gibbon's appraisal of the character of
Mohammed leads him to a more complex mode of characterization, in which an
assumption of the uniformity of human nature has given way to an appreciation
of the different roles Mohammed had to play and a refusal to reconcile or flatten
them out into a "consistent" historical portrait. Appropriately enough, in an account of the First Crusade a few chapters later, Gibbon makes some of his most
positive remarks about romance and heroism, footnoting his appreciation of the
sincerity of the crusader belief that the Holy Land should be liberated with an
interesting double reference:

> If the reader will turn to the first scene of the First Part of Henry IV., he will see in
> the text of Shakespeare the natural feelings of enthusiasm; and in the notes of Dr.
> Johnson the workings of a bigoted though vigorous mind, greedy of every pretence to
> hate and persecute those who dissent from his creed.[20]   (VI, lviii, 266, n. 21)

In concert with Gibbon's growing interest in defining a narrative voice characterized by its appreciation of variety and complexity rather than by its disembodied and magisterial purity, he becomes attuned to new thematic rhythms in his
materials. A defence of the absolute or hereditary right of the monarch, for example, gives way to a sensitivity to the monarch's personal virtues and how they
fulfil or change, adequately or not, the inherited form. So the more flexible causalities of fiction begin to undermine the deductive morality of humanist historiography. So too Gibbon places his own construction on the central literary questions
of the eighteenth century: how do we discover what we know? what literary shapes

best express what we know to others? and—most important—how do those shapes create the conditions for the knowing itself? In writing the first chapters of the *Decline and Fall* Gibbon discovers a rhythm that can express a private sensibility going public. But it is only in the second half of his great work that he capitalizes on the freedom of his own style. The success of the 1776 and 1781 volumes of the *Decline and Fall* gave Gibbon the security to present himself more individually in the later volumes. By both purchasing and appreciating the fictions Gibbon either invented or discovered, his audience allowed him to create an authority for himself beyond the validation of humanist historiographical tradition. In contrast with the humanist view of public luxury and corruption heroically condemned by the historian's private purity and innocence, Gibbon moves toward a mercantile view of history and civil society that reflects his own new perception of himself as an author sensitive to the legitimate interests of his audience. The classical theme of corruption, and even of the "Fall" of Rome, must therefore mutate into a series of distinctions between worthy comfort and unworthy excess, at least in part because *corruption* had long since become an antimercantile codeword. Commerce, Gibbon argues in the 1788 volumes, is a motive for action that performs the admirable social function of spreading cultural advance, and, in the *Vindication,* his definition of himself as a writer summons up the imagery of industrial capitalism:

> If my readers are satisfied with the form, the colours, the new arrangement which I have given to the labours of my predecessors, they may perhaps consider me not a contemptible thief, but as an honest and industrious manufacturer, who has fairly procured the raw materials, and worked them with a laudable degree of skill and success.[21]

This is not the voice of humanist abstraction but of a writer who recognizes that while a book may aspire to the heights of speculation and philosophy, it is still also a *product* that is delivered not *ex cathedra* but as part of a "transaction" (Gibbon, like Hume, uses the word often) between an author and his public. It may have been a corrupt or at least unmindful society that chose to import silk from the East rather than the art of printing: "I am not insensible of the benefits of elegant luxury; yet I reflect with some pain that, if the importers of silk had introduced the art of printing, already practised by the Chinese, the comedies of Menander and the entire decads of Livy would have been perpetuated in the editions of the sixth century" (IV, xl, 234). Money, like commerce, creates a larger context for cultural activity and helps fashion meaning from otherwise isolated objects and persons:

> The value of money has been settled by general consent to express our wants and our property, as letters were invented to express our ideas; and both these institutions, by giving more active energy to the powers and passions of human nature, have contributed to multiply the objects they were designed to represent.[22]   (I, ix, 220)

Our ideas of the Enlightenment are generally received from the practitioners of the history of ideas, who tend to value fiction only for its ability to parrot or reflect the explicit themes of nonfiction. The polemical intent, therefore, of what I argue above emphasizes instead how ideas work through fictions and are changed by the methods of expression, connection, and authorial self-presentation, even in such seemingly "nonfictional" works as the *Decline and Fall*. The official Enlightenment defined by the historians of ideas is being increasingly challenged by the dark Enlightenment of eighteenth-century fiction. But perhaps, if we do not make the cleavage so extreme and search out modes of integration rather than of separation and self-sufficiency, we will learn more about the links and resemblances between, for example, the fictions Gibbon mines for truths, and the truths he can best express through fictions. In this way the attack against Christianity is not "a serious structural weakness of the *Decline and Fall*" but a necessary clearing of the ground in preparation for the literary–historical (rather than Christian–historical) narrative to follow.[23] As Gibbon writes, "In the connexion of the church and state I have considered the former as subservient only and relative to the latter: a salutary maxim, if in fact, as well as in narrative, it had ever been held sacred" (V, xlix, 244).

In the narrative metamorphoses of the *Decline and Fall* the absorption of Christian narrative into humanist narrative is only a first step, as humanist narrative is itself superseded in its turn. If Gibbon emerges from his labors with any unblemished virtues still to celebrate, that virtue may reflect another preoccupation of eighteenth-century English fiction—domesticity. Domesticity is the midpoint, the mediation between public and private virtue. It makes its appearance in the *Decline and Fall* not just in Gibbon's remarks on specific individuals but even more significantly in his growing interest in the history of a family as the appropriate nexus for a general historical study. In the last volume this implicit dissension from the moral themes of the humanist orators is fulfilled by the "Digression on the Courtenays" and by the extended remarks on the Colonnas and the Orsinis. After the *Decline and Fall* Gibbon pursues this new interest with "The Antiquities of the House of Brunswick" and a proposed volume dealing with illustrious English men and women from Henry VIII to the present: "the most eminent persons in arts and arms, in Church and State . . . a rich display of human nature and domestic history."[24] With domesticity to ameliorate the ravages of individual nature, Gibbon can accept the importance of biography, his own and that of others, and designate family as a personal order of emotional and social connection through history. Like many of the eighteenth-century novelists, he also seems to envisage domesticity as both a protection from the public violence of history from without and the frenzy of rampant individuality from within—again a third term.

With Gibbon's complex view of the importance of personal nature in mind, it therefore grieves me to read attacks on his manners, his self-importance, his clothes, his eating habits, and his sexuality—attacks in which his critics show so much less sense than he of the interplay between man and writer. I would rather see Gibbon, as I have described his work, as equally committed to the personal and to the general, to the Epicurean and to the Stoic. Literature for Gibbon was preeminently a social act, and Sheffield's personal estimate of him may serve as a literary estimate as well:

Perhaps no man ever divided time more fairly between literary labour and social enjoyment; and hence, probably, he derived his peculiar excellence of making his very
extensive knowledge contribute, in the highest degree, to the use or pleasure of those
with whom he conversed. . . . He united, in the happiest manner imaginable, two
characters which are not often found in the same person, the profound scholar and the
peculiarly agreeable companion.[25]

Gibbon would no doubt have appreciated this estimate of him, with its deliberate
echoes of his own view of Julian the Apostate, who "solicited, with equal ardor,
the esteem of the wise, and the applause of the multitude" (II, xxiv, 480). What
influence the contemplation of Julian and other complex heroes had on the historian of the Roman empire I cannot say. But it would suit the Gibbon I have
described if the literary expression of such traits was intimately connected to their
personal development. May we ourselves be so amiable, and our own studies so
replenished by our private and domestic lives.

[1980]

Notes

1. All references to the *Decline and Fall* are to the J. B. Bury edition, 7 vols. (London: Methuen,
1902–9).

2. *Gibbon and His Roman Empire* (Urbana: University of Illinois Press, 1971), p. 110.

3. *The Rhetorical World of Augustan Humanism* (Oxford: Clarendon Press, 1965), pp. 7, 9.

4. *Gibbon's Journal to January 28, 1763. My Journal, I, II, III and Ephemerides*, ed. D. M. Low
(New York: Norton, 1929), p. 129.

5. Leo Braudy, *Narrative Form in History and Fiction* (Princeton: Princeton University Press,
1970), pp. 213–71.

6. *Memoirs of My Life*, ed. Georges A. Bonnard (London: Nelson, 1966), p. 47.

7. *The Dramatic Works in the Beaumont and Fletcher Canon*, ed. Fredson Bowers (Cambridge:
Cambridge University Press, 1966), I, 86. (Act V, line 313). *The Knights of the Burning Pestle* is
rife with jokes, both simple and sophisticated, about the collision of a literal-minded audience with
highly artificial theatrical conventions.

8. *The English Essays of Edward Gibbon*, ed. Patricia B. Craddock (Oxford: Clarendon Press,
1972), p. 150.

9. Compare, for example, the practice of Richardson in the later editions of *Clarissa*, where he
asks the reader to make similar excursions into the text to underline the "truth" of his negative view
of Lovelace's character.

10. See also *Narrative Form*, pp. 66–75; J. G. A. Pocock, *The Ancient Constitution and the Feudal
Law* (New York: Norton, 1967); Edward Gibbon, "Abstract of *Commentaries on the Laws of England
Book the 1rst* by William Blackstone," in *English Essays*, pp. 59–87.

11. "Gibbon and the Church Historians," *Daedalus*, 105 (Summer 1976), pp. 117, 118.

12. "Marginalia in Herodotus," in *English Essays*, p. 367. Patricia Craddock dates these notes to
1789–90.

13. "A Collection of his Remarks, and Detached Pieces, on Different Subjects," in *Miscellaneous
Works of Edward Gibbon, Esquire*, ed. John, Lord Sheffield (Dublin, 1796), 3:78.

14. "A Vindication of Some Passages in the Fifteenth and Sixteenth Chapters of the History of the
Decline and Fall of the Roman Empire" (1779), in *English Essays*, p. 235.

15. *The Library of Edward Gibbon* (London: Jonathan Cape, 1940).

16. *A Journal of the Plague Year,* ed. Anthony Burgess and Christopher Bristow (Harmondsworth: Penguin, 1966), p. 255.

17. *A Journal of the Plague Year,* p. 256.

18. See especially *Decline and Fall,* III, xliii, 639–41, for Gibbon's account of the tremors and plague during the reign of Justinian.

19. Gibbon's generally positive remarks about Cromwell in the 1788 volumes may further specify his awareness of the lesson of the English civil wars that history could be successfully engaged by the private and unanointed hero. See, for example, *Decline and Fall,* IV, 1, 397; V, lxx, 509, n. 29; and 534.

20. Compare Gibbon's sneer at the lack of psychological realism in Johnson's play *Irene* (*Decline and Fall,* V, lxviii, 435, n. 53). For a further comparison of the critical methods of Gibbon and Johnson, see my review of Craddock's *English Essays of Edward Gibbon* in *Studies in Burke and his Time,* 17 (1976), 59–61.

21. "Vindication," in *English Essays,* p. 277.

22. Among many such sentiments, compare also Gibbon's remarks to Sheffield, who had protested the sale of his library: "I am a friend to the circulation of property of every kind, and besides the pecuniary advantages of my poor heirs, I consider a public sale as the most laudable method of disposing of it" (Keynes, *Library,* p. 26). Make what you will of the fact that most of the library was bought by Gibbon's unfriendly neighbour, William Beckford, the author of the gothic oriental romance *Vathek* and a great denouncer of what he considered to be the pomposity of Gibbon's learning.

23. This is Arnaldo Momigliano's formulation of a commonplace in the criticism of Gibbon by historians. See his contribution to the Summer 1976 *Daedalus* issue on Gibbon, "Gibbon from an Italian Point of View," p. 130.

24. *The Letters of Edward Gibbon,* ed. J. E. Norton (London: Cassell, 1956), 3:312.

25. "Lord Sheffield's Continuation of the Memoirs," *The Memoirs of the Life of Edward Gibbon,* ed. George Birkbeck Hill (New York: G. P. Putnam's Sons, 1900), p. 250.

■

Mad in Pursuit
*Visits to Bedlam: Madness and Literature
in the Eighteenth Century,*
by Max Byrd.

*Nightmares and Hobbyhorses: Swift, Sterne, and
Augustan Ideas of Madness,* by Michael V. DePorte.

Increasingly in the eighteenth century, feeling and reason traveled separate and
skewed roads, the one hidden in the dark forests of solitude, the other striding the
heroic turnpike road to progress and social prosperity. Like most revolutionary
changes in the definition of human nature, the new imperatives of eighteenth-
century scientific empiricism and social organization offered many rewards. Physical processes and social institutions might be observed and corrected with clarity
and efficiency. The mechanical model of knowledge might purge or at least control both the diseases in the body and the disruptions in the state.

But the separation within the self necessary to create the good scientist and the
good citizen was a separation between subject and object, observer and material,
individual and society, that directly affected the eighteenth-century attitude toward
mind in general. If what I observe is separate from me, what in me affects and
what in me does not affect my vision? If I observe myself, is that a separation
within myself? The Platonic continuum between the physical and the spiritual had
fully given way to an Aristotelian and Cartesian division and categorization of the
kinds of identity—physical, mental, and spiritual. Since the brain was physical, it
could be subject to physical ills, and thereby have its search for a truth beyond
the individual disrupted by physical causes. Or, in another formulation, if reason
were the highest goal of man, then madness or an insufficient social and personal
commitment to the goal of reason argued the presence of a diseased and culpable
will.

The desire to compartmentalize and to specialize the self for social harmony
and individual success contributed to the growth of a belief in the fatality of
feelings, the uncontrollable waves of potential frenzy and madness that threatened
the fragile structure of control. When madness is identified with the antisocial,
then the only reaction one can have to individuality may be despair. Traditional
psychoanalytic criticism hardly disputes the eighteenth-century view that society
knows better. As Max Byrd shows in his excellent and suggestive *Visits to Bed-*

lam, by the eighteenth century, madness had lost its association with insight and divine inspiration to become instead an emblem of the inability to get along in the new world. Confinement was not so much to treat the patient as to separate him from society and its benefits until he might cure himself, whether voluntarily or by punishment. The fruits of that attitude toward the self and society are still with us. Alexander Cruden remarked in 1739, in a prescient anticipation of Erving Goffman, "The way to be mad was to be sent to a Madhouse." As Locke had argued that the legal definition of identity was the most clear and workable, so the eighteenth century decided that to be in a madhouse, legally committed, was the badge of your madness.

But in the early years of mass industrial society, what Byrd calls "the struggle for social self-control" was not an easy matter, and the image of madness and the madman permeates the literature of the period. Until fairly recently, however, the English and American desire to forget the darknesses of the self has caused scholars and critics to concentrate primarily on the bright side of the Enlightenment, ignoring the wallflowers at the Festival of Reason to consider instead the sheet music for the dance. The antiaffective and antibiographical emphasis of the 1950s effectively squelched any inquiry into the varieties of feeling by asserting that, while intellect had many gradations, feeling was undifferentiated and took place behind double-locked doors. Like the beliefs of the eighteenth century itself, such a view considered the world of feeling to be a fatal place, unless, of course, the feelings were tied to literature. But the slightest inkling of despair or self-loathing would send Samuel Johnson to his prayers or his chains; the slightest step outside the garden gate insured Clarissa's ultimate death. Feelings were fatal; only intelligence could hold back, detached, observing, efficient, clear, and distinct.

In the last few years, with the ending of the cold war and the monolithic sense of self it encouraged, writers have turned to a closer exploration of the affective side of the eighteenth century, perhaps to learn the links between individual behavior and social expectations, and to understand the elements of personal desire and social control that contribute to the creation of what we call character. If the only choices are to avoid feeling totally or to indulge it totally, then there is little sense of the twilight between reason and feeling, or sanity and insanity.

One of the most prominent areas in this new exploration has been the study of madness, which received a special impetus from the publication in 1961 of Michel Foucault's *L'Histoire de la folie.* Foucault's main argument is that madness in seventeenth- and eighteenth-century Europe gradually replaced leprosy as the primary means of separating individuals into the socially useful and the socially unnecessary or threatening. Essentially following Durkheim's idea that a society is defined as much by what it excludes as by what it includes (itself an eighteenth-century distinction), Foucault collects a mass of materials about French attitudes and practices in the treatment of the mad, the founding of the first public asylums, and the gradual definition of a society founded on reason. (I might also mention here George Rosen's *Madness in Society: Chapters in the Historical Sociology of Mental Illness,* which begins with ancient Palestine, Greece, and Rome and contains much fascinating material, although, like Foucault's book, it spends little time on England.)

Foucault generalizes almost totally from the French experience and so his book can be easily faulted for its assertive sweep. (The shorter American edition is called *Madness and Civilization*.) Most important, he leaves out the special English attraction for the mad as objects of awe and insight, despite the social prohibitions. The label of "eccentric" is available to anyone in England who is dogged enough to carve out his right to his own mannerisms; in France it is generally a matter of class. (I gloss over the way those mannerisms may themselves be warped by the fight to assert them.) Foucault also tends to view the repression of madness through public policy as simply a means to keep idiosyncrasy out of the normal way of life and to spare the normal, conforming citizens unpleasant sights. But this view contrasts with the English and American inclination to create ambivalences: simultaneously to hide and to expose whatever is most disconcerting and upsetting— the election and fall of Richard Nixon being only the most recent example.

Max Byrd and Michael V. DePorte deal primarily with England in the eighteenth century. Their view of madness might be compared with Foucault's in the way Johnson's treatment of the problem of evil in *Rasselas* might be compared with Voltaire's in *Candide*. The Frenchman brings the reader through more horrific and disruptive experiences, a whole world in flames, but finally ends with calm philosophy, labor, and a portable moral. The Englishman seems calm all the way through, but his meditation, his abstraction, is always inconclusive, and his message, if there is one, is the irresolvable conflict between individual compassion and divine, fatalistic perspective.

Byrd's book and DePorte's book themselves form a kind of matched set. Byrd's tends toward the literary and meditative, while DePorte's is the more historical and factual. But Byrd's is obviously the superior work. Byrd concentrates on Pope, Swift, Johnson, Cowper, and Blake to trace what he calls the eighteenth-century assault on both the idea and the body of the extraordinary madman. Using *King Lear* as his touchstone, Byrd argues that the loss of the concept of holy madness succeeds in "taking away the sacramental element from all common vital acts of experience" and supports "the tenacious belief of the Augustan mind that the madman is basically hostile to the bourgeois order." Whatever hesitations Pope and Swift may have had about the new economic and political order, according to Byrd, they shared its basic distrust of subjectivity and subjectivity's most obvious efflorescence, madness: "Madness is a failing of the aristocracy and the poor; the middle class cannot accept it." Byrd associates this belief with Locke's distrust of private style and insight as a way to truth, and one of his main texts (as is DePorte's) is Swift's *A Tale of a Tub* with its excoriation founded in guilty knowledge of originality, subjectivity, and self—all the ills Swift considered typical of the modern age.

To his credit, Byrd is as interested in the despair as he is in the attack, and he discusses the difference between Pope's acceptance of the conclusion that madness is willful folly (in the Dunces) and Swift's emphasis on the role of human physicality, the natural tendency of the body to decay and madness. Around the mad, Pope arrays images of excrement and animality, poverty and stupidity, while Swift is preoccupied with the madness of thwarted and excessive sexuality, and his attack on the mad often appears coupled with his misogyny. Hysteria and hypo-chondria walk together in the eighteenth century, and Byrd points out that many writers in the early decades of the century worried that melancholy, "the English Malady," would create an England depopulated by suicide.

After a horrific description of the practices of Bedlam, Byrd carries his story into the emblematic figure of Samuel Johnson. So sensitive to his own tendency to madness and despondency and so intent on constructing a literary self that would help him control it, Johnson moved from the darkness of his room and his "black dog" (Johnson's phrase for his frequent depressions, appropriated by Winston Churchill to describe his own) into the clearer light of *The Rambler,* where such personal problems could become a variety of "intellectual malady." After John-son, Byrd considers Cowper and Blake as examples of the late eighteenth-century effort to turn toward subjectivity and madness as sources of inspiration and knowl-edge, an explicit attack on the Augustan demands for public order and clarity. But their interest in extreme states of feeling is not the same. Cowper hated his mad-ness, but used it as poetic subject matter, presenting himself as a weak, wounded figure to be pitied for his faults. Blake is more triumphant, embracing the charge of madness as a badge of honor, proclaiming the freedom of the mad and the enslavement of the rational.

Michael DePorte's book is somewhat more pedestrian than Max Byrd's, al-though it is more beautifully printed (Byrd should object violently to the bad typography of his book and the vague way the illustrations have been reproduced), and handsomely embellished by the author's own line drawings. But DePorte's book is finally not so much an effort to understand the place of madness in eighteenth-century culture as it is a large, well-organized collection of discursive references to madness in the period that attempts to focus its material by chapters on Swift and Sterne. However well handled the research might be, therefore, DePorte's book gives the impression of preliminaries rather than the thing itself. Byrd seems to have read many of the same background works, but he goes on to enlarge upon their meaning, while DePorte is intent on pinning down the elusive detail. DePorte emphasizes his scholarship in long footnotes and an extensive appended bibliography. But he falters when it comes to any sensitivity to what is being said in the literary works he discusses. Whatever the wide net of his read-ing, Swift and Sterne slip through its meshes, perhaps because his view of them is essentially reductive. DePorte seems out of imaginative sympathy with the pe-riod and its writers and he substitutes for his lack of connection a minute knowl-edge of the ideas and commonplaces of the age. He has some interesting remarks to make about Swift's efforts to keep the reader uncomfortable by upsetting his identification with Gulliver, and about the emblematic importance of Don Quixote in the eighteenth-century attitude toward madness (paralleling a similar discussion by Byrd about eighteenth-century attitudes toward King Lear). But DePorte's knowledge of ideas finally serves primarily to narrow his sense of literature. To say that "of course . . . Gulliver is not developed as a character in a novel; he is used as a rhetorical device," makes me wonder why the theme of madness was brought up at all. In the same way, I don't agree that *Tristram Shandy* shows "the final smallness of all things human," nor that an important part of Sterne's purpose is that he "wished to reveal the hollowness of conventional criteria for sanity." In his urge to discern clinical traits in the works of Swift and Sterne, DePorte, like the brothers in *A Tale of a Tub*, tailors the language of ambiguity to fit the specific demands of a moment's context. *Tristram Shandy* is neither a novelistic version of *The Vanity of Human Wishes* nor a clinician's textbook. DePorte has turned the history of ideas into mere chronology, a series of isolated moments of intelligence, bound together by words, categories, and verbal motifs, as if they were voices in a vacuum, or a psychology without people.

Byrd, more than DePorte, catches the feeling between people as well as the feeling within. He may distance himself from his material by a well-formed and often elegant style, but he allows the passion to come through, since the style finally is personal and the involvement is with authors and subjects as much as with ideas. DePorte distances through scholarship, and the result is less happy, both for his handling of literary texts and his understanding of why some writers (such as the many mechanistically oriented physicians) should have held such "naive" ideas. DePorte is conducting a study in sources, while Byrd is attempting to suggest the centrality of madness to the eighteenth-century vision of the individual in society. To make his case, I think Byrd exaggerates somewhat either end of the continuum. His Pope is a little too "urbane and self-possessed" for my taste, primarily because Byrd concentrates on *The Dunciad* which, like *The Essay on Man*, its more ambivalent brother, may show Pope at his most inhumane, so intent is he on establishing a cosmology that won't fall apart in his hands.

I also depart from Byrd's analysis when he claims that, in the fascination with melancholy and sublimity in the later eighteenth century, we see "the beginnings of the dissolution of the Augustan fear of madness, and the modern embracing of it." Perhaps in literature, and primarily in popular literature at that. But no matter what kinds of madness we may be willing to experience vicariously in fiction, poetry, or films, we are still personally afraid of madness and still tender about exposure of extremes or even of many gradations of feeling. By the end of the eighteenth century the separation of reason from madness, of aspiring mind from frail body and feelings, has become socially institutionalized, not only in the asylums but in cultural iconography as well. Just as Samuel Johnson showed how one could be depressed, consumed with an appalling collection of self-hatreds, and also a great critic, so the Romantics allowed madness into the socially acceptable realms, so long as you were a poet. Despite the early eighteenth-century images of a universal Bedlam, by the end of the century the belief that the individual was more crazy than the society has been fixed. Madness was still a deficiency and a blot on human nature (as in different ways were physicality and feeling), but if it were combined with certain talents, usually those of performance, in poetry or politics, it would be allowed. The rampaging but grand horse of madness and imagination in the *Phaedrus* had degenerated into the distracted and spavined hack of *A Tale of a Tub*, simultaneously tolerated and scorned.

So many of the older issues of literary criticism arose from personal interests, but wore the formal clothes of objective analysis. Now I think we should look for a realization of personal interest that allows the interpenetration of individual, work, idea, and age much more intricately than would yet another addition to our knowledge of detail or imagery. Michael DePorte's *Nightmares and Hobbyhorses* offers an awareness of an aspect of a vital problem the reader may have previously dismissed from his picture of the eighteenth century. Max Byrd's *Visits to Bedlam* allows us to speculate and expand beyond its reaches. DePorte excites only argument or agreement; Byrd inspires the reader to thought and feeling of his own.

[1975]

V

THE SWAY OF GENRE

Framing the Innocent Eye:
42nd Street and *Persona*

In the history of every art, there are moments when artists choose to comment either on their own form or on another art. Such comments invariably have a polemical purpose: to assert the superiority of one art to another, the container to the contained, the self-conscious to the unself-conscious. What cannot be included—what cannot be framed—is implicitly larger than the frame. What can be included is in some sense subordinate. If the containing art also focuses on the processes and assumptions of the art contained, it both reveals the art's inner workings and asserts its own larger perspective. A movie biography of a painter, for example, like *Moulin Rouge,* tells us more of Toulouse-Lautrec's craziness than of his art. On the other hand, if an art work contains some reference to its *own* processes, we are invited to see a new depth within that art as well as to separate the particular work from those others less conscious of their potential. To place an art within another art therefore creates an aesthetic perspective. As perspective in painting leads us into inner space, this aesthetic perspective leads us into history, supplying a depth in time to what might otherwise be only an individual work.

So long as Christian motifs determined the materials available for art, there was little need for such depth. But with the search for new subject matter that followed the secularization of painting, art could propose itself as its own subject, and the artist was ready to become a creator whose formal techniques were as worthy of dramatization and analysis as were the designs of God himself. Along with Renaissance painting appeared as well an increasing number of treatises about the science of painting (perspective, proportion, etc.), a fascination with the painter as a unique product of human nature, and a virtually evangelical belief that painting has a special insight to give into the heart of things. Such artistic self-consciousness asserts both the skill of the maker and the importance of the art form. By including false or distorted or diminished versions of itself, it implies its own greater truth. It only seems to question itself. In fact, it questions its precursors, in an effort to define art history not as an increasing mimetic progression but as a deepening formal awareness. The new self-consciousness, it implies, is better than old rhetoric, or the imitators to come.

The motif of art-within-art therefore in general signals a polemic assertion of an art's claim to reveal "reality." Whatever the details of the polemic, it also broadly invites its audience to savor the experience of one art above all others as an essential human activity. It highlights the crucial sensitivity of the artist (as opposed to the artisan) to necessities of form and the sophistication of technique. And it makes such sensitivity a prerequisite for true understanding. When art replaces or at least competes with religion for acolytes, then technical virtuosity and formal self-awareness signal the path to spiritual as well as human truth. Art-within-art wants to be paid attention to—as art. And its practitioners are like those magicians who perform the trick even while they reveal that it is a trick and the audience deliciously, and complicitously, fooled. Only then does the artist move beyond the mere magician by implying that trickery is *itself* something to be learned, and that awareness of the processes by which art achieves its magic can turn an audience of gulls into the wisest of the wise. Instead of transparently opening a window on another place, art-within-art thus creates a commerce between the work and a newly active audience that must be willing to discover ultimate value not so much in what the art work shows about the world as in the ways the world supplies material for the work. (Which is why academics and metaphysicians are especially drawn to art-within-art, eager to supply the explication it requests and eager to accept its assurance that explication is also an essential activity of the human spirit.)

But what does such formal self-consciousness have to do with the aspirations of art to create a heightened human image and sensitivity? It is a characteristic of the arts of human presence that perspective on the form is interwoven with perspective on the self. Looking into a painting may imply looking into the history and meaning of painting as well. But it also involves a look into the inner life of both its subject and potentially its creator. We may call art-within-art formally self-conscious and historically self-aware. But we can also read that self-consciousness and self-awareness as an aspect of the painter's character as well as the sitter's, the playwright's as well as the character's, the director's as well as the performer's. Thus, the self-consciousness that arises from art-within-art can be directed toward the medium and its possibilities as well as toward the ways (especially in the visual arts) one would and would not like to be seen. I think of many Renaissance paintings, for example, in which the hidden mind of the subject is externalized into the books and objects that surround him, while his inner nature, the self to which the painting has given us the more direct access, is in the depths of his eyes and the lines of his face. In other Renaissance works of the same period, the existence of an inner text validates the frame text and vice versa. Stories within stories, paintings within paintings, plays within plays—all assert that there are important distinctions to be made between levels of fictionality— and that those distinctions imply that artistic fiction itself is not the opposite of reality but a crucial version of it. That Antony and Cleopatra can imagine themselves being played by actors in some diminished future implies that they are more than mere actors in the eternal present of Shakespeare's play. In the second part of *Don Quixote* the Don and Sancho similarly affirm their own reality by vanquishing the false Don and the false Pancho who have emerged from Avellaneda's unauthorized continuation of the original.

A simple distinction here suggests itself. An art can appear in the midst of another art either as *contrast* (books in paintings, poems in novels, plays in movies) or as *doubling* (paintings hanging on the wall in paintings, tales told by characters within novels, people in movies going to the movies). Both involve framing—a stepping back, an establishment of perspective not on the world so much as on the way the work makes a world. But their implications are somewhat different. *Contrast* usually implies an artistic hierarchy. Whether to serve Pateresque sublimity, humanist pedagogy, modernist collage, or multimedia versatility, the contrast of art-within-art opens an argument about the relevance of artistic perception to action in the world. *Doubling,* on the other hand, more often turns inward, exploring art less as social event than as psychological revelation. As we shall see, the distinction is hardly absolute. But as a way of approaching similar moments in the history of an art form with equal respect for their formal qualities and their historical context, it is useful and, within measure, accurate.

❏ ❏ ❏

As the newest art, movies have available to them correspondingly more resources for commenting on themselves and on their relations to the other arts. Born from a ferment of reportage, magical transformations, and avant-garde self-regard, the movies quickly rushed out to absorb and include as much of the world as possible and then to make up more. But the recording of images of all kinds retained an air of encyclopedic inertia until the coming of sound.

I think it is difficult to overemphasize the distinction between silent film and sound film. Historically, critics and theoreticians have generally preferred silent film, the "purer," "more essential" form, and deplored the degenerate eclecticism of sound film. But I would like to argue instead for the superior self-consciousness, the greater perspective, and the new artistic depth that became possible with the advent of sound. Like perspective in painting, sound was a technical innovation with psychological and epistemological dimensions. Every such advance allows itself to be ignored as well as used. Once sound was possible, so was silence. Invisibility became the complement of what was so easily shown and seen. Sound thus allowed film to free its surface of unnecessary magical and illusionistic techniques because the sound track by its nature could itself imply a world unlimited by the visible, an invisible place from which visual forms might gain an inner energy. With sound, film could meditate directly on its own nature as well as compete more directly with other arts, which before had been either ignored or imitated.

It is therefore no accident that music and theater take a central role in the film that most memorably made the transition from silent to sound—*The Jazz Singer*—in which the story itself, with its passage from religion to theater, from tradition to innovation, echoed the evolution in technique. Of course all genre films—horror films, war films, science fiction films, even women-in-prison films—crucially evoke the question of artistic self-consciousness, because all call upon a history of previous films with which they share important characteristics and against which they define their own originality or fealty. (Which may help explain why, in *The Jazz Singer,* the son of a cantor makes his most notable stage appearance in blackface.)[1] Musicals, of all genre films, place that self-consciousness at the heart of their plots, themes, motifs, and characterizations because by definition they include music, dance, and, very often, the stage itself. Singing or dancing in musicals does not, of course, have to occur on stage. But, wherever it happens, it is still a performance, a setpiece that raises our sensitivity to the artistry of the rest of the film. If there is an audience within the film, they watch, they listen, and they may even join in, while the music bridges the gap between what is onstage and what is offstage—what is seen and what, for the moment, is unseen. Similarly, the sound track knits the audience outside the film to the performers within the film. Onstage, it is the frame of their professional energy. But when song and dance do not take place on a stage, they are perceived as projections of inner states. The music, the song, the dance tell us what they feel. When the same film contains songs and dances offstage and songs and dances onstage, a conflict between the public and private sides of a character's nature may be the theme. A musical about singing and dancing onstage is realistic, while a musical about singing and dancing offstage is an occasional poetry, in which the poetry must create the occasion as well as celebrate it. The frame of theater within film allows an unthreatening intensity; if the frame is broken, if the boundaries between the arts disappear, disruption and danger wait in the wings.

42nd Street, in which Busby Berkeley directed the dance sequences and Lloyd Bacon the offstage framing story, is an excellent example of what can occur in films when the methods of one art (the stage) are framed, included, and thereby commented upon. About thirty years later, Ingmar Bergman's *Persona* embodies another phase in film's artistic self-consciousness by its use of film fragments (as well as television and photographs) as crucial elements in its story. I juxtapose them in part to show how one seemingly more frivolous "entertainment" film and another seemingly more serious "art" film can share similar concerns about what makes film different from the other arts.

The beginning sequences of both films introduce the viewer to the way of seeing each film embodies. Both include montages of often very quickly juxtaposed images, and both are accompanied by an appropriate musical sound track. In *42nd Street* the rapid series of images evokes the excitement and energy of New York, especially the theater district. The rumor of the new play is flying across town: people report it to one another, telephone operators listen in and pass it on. It's one great buzz of communication, each shot leading to the next, with never a worry about the accuracy and value of the information conveyed or of the process that speeds it on its way. The early images of *Persona,* on the other hand, are enigmatic. They raise into awareness aspects of film presentation that we usually don't pay attention to (the countdown on the leader, the arc igniting in the projector), and they invoke the primitive history of film as well (cartoons upside down, a skeleton in the speeded-up style of silent films). Moving past our eyes with as much frenetic energy as the early images of *42nd Street,* the early images of *Persona* also make us aware of the way film can stop time and its fascination with images not of vitality but of violence and death. The music underlying *42nd Street* sweeps us jubilantly forward. The music of *Persona* has no melody; like the images themselves, it is a disturbing pastiche that leads to a cold silence into which the sound of a telephone intrudes. Everything that *42nd Street* exploits as its aesthetic due, *Persona* presents as a dubious legacy. In *42nd Street,* at the end of the sequence we share the voyeuristic point of view of a man who looks at a woman's legs reflected in a mirror. She is reading the *New Yorker,* with its traditional cover of the fop Eustache Tilley observing a butterfly through his monocle. The references to peeking and observation are gentle and mocking. In *Persona,* at the end of the sequence, a young boy wakes up, puts on his glasses, and begins reading Lermontov's *A Hero of Our Time.* Then he discovers the camera watching him. He peers into it and puts his hand on it. From behind him we see that he is looking at a gigantic, undulating image of a woman's face. Here then the references to observation and voyeurism are more disturbing, and we do not escape being looked at ourselves.

In general these two films illustrate the distinction I have made between contrast and doubling. In *42nd Street,* film asserts a perspective larger than that of theater in two principal ways. First, it unmasks the backstage life, the preparations and difficulties in putting on a show. This is Lloyd Bacon's part of the film. Then Busby Berkeley demonstrates the limits of theatrical space in comparison with that of film by penetrating and thereby expanding it with his plunging, pirouetting camera and his multidimensional staging. In fact, *42nd Street* was as much a historical propaganda piece for films as an aesthetic one. Warner Brothers, which had made a tremendous success with *The Jazz Singer* in 1927, was, like the rest of Hollywood, in the early Depression doldrums. Film attendance had slumped and the number of radios had gone way up. To drum up business, Warners sent a promotional train around the country, packed with stars, musicians, dancers, and lavish costumes and sets. *42nd Street* emerged almost directly from that tour. For audiences dissatisfied with silent films and static sound films, it would provide enough music and visual energy to capture both the radio stay-at-homes and the more affluent theatergoers, sweetening the lure immeasurably with a gossipy demystification of backstage life.

Theatrical art-within-art makes us think of the playwright; cinematic art-within-art makes us think of the director. When Hamlet instructs the players, he speaks with Shakespeare's professional awareness, if not his specific opinions (unless we are in the audience of the film *Hamlet,* when we may hear instead the voice of the actor–director Laurence Olivier). The story of *42nd Street* seems at first social: the group working together to create the show, the nuts and bolts of show business, the camaraderie of show people, the individual training and talent that goes into the public production numbers. But its larger story is the need for a supervising control that will bring out what is best in every individual.

Two later sequences from *42nd Street* and *Persona* indicate the central importance of the question of direction and authority to both films. In *42nd Street* the director, Julian Marsh (Warner Baxter), sits on a runway on a level with the stage but outside it, over the orchestra pit. Onstage the performers are walking through a production number, gossiping about personal matters. Then Peggy Sawyer (Ruby Keeler) leads a more energetic dancing sequence. Marsh is totally dissatisfied and exasperated, raging at the performers for their lack of professional polish and gloomily predicting that the show will never come together. But, by a repeated shot from above the stage, we are also reminded of the point of view from which the film will be coherent. In the sequence from *Persona* the theatrical separation of director from performers, the standing outside the proscenium, is presented in more domestic and psychological terms. Elisabet (Liv Ullmann) begins the sequence by taking a picture of the camera/the audience with a small camera of her own. Then she writes a letter, which she asks Alma the nurse (Bibi Andersson) to take to the post office. On the way, Alma reads the letter and discovers that in it Elisabet has told her husband about Alma's sexual experience on the beach. Alma feels used, an object of Elisabet's witty anecdote and condescending observation. She stands moodily beside a forest pool, her image reflected in the water. Returning to the house, she becomes a director, or at least a kind of set decorator, herself, vengefully leaving a shattered piece of glass where Elisabet can step on it. Both situations allude to the way the director endangers the performer by treating her as an object of manipulation. By looking at another, by interpreting another, Bergman implies, we all participate in the relation between director and performer. Intriguingly enough, we watch Alma from a distance, like a theater audience, and her action is framed by an almost proscenium-like arrangement of house and trees. As the sequence continues, Elisabet (off-camera) does cut her foot. Alma looks at her, she looks at Alma, and the film itself splits before our eyes, revealing again the fragments of primitive cinema, and concludes with a close-up of an eye. Elisabet appears, out of focus and in slow motion, until gradually the "normal" style of unself-conscious movie realism reasserts itself.

In their different ways, both films thus invite us to become aware of the processes of direction—the varieties of control both inside and outside their stories. Within *42nd Street* the director of the stage musical "Pretty Lady" is sentimentally presented as a dying man who ruthlessly and singlemindedly is creating a last grand effort, for which others—the flashy and public performers—will get the most credit. Peggy Sawyer might come out of the chorus to be a star, but it is Julian Marsh on whom the camera rests its final eye—the director who has brought the show into being, now disappearing into the shadows, sinking into death. This final emphasis on the fictional director, within the film but behind the scenes of the show, indicates the perspective *42nd Street* takes on the world of theater. The director outside *42nd Street*—and here I am talking about Busby Berkeley rather than about Lloyd Bacon—both relishes this martyr image and yet casts a God's eye of condescension on the stage director's limited materials. Working for precision and uniformity, putting people together from fragments and forming them into patterns, Berkeley announces the superior intensity of film to theater as a showcase for song and dance, as well as its superior ability to extend the power of song and dance into realms that theater could hardly hope to enter. The main story appears to be that of the overnight star, whose leap to fame embodies the chance that we will all someday be recognized for our talent and thereupon be invited into a world of harmony and self-realization that was previously closed. As the kid from the chorus, Ruby Keeler, with her endearing naiveté and awkwardness, allows an empathy that the more polished star she replaces (Bebe Daniels) resists. But, by including the theater within the film, and by making the story of the film the creation of the musical "Pretty Lady," *42nd Street* also points us away from the star and toward the show. The successful channeling of energy away from the chaos of rehearsal and private life and toward the higher reality of performance is accomplished entirely by the dying director, whose final indignity is to hear the star praised while he remains either insulted or anonymous.[2]

Outside the theater the stage director Marsh may collapse and die unappreciated. But Busby Berkeley is the film director as New Deal wizard, breaking the frames of the past and creating new patterns of people for a newly energized America. Viewed now, the film is strikingly wide-eyed and optimistic both about the way true talent shines through as well as about the communal harmony, the group solidarity, of the backstage world. Some years later (1949) Judy Garland left the filming of *Annie Get Your Gun* with emotional problems heavily contributed to by Berkeley (the director, later himself replaced). Berkeley had also been the fatherly force behind Garland's youthful films with Mickey Rooney. But now her fight was not to put on a show in the barn but to become an adult on her own. Thus the later conflicts between Berkeley and Garland flow easily from the darker potential of *42nd Street*'s story of a dying director and fledgling star. Bebe Daniels may magnanimously welcome Ruby Keeler as her replacement and assure her that "people want to like you." But Berkeley's swirling patterns and his costuming of the final chorus as multiple images of Keeler sound a note of muted aesthetic vengeance against the all-too-visible star by the all-too-invisible director.

The clear causality of *42nd Street,* the straightforward sureness of its plot, seems inseparable from its optimism about American progress in general. Film form had of course been an explicit concern of filmmakers since the early days, particularly pushed forward by French and Russian theoreticians after World War I. The questions they most often discussed attempted to discover the special nature of film reality in cutting and camera movement. Berkeley, in his professedly unselfconscious and empirical American way, nevertheless shares their exploration of the new aesthetic freedom made possible by film. But after World War II, another era of film self-consciousness had been reached, this time not in terms of formal causality and the special ways films tell stories but in terms of the significance of acting and performing.

Persona, thirty years and a World War after *42nd Street,* is much more uncertain about its ability to tell a story so simply and directly. Similarly, the nature of performance has become an issue and the relation between director and performer no longer so blithely assured. For a European, especially after the experience of Hitler, Mussolini, and Stalin, the question of aesthetic authority can hardly be so simple. Even though many of the preoccupations of the two films are similar, the self-confident Berkeley has been replaced by Bergman, the Kierkegaardian artist, plagued with doubt about his ability to supersede the past and create authoritatively and anew. "As a human being," Bergman once said, "I have made an enormous fiasco. Therefore I must become a good director." Many Bergman films focus on the self-deception of the artist who finds strength from controlling others and using them as material for his art. Berkeley's rampant director, like his swooping camera, has not a moment of self-doubt; he celebrates the freedom of movement that film allows, first sketching, then ignoring, the stage proscenium to tell us in what order its contents should be read. But when films (and television and photographs) appear in *Persona,* Bergman is signaling a relentless critique of the ways in which those arts of vision have influenced how we see ourselves and others. In such a critique the artist of the visible cannot stay blameless, for in creating his work he has destroyed something of the private identity of the real people who are his materials.

In *42nd Street* the people who seek the spotlight and bask in the audience's eye are rewarded with fame and success. They are characters and, we assume, performers, who seek the camera's/audience's gaze and glory in being observed. The camera realizes them, it justifies them. They grin at it cheerily, with an almost manic exuberance. Through the 1940s and into such postwar films as *Singin' in the Rain* and *All about Eve,* there is more uncertainty about the characters who like to be looked at, a friendly self-irony about the early days of film in *Singin' in the Rain,* a satiric bitterness about the infighting of postwar theater in *All about Eve.* In Anne Baxter's Eve, the eager amateurishness of a Ruby Keeler is reinterpreted as the mask for a vicious desire to get to the top by trampling every normal feeling in sight. Yet *All about Eve,* like *The Bad and the Beautiful* and other Hollywood mea culpas, implies that there are only a few bad eggs around. Most of the time it's like *The Band Wagon* or *Babes on Broadway,* with everyone pulling to put the show together. In *Persona,* on the other hand, the desire to be observed—to be seen in order to be—is hardly so benevolent or so easily rewarded. Elisabet the actress, whose career requires being looked at, goes mute during a performance of *Electra* in order to escape to some more secure inner world. She knows well that sight is power over the seen. Alma the nurse, trained to tend and serve, does not know, and so she is horrified to discover in Elizabet's letter that what she had thought was an intimate exchange has been turned into an amusing anecdote.[3]

In the last scenes of *42nd Street* we are finally allowed to see the three production numbers from the show that is being put together throughout the film. In a line of rising intensity, all three simultaneously flirt with and then aesthetically anesthetize sexuality and physical violence. In the first, "Shuffle Off to Buffalo," the audience of passengers on a sleeper train sing innuendos about a newly married couple. In the second, "I'm Young and Healthy," Dick Powell and (a silent) Toby Wing are the centerpiece of Berkeley's patterns of legs and bodies, viewed from overhead and resembling the giant, vaginal flowers of Georgia O'Keefe's paintings. In the final sequence, "42nd Street," we begin on stage with Ruby Keeler, then move to what seems like a real street scene in which there is stylized violence and even death. Meanwhile Dick Powell musingly sings about the action while he observes it from a window. The chorus appears, all dressed as Keeler, while she dances in front of them. Then, through a collage of cards they turn into the buildings of New York. The camera zooms to the top of the Empire State Building to focus on a grinning Powell and Keeler, who pull down an asbestos curtain over their final kiss. Outside the theater, we look down on the exiting audience commenting on the success of the show. The camera moves down to focus on Julian Marsh, the forgotten director, who listens, then walks into an alley and collapses.

Berkeley's camera in *42nd Street* is a kind of ideal self, letting us look into whatever public and private worlds we'd like. Bergman's camera in *Persona* is a more questioning, intrusive viewer, forcing us to look at some things we'd rather not. Its goals are finally more psychological than dramatic, telling us not what film can do better than theater but what film can do that theater cannot. When Alma tells the story of her sexual adventure on the beach, we see nothing but her talking and Elisabet listening. It is an intensely erotic sequence that explicitly avoids using most of the usual theatrical and visual resources of film—a sexual adventure told by a quiet-voiced woman sitting in a semidarkened room. Sexual dialogue in *42nd Street* is primarily composed of innuendo that goes nowhere, while in *Persona* it is a structure of implication that the viewer's own imagination must complete. In his elaborate visual patterns, Berkeley eroticizes the scene of his films, while Bergman through his dialogue reveals the inner erotic life of the teller.

In *42nd Street* film celebrates itself by including theater. In *Persona* film explicates and even criticizes itself by including film. Film-within-film in *Persona* turns us away from a social definition of the individual and toward an inner nature reflected by the film's aesthetic self-consciousness. Yet Bergman's problem is that film can invoke the invisible and inward only by the visible and external. Thus, his formal self-consciousness does not privilege his film over past films so much as it questions the way film shapes sight in general. The arts of vision and performance, Bergman implies, too easily package and trivialize anguish even as they convey it to us. The eye turns everything it sees into an object, whether it is the Vietnamese monk willfully setting himself ablaze on television to make a moral point or the young Jewish boy with hands raised being led away to a concentration camp. Such intense images invoke a human captivity and death that they also embody as objects of contemplation. But the danger is that the technology of vision only pretends to expand while it actually cuts us off from both intellectual and emotional understanding.

Self-awareness leads too easily to self-preoccupation. So the formal self-consciousness of *Persona* implies that the desire to be observed is by its nature suspect and the act of observation an assertion of power, whether the observer is the director who has actively put together the action or the audience who is passively receiving the action. Certainly the theme of voyeurism is an ancient one wrapped tightly around the roots of film. But I want to stress here its function in films that are explicitly about people *who make their living as performers*. *Persona* begins in the refusal to perform, in Elisabet's confusion about the relations between performance, images, and real life. Thus, in her hospital room, she is both fascinated and horrified by the spectacle of the monk immolating himself, serenely dying in a performance for the television cameras that is clearly linked to a moral principle. *42nd Street* assumes without question that messy life should be realized in perfect performance. No matter the fact that Dick Powell used to come over to Ginger Rogers's house during the filming to weep and complain to Rogers's mother that he was only making $75 a week. As far as the film is concerned, making it, getting to the top, is an uncomplicated goal. But in *Persona* each successful playing of a role plotted by someone else erodes the core of the performer's nature still further. With a horrified look in her eye, Elisabet on stage turns from one camera to look at another. Can she ever escape? Bergman must doubt it because after all his eye is always there. Perhaps all that she or we can do is shed levels of fiction endlessly. One can never escape the director because he cannot escape himself: his self-consciousness is a mirror of our own.

Film divides its audience's allegiance between the director who controls our eye and the performer who engages our feelings. Usually the director is an invisible shaping force. But once the presence of the medium has been asserted, we are invited to question the sufficiency and the meaning of that force, to reinterpret technical mastery as totalitarian control and to discover the psychological roots of aesthetic form. Too often, the psychological meaning of a work of art is derived entirely from its explicit plot and themes. But psychological exploration in film often takes the form not of an explicit analysis but of either a clear contrast with older, more limited, conventions of performance (as is often the case with genre films) or an invocation of the limits and liabilities of the cinematic eye on the world (as is often the case with "classic" films). In both methods, the transparency of the film, its request that we consider it a window, is darkened and disturbed. No longer can the director play an unruffled God. "I love the people but do not like to stage me to their eyes," says the Duke in *Measure for Measure,* Shakespeare's ambivalent attack on such behind-the-scenes power. Thus Bergman's preoccupation with his art does not assert its superiority to other arts so much as it questions its (and his own) authority. Descending to the plane of his characters, he is to be judged as well. Elisabet takes pictures of the camera (and of the audience?) with her camera. As an actress, she is constantly aware of its intrusive presence, and so tries to outstare and thereby master or at least become equal to it. Even as she recognizes its role in her own self-definition, she resents her dependence on it. Although by withholding her voice she has become even more totally a visible object, she makes its absence ring loudly. We are reminded of what we expect from a film and therefore we are reminded of film, and we may feel that odd aesthetic shiver that occurs whenever a character appears in an art that he cannot fulfill or appreciate: the blind in film or painting, the tongue-tied in drama, the illiterate in fiction, the uncoordinated in ballet, the tone-deaf in opera, to name only a few. In light of Elisabet's resistance, perhaps I should change the title of this essay to "There is no innocent eye in a film-framed world."

So far it seems that the cinematic paradox posed by *Persona*—escape from being an object by turning someone else into one—can be dissolved only by the good-faith gesture of criticizing (and thereby excusing) the nature of film itself. But a final element in the psychological ramifications of film aesthetics must be explored as well: the sexual roles that both the eye of the audience and the camera of the director play in the two films. In both the camera is primarily perceived as the vehicle of sexual power, welcomed for its attention in *42nd Street,* resisted in *Persona*. Specifically it is a voyeur, a penetrator, plunging into space from which we are usually barred, across the proscenium and between the legs of the dancers in *42nd Street,* through the eyes and into the private fears and desires in *Persona.* Of course such a camera must be called male, and the pressure of the eye in both films (I should say most films) is that of men looking at women. In *42nd Street* the eye belongs to a self-assured male, whose doppelganger within the film dies almost as a sacrifice to the greater visual appeal of women.[4] In *Persona* the eye belongs to an uncertain, self-questioning male who both indulges and attempts to undermine his power. Revealing the camera's methods, calling attention to its presence, allows Bergman both to qualify the camera's authority and feminize its aggressive and coercive patterning. The cinematic manipulation of emotion must give way to an insight into emotion, nowhere more acutely than in the climactic sequence when we first watch Alma telling Elisabet's story from Elisabet's point of view, then hear the story again, watching Elisabet from Alma's point of view— until at the end the two faces become one. The camera as accuser has merged with the camera as accused. Viewer has merged with viewed, and the audience's privilege of separation from the action has itself been called into doubt and criticized. Berkeley's camera, drunk on its own self-esteem, has evolved into Bergman's camera, by turns the assaulter and the assaulted.

In the contrast between *42nd Street* and *Persona,* we see first a film whose celebration of itself is inseparable from its celebration of human energy and enthusiasm, and then a film whose questioning of itself is inseparable from its exploration of human frailties and doubts. Too often the critical fascination with the framings and unframings of art obscures what *42nd Street* and *Persona,* in their different ways, indicate quite clearly; the invocation of the frame, the containing of one art by another or by itself, allows a more intense glimpse of those perennial themes— sex, violence, and death. Frames, like criticism, domesticate what they help us to discover. They protect us from disruption even while they teach us to cope with it. But although the act of interpretation pretends to solve the puzzle and dissolve the frame, the basic question still remains: do we map the labyrinth in order to find the Minotaur or to escape from it?

Audiences notoriously look to popular art for solace and entertainment, and art in general creates a series of moments in which we can experience the incompleteness and even the jaggedness of life not as inadequacy, disorder, or decay, but as a different kind of order. Those works that call the frame into question polemically emphasize the substitution of artistic order for the "normal" modes of political, social, religious, and psychological explanation. In *42nd Street* the love/ hate competition between film and theater yields a contrast between the tight world of the proscenium and the expansive grandeur of the film. In *Persona* it is expressed in the opposition between theatrical tyranny over the performer and cinematic empathy with her. As befits our more self-conscious times, *Persona* comes to a much less conclusive ending than does *42nd Street.* Yet both turn toward their audiences in their final moments, as if to acknowledge that pressure of audience presence that is always an integral part of art-within-art, the final term in its equation. At the end of *42nd Street* two audiences are distinguished: the unaware one that has seen "Pretty Lady" and applauded its star; the sophisticated one that has seen *42nd Street* and understands the importance of its director. At the end of *Persona* two audiences are again distinguished: Alma, who seems to have packed up Elisabet and absorbed her as she has packed up the island house and then herself is taken away by the bus; and ourselves, who realize that both Alma and Elisabet are images in a film that lives and moves only so long as the arc lamp is ignited.

Neither ending enables us to escape its film quite unscathed by the possibility of being found in the wrong audience. Both invite us to complete them by becoming better audiences the next time. Yet *42nd Street,* with its easy supersession of theater, retains a casual optimism that improvement is possible, just as its credits— "Ruby Keeler as Peggy Sawyer," "Warner Baxter as Julian Marsh"—assume an unproblematic equation of actor and role. In *Persona,* personal identity is hardly so casual or so simple. And we might well ask, at least in terms of *Persona* and films like it, whether there can be any real optimism in an art that contains and questions itself. Or is its glimpse into its own interior forever doomed to be caught between self-congratulation and self-loathing?[5]

Bergman evades such smarmy schizophrenia by simultaneously criticizing and exploring the connections between theater and life for which film is the bridge. To be a person, he implies, is to be a performer, and even out on a rocky beach far from the technology of cities, once there are two people, there is a show and an audience. The cleansing of the eye is therefore a never-ending task and one for which film is eminently qualified. The original title of *Persona* was *Kinematography,* and in it Bergman strives to validate his belief in film as an art by testing all its pretenses to be "real" and exposing all of its tricks. Berkeley breaks the proscenium but preserves the frame. Bergman pushes his story out to the beach, the edge of man's building against nature, and, not coincidentally, Bergman's own house. From the witty urban frames of *42nd Street,* we have come to the natural boundaries of *Persona.* Art-within-art in *42nd Street* is a polemic of film against theater. Art-within-art in *Persona* begins that way by calling attention to Elisabet's sense of personal inauthenticity onstage. But Bergman has no illusions that stages finally end. Like the interpolated tales in *Don Quixote* or the paintings and mirror in Velázquez's *Las Meninas,* the films within the film of *Persona* place the artist on equal footing with his subjects—equally strong, equally vulnerable. By revealing the processes of their arts, such works face their audiences more directly as well. Their exposure of artistic illusion marks not a despair over art but an assertion of its continuing human relevance, its willing self-criticism, and its determination to gain the imaginative consent of a free and newly aware audience.

[1983]

Notes

1. *The Jazz Singer* is in fact a melodramatized version of Jolson's own career, linking by its story some of his most popular songs and scattered bits of biography and gossip. Its form exemplifies the

close relation between musicals and show business biography that appears most recently in *Honeysuckle Rose* starring Willie Nelson and may go as far back as the fourteenth century, when compilers of the songs of the Troubadour poets sought to find in them a continuous life history.

2. That Ruby Keeler had become the wife of Al Jolson only a few years before *42nd Street* might generate some cynicism in the gossip-minded observer. On the other hand, since Jolson had married her out of the chorus of his own show, it could lend a note of reality to the sentiment. The recent Broadway revival of *42nd Street,* the death of its director Gower Champion on the day of its first performance, and the announcement of his death by producer David Merrick as the cheers for the show were dying down, compounds the ironies of Broadway self-consciousness beyond my ability to comment.

3. Bergman and Liv Ullmann had begun living together sometime before the making of *Persona,* and so the collusion of director and "actress" has a biographical component as well. For a very different way of thematically exploiting the emotional relation between director and actress, consider Godard's *Pierrot le Fou* (1966), starring his then-wife Anna Karina.

4. In its story about the opening of the play version of *42nd Street,* the *New York Times* noted that the woman who played the Keeler role was herself virtually picked out of nowhere by Gower Champion and had been his intimate companion for most of the rehearsals.

5. In light of recent backstage musical plays and films, I might rephrase this question as "does *42nd Street* plus *Persona* equal *All That Jazz?*" Bob Fosse, the director of *All That Jazz,* does let his alter-ego star, Roy Scheider, take a good deal of abuse in the film, including death. But he preserves the musical film tradition of letting Broadway ambition be an emotionally and aesthetically limiting business, even though there are a few perfunctory nods toward the danker swamps of Hollywood.

Genre and the
Resurrection of the Past

Anyone who watches television, goes to the movies, or listens to the radio is aware how much his or her sense of personal time is linked with those activities. We date our lives and loves, our depressions and elations, by the songs and stars that were popular when we passed through those moments. We map our own existence in time by those coordinates of a fantasy time that makes nonsense of any rigid division between public and private life. They tell us how history fits into us as much as how we fit into history. And when the stars die and the songs are no longer played, we feel their loss as a loss inside, to commemorate with nostalgia the way we used to be and in some crevice hope we still are.

But in the unending bombardment of words and images that is so characteristic of the present, there is also a disheveled uncertainty about which are truly valuable and permanent: what will last? what really tells us the most about ourselves, as individuals and as a nation? To try to get at this question, I want to talk about films as seemingly different as *Chariots of Fire* and *E.T.*, *Reds* and *Shoot the Moon, Pennies from Heaven* and *Poltergeist, Star Trek II* and *Gallipoli.* But two trends beyond the specifics of individual films have to be mentioned first: the way in which horror has become the dominant genre, even invading with its images and motifs films that are otherwise not "really" horror films; and the inclination of filmmakers to believe that nothing succeeds like sequels.

In both of these trends can be found what I have elsewhere called the pervasiveness of soap-opera sense of time in American life, in which stories never end; they only continue. After wars, assassinations, and a steady diet of the deaths and murders of the famous or the merely local, we know that there will be no apocalypse on television because the nature of the medium works against it. There is always another program, another season, another bridge of music, voice, and computer graphics to make the audience feel it is not alone in the void.

It would be safe to say that the present movie audience is the most formally sophisticated in history, and for that sophistication we must thank television. Many films have been made by directors who are highly educated in film history and therefore apt to pack each scene with layers of allusion, often in direct proportion to its thematic emptiness. But audiences make films as much as do filmmakers, and years of watching television have made them ready and eager for the current genre bombardment, in which past stories, images, and motifs of all sorts are repeated, revised, and revaluated in an endless reflection on a past that seems entirely made up of previous motion pictures. In the 1950s no horror film required that you had seen other horror films. If you had, you might have a more interesting time, but it wasn't necessary. Now, almost every film in every genre—horror, science fiction, musical—virtually insists that you be aware of previous films so that you can properly savor the nuances this one adds. The way a genre film invokes its own artistic tradition is always a variety of comfort. It can mingle several traditions at once (*Star Wars*); it can reveal what previous works have kept decorously hidden (*Body Heat*); or it can mockingly parody (*The Life of Brian*). But no matter how explosive its material, no matter how it ups the ante on sex, violence, and self-consciousness, the genre film inescapably dramatizes its commitment to a quest for clarity and understanding possible only through the contemplation of history.

The audience that appreciates genre films, remakes, and sequels is one that wants to be both shocked and knowing, to be in on the details of repetition and variation within the films as well as all the interviews, films about the films, and biographical material that surround it. Such an audience wants its awareness catered to and confirmed, for the irony generated by its knowledge of films is not savage or satiric but cozy. In the midst of the most extreme movie violence, there is now a family of dedicated viewers, safe in its knowledge of the patterns of form and story, self-satisfied and detached in its bemused contemplation of special effects and production tricks. To talk about the media manipulation used in the Kennedy or Nixon Presidential races could ten years ago seem like a great revelation. With Carter and Reagan the manipulation became part of the story. Just as soap-opera audiences are invited to immerse themselves in the intricacies of the *Dallas* plot even as they watch Larry Hagman on talk shows pondering the nature of the character he plays or read fan magazine articles about what Larry ("J.R.") Hagman is really like.

The audience that can appreciate all those nuances without the slightest self-conscious twitch is an audience that has become skilled in all the ways Hollywood tells stories and all the ways stories are told about Hollywood. By now everyone is a member of many different audiences, and there is no movie star left who was not once a fan. Thus the most common emotional appeal movies make today is not to fear or curiosity or desire but to self-congratulation, that species of pride one takes in being a professional member of the media audience, like a sports freak with his statistics, completely *au courant* with the latest new careers, hair styles, and methods of simulating decapitation, as well as with the traditions that stand behind them.

The present popularity of sequels makes the appeal to being "with it" only more obvious. Each genre movie is part of an implicit series, and "Kharis still lives" could be the motto of any filmmaker who wants to tap the energy remaining in the images and stories that had captivated audiences before. But now, urged on by the desire to keep the money safe and bent on exploiting the knowing audience, the filmmaker spawns sequels of his own, creating instant cults whose uniform is the T-shirt and whose relics are available at participating toy stores. So the trailers for *Rocky III* proudly proclaimed "An American Tradition." In Hollywood, it seems, twice is a sequel; three times is a tradition.

I am not being snide about sequels (or genre films) in the name of some ideal of the high-class individual work of art. The old high culture/popular culture distinction, never very compelling, seems to me to have even less point when we look at what has been produced in Hollywood and consumed in America over the past few years—the films of the early 1980s. In these films there is a common preoccupation with the pressure of time and history on the individual, and, depending on whether the film's view is optimistic or pessimistic, the freedom of the present or the claustrophobic pressure of the past.

Like the proliferation of genre films, the overwhelming number of remakes and revivals, as well as the supposed resurrection of traditional political values represented by Ronald Reagan, the popularity of sequels indicates that we are in a period when the question of the past and what to do about it weighs heavily on a present that is in danger of both ignoring it and treating it too seriously, without sufficient distance and irony. Sequels and the newly ironic genre films allow just that kind of distance. Their stories, built on a core of characters, never really end. When you see them, you don't buy a ticket to a film; you buy a ticket to a world, and a cozy world at that. Thus, even horror films become for the fan familiar treats, and fright becomes a welcome variation on familiarity. Film critics may debate about the essential nature of the western or the musical or even the boxing film. But if there is any pure genre still afoot now, it is the genre of self-consciousness about genre, the genre preoccupied with facing up to or facing down its own past.

But the question still remains whether this formal sophistication actually constitutes cultural progress or is merely cultural accumulation—and the raids on the greatness of the past less an enshrinement than a rummaging in the garbage heap of broken images. Remakes at best are commentaries that gain in self-consciousness what they lose in freshness. To remake *The Thing* complete with the politics of 1951 that permeated it would be ridiculous or at least strangely archaic. So John Carpenter, in the name of going back into the past, goes back still further to John W. Campbell, Jr.'s original story, and serves up a film with no politics and virtually no plot at all—whose ending aches for the sequel that as yet has never come and perhaps never will. In an age preoccupied with the search for originality and personal style, the deluge of sequels, remakes, and genre irony dissolves the anxiety of creative aspiration by implying that there is no need to reinvent from scratch; just repeat, vary, continue, go on. Such works preserve us from constant comparison with the mighty dead, and yet they insist upon that comparison as well. They let us step back and congratulate ourselves for knowing how they work. But then they pull out the rug: if you know so much, you must be old; and if you are old, you are closer to death.

Thus the almost invariable tones of melancholy and gloom in many current films. Sequels may plunge on: Rocky Balboa wins again; Luke Skywalker learns a little bit more (about his past, of course). But in other films the note of desperation, the pipings of creativity on the brink of the abyss, are much shriller. *Pen-*

nies from Heaven, for instance, with its brilliant parts and overall incoherence, reminds me of those fantastic concoctions served up at restaurants that feature no coherent cuisine, just all the most expensive ingredients: filet mignon coated with caviar and garnished with kiwi fruit. In *Pennies from Heaven* Busby Berkeley and Fred Astaire slug it out with Walker Evans and Edward Hopper to see who deserves the prize for telling us what the 1930s were really about. Steve Martin is the appropriate star for such a film because his main comic gesture is a smirk. On stage it tends to mean "I'm doing something stupid, but I know it and therefore it's funny." In films it tends to mean "I know I'm just a kid, but I'm up here playing in the fast lane." In both situations Martin insists on how aware he is. In *The Jerk* he seems to take seriously what no one else would, even while his eyes and his voice and his smirk let us in on the secret that he's not really taking it seriously at all, just acting. Unlike Robin Williams, whose awareness turns him into Mr. Media, an antenna that grew up where all the television and radio and movie waves in the universe converge, Martin never attempts sincerity or emotion without jutting his jaw and curling his lip and telling us he really didn't mean it; what do you think he is, a fool?

Yet even though Martin is cool, he wants to be sincere as well, especially if sincerity is defined by the total commitment of Astaire and Rogers to their craft in a lost time when the seam between person and performer rarely showed. With all his standing back, Martin still wants to play with the big kids, and if Fred and Ginger are not yet the mighty dead, they might as well be, for their films represent a lost ideal of order, elegance, and security. But finally we must admit that their world is forever lost, and so the character Martin plays in *Pennies from Heaven* also learns that, whatever your fantasies, whatever your cool, you can't change your place in history. In the crucial sequence, Martin and Bernadette Peters dance on a stage under a film of Astaire and Rogers. True, Astaire and Rogers are in black and white, and Martin and Peters are in color. But the fantasy stars of the past loom over the diminished forms of the seemingly more realistic fantasy stars of the present. Even when Martin and Peters are techno-magically transposed into the black and white film, "becoming" Astaire and Rogers, the sense of loss is the dominant note: the present is a weak imitation of the past—in lip sync.

Pennies, like the "new" genre film it is, breathes deeply in the history of visual imagery, especially that of musicals; its past is a past made up of other films, even while it nervously pays tribute to the imagery of painters like Hopper whom it considers to be more "real." *Reds,* or *Chariots of Fire,* or on the other hand *Gallipoli,* step outside of that kind of self-conscious genre history to present themselves as "original" works. Yet they are curiously involved in very similar issues of aspiration and loss. Instead of doing the old-fashioned thing of staying within the past he seeks to reconstruct, Warren Beatty in *Reds,* for example, intersperses bits of interviews with the survivors of a past that also included John Reed and Louise Bryant. It really happened, he seems to be saying: past and present are linked; these people and their passions were once real. But paradoxically this effort to ballast his characters with a documentary and anecdotal reality succeeds only in underlining the marionette quality of the screen Reed and Bryant. How amazing, we are invited to wonder, that these ancient faces and bodies once lived in the gaudy past. But why, we might continue to ask, are all these real people unidentified (except in the credits) and why, counterwise, are the well-known faces of Beatty and Diane Keaton adorning characters that now seem so unreal? As he shows by casting other familiar faces (George Plimpton, Gene Hackman) in cameo roles, Beatty wants to have it both ways: respect the truth of the past as much as possible; then rip its fabric by in-jokes whose only point is to remind the audience of the fictionality of the reconstruction.

The old way to do such historical melodramas—for which Lubitsch, say, was so criticized by Siegfried Kracauer—was to place the individual against a large historical canvas and then show that everything that happened could be explained by the personal emotions of the participants—the Cleopatra's nose theory of history. But *Reds* is more torn between the claims of individual desires and those of public issues. Toward the end of the film, for example, Reed argues impassionately to Emma Goldman that she shouldn't give in to her feelings. Then, in quick succession, he decides not to resign from the International, goes off to help propagandize the Tartars, and then denounces Zinoviev et al. for killing the individual in the name of the Revolution and thereby killing the Revolution. He has come around to a way of thinking the film originally characterizes as Bryant's. Emotions and conscience seen to win out over principles and the March of History—suitably capitalized. But the recantation comes too late, and Reed dies of a typhus contracted in the service of the Revolution. Bryant's views of personal politics may finally prevail, but she is important only insofar as she fits into Reed's life, and he only insofar as he has been touched by history. Their consolation is that at least neither will ever grow old and vague like the ancient witnesses rounded up by Warren Beatty to authenticate their story.

Thus both *Pennies from Heaven* and *Reds* ruefully contrast the diminished present with the glorious past, even as they imply that we have superseded that past in understanding. Now we know that Fred Astaire's films were fantasy escapes from Depression realities (authenticated by Edward Hopper). Now we know that John Reed and Louise Bryant should have been praised and celebrated rather than attacked and harassed. Thus the execution of the Martin character in *Pennies* and the death of Reed in *Reds* resemble happy endings because they preserve the purity of our new illusions of knowingness. Surviving, John Reed would have been like the *Reds* chorus of ancients—feisty, fascinating, but somehow unfortunately alive and old. And a flash forward to the last days of Louise Bryant as a kind of Parisian bag woman in 1936 (had she heard the news of O'Neill's Nobel Prize?) might have made the links between romantic past and fallen present much too uncomfortable.

Like the genre films that self-consciously announce their freedom from tradition by superseding it, *Reds* is fatally caught between bowing to history and desperately attempting to escape its power. Until fairly recently, time in musicals seemed outside history because it was always perfect, rhythmic, synchronized, and harmonious, an elegant ritual that would never die. It was the quintessential movie time unconnected to the ragged world of facts and events. But *All that Jazz* and *Pennies from Heaven* showed how death could be made part of the timeless rhythm as well. And in this sense *Reds* is a variety of musical. Louise Bryant after Reed can't be an issue because that would undermine the enclosed and virtually utopian idealism of the film, which is constantly at odds with its desire to demonstrate its intellectual seriousness, its engagement with real history. I am fascinated that Beatty left out Reed's production of the Paterson Strike Pageant in Madison Square Garden in 1913. Perhaps he thought it would cut too close if Reed were so obviously, like Beatty, the impresario of history, rather than a reporter, participant, and finally, the nobly dying victim of great events. Milos Forman in *Ragtime,* with his Eastern European cynicism about history, makes it even more obvious who wins: the hero of action (Coalhouse Walker) and the hero of sensibility (Father) are in different ways destroyed, while the hero of artistic detachment, the filmmaker Tatiyeh, flourishes, complete with Mother at his side, leaving the dead past behind.

"The way you deal with death is just as important as the way you deal with life," counsels once-Captain, now-Admiral Kirk to his ambitious daughter in *Star Trek II,* a film that makes the aging and even the death of its previously ageless characters an essential part of its plot. In fact, the presence of death—challenged, evaded, succumbed to—has been so pervasive in recent films that it's surprising (or appropriate) that so little mention has been made of it. On the most explicit level, films like *Sergeant Pepper's Lonely Hearts Club Band, Superman I,* and *E.T.* lead us up to and beyond the point of death and decay only to reverse the process magically. Sergeant Pepper's magic horn turns the corrupted Pepperville back to the idyllic small town (Andy Hardy's Carvel) it once was; Superman turns the whole world back on its axis to resurrect Lois Lane; Elliott's love for E.T. revives the inner glow of life that the most up-to-date medical technology could not maintain. All our national mythology emphasizes freshness and innocence as the great virtues, and age and experience as the portents of death, the ultimate winding down of things. But a film like *E.T.* promises that even with this burdensome wisdom we might participate for a moment in the fantasy of renewal. And every adult who has stood in a hospital room and watched the blood pressure drop and disappear in a loved one, young or old (and E.T. conveniently is both), happily cries along with Elliott: this time love worked.

In a very different way, *Chariots of Fire* attempts virtually the same denial of death and time as *E.T.* Unlike Beatty's John Reed, whose action in history is compromised by his good looks and his theatrical personality, the runners Liddell and Abrahams are performers either unaware of or unconcerned about being seen, even while other characters try to impose nationalistic or religious significance upon their actions. No matter what the movie tries to tell us, neither man runs his race for the state, for society, or even for the usual audience in such cases—the loved one. Abrahams has his coach, but the coach is less a personal audience than a witness to a perfection of form, equivalent to Liddell's pronouncement that God watches him run and takes pleasure in it. I wonder if the Best Picture award *Chariots* collected doesn't indicate less about its quality than about the Hollywood desire to believe that somehow, somewhere, there are people of ferocious ambition who nevertheless don't care if anyone watches them: like Liddell who runs for God, Abrahams who runs in the name of self-achievement; Gandhi (in *Gandhi)* the political saint, or Mozart (in *Amadeus),* the genius in spite of himself.

The character of Schultz in *Chariots of Fire,* with his American sense of public performance, says that he can't understand either Liddell or Abrahams. Like Salieri in *Amadeus,* perhaps he has discovered that the fame to which he aspires may not be the fame he really wants.

In their different ways, *Amadeus, E.T.,* and *Chariots of Fire* embody a dream of escape from time and its final trumpet, death, into some kind of transfiguring fame. The defeat of time, like Elliott's revival of E.T. or Superman's disinterring of Lois Lane, will be a victory of the purified self over the corruptions of the body. But the assurances are not always so visionary. If we keep our eyes for the moment fixed on those films where bodies running against the clock become a general metaphor for the ambition to defeat death, *Chariots of Fire* takes a middle ground between the fatal history of *Gallipoli* and the blithe optimism of *Personal Best.* In the golden-glowing England between the wars, it might still have been possible to be ambitious, to race against time and win. Running is a compelling image for ambition not just because there are so many joggers around now or because *career* originally meant a race course. Of all sports captured on film, running especially conveys the impact of an individual relying solely on his or her body—without teammates (too social) and without special equipment (too technological). It translates ambition into the bare facts of body, mind, and motivation. But *Chariots of Fire,* despite its Academy Award, is a little too ironic about the paraphernalia that surrounds running to embody the American ideal of personal ambition (as does *Personal Best),* and it is too nostalgic about the England of afternoon sherry and hedgerows to have any political bite (as does *Gallipoli).* Both *Personal Best* and *Gallipoli* also feature running and runners, but their attitudes toward time could not be more different. In *Gallipoli* the time is war, and the fatalities of history channel the two young runners into a march toward inevitable death that they suspect and the audience knows must come. In the last moments of the film one of the runners uses his talent to try to avert a suicidal advance into the guns of the enemy. He runs and runs and runs, but still the message never gets through and his friend, with thousands of others, dies fruitlessly. Anyone with a bit of history might remember that the blame for the disastrous campaign at Gallipoli has usually been laid at the door of the young Winston Churchill. But Peter Weir's imagination is set into motion less by a desire for revenge on Churchill or the British military mind than by the more general theme of a doomed human struggle against fate. The past cannot be changed. The life given for society is a sacrifice at an empty shrine.

Personal Best, with its American-style optimism, implies that there is always enough time, especially when the pressures of the big race or the big game can be removed and competitors turned into lovers. Running against time is simply running against the worst and realizing the best about oneself. *Personal Best* is thus like *Chariots of Fire* or *Gallipoli* with all the business about empire and war and social pressure and antisemitism left out. The most socially explosive content—the relation between the two young women—is, like everything else in the film, shown as a personal choice, not a cultural or cosmic problem, nor the subject of moralizing and judgment. The political question of the boycott of the Olympics is there only to set the stage for the individual struggle.

But the bright lights and the unself-conscious bodies of *Personal Best* serve mainly to indicate how rare such optimism or obliviousness is in most recent films, where one is more likely to find a monster festering within than a pure urge to win. *Gallipoli* manages to keep its main characters pure by putting the blame on history, and *Chariots of Fire* is ambivalent even about that. But characters like Steve Martin's Arthur in *Pennies from Heaven* or Reed and Bryant in *Reds* are aching to be discovered, to be known for what they are—great spirits—usually independent of any particular talent or ability. Beatty gives such a role some substance because so many of his best performances (*Bonnie and Clyde, McCabe and Mrs. Miller, Shampoo*) have been as self-dramatizing small men who try to rise to a heroic status always tinged with play-acting and personal myth-making. Perhaps such ironies still exist in *Reds*. But if we are being asked to consider Reed as yet another public figure who has confused action with acting, the clues may be too deep to be extracted. In fact, Reed seems much more like an adult version of one of the new teen-age heroes—the young King Arthur, the prince in disguise who can pull the sword from the stone and reveal himself as the natural leader, before whom all fall down in fealty. John Reed grasps the sword of history; Luke Skywalker sets forth against the empire. The promise of time is fulfilled in the young idealist, the great man in the disguise of youth.

The most recent wave of films with medieval settings, unlike their socially oriented forebears in the 1950s, summon up a past world that authenticates war and violence by its relation, through magic and Christianity, to the eternal truths of the universe. Yet too often their heroes, like those of films with more modern settings, seem motivated primarily by the desire to be celebrated enough to conquer death through fame. But history is a double-edged sword. Even in the most positive film images of the past, the gloomy shroud of time and fate waits to fall on the hero's shoulders. The race for honor, the desire to make a difference, and thereby escape from time, is revealed to be the surest path to being swallowed up by it. The pursuers of fame and honor may race against time toward a perfection of body and spirit. But those who flee from horror live in a world where personal energy often wears the face of violence and mania.

Understanding the appeal of horror films these days is crucial to understanding films in general, because the motifs and themes of the horror film have so permeated films of quite different sorts. The Vangelis music for *Chariots of Fire,* for example, with its horror-film combination of menace and nostalgia, accords perfectly with the theme of spiritual self-absorption the plot dramatizes. In *Chariots of Fire* the heroes run against time and seem to succeed. But films where the horror element is more pervasive leave behind their origins in other genres or in "realism" to become infused by the horror film's focus on the fragile individual or the embattled group, menaced by the intangible and all-powerful forces of the past. This past has been forgotten and ignored, rather than praised and revered, and it will now therefore take its revenge. In such "horrified" films the forward, ambitious youth who grasps the sword from the stone learns that his own conviction of newness and originality is an affront to time. In the ensuing combat the odds lies not with the individual but with an implacable fate. (Thus the recent prevalence of films in which seekers of media fame are threatened or threatening—*Pennies from Heaven, The Howling, Shoot the Moon.*) In the 1950s the horror tended to come from the outside—in the shape of The Thing or the Creature from the Black Lagoon. But in our own time it either incubates within (as in *Alien* or the remake of *The Thing*) or distressingly wears the guise of familiarity as in *Shoot the Moon* or *The Shining*). "Who are you?" one hero asks the beautiful woman/skeletal monster in *Ghost Story.* "I am you," she says. "I am you."

Jean-Luc Godard once said that to make a film was to photograph death at work. And horror movies especially exploit one of the basic elements of the movie experience—its insistent irreversibility. Just as the camera pulls us inexorably down the hallway to the door we would rather not open, it also forces us to face a future we would rather forget, the future that holds our own deaths. The horror film takes its revenge particularly on those who have forgotten the past, the ancestral house and land, and the dead who inhabit it. In more benevolent versions, involving strange beings, the older than old can be loved, like E.T., and even consulted, like Yoda, the Jedi guru. But in the stories of more earthly horror, the dead have been forgotten entirely, murdered, and left to rot, or their sacred burial places built over with fancy hotels and tract housing. In such places, there is neither memory nor respect among the living, only the unearned energy of merely being alive. As films such as *Ghost Story, The Fog,* and *Poltergeist* emphasize, only after the dead have been remembered will the sin against them begin to be expunged: knowing the past is the first step to release from it.

But what is this past that must be remembered? The past that is closest to us and the death we try best to forget are both our own. The great gap in our recent national past, now only tentatively being explored, is of course the experience of the Vietnamese War. But the horror-tinged films of the last several years return instead to a past that is much more personal—a forgotten past that from the beginnings of gothic fiction has been characterized as a tangle of genealogy and family. In our own time the chains may still rattle in the ancient crypt, but from *The Exorcist* on, many more familiar experiences of family disruption have been the precondition for the possession by an alien horror. In particular it is the fathers who have failed, the fathers who should preserve the sacraments of family and local tradition but turn out instead to be either missing, dead, or crazy. Even *Apocalypse Now,* nominally about the political nightmare of Vietnam, uses the shape of Joseph Conrad's *Heart of Darkness* to move the story further and further away from any political reality into its tale of the search for the enigmatic Kurtz, whom the narrator finally kills in an explicitly Oedipal battle. Similarly, by the end of *Shoot the Moon* the film has given up all its pretensions to being a realistic picture of a family broken by divorce to become what is in essence a horror film: first, the mother with her children in a lonely house out in the woods menaced by an irrational monster (who happens to be her ex-husband); then the monster's subsidence into what seems like normality; and finally the monster's violent return, in a total demolition of all previous claims to civilized behavior unmatched since the James Mason of *Bigger than Life*—the original "Daddy is crazy" movie. Plucky mothers (in *The Shining, Close Encounters, The Secret of NIMH, Poltergeist, E.T.*) take up the slack when their absent, weak-willed, or murderous husbands fail. But over each film hangs the only truly final ending—death, which for a time the story has managed to keep away. No matter how decisive the ending, how final the heroism, how absolute the defeat of horror, there is always the possibility that escape was merely a dream, and we must return to fight or flee another day. The skull gleams alluringly beneath the skin, the films are made and remade, and the audience is locked in a never-ending test of its self-esteem and its fear: Am I one of the elect? Can I look into the face of death and survive?

Church attendance, we are told, is falling. But horror film attendance remains high, for in the horror communion the audience can experience a terror akin to personal death and yet be granted a reprieve, even a resurrection, like that of Lois Lane, E.T., or Mr. Spock in *Star Trek III*. The audience's knowledge of genre convention, like its awareness of sequels and remakes, helps perform the same function as a funeral service does for mourners: turning discomfort, fear, and anxiety into matters of ritual, elegance, and even routine. There are periods in which artists of the eye and the ear are intent on not being dismissed as formulaic and so exhibit an urgent originality. But there are also periods—and we seem to be in one now—in which artists glory in their exuberant inhabiting of formulas and genres, their close acquaintanceship with the social and aesthetic ritual by which clichés become revelations. Thus they gain their cultural authority and popularity by the skill with which they raise and then dramatically organize our fears and doubts. What is particularly striking about many films now is their desire to have it both ways—to indulge in the absoluteness of catastrophe and apocalypse while promising the audience that everything is all right: come back next week for another version. Those who seek to forget the past are swallowed up by it. But those who know the past try to placate its power by repeating it in as many variations as possible. In so many areas of our culture, the lavishness of presentation, the amount of money and technological expertise spent on the work, only underscores the feeling that the present must make up in material wealth what the past had in genius. Even such a summery film as *E.T.* cannot avoid the conclusion that winter is coming. Why else should Spielberg release it at the same time as *Poltergeist,* whose prime message is also to reconcile us with the fact of death, totally shorn of the usual horror film trappings of personal or familial sin?

The poet of democracy, Walt Whitman often intoned, will be the poet of death— death as the end, death as the all-embracer. Films now seem both preoccupied with death and intent on escaping it through their intricate reweaving of the patterns of the past. As there is a casualness about violence and destruction, so there is also an almost millennial longing for the incandescent moment when one achieves absolute success and burns out at the same time. One of the most brilliant recent explorations of these themes is *The Terminator*. In the future, tells the film, the machines take over the world, only to be defeated by a hardy remnant of human beings who have been rallied by a charismatic leader. But at the last moment the machines send a humanlike robot into the past (our present) to murder the mother of the human savior and thereby change their defeat into victory. Simultaneously the humans send their own emissary to warn her. The story of the film is the process by which this normal woman of the present grows into the heroine that she is remembered as being by the man who, by returning to help her, becomes the father of the son he had originally admired as his leader. Thus, in a much more intricate way than the defeat of Darth Vader by Luke Skywalker or the resurrection of Spock in *Star Trek III* (at the expense of the death of Kirk's son), *The Terminator* interlaces past, present, and future as an image of the round of generation and regeneration—male and female, parent and child. For all its atmosphere of fatality—the onrushing robot of future dread, the eternal ring of the plot—the final image of mother and child driving towards the mountains suggests that some bittersweet victory may still be wrung from the inexorable rush of time.

The Terminator is in part so successful because it is self-aware without being self-conscious, exploring its traditions without condescending to them. For an audience threatened by impersonal History and personal death, the defeat of the robot is a victory of love and human connection over a mechanical and inhuman future. Its knowledge of genre convention, the awareness of the past exploited by filmmaker and audience alike, furnishes a way to lighten the burden. Possessed by genre, obsessed with the revision of its past, and encouraged by an audience eager to show its own expertise, Hollywood now seems unwilling and unable to leave its patterns behind. The innocent hero may go down that corridor and open that door. Our superior knowledge of such corridors and doors implies that we will never be so trapped And yet we return, to be lured down that path and forced through that door again and again. The film characters are motivated by innocence and curiosity. But we are moved by experience. We remember the form and, by fulfilling it, hope we shall be purged.

[1985]

◻

Newsreel: A Report

What we demand is the unity of politics and art, the unity of content and form, the unity of revolutionary political content and the highest possible perfection of artistic form. Works of art which lack artistic quality have no force, however progressive they are politically. . . . We must carry on a struggle on two fronts.

MAO TSE-TUNG, quoted at various moments by Kirilov and
Véronique in *La Chinoise*

In the approximately nine months of its existence, New York Newsreel has completed fifteen films, with several more almost ready for release. The films are frequently very good and always interesting, although sometimes much good will is necessary to disentangle the web of aesthetics and politics at a particular film's center. But Newsreel shows in general a vital and aggressive willingness to experiment with traditional documentary methods in a concerted effort to work "on two fronts" and integrate its political commitment with the movie-making techniques.

The earlier Newsreels are closer to usual documentary form. They do imply that the viewer has some knowledge, for example, of the antiwar, antidraft movement. But they generally take the expository approach dictated by the documentary assumption "I was there and you weren't." This method is best exemplified by *Boston Draft Resistance Group,* done mostly in synchronized sound with some narration that describes and explains the group's activities. It is clean and straightforward in a kind of BBC manner that perfectly suits the incessant reasonableness of the Boston Draft Resistance Group's arguments and their decision to look fresh-faced and shorn. This familiarly professional documentary form (even down to the detailed credits, the only such in the Newsreels I have seen) with its radical content is one way of attacking the problem.

Two less successful films about draft resistance are *Chomsky* and *Resist and the New England Resistance.* The frame of the first is an interview with Noam Chomsky that is then interspliced with antiwar and antidraft activities. It was made just after the Coffin–Spock indictment, but still has a sense of immediacy in its combination of shots from the first Call to Resist meeting several months before, an interview with Coffin, and the actions of several individual resisters. *Resist and the New England Resistance* uses the same Call to Resist footage, but relates it more directly to individual decisions to turn in draft cards and the political implications of such acts.

Except for some close-ups, the camera in *Boston Draft Resistance Group* only records. It is a witness, not a participant or a commentator. Such an approach appears more purely in a film called *Four Americans* released by Newsreel but edited and synchronized from Japanese footage. Before a dark backdrop the four deserters from the *Intrepid* make joint and later individual statements about their decision. The setting is very stagy and frontal; the camera never moves. But gradually the men emerge in contrast to the rigid aesthetic format.

Later Newsreels do not completely drop this more "objective" and traditional approach because the group preserves a sensitivity to the special kind of treatment each subject demands. A comparatively recent film like *Meat Cooperative* again has a fairly straightforward chronological form, while it describes in a *Consumer Reports* manner the growth of a Lower East Side community meat cooperative that successfully does away with the bad meat and high prices of the local supermarkets until OEO funds are cut off and it must close. The second section, in which the leaders of the cooperative try to get help from the local congressman to have the funds renewed, is inconclusive and abrupt, like the action itself. But the promise of the cooperative, and its potential as an example, carry the weight of the film. Although *Meat Cooperative* like *Boston Draft Resistance Group* is aesthetically traditional, it is politically part of a propaganda of possibilities that stands opposed to what one Newsreel member called "the aesthetically and politically mindless propaganda of the thirties."

The more pervasive trend in Newsreel has been films that demand much more from the audience in both aesthetics and political response. *Meat Cooperative* can be called open-ended because it suggests the possibility of other cooperatives on its model. But films like *No Game, Garbage, Riot Weapons, I.S. 201,* and *Chicago* abandon the familiar documentary explicitness and chronological linearity to demand more of the audience's attention and engagement. The assumption of these films seems to be that a TV-conditioned desire for pleasant sound and sync dialogue is related to a desire for easy and unabrasive answers to distant problems. Their soundtracks and frequently their spray of images are irritating and confusing. The nonsync film becomes more radical than the sync because sync suggests easy solutions, the effortless marriage of word and image. But these films imply that neither the problems nor the solutions are easy. Earlier propaganda frequently had little aesthetic appeal, while its political content was simplistic, schematic, and therefore easily ignored. These more experimental Newsreel films attempt to achieve a more open-ended political result by aesthetically radicalizing the audience as well. The understanding needed to bring together sound and image mirrors the understanding necessary to translate accurate analysis into appropriate political action.

No Game, Newsreel's Pentagon film, stands uneasily between the "witness" films and the more experimental ones. The camera moves about the Lincoln Memorial, recording parts of speeches, incidents, and faces, and then follows the marchers to the Pentagon. The soundtrack is a frequently hard to understand mix of statements by the speechmakers, hubbub, and marching noise that synchronizes momentarily in a Peter, Paul, and Mary song. Finally, when the camera sweeps down a line of troops before the Pentagon, a studio voice authoritatively addresses the soldiers about the War, and the image shifts to Vietnam footage. Although some audiences have complained about this voice and the way it disrupts the more documentary tone of *No Game,* I found it much less annoying than the many pointless wide-angle shots. The shift in images is, however, very effective. The confused charges around the Pentagon give way to the overexposed blacks and whites of the war scenes; the familiar bushes and trees change into the landscape of a lunar world; and the helicopter that hovered over Arlington Bridge is transformed into an image of malevolent destruction.

Despite these striking images of the dream-world of evil that the marchers are trying to fight, the studio voice in *No Game* does detract from its final effect; it is too authoritarian and its final optimism about the value of the march is too easy. The explaining and interpreting overvoice is feasible for films like this primarily because it's cheap. Politically, its effect can be dogmatic and abstract, without a feeling for the nuances of the concrete situation. Films without the direction of an overvoice, on the other hand, risk fuzziness or the imposition of even more simplistic devices. *The Jeanette Rankin Brigade,* which details a trip to Washington by a group of militant women, falls too easily into a series of heavy ironies that juxtapose the resolute women with a supercilious world of men—cops and otherwise. The effect of the march is politically inconclusive, and could lead to more understanding of the proper use of this kind of protest. But without an appropriate or compelling artistic form, inconclusiveness appears only as confusion.

In *Riot Weapons* the last image makes a direct appeal to the audience to engage the film and the problems it depicts: two black New Jersey National Guardsmen point out of a billboard in Newark, while the camera closes on the pointing hands. But the direction of the film that precedes this image is unclear. Gun advertisements in police magazines, publicity shots of police tanks, and scenes of riot training alternate with footage and stills of riots and their aftermath. The contrast is heightened by the soundtrack: behind the ads is the clatter of guns and the shriek of sirens; behind the riot scenes, only silence. But the riot sequences generally lack any bite or point, in addition to being repetitious. What are the demands that the final image is making on the audience? If the contrast between the two kinds of sequence is the main point, what choice has been made about the length of the film? Does *Riot Weapons* merely document trends in police militarism or does it also imply that black and white radicals should arm themselves too? Is there, for example, a progression from ads for police weapons to ads for ordinary weapons? (I could not tell when I saw the film.) *I.S. 201,* which deals with a memorial parade in honor of Malcolm X and other commemorative activities in a New York public school, similarly tries to find some form other than the chronological narrative of the observing documentary camera. The titles for the separate sequences have a screechy soundtrack behind them (and follow rather than precede the events they describe). The film does capture some sense of the rush of these activities and the energy liberated by Malcolm's influence. But once again there is a lack of effective rhythm in the film itself, an inability to set up its own terms securely enough. For a film that deals with potential action and movement, *I.S. 201* has a curious lethargy, especially in the shots of the destroyed areas of Newark, while an I.S. 201 panel discussion occupies the soundtrack.

Talk, as it is embodied in the discussions that swirl around political action, forms an increasingly important part of Newsreel's films. The films now in progress concentrate even more on developing a kind of "follow" documentary, a film about the dynamics of different groups as they get into, learn about, and try to deal with the society they live in, to bridge the gap between talk and action. *Garbage* and *Chicago* are the two most interesting and most successful attempts I have seen so far to document this process of thought and action and produce a film that has aesthetic form without political finality. *Garbage* follows a Lower East Side group called "Up-Against-The-Wall-Motherfuckers" on a trip to throw garbage into the central fountain of Lincoln Center as a statement about the cultural garbage Lincoln Center purveys and the mounds of real garbage people are living in because of the New York garbage strike. The soundtrack is full of talk—jokes, arguments about the project in earlier discussions, commentary during the trip itself, "America the Beautiful" in falsetto, and discussions afterwards, and more talk about later action to relate the existence of Lincoln Center to the problems of the Lower East Side as a community. *Garbage* was shot by many Newsreel cameramen and therefore embodies many points of view, in its images as well as in its soundtrack, about the appropriateness of the garbage dump as a reaction to the fact of Lincoln Center. One especially ambiguous shot of a black janitor with a broom watching the exuberant Motherfuckers go by introduces the idea that those in power will never be touched by something as whimsical as this; the only effect will be extra work for the people who have to clean up.

Chicago deals with the late March conferences at Long Villa outside Chicago to plan for radical action during the Democratic convention. Most Newsreels start with a "teaser" before the logo and title. In *Chicago* it is a seemingly pointless ride down a long Chicago street, faster and faster, with jumpier and jumpier cuts, until the street deadends in the International Amphitheater, site of the convention. This trip appears several more times in the film, together with approaches from other streets, and rides around Chicago by car and elevated. The camera is restless—not content, as in, for example *Boston Draft Resistance Group,* to follow along and listen to explanations, but dodging in and out, breaking away from the conference discussions with their endless cups of coffee, speakers, and uncomfortable chairs, looking out into Chicago for the relevance of all the talk, for where it connects. The two longest sections devoted to speakers underline this problem. A white committee leader reports on the arguments, the irresolution about what exactly should be done at the convention. Then, towards the end of the film, a black speaker lists in numerical order the demands the convention has decided on and phrased with a rigid certainty, while the camera keeps cutting back to the elevated train ride. Is this the way to Chicago? Is this what should be done?

Films like *Garbage, Chicago, Boston Draft Resistance Group,* and *Meat Cooperative* have a richness and vitality that repays seeing them several times. Even the less successful Newsreel films are provocative in their deficiencies. Ideally, Newsreel is a community of politically committed filmmakers who can progress in artistic ability and political understanding at equal pace. But practically, people come into the group at different levels of sophistication in both filmmaking and politics, make films, and then change to varying degrees. Making films that strive for some immediacy, with a large group and possibly interminable discussions, forces the need for a series of compromises, with many bad choices being made about both subject matter and treatment. Newsreel members admit that many of their films contain "cheapies"—bald ironies, badly conceived footage, muffed effects. But more important is that many Newsreel films work fruitfully in the terms they have set for themselves. The Newsreel logo is the words "The News-reel" flickering violently to the sound of a machine gun—the cinematic equivalent of Leroi Jones's line "I want poems that can shoot bullets."

[1969]

In the Criminal Style

Crime Movies: From Griffith to the
Godfather and Beyond,
by Carlos Clarens.

Film Noir: An Encyclopedic Reference
to the American Style,
edited by Alain Silver and Elizabeth Ward.

What's a genre film? Up until the genre explosion of the 1970s the answer might have been "any well-made, unpretentious, but memorable film that never gets nominated for an Academy Award." Never, that is, unless the film is a musical, where the lavishness of production (epitomized in the Freed days at MGM) can assure the fainthearted that something important is being said in the name of show business.

But most of those other genre films—gangster, detective, science-fiction, western, horror—that haunt memories and dreams more often than they appear in critical monographs or praises of the industry, have begun at the bottom of a double bill and ended in job lots sold for late-night reruns. They were rarely the films that Hollywood was officially proud of. When anybody talked about them, it was usually to condemn/excuse with the favorite term for all genre films—"escapist."

Understanding escapism, however, requires some knowledge of what's being escaped from. Carlos Clarens, in his intricate and often wise new book, *Crime Movies,* points out that genre film (like all art that plays on conventions) is based on consensus—a shared collection of cultural values. I would add that such a consensus is often about where to find the areas of important conflict: the heart of any vital genre art lies in the continuing contradictions of a society. When the contradictions vanish or (more often) when attention is focused elsewhere, the genre will go underground as well, until a world with similar problems awakens it to relevance again.

Clarens argues that the movie dealing with crime and criminals has had the most tenacious hold on the screen from Griffith's *Musketeers of Pig Alley* (1912) down to the present, because at its best it deals with a trinity of elements—criminal, law, society—whose shifting relationship articulates the changing shape of American attitudes toward social norms, those who transgress them, and the penalties they do or do not pay. The western, says Clarens, lost its mythic lure in the early 1970s after *Little Big Man* and *McCabe and Mrs. Miller,* while the crime film is still defiantly current. Neither obliquely historical like the western, nor ahistorical and psychological like the horror film (to which Clarens devoted *An Illustrated History of the Horror Film* in 1967), the crime film has constantly maintained an effort to connect in *some* way with a real and contemporary social history.

Unlike the history of other genre films, in which plots motifs, themes, and characters costume the "real world" in heightened forms, the history of the crime film can serve as an only slightly heightened documentary of what criminals were actually doing. Clarens's discussion therefore moves subtly between the films themselves and the history of crime outside the movies. He even includes episodes in the criminal history of Hollywood itself (founded in part for its proximity to the Mexican border), from the early use of gangsters as strikebreakers to the later control of the International Alliance of Theatrical Stage Employees (IATSE) by the Chicago mob in the persons of Willie Bioff and George E. Browne.

Two defining perspectives already appear in the first major films to deal with crime: the emphasis on environment in Griffith's *Musketeers* and the fascination with the psychic atmosphere of the antisocial and the illegal in Sternberg's *Underworld* (1927). Their titles give them away: Griffith was romanticizing a lower-class experience in images akin to the photographs of Lewis Hine or Jacob Riis; Sternberg was looking into darkness itself by setting Ben Hecht's story of the charismatic, doomed gangster in a hallucinatory studio world first cousin to that created by such German directors as Robert Wiene, G. W. Pabst, and Fritz Lang.

With the sound film arrived a group of actors who would give their own shape and voices to the fascination with the criminal. Edward G. Robinson, James Cagney, and Humphrey Bogart are well known for their criminal roles. But the type was a fruitful field of expression for almost every major male star of the period, and Clarens makes the useful observation that Spencer Tracy and Clark Gable both came to Hollywood notice for their stage performances as Killer Mears in *The Last Mile.* (Preston Foster finally got the screen role in 1932.)

The association between male stars and gangsters in the 1930s had a strong metaphoric truth. In the celebrity world of café society in the 1920s, the rich and the criminal clinked glasses with the stars for the wide-eyed audience of the press. Then, in the Depression years, the willful gangster could be both surrogate and cautionary example to the moviegoer, as he climbed his way up the ladder of success only to tumble into the gutter in the last reel. The formula was as old as Fortune's Wheel, and its exploitation went back at least to the eighteenth century, when the confessor at Newgate Prison would rush the scabrous deeds and last words of the recently executed into print, complete with a moral conclusion: identify as far as the gallows, then cut yourself safely loose.

A sympathy with criminals can be maintained so long as they attack people and institutions one dislikes or doesn't care about. But it's much more difficult to cut oneself free of the attraction of the actors who played their doomed roles. For all its emphasis on the grimy details and the historical realities of crime, the crime film also could never be free of a double view of its central figures. Like the journalists who prided themselves on their underworld contacts, the films were unable to purge themselves of a simultaneous psychic hankering and moral disdain for those figures of will whose urge to action and violence meshed so completely with the visual needs of films themselves.

It is hardly surprising then that films were drawn to the dynamic individual rather than to the faceless Mob. Society was always the most immediate enemy. But the right it finally had on its side could vary tremendously. When gangs became more organized and even corporatized in the wake of Repeal, the single-minded gunmen began taking on the air of the more eccentric western outlaws. In the face of John Dillinger the features of George Raft and Clark Gable found a real-life echo. But the FBI, with its scientific laboratories and its national web of agents, was on the move. In such an atmosphere of official and unofficial organization, a character like Bogart's Roy Earle in *High Sierra* (1940) is the last of a dying breed of individualist, "a farewell to grassroots America" says Clarens, although he might also have mentioned the debt Bogart's characterization owes to the "existential gangster" of *Petrified Forest*.

Clarens contends that the crime film itself has no ideology but easily takes on political shape, depending on who works on it. But it is hard for me to agree that films whose main focus is on the conflict between individual desires and social norms can ever be without some inherent ideological point. From the 1930s into the 1950s the crime film attracted the talents of some of Hollywood's most polit-ically aware writers and directors—John Wexley, Albert Maltz, Francis Faragoh, Edward Dmytryk, Rowland Brown, Abraham Polonsky, Sidney Boehm, Robert Aldrich, John Huston, to name a few. Most of these are men on the Left. But a conservative like John Lee Mahin was also a major writer of crime films, because in them Right and Left can similarly condemn an oppressive society in the name of the individual, forced to live as a criminal because there is no place in which he can live as himself.

This individual dilemma becomes most acute in the films of one of the most fascinating periods in film history—the time of "film noir," the films of darkness and moral ambiguity that held the screen particularly from the middle 1940s to the early 1960s. Clarens devotes an excellent chapter in his book to noir films (true addicts always use the word as an anglicized adjective). But an even grander presentation and somewhat more grandiose claims are made in *Film Noir: An Encyclopedic Reference to the American Style*. From Sternberg's *Underworld* to Scorsese's *Taxi Driver,* Alain Silver and Elizabeth Ward, the editors, have in-cluded more than 300 detailed accounts of individual films complete with credits, synopsis, and an analysis of how the film fits into a general conception that has been laid out in an introduction and a group of appendices that discuss hybrids of noir with the gangster film, the western, the comedy, and the costume film. In addition, Silver and Ward furnish a breakdown of films by year as well as lists according to director, writer, director of photography, composer, producer, per-former, and studio.

In discussing works of this kind, it is always easy to argue about omissions and inclusions. (Clarens would no doubt ask why *The Story of Temple Drake,* 1933, is missing.) But the claims made for the films can be separated from the particular elements in the list. *Film Noir,* so preoccupied with purity, so intent on celebrating and explicating every detail of those films on the honor roll, proclaims that a second generation of scholarly romancers have replaced the often blandly appreciative film buffs of the past. Silver, Ward, and their encyclopedists want to keep film noir in its own special world. Although they argue that it transcends genre because of its moral ambiguity and the inner corruption of its characters, they go about their task of marking gradations of noir with as mathematical an eye as any generic Linnaeus.

Silver and Ward are certainly right when they say that there is a lack of social consciousness in the films they admire. But Clarens makes this absence much more understandable, through both his general historical approach and his sense of the debt film noir owes to the gangster film. Silver and Ward argue that film noir is not a genre because it is time-bound, but their own interest is less historical than formal, and their contributors explicate motifs and iconography with the enthusiasm of art historians. Clarens's chapter title, "Shades of Noir," illustrates his unwillingness to be too finicky about definition. In his definition of genre, the audience supplies what is necessary "to fill in the empty spaces," and my own sympathies are much more with his perhaps overexuberant inclusiveness than with Silver and Ward's desire to establish precision where there is primarily overlap. Yet *Film Noir* is a handsome book, its collection of information is welcome, and its explications of specific films are often very interesting (depending on the contributor and assuming "noir" isn't slathered on as an all-purpose honorific).

Clarens's book, on the other hand, is a major work (and it even contains many more interesting stills). While *Film Noir* aims to exclude, Clarens is often very enlightening about films (like *On the Waterfront*) that at first glance wouldn't seem to be part of his subject at all. It is his sense of history, both inside and outside the films, that allows Clarens to release genre from conceptual rigidity. Yet he also maintains an inclination for the unpretentious and direct and against the overblown and poeticized. He dislikes those who try to make crime films into "Something More Meaningful," and so will compare *Serpico* unfavorably to *Walking Tall,* or rank *Bonnie and Clyde* lower than *Bloody Mama.*

Yet one of the lessons of film history is that self-consciousness also appears in various stages. Since the 1940s the crime film has almost invariably contained a measure of nostalgia, if not for the old criminals, then for the old crime films and the heroes they both celebrated and condemned. In the 1970s the real fear seems to be directed not at the syndicate, the underworld, or the slums, but, as Clarens remarks, at the giant corporation and the giant government agency. Now, of course, Hollywood itself has become absorbed into such corporations, and genre films with B ancestors appear burdened with multimillion dollar budgets. In this mood of aesthetic elephantiasis, the eccentric individualist—a cop named Dirty Harry, Serpico, Buford Pusser, Popeye Doyle, or Bullitt—is totally isolated, dreaming perhaps of becoming an aide to the Godfather (Vito Corleone, that is, not Michael) where real family and community might be found. With his delicate sense of the complex historical and aesthetic forces that create films, I wonder what Clarens would say about the almost simultaneous appearance of Al Pacino as the sexually masquerading affectless cop in *Cruising* and the morally aggressive and emotional lawyer in *And Justice for All*. Clarens, like the contributors to *Film Noir,* remind us of the force and imaginative power of a remarkable group of films out of Hollywood's past. Nowadays, it's often more rewarding to watch reruns of *The Rockford Files* and *Harry O*.

[1980]

◻

Western Approaches
Sixguns and Society, by Will Wright.

Social psychologists and anthropologists made their first impact on the study of film after the Second World War through the work of such writers as Hortense Powdermaker *(Hollywood: The Dream Factory,* 1950), and Martha Wolfenstein and Nathan Leites *(Movies: A Psychological Study,* 1950). Unlike the art historians and visual formalists of the 1930s, who wanted to explore (as in the title of Rudolf Arnheim's 1933 work) film as art, these later writers searched films for data about public and private social attitudes. Because their interests were shaped by their observation of the ideological impact of films before and during the war, they focused on the popular film rather than the "art" film, and they usually concluded that it was a Marxist–Freudian opiate, expressing, exploiting, and thereby allaying the fantasies of its audience.

Like the formalists, then, the social psychologists considered the most interesting part of the films to be their static patterns. But, whereas someone interested in visual pattern might also speculate upon new ways to elaborate the image, films for the social psychologists changed only as they expressed more and more accurately the dark pathways of the collective psyche. For the formalists, the way to new films might be forged by a more intricate technology; for the social psychologists, their own studies would be aided by a more lenient censorship. The formalists, in other words, appealed to the artist; the social psychologists examined the audience. Somewhere in between, the film itself was often lost and with it the special quality of the individual experience. Avant-garde formalists might praise, and conservative formalists deplore, the introduction of sound; radical sociologists might deplore, and conservative sociologists praise, the elaborations of genre. But all, whether with approval or disapproval, considered the film itself to be a product, either of artistic imposition or audience catharsis, with little that was interesting apart from the dynamics of its creation or the passivity of its acceptance.

Will Wright's *Sixguns and Society,* subtitled "a structural study of the western," falls obviously in the sociological camp. (Wright himself is a professor of sociology at the San Diego campus of the University of California.) But Professor Wright is less interested in the Freudian categories that animated many of the earlier writers than he is in the patterns of Lévi-Strauss, and the possibilities they offer for relating the shape of the American western to the social structure of American society rather than (might he say "merely"?) individual fantasies of self and relationship. To affirm the method, an adjustment must be made, and Professor Wright argues cogently against Lévi-Strauss's distinction between historical societies and nonhistorical or myth societies by showing that the myths of historical societies are primarily myths about history itself. In history, he implies, the past causes the present; in myth the present causes the past: "myths provide a ground for action excluded by the logic of history." One therefore need only turn to the western to discover the patterns of America.

But if Lévi-Strauss had not made his distinction so absolute, would anyone have needed to argue such an obvious point? Perhaps only in the worlds devoted to intellectual patterns does one have to assert that there are emotional patterns as well. This interplay between myth and history is basic to our understanding of the popular genre film, which bears a self-conscious relationship to a tradition of films similar to itself, as distinguished from the "serious" film, which presents itself as a unique, finished product, artistically self-sufficient, self-contained, and responsible only to its own internal workings.

Genre films thus would seem to be an appropriate area to test structuralist assumptions about the patterns of popular art. Their pleasures are the pleasures of familiarity, perhaps even ritual, where we know virtually everything that is going to happen but want to see it happen again in this particular set of nuanced ways.

Everyone connected with the creation of a western—director, scriptwriter, cameraman, and actor—is therefore a structuralist by necessity, implicitly or explicitly insuring that this particular work is a variation on the basic pattern, combining fidelity to genre form with the integrity of this individual expression. To state the basic thematic terms of any western—the individual and the group—immediately suggests the lure of conflict inherent in its stories and the ease with which it can project into large heroic shapes the kinds of conflict the moviegoer (especially the male or working moviegoer, a side issue Professor Wright never raises) faces in his daily life. If the problems are not resolved, as by definition they cannot be, the audience is at least solaced by the grandeur of their expression. The emotions raised by popular art perform their first function by conveying to the audience the basic message: "you are not alone."

Professor Wright begins his analysis by attacking the incomplete accounts of all those critics who have seen in westerns one or another invariable motif. Beyond these static patterns, he asserts a more integrative historical view: the changing patterns of western plots, he argues, reflect the changing patterns of American social institutions. I certainly agree and I would expect anyone who has followed any film genre to agree as well. What after all does popularity mean, if it does not mean a continuing relevance to the beliefs and feelings of the audience? But Professor Wright is less concerned to introduce a historical element into what had previously been more isolated and static studies than to substitute an increased number of static patterns. His basic "stages" of the western (no pun from him here) are four: the "classical plot" (most classically *Shane*), in which the hero, although separate, helps society; the "vengeance variation" (*Stagecoach, One-Eyed Jacks,* etc.), in which the hero is antagonistic to the values of society; the "transition theme" (*High Noon* and two other films of the early 1950s), in which the hero and a woman join forces as an outlaw couple; and the "professional plot" (*Rio Bravo, The Wild Bunch,* etc.), in which a group of heroes defend society only as a job or because of a love of fighting.

Professor Wright supplies many more details in these patterns and somewhat fuzzily periodizes the classical plot from 1931 to 1955, with the vengeance variation overlapping from the early 1950s to about 1960, and the professional plot taking hold from 1958 to 1970. But authority and framework are most important to him than the actual experience of individual films. He says in his dedication that he has learned to love westerns (appropriately enough through the teaching of his father), and it is the plural that seems most important to him. Each section of his book brings in the most dashing authorities to support his daring variations on Lévi-Strauss: Kenneth Burke, Vladimir Propp, Arthur Danto, C. B. MacPherson, Karl Polanyi, John Kenneth Galbraith, Jurgen Habermas. Professor Wright's method cannot be separated from his subject. He stands in relation to his honored authorities (all invoked as exemplary framers) as he believes the individual film stands in relation to the genre, the detail to the plan, the actor and cameraman to the scriptwriter and director. Only large-scale differences count as real. The individual fits his way cautiously into the big picture; the actor only inhabits the shell of his character; the individual western must fit its way into the great structures of the genre—or all will necessarily fail.

The history of ideas as a discipline assumes that the respectability of a literary work will be assured, so long as the critic can point to contemporary works in which many of its subtly presented ideas and attitudes appear with boring but verifiable clarity. Sociological views of literature often have the same goal: the otherwise *outré* work is validated because analogies can be made between its details and an array of authoritatively defined socioeconomic "facts." Either ignored or mocked is the possibility that the artistic work may develop and transmit the ideas better than a more explicit "nonfiction," or—the more radical position—that both intellectual and social structures may be more dependent on aesthetic structures than they are influences on them.

Most recent books on the image of women or blacks in films, for example, are so eager to deplore the stereotypes of the past that they fail to consider that those stereotypes may not have been superseded, and the critiques might not have been written, if those older views had not been expressed, exposed, and thereby purged.

Professor Wright's dogged tracking of pattern blinds him to the varieties of expression his patterns might discover, if they truly had the interpretative power he claims. The social interpretation of the genres of literature was an especial preoccupation of the Renaissance. Hobbes, who in this and other ways might be called the grandfather of structuralism, says in his response to Davenant's preface to *Gondibert* that there are three basic modes of literature—the heroic, the dramatic, and the pastoral—corresponding to the court, the city, and the country. Hobbes thought therefore that the hero should be as uncomplicated as possible, the better to carry the weight of meaning relegated to him by the design. Individuality in art, like individuality in the state, had to be masked and repressed; otherwise it was the first step to chaos and confusion. But unlike Hobbes, Professor

Wright is part of a culture that has historically emphasized originality as a criterion of artistic value, and he is dealing with an art form that somehow mediates
the contributions of many people. Yet he is so committed to pattern that his explanations tend to be paranoid and reductive, because in his sense "a myth *explains* social interaction."

But how can one come to such conclusions about a visual art primarily in terms
of plot synopses? And how can a theory that purports to discern the changing
conflicts between individual and society ignore the importance of stars? *Sixguns
and Society* may be one of the only books on film that uses the names of characters rather than those of actors and actresses, and Professor Wright consistently
ignores the way in which actors and actresses are like plot conventions—paths
through which we enter into empathy and affinity with the world of the film.

The essence of genre film lies in the interaction of flexible narrative and frozen
types, rich character and rigid plot. But Professor Wright's sense of history, plot,
society, and genre are all equally invariable and abstract. Is it really possible to
discuss the mythic purity of *High Noon* without at least mentioning the historical
reality of the Hollywood blacklist, to which it so obviously alludes? It is possible
to discuss the theme of the returning gunfighter in the late 1940s and early 1950s
without mentioning the Second World War or Korea? Nothing in Professor Wright's
theory or his analysis suggests how Gary Cooper throwing away his badge at the
end of *High Noon* (1952) can metamorphose into Clint Eastwood throwing away
his badge at the end of *Dirty Harry* (1971), nor does his plan of historical "progression" or his restrictive sense of genre allow us to wonder why the "professional plot" seems to be characteristic of both 1930s and 1960s westerns.

When Professor Wright sees in the professional plot "a deep conceptual corre-
lation between his narrative structure and the ideological requirements of modern
society," I can agree about the analogy and then disagree about almost every
detail and causality he arrays underneath it. It is not enough to juxtapose the social
and the aesthetic: one must be sensitive to the dynamics of their interaction. Otherwise, as in most structuralist or semiological studies, the movies become fodder
to enlarge the theory, and the result is just another form of the old style of condescension, in which the critic is unwilling to believe that the material may be at
least as sophisticated about itself as he is, or perhaps more so.

At the end of *Sixguns and Society* Professor Wright explicitly denies the beset-
ting assumption of much structuralist and semiotic analysis that criticism is a moral
calling superior to creation because it is cleaner, better ordered, and an excellent
method for generating articles. But at the center of the book is the unexamined
assumption that aesthetic structures at most only illustrate intellectual structures
and political structures (unless, of course, those aesthetic structures are by "individual artists," the hallmark of true value).

Professor Wright therefore never reaches the basic questions of genre art: to
what extent do popular films reflect social beliefs and to what extent do they shape
them? To what extent do they affirm them and to what extent do they criticize
them? A genre or a set of conventions is popular so long as it can encompass
ambivalences. Works of popular culture may therefore less usefully illustrate a
theory than they may define the conflicting terms that the theory has flat-footedly

tried to resolve. Genre study in literature has generally searched for the pure form by which individual works should be tested. Professor Wright makes such a neo-Aristotelian effort a social necessity as well.

Professor Wright has a larger sense of what he wants to do in his study. But he is totally hampered by his desire to assert the social role of the critic along with the originality of his own ideas. If he could understand the similar interplay in the western between the demands of self and the demands of society, the demands of individual expression and the demands of genre convention, the personality of acting and the impersonality of plot, his book would be much more compelling. *Sixguns and Society* takes a tentative look around that I might wish had been taken by someone more attuned to the uncertainties and specificities of sights and sounds than to the rigidities and solemnities of structure. As the eighteenth-century novel never tired of pointing out, the blinkered search for pattern easily leads to the creation of a pattern waiting to be discovered. Walter Shandy may tell us more than Lévi-Strauss about the interaction of mind, art, and society. The true test of an aesthetic theory is its ability to expand and enrich our experience of art. When everything comes out sausage, it has failed that test.

[1976]

The Sacraments of Genre:
Coppola, DePalma, Scorsese

"An aesthetic of reality," André Bazin called the Italian neorealist films of the immediate postwar period, and the description has stuck. Whatever the changes in style and approach that directors like Rossellini, DeSica, Antonioni, and Fellini made later in their careers, there is still a critical tendency to root them in filmmaking that stayed close to the stuff of everyday life. By respecting the integrity of the actors and objects within its gaze, neorealism sought not to turn them into something thematic or symbolic, but to maintain their separateness and their unalloyed reality—if we take "reality" to mean that which is constantly evading our final interpretation and our subordination of it to our interpretive systems.

The now-aging younger generation of Italian–American filmmakers—in which I include Francis Ford Coppola, Brian DePalma, and Martin Scorsese—at first glance could be hardly more different from the generation of neorealists in their style and preoccupations.

Most striking is their commitment to genre formats in plot and style, an indication of their rootedness in an American rather than a European tradition of filmmaking. Genre has always been the prime seedbed of American films. The neorealists and the European school in general, with the great exceptions of the early works of the French New Wave and the more recent New German cinema, have usually treated the individual film as a work situated in the history of art, or in the eternity of nature, while even in the most ambitious as well as the most perfunctory American films it is the pressure of the history of film displayed in genre form that has been the most crucial factor. Neorealism particularly, at least in Bazin's account of it, is explicitly presented as a statement of freedom against the stylization associated with expressionist film (as part of an attack on German politics and Nazism as well). This kind of film, Bazin argues, exhibits the "true" aesthetic of the medium, while the stylized sets, directorial control, broad-gesture acting, and melodramatic plots of film expressionism are a falsification of its essential nature.[1]

In such an argument the films of Coppola, DePalma, and Scorsese, with excep-

This essay is dedicated to the memory of Dennis Turner.

tions I'll note later, almost entirely wind up on the side of the tradition that Bazin believes neorealism is attacking. They are fascinated with artifice—with genre plots, characters, and motifs that delve into the roots of popular forms—as well as with stylized sets, lighting, and an expressionist use of color that convey the emotions of the characters and the situations rather than the "reality" of the objects. In contrast to the neorealist and Soviet use of nonprofessional actors to energize the film with a "realistic" sense of character, these directors focus on both the self-stylized character and the character whose psyche film and popular culture has taken over—characters for whom all experience must be mediated by the shapes of film artifice. Instead of imitating the dynamic reticence of the ideal neorealist director, who lets reality unfold before his camera, these directors are drawn to the implications of directorial imposition and tyranny: the director as aesthetic master of his material, shaping it to his will. Rather than Renoir or Rossellini, Antonioni or DeSica, their heroes are the great independent stylists: Welles for Coppola, Hitchcock for DePalma, while Scorsese invokes the eccentric combination of Michael Powell and Sam Fuller.

Yet of course the neorealist ideal against which I am measuring the deviations of this trio of Italian–American directors who have become so prominent in the seventies and eighties is itself a myth. If there ever was a neorealist consensus, it was in the eye of the wishful-thinking observer Bazin. The operatic structures of Visconti and the directorial flamboyance of Fellini obviously also play paterfamilias to *The Godfather* and *New York, New York,* where realism is heightened rather than negated. Similarly, Bazin's too easy equation of neorealism and liberation on the one hand and totalitarianism and expressionist distortion on the other is belied by the fact that so many of the directors who came to prominence after World War II received their technical training and a certain amount of their aesthetic underpinning in Mussolini's documentary film office.[2] In fact, the neorealist commitment to "an aesthetic of reality" was never so wholeheartedly polemical as Bazin argues. Rossellini is of course considered to be the one who strayed least from the fold, descending into neither Felliniesque bravura, Viscontian theatricality, nor Antonionian modernism. But from the first, Rossellini himself problematized the "reality" he was observing with calculatedly stylized effects. I mention just one example here: the torture scene in *Open City,* set in a room that, with total spatial illogic and psychic logic, is right next door to the main office of the Nazi chief as well as to the clubroom of his dissipated pleasures. Such a juxtaposition creates a rift in the documentary discourse (with its assumption that what is observed is truly happening) and makes us aware instead of the perceptual variations on "reality" through which the film is constructed. It is an incantatory moment, a mode of suprarealistic perception that I would like to call a sacramentalizing of the real, not so that it be worshipped but so that its spiritual essence, whether diabolical or holy, inflect what is otherwise a discrete collection of objects in space. Such a moment in Rossellini's early films connects them with preoccupations that appear with more elaboration later, for example, in his analysis of the signs of material status in *The Rise of Louis XIV,* or the signs of personal self-definition in such seemingly different films as *The Little Flowers of St. Francis* and *General della Rovere.* The commerce between such moments of psychological or expressionist eruption and their surrounding documentary format can suggest as well a closer lineage between, say, Rossellini's generation of neorealists and the mingling of documentary and expressionism in Scorsese (*Raging Bull, King of Comedy*) as well as the historical melodrama of Coppola's *Godfather*.

But my purpose here is less to argue (except by suggestion) the links to an older generation of Italian filmmakers than to explore the different ways Coppola, DePalma, and Scorsese adapt to the special situation of the American film what I would like metaphorically to call a Catholic way of regarding the visible world. In varying biographical degrees, they come to film, I would argue, with a specially honed sense of (1) the importance of ritual narratives, (2) the significance of ritual objects, and (3) the conferral of ritual status. Unlike the Protestant (and often Jewish) denigration of visual materiality in favor of verbal mystery, these directors mine the transcendental potential within the visual world. Objects, people, places, and stories are irradiated by the meaning from within, which as directors they seek to unlock. Sometimes the meaning, as in the work of another Catholic director, Hitchcock, is beyond the visual. But it is still linked to an effort to make visual style a mode of moral exploration, an almost priestly urge to reeducate the audience in the timelessness of ritual stories, along with the attitudes necessary for their reinterpretations.

This process takes place, as I have said, within an American film context that has always stressed the armature of genre and of film history as the presupposition of every film. It is an aesthetic approach enhanced of course by the long-lived existence of a studio system. But even with the end of the studio system, we find professed anti-Hollywoodians like Coppola and DePalma seeking to set up their own version of Hollywood and in essence beating Hollywood at its own genre game. All three directors, along with most other American filmmakers of their generation, received their technical training at the same time that the *auteur* theory of film was a force of radical upending of the official system of value. "No more European films of the grand style and no more Hollywood films of pretension" was the battle cry. The great American director would be defined instead as a man of personal style and vision, often working in the lowliest ranks of the studio, turning out masterpieces of tension between studio demands and personal urge. "Art" here was not the grand assertion of the European artist with his tradition of craft and guild connection on the one side and masterpieces and originality on the other. *Auteur* "art" came instead from a subversive use of the paraphernalia of studio complacency to articulate a personal vision.

All three also did some or a good deal of their journeyman work with that institutionalized representative of the Hollywood antisystem, Roger Corman, whose stock in trade was taking marginal film genres like horror or biker films and mixing them into an almost surreal concoction of flash and action. In the midst of Hollywood, Corman represented a knowing "bad taste" that simultaneously mocked Hollywood's upscale liberal pieties even while it studiously learned all its techniques. Corman produced Coppola's first film, *Dementia 13,* Scorsese's first substantial feature, *Box Car Bertha,* and released DePalma's *Sisters;* he also offered a place where talented film-school graduates like George Lucas, Steven Spielberg, and Jonathan Demme could learn their craft at low pay. The previous Hollywood generations of directors had come from live television (Lumet, Frankenheimer, Penn) or filmed television (Altman, Pollack), with its symbiotic relation to New York theater (especially in the days of the blacklist). This new generation came out of the film schools—USC, UCLA, and NYU. If the California contingent of Lucas, Spielberg, and Coppola were more oriented to Hollywood genres and studio expertise, it came in part naturally from the prejudices of their instruction, which stressed the need to fit in, if not with the Hollywood system, then with the Hollywood way of doing things—melodramatic plots and technically advanced visual style. If the New York contingent of DePalma and Scorsese was more dubious about the ultimate uses of technical expertise and often included a questioning of their own procedures, it came naturally from their nurturing in the *cinéma vérité* documentary world of New York in the fifties and sixties, with its constant arguments over the nature of cinematic truth and its New Wave city-film ambience of street-theater strutting.

But I must return from this entire generation of new directors to Coppola, DePalma, and Scorsese in particular because I believe their Catholic upbringing, literally or metaphorically, makes them the most salient filmmakers of that group, heightening a self-consciousness about all aspects of filmmaking that is already inherent in the historical–aesthetic moment in which these young directors began to work. Each of the three emphasizes a different aspect of film self-consciousness as his own. In Coppola it is the sense of genre, which for him is attached to a feeling for family situations and family betrayals, much as the latest genre examples turn against the past in the name of bringing that past to some higher perfection. Genre for Coppola is like the rituals of religion. But in the family context those rituals are poisoned by the shadows of death and ambition, just as the christening of Michael Corleone's child in *Godfather I* is intercut with the bloodbath wave of assassinations he has ordered. The old must die so that the young can move into their places, as Brando, sinking into the garden while making faces, gives way to Pacino and DeNiro, his inheritors and his younger selves. Fred Astaire in Coppola's *Finian's Rainbow* may still spryly head off across the fields, but his day is clearly over, and like Martin Sheen contemplating Brando's Kurtz in *Apocalypse Now*, it seems easier to kill him off than to fathom his meaning. In *Godfather II* Michael the inheritor is a cold avenger whose sword turns finally upon those he has vowed to preserve. Hymie Roth, the old Jewish gangster, may be defeated, but by the end the family has disappeared as well and Michael sits alone, while the lost voices of Sonny and Fredo and Kay echo in the empty room.

I have been recounting those elements in Coppola's films that lend themselves to an allegorical reading of his own relation to Hollywood and his past masters: a deep homage along with a simultaneous effort to replace them with his own aesthetic family—his father the composer, his sister the actress, and of course all his friends and coworkers at the (now defunct) American Zoetrope. Always there is a dream of camaraderie, and invariably that dream turns sour, often with a sentimental heaviness, for example in *The Outsiders*, where the bad boy Matt Dillon maintains his friendship with the younger boys to the point of sacrificing himself in a needless theatrical gesture. Much more than either Scorsese or DePalma, Coppola is committed to storytelling and narrative of an older sort, in accord with his commitment to genre and family ritual as structures of feeling that he wishes would still retain their ability to compel belief. But Coppola's commitment is undermined by his general unwillingness to question his own role as the director and *Wunderkind* who will pull all this together and make it work. Orson Welles is his progenitor and Wellesian control is really his ideal. But he lacks Welles's self-critical fascination with theatrical windbags and greedy fakes. In *Godfather II* Michael Corleone has clearly lost all the vitality of the past even as he has superseded it in efficiency and ruthlessness. Like Coppola's own grand projects that never quite work out—*Apocalypse Now* and *One from the Heart*—the recreation of past stories in order to squeeze them of all their possible meaning never quite gets to the core that gives them life. Too often they remain only stories, and even at his best Coppola is more a virtuoso stager of their gestures than an expounder of their meanings. *Finian's Rainbow* effectively ends one major musical tradition in film; *Godfather II* systematically dismembers and calls into question every feeling and value that animated *Godfather I; Apocalypse Now* attempts to say the final word on the whole history of European and American colonialism; *The Outsiders* will be the ultimate "bad kids are really good kids" movie, etc., etc. Instead of being energized by his self-consciousness, Coppola too often is swamped by it. His detachment from his tradition leads not to sympathetic analysis so much as to cold compendium.

The only film that Coppola made for the short-lived Director's Company (made up of himself, Peter Bogdanovich, and William Friedkin) is *The Conversation*, a smaller film than most of his, and one that intriguingly situates Coppola in relation to the earlier generation of Italian directors, as well as to Brian DePalma. Even though, as it has often been noted, *The Conversation* owes an enormous amount to the editing and constructive skills of Walter Murch, I will treat it as connected to Coppola's own interests because, as Michael Pye and Linda Myles point out, it proceeds directly out of an intellectual context at Zoetrope where Antonioni's *Blow-Up* was constantly being discussed as a key to all the most intriguing questions about the filmmaking process and the meaning of film that the young filmmakers were setting about to explore.[3]

Blow-Up was more appealing to the self-conscious young filmmakers than any of Antonioni's earlier films because its theme is specifically the problematics of vision: how seeing is mediated by the camera. Within a mystery plot featuring a Hitchcock-style innocent bystander who catches a glimpse of a crime, Antonioni explores similarly Hitchcockian themes of moral entrapment, in which the bystander becomes culpable through his particular way of seeing and interpreting the world. Like Scotty in *Rear Window*, Antonioni's Thomas has moral flaws that come specifically from the impulses that animate his career as a photographer. Moodily alienated from fashion photography, in which he is clearly the master over fawning, posturing women, he seeks some moral exoneration by frequenting flophouses and surreptitiously taking pictures of the bums and outcasts who are their inhabitants. By this ambiguous penance he delves into what he considers to be the "truth" of life. And he shows the photos to his agent as part of plans for a new book that will supposedly allow him to be seen as a "serious" photographer.

With his unquestioned commitment to the morality of his own perspective and style of vision, Thomas is fair game for the events that follow. By accident, he photographs what seems to be a crime and then continues to blow up his photograph in search of the elusive, consummating detail that will reveal the truth—a detail that becomes more indistinct, the closer he comes to it. In *Rear Window* the newspaper photographer Scotty is similarly drawn into the lives of the people he thinks he observes with detachment. The crucial emblem of his involvement is his discovery that he has witnessed a murder without knowing it. But there is no problem of sight for Hitchcock except for its moral valence. You have to pay for seeing; you can't be detached. In *Blow-Up,* on the other hand, seeing is itself called into question, along with the minute amassing of facts that purport to lead to a solution. Unlike Hitchcock's, Antonioni's narrative does not follow even a pseudocausal unfolding. Its story is more like a collage, a cubistic refocusing on the protagonist, who, like characters in Antonioni's earlier films, only sporadically follows his first goal. Hitchcock minimized the lost, strayed, or stolen object that was the *pretext* for so many of his plots by calling it the McGuffin. But it nevertheless existed. In *Blow-Up* the photographer tries to turn the pretext into a text and fails miserably.

Yet, although Antonioni goes beyond Hitchcock in questioning the sufficient reality of the visible world, he shares Hitchcock's final unwillingness to demystify the visual image and the director's privilege of presenting it. Thomas the photographer is not, I think, a surrogate for the director because *Blow-Up* specifically characterizes the photograph as a still picture and so necessarily inferior to the cinematic way of seeing the world. By satirizing the fashion photographer's pictures of the down-and-out in a mockery of the naive neorealism that dwells only on the surface of reality, *Blow-Up* especially implies that the photographic fetishizing of the visible is less "insightful" than that of film. Antonioni's perspective—*as director*—resembles a modernism of the Flaubertian and Joycean sort: God pares his fingernails while his characters squirm in their limited universe of immediacy. It keeps intact one of the most basic assumptions of film: that the directorial perspective is privileged, unquestioned, and almost by definition unquestionable. Hitchcock varies this assumption by making the audience, like himself and his characters, complicit in the strange goings-on because of their own personal darknesses. But still it is the director who retains the edge of authority sufficient to demonstrate to us our moral lapses and epistemological blindnesses.

In Coppola's *The Conversation,* however, the crime is real and the mystery can be solved—if one interprets the data properly. But Harry Caul, the sound man, who thinks that his equipment allows him to control and understand events, is in fact manipulated by his own belief in his godlike detachment. Much more than the photographer in *Blow-Up,* he is a figure of the director, especially the director whose technical mastery has been his passport to success. The crucial sentence Caul has recorded he has also misheard, misread, and thereby totally mistaken who are the murderers and who are the victims—encouraged by his own outsider's desire to believe that the wealthy prey tyrannically on the innocent. His moral preconceptions, his belief in himself as a controlling intelligence through his expertise, and his manipulation of his technical skills themselves all turn into the agents of his failure.[4]

Yet, despite its critique of the director's technological detachment, the fact that Coppola gave up effective creation of *The Conversation* to Murch indicates that there is some sense in which he has himself tried to escape unscathed from the film's *mea culpa*. One wonders if the maker of *One from the Heart,* with its elaborate paeans to the technology of emotion, has really watched *The Conversation* with the attention it deserves. The similarly divided aims of *Apocalypse Now,* with its simultaneous satire of American technological warfare and its exploration of dark spiritual forces in the Vietnamese jungles, follows *The Conversation* in replicating Coppola's own division between the desire to control through technique and create through imagination.[5]

I have called this interplay between the technological future and the mythic past in Coppola's films a tension, a dialectic, a Jekyll-and-Hyde split in his commitments as filmmaker and moral storyteller. But in the films of Brian DePalma, it becomes a prime theme on its own. Coppola is the genre storyteller, big daddy director, studio magnate. DePalma believes in the myth of Hollywood with a capital H and, according to all his interviews, loathes it. Yet he has become very successful making films that raise the ante in horror violence beyond even the Corman level, while mixing them with an irony about his own position as the outlaw little kid director now armed with all the technical resources and a good deal of the money of the big guys. Although brought up as a Presbyterian, DePalma acknowledges a strong Catholic cultural background. Of the three directors, he is the most fascinated with significant objects, especially the knives and other instruments of cutting so favored by Hitchcock, which take their places in the rituals of the deranged. Neither Coppola nor Scorsese lavishes the attention DePalma does on a table or desk top with its array of objects that create a mood or express a personality. Objects for DePalma are close to icons, and one central icon in his film may be the statue of St. Sebastian in Carrie's closet (not present in Stephen King's novel *Carrie*), the Saint pierced by arrows just as Carrie will by the powers of her own mind later skewer her mother with every kitchen gadget available, murdering and sanctifying her at the same time.[6]

In both *Carrie* and *The Fury,* as well as *Sisters,* DePalma celebrates the power of the mind and the imagination to move the otherwise inert objects of the world and thereby create its own reality. Telekinesis plays the same role in DePalma's films that genre references do in Coppola's and allusions to film history in Scorsese's: it invests the normal and the repetitive with the transcendent spirituality of ritual power. And DePalma particularly vests that imaginative power and strength of mind in a human being, a character, and invariably a young character at that. The young, in Coppola, can never reach the greatness of the past. They succeed primarily in turning it into a machine-like efficiency. The young in Scorsese are burdened immeasurably by their own desires for recognition and justification as dictated by movie stances and gestures from the past. But the young in DePalma have a kind of almost Wordsworthian energy that the adult world is bent on corrupting, not sexually so much as by its superior knowingness and its institutional absorption of their vitality for its own needs. The teen-age computer whiz in *Dressed to Kill* is going to use his own command of film technology to find out who killed his mother. The sound technician in *Blow-Out* is going to face down the entire police department and city government with his revelation of the criminality of a public figure. Carrie, the schlumpy teenager, falls into experience with her first menstrual period and becomes the butt of the more knowing girls around her. When she is humiliated at the prom, she destroys everything in her path; there is no time for small distinctions about who was nice to her and who wasn't. It is personal power without an adult moral monitor, but also without the adult willingness to conciliate and compromise.

But whereas Carrie's natural magic and that of the young boy and girl in *The Fury* cause disaster to the evil (as well as a few of the good), the technical magic of the computer whiz in *Dressed to Kill,* and even more so that of the sound technician played by John Travolta in *Blow-Out,* really doesn't work. Both are more personally involved in the crime than either the photographer in *Blow-Up* or the professional eavesdropper in *The Conversation;* neither has any illusions about the detachment their technology allows; both are using that technology for highly moral ends—to solve a murder or to reveal corruption. But both find their technical command to be fallible. The kid in *Dressed to Kill,* for all his minute tracking of the psychiatrist's patients, fails to understand that the killer walked out of the office rather than into it; his expertise is undermined by his youthful inability to imagine the adult depravity of the schizoid psychiatrist. The sound man in *Blow-Out,* even though he has witnessed the crime and has it on tape, is powerless to prevent the killer's erasure of his taped collection of the world's most significant sounds, just as he is powerless to prevent the murder of the prostitute who has helped him and believed in him. All he can do finally is use her scream in a horror movie—her naturalness, youth, and energy swallowed up by his own now adult and affectless purposes. The difference here is that DePalma himself—unlike Hitchcock, unlike Antonioni, and unlike Coppola—is not left out of the indictment. The prostitute is played, in perhaps a Godardian nod, by his own wife, Nancy Allen. And there is more empathy between himself and John Travolta's sound technician than there is dissociation. Antonioni at the end of *Blow-Up* makes David Hemmings disappear, blanking him out of the frame to imply his own more inclusive perspective. But Travolta at the end of *Blow-Out* resembles DePalma, sitting in the studio, opportunistically putting together a film from everything at hand.[7]

There are truths inaccessible to technique, the ending of *Blow-Out* seems to imply, and unmimable by the seemingly lifelike creations of a spiritless technology. In DePalma, as in some Hitchcock, there is a sense that film technique, film style, the film way of seeing, can never penetrate to the real truth, which in essence is invisible. At best we have only symbols, significant objects, details, gestures, that at the crucial juncture reveal their emptiness as ways of explanation and modes of power. As Coppola hankers after the charisma of a Brando that disdains technical firepower, so DePalma celebrates the psychic power from within, which technical mastery seems to corrupt or at least to stifle and to warp. He places the Hitchcockian distinction between moral control and aesthetic control further into doubt by bringing (again a bit like Godard) the filmmaking process itself in for some severe questioning—even of course as he glories in his manipulation of the audience as God–director.[8] In a sense DePalma's aesthetic and moral vision is closer to that of Paul Schrader, the Dutch Calvinist, than to those of Coppola and Scorsese. But his sense of sin includes neither Schrader's moral reversal of established norms nor his puritanical preoccupation with the body and its messes. Instead it is illegitimate authority, aesthetic even more than political, that is the sin for DePalma—and at his best he does not exempt his own.

Every director solves the problem of authority, on the set and in the film, in a different way. And in the unwinding of that way is his or her sense of what constitutes a coherent story. I have been characterizing the approach of Coppola as filled with an anxiety about his own authority, drawn to genre and family rituals as gardens of nostalgia amid decline; and the approach of DePalma as mocking its own authority, especially its derivation from technical mastery, even while he celebrates a psychic energy that ideally makes an otherwise inert technology actually work. In this array, Martin Scorsese is the director who most thematizes his own authority even while he explores the final and perhaps most pervasive aspect of the intersection of film with Catholicism—not ritual or significant objects, but the structure of sainthood. These distinctions are of course not hard and fast, and DePalma especially is fascinated by saintlike figures, especially the natural freak-marvels, while Coppola casts his melodrama of the generations with iconic stars like Brando. But Scorsese much more concertedly places the performer/saint/devil at the center of his films. As the first lines of *Mean Streets* insist, "You don't make up for your sins in church: you do it in the streets; you do it at home. The rest is bullshit and you know it." Like the saint in the church, the saint in the streets of Scorsese's films, so often incarnated by Robert DeNiro, makes the institutional forms into a personal order with an almost monastic fervor.

Scorsese's sense of film relies on film history and especially on the ways the film version of reality warps the consciousness of those without sufficient detachment. Saintlike in their self-sufficient isolation from the normal world, characters like Travis Bickle in *Taxi Driver* or Rupert Pupkin of *King of Comedy* model their own actions and responses on a world of film melodrama. They are enlarged versions of the uncle in *Mean Streets,* who is watching Fritz Lang's *The Big Heat* almost for hints on how to be a gangster, while Johnny Boy, the DeNiro character, is outside being shot. Less willing even than Rossellini to separate the natural world from his perception of it, Scorsese places his characters at the center of his films, and the look of the film radiates out from them, just as their moral conceptions of reality and their self-constructions come from the films they have already seen. Like Rossellini, Scorsese is interested in the figure of the saint as a character who moves beyond "realistic" norms, transfiguring his marginality into a kind of transcendence. The extraordinary calm of the Franciscan emissary in *The Little Flowers of St. Francis,* while he is being brutalized by the bandits, embodies a divine spirituality that can subsume earthly violence. In the much more pervasively violent films of Scorsese (who first wanted to be a priest because his asthma prevented him from being a gangster), the stylization of the visual form becomes a kind of skin over the eruptions within, as if to demonstrate how much chaos the rituals of seeing and storytelling can actually subdue. In a certain sense, one can thus place Scorsese in a European line that stretches from Sade to Pasolini, in which the stories of violence and death paradoxically point to the patterns of the form that contains them and the rituals by which they are distanced and turned into meaning. Like the Neapolitan paintings of Caravaggio and others, with their incessant heads of John the Baptist and Holofernes, their pin-cushion Sebastians, and their massacred Innocents, such works disrupt in order to reestablish, breach in order to heal and reauthorize.

But Scorsese, more than Coppola or DePalma (or Sade and Pasolini, I would say), considers the formal self-questioning of his own authority and complicity to be part of the story he tells. Perhaps, in delivering the sacrament, the individual priest has been made eternal in his role. But Scorsese, with a modern's sense of the ersatz sainthood conferred by the media, cannot stop there. In contrast with DePalma and Coppola, and even more sharply with the blithe, control-celebrating Lucas and the director-worshipping Spielberg, Scorsese continually characterizes himself in his films as an inciting force. In *Mean Streets* he is the killer who shoots DeNiro at the end; in *Taxi Driver* he is the murderous misogynist whose appearance triggers off Travis Bickle's breakdown; in *Raging Bull* he is the barely offscreen make-up man who is preparing Jake LaMotta for his stage appearance reading Shakespeare; and in *King of Comedy,* he is the a.d. who mockingly tells Rupert to ask the director if he really wants to know what's going on.

Interestingly enough, in the successive interplay between Scorsese and DeNiro, there is also a gradual emptying of the main character's moral pretensions and physical courage. With each step he turns more and more into a media figure, hungering for his place in the public eye. In the contemplation of the Italian–American director, there is some irony to be mined from the fact that in the year of *Taxi Driver,* Sylvester Stallone appeared in *Rocky.* Stallone/Travolta are an intriguing contrast with Scorsese/DeNiro: the main stream vs. the outsider Italians, the middlebrow vs. the highbrow filmmakers. The most relevant contrast to draw here is the unproblematic quality both of Stallone's thematizing of success and his celebration of winning through the self-conscious creation of a great body. True, Stallone admits that success has its pitfalls, and bodies age. But somehow those problems will be overcome. Scorsese's vision of both fame and physical fitness is much darker. In each of his films with DeNiro there is a progressive defacement of the star—the mohawk haircut in *Taxi Driver,* the bloated weight-gaining to play La Motta in *Raging Bull,* and the odd shot of hands wiping across a window-reflected face in *King of Comedy.* Like the implied and actual mutilations in *After Hours,* these images embody the tangled relation between audience response and personal identity. *Raging Bull* particularly seems to be a direct response to *Rocky,* similarly contemplating the boxer as a figure in working-class and lower-middle-class Italian–American culture. In contrast to the sweet color melodrama of *Rocky,* it is shot in a lusciously harsh black-and-white neorealist documentary style. Unlike Stallone, Scorsese does not blandly approve the benediction of visible success. In the figures of Bickle, La Motta, and Pupkin there resides instead a sense of the gaping uncertainties of public appearance and the desire for personal fame, along with a raging iconoclasm toward the performer—as if Scorsese wanted to undermine his own inclination to trust too much in the substantiality of images.

All such characters in Scorsese's films are saints of a sort, but saints as heroes *manqués*. In a way they are reminiscent of Rossellini's false General della Rovere, the common man who becomes a hero because others think he is. But Scorsese's saints have an urge to be different and to make a difference that has been totally warped by the culture of visual media in which they try to find themselves. In Rupert Pupkin's fantasy wedding, television has become the church. As Scorsese has said of Travis Bickle's more malevolent version of this urge, he's "somewhere between Charles Manson and Saint Paul. . . . He's going to help people so much he's going to kill them." Scorsese's exploration of such upside-down spirituality is part of his own particular inclination toward the performer as the key to a social and cinematic vision. But it is the performer not in the sense of Coppola's ritually murdered Brando, but the performer as the lightning rod for all the crazy pressures on the effort to construct a self in America today. Johnny Boy and Jake La Motta are specifically Italian; Travis Bickle and Rupert Pipkin are not. But all four, like Alice in *Alice Doesn't Live Here Anymore,* as well as many minor characters in Scorsese's films, are infused with the desire to be somebody.[9] That desire, as perhaps it must be in film, is predicated specifically on being seen and paid attention to by an audience. Johnny Boy dies among friends. But Jake La Motta leaves the film to greet a waiting audience, his career now revived, while Travis Bickle's insane shooting spree is turned by the newspapers into a heroic vendetta. Rupert Pupkin emerges from prison for kidnapping the talk-show host to discover that he has become a celebrity, and Paul Hackett in *After Hours* is finally turned into an absurd art object himself. In *Taxi Driver* and *King of Comedy* especially, such endings are presented as part real, part fantasy, like the ending of Murnau's *The Last Laugh,* the director's salvation of characters he has otherwise presented as doomed by their own obsessive despairs. The transcendences in *Taxi Driver* and *King of Comedy,* though, are specifically examples of a media grace, as false and as true as the spotlight for which the protagonists in such different ways always longed. In *Taxi Driver* the saint has become the scourge; in *King of Comedy* he is a stand-in for all those in the audience who want to be celebrated merely for being themselves.

What I have been arguing here may perhaps be extended and deepened by a consideration of the role of actual ethnicity in the works of these directors. But I'm not sure. In many of these films the ideology is not ethnicity or religion per se so much as it is the way in which those social and psychological forces are mediated by and even subordinated to visual style. The crucial issue is not ethnicity but the *representation of ethnicity* by members of minority groups whose particular angle on the world has been nurtured by the world of films that they now choose to influence in their turn. In a sense, these directors and their films may therefore signal some final stage of actual ethnicity in the interplay between a specifically Italian–Catholic sensibility and the general cultural system of American film history. Instead of taking a more sociological view of evolving ethnicity, I have chosen instead to explore the possibility that the three most prominent young American directors of Italian background have a common set of aesthetic preoccupations (and therefore a thematic ideology) that may be at least metaphorically considered to invoke traditionally Catholic attitudes towards the visible world. The neorealists in great part wished to step away from a cinema of stylization and control that Bazin, Rossellini, and others identified with political tyranny. They sought to create films closer to nature and thereby to natural truth. Even in their moments of stylization and artifice, they attempted to preserve the connection of their people, places, and things to a world without mediation (or at least without the mediation of the past). But for these young directors the past cannot be avoided. There is no liberation and little resistance. In this way they are similar to other directors of aspiration ever since the New Wave. The American directors especially are bound up in both the pressure of contemporary media and the need to come to terms with a film past. There is no question of being freed from history, only how to gain control of it (Coppola), mock it (DePalma), or meditate upon it and revise it (Scorsese). Thus Coppola, like Lucas, gives aid and comfort to the greats of the past (Welles, Kurosawa), Scorsese busies himself with committees to discover ways of preserving film stock and color dyes, and DePalma gives interviews denouncing Hollywood.

At the pure moment of neorealism described and idealized by Bazin, the God of nature was appealed to as an escape from the devil of History. But history is now less God or devil than an accumulation whose compulsions can be deflected but not avoided. The only final authority is therefore not outside but within the work. Unlike the so-called "invisible" style of the neorealists, style here is the necessary signal of personal vision. But each of these directors, in contrast with Lucas and his northern California lack of an ethnic self distinct from movie myths, has a fruitful guilty conscience about the assertion of style and the usurpation of divine or parental authority it implies. It is just that guilty conscience—that sense of the gap between secular metaphors of ritual, sainthood, authority, and their religious counterparts—that generates so much of the aesthetic and ideological richness of their films. Like so many other artists these days, Coppola, DePalma, and Scorsese are more entrepreneurs and explorers of entrapment than of freedom. But from their very best works we nevertheless emerge to puzzle out endlessly what key it was that so lavishly allowed our release.

[1986]

Notes

1. The general assumptions about the basis of the neorealist aesthetic and particularly Bazin's version of what he believes to be Rossellini's practice has been recently challenged by Peter Brunette. See especially "Rossellini and Cinematic Realism," *Cinema Journal*, 25 (Fall 1985), 34–49. Brunette here and elsewhere in his view of Rossellini is specifically concerned with the way in which every discourse is constantly subject to erosive counterdiscourses that ultimately threaten any classical sense of "unity" in the films, along with, it is implied, the conventionally moral implications of such unity. The connections I shall argue between the seemingly distinct aesthetic of the postwar neorealists and the "school" of Coppola, DePalma, and Scorsese complement some of Brunette's views, although from the angle of film history rather than that of critical theory. On the influence of Fellini's melo-

dramatic style, see Naomi Greene, "Coppola, Cimino: The Operatics of History," *Film Quarterly,* 38 (Winter 1984–85), 28–37.

2. Connecting a particular style with a particular politics is tricky business at best, even though theater has traditionally been the mirror of social structure, and film to a certain extent follows in its ideological wake. But I still wonder why the Nazi tendency in propaganda (with the prime exception of Reifenstahl) was toward historical melodrama, while the Fascist was toward documentary. Perhaps it has to do with the relative positions of Nazism and Fascism on the Great Man/Everyman axis, and the way each defined its audience.

3. Michael Pye and Linda Myles, *The Movie Brats: How the Film Generation Took Over Holly-wood* (New York: Holt, Rinehart & Winston, 1979), 101.

4. Caul's mistake has been psychologically interpreted as caused by his paranoia. But to root the explanation exclusively in his character diverts attention away from the aesthetic self-criticism of *The Conversation.* In art, paranoia may be just another name for aesthetic unity.

5. The successful Ewok siege of the Death Star substation in *Return of the Jedi* contains the film's only energy because it arises from a similar tension in the imagination of George Lucas.

6. Compare the very un-Coppolan moment in *The Conversation* when we discover that Caul has hidden the crucial tape inside a hollow crucifix.

7. The relations between directors and stars can be arrayed on a spectrum from conflict to conspiracy. The basic question remains who is left inside the film and who is allowed to escape. With the examples mentioned above, compare Robert Altman's "erasure" of Paul Newman at the end of *Quintet.*

8. See Pye and Myles, 168.

9. The modernist and minimalist Soho of *After Hours* of course geographically overlaps with the Little Italy of *Mean Streets.* Perhaps the title should appear as *After (H)ours,* to emphasize the denaturing of any ethnic characteristics in either its setting or its hero.

VI
MYTHS OF HISTORY

G. by John Berger

Of all the discarded masks in the steamer trunk of cultural history, none seems less promising to wear or to meditate on than that of Don Juan. Every popular psychology book for years has minutely explained that under the Don's omnivorous sexuality lurks impotence and death, the objectification of human relations, and a childish ego forcing the world to make up for not being an extension of himself. Especially in 1972, when no one wants to be treated like an object, Don Juan would seem to be the arch-villain, his sexual pride an index of his emptiness.

But in John Berger's excellent and fascinating new novel *G.*, "a novel on the theme of Don Juan," dedicated to "Anya and her sisters in Women's Liberation," there appears not the sexual coup-counter of the Freudians, but the Don Juan who captured the European imagination for more than 200 years—Tirso da Molina's Don Juan, Molière's Don Juan, Mozart's Don Giovanni, Byron's Don Juan—the symbol of personal freedom, the eternal rebel against God, against nature, against society, against culture, in the name of a world in which the only complex and authentic elaborations of identity and relation are made sexually.

In the thick mulch at the roots of the English novel, the Don Juan figure, the libertine, played a central part. He was a self-justifying, self-contained character as pure in his way as the moral and spiritual woman who so often opposed him, each attempting to assert a personal definition of the self-sufficient personality. But Berger, who has been the art critic of the *New Statesman* and most recently the author of *The Success and Failure of Picasso* and *Art and Revolution,* makes his Don Juan more similar to Byron's—the boyish and fallible voyager after sexual adventure who sardonically but compassionately observes the shams and deceits of the societies he moves through.

The hero of Berger's novel is G. (for Giovanni), the illegitimate son of an English mother and an Italian father. Rich and privileged, he is free to travel. He was conceived four years after the death of Garibaldi in 1886, born in Paris, raised by an aunt and uncle in England—and he was dead in Trieste on the day war was declared by Italy and Austria-Hungary. The events of European history swirl around G., counterpointing our view of his personal destiny. History in this book is often a matter of crowds: Garibaldi's ragged army entering Naples in 1860; the rioting workers in the streets of Milan in 1898; or the crowds of Bosnian nationalists, Italian Irredentists, and Hapsburg soldiers in the streets of Trieste in 1915.

Part of the power and fascination of *G.* comes from this extraordinary mixture of historical detail and sexual meditation, for at the intersection of G. and history is Berger's attitude toward heroism. G. is neither the public romantic Garibaldi, who galvanizes an entire people, nor is he a private romantic like his friend Chavez, who in 1910 won a prize for being the first man to fly over the Alps. Garibaldi is already dead before G. is born. While Chavez, the aviator, that type of the modern hero so mocked and mourned from the Cubists to Renoir's *The Rules of the Game,* attempts his great action (to the awe of crowds of peasants), G. seduces a chambermaid in a nearby hotel. In another scene, while Chavez lies dying for no apparent reason, G. is superficially wounded by the Peugeot representative at the competition, who has become irate at G.'s attentions to his wife. My crude parallels here convey little of the rich elaborations Berger makes of these events, which take up a large part of the center of the novel.

G. is not a hero like Chavez or Garibaldi. We never see him conquering women in hordes, although that may be perfectly consistent with his character. Berger focuses instead on a very few of his relationships with women. G. is not a victimizer but a willing victim whose nature is a release for the nature of others. He has the ability to evoke more reaction in others than he feels in himself, but always on the sexual basis of a one-to-one encounter, not on the grandiose scale of previous standards of heroism.

"The stranger who desires you and convinces you that it is truly you in all your particularity whom he desires, brings a message from all that you might be, to you as you actually are." Through what in *The Success and Failure of Picasso* Berger calls "the shared subjectivity of sex," G. establishes a perspective apart from the subject–object and object–object relations of public history. He is a vessel into which others may pour themselves to learn their shapes.

Sexuality is central to *G.,* but in this book the timeless moment of sex must always be considered within the context of history. When Berger is not writing novels, he is a painter and Marxist art critic with a keen sensitivity to the unique psychological and esthetic moment of a painting as well as to the historical, social, and cultural setting that conditions its creation. In *Picasso* he says, "Only in fiction can we share another person's specific experiences. Outside fiction we have to generalize." Berger's decision to write fiction is dictated by a choice of subject matter, a desire to express himself in a way criticism might not allow. The urge of the critic to explain becomes transmuted into the urge of the novelist to be baffled. As Berger remarks in *G.,* "All generalizations are opposed to sexuality."

Of the novels written since World War II, those I have been most moved by have been concerned with character, and in the last 10 or 15 years with character amid the opaque rhythms of history. Who would have predicted, watching the flood of Frank Yerbys, Kathleen Windsors, and Taylor Caldwells pouring from the book clubs of the 1940s and 1950s, that a good proportion of the great imaginative works of the 1960s could be called, without too much stretching, "historical novels": *Catch-22, The Sotweed Factor, Little Big Man, V, The Tin Drum, The Armies of the Night, One Hundred Years of Solitude*? In these novels, unlike the earlier historical novels, history is not a refuge for a passion and jollity the modern age denies, a primitivist playground or a Joycean nightmare from which we wake relieved in the present. It is an arena for understanding of the self through what lies outside and tries to determine it.

Because G. is also self-conscious about the act of its own creation, some readers might think it superficially resembles *The French Lieutenant's Woman*—i.e., historical novel, intrusive author, passion in the twilight of Victoria. But G.—in addition to its vividly portrayed characters and the crashing immediacy of its historical settings—is a complex novel of ideas that sets off in the reader meditations about sex, history, and the nature of the novel that could never have been excited by the flaccid ironies and self-important complacencies of John Fowles's work.

Literary self-consciousness, for Berger, is a metaphor for human self-consciousness, the necessary partialities and deceits involved when one person tells you about a third, even when that third is himself. Time and again, Berger intervenes to allow his characters to escape from a control he never meant to wield. Oddly enough, for all such intervention, G. is less loose (almost less personal) than his critical works. But the coldness, the detachment in the prose gradually reveals itself as an unwillingness to control, and the insistence of his voice becomes more and more hypnotic, until the reader is increasingly guided by its perceptions, its stories, its asides, even its reticence.

Part of my pleasure in reading G. arises from just such a growing feeling for the intricate relations between its characters, settings, ideas, and form—a kind of interdependency that great novels always exhibit. G. puts the reader in contact with someone for whom writing a novel is a special way to think about the problems that most vitally concern us. The hermeticism of the Nabokovian novel, with its equal attack against history and character, is the quintessence of the modernist lure: the novel that finishes novels, literature telling us that literature is basically worth nothing; it's all parlor games, fans, and now back to the real business.

G. belongs to that other tradition of the novel, the tradition of George Eliot, Tolstoy, D. H. Lawrence, and Norman Mailer, the tradition of fallible wisdom, rich, nagging, and unfinished. To read G. is to find again a full commitment to the resources and possibilities of the genre—and a writer one demands to know more about. Not to sit at the feet of his aphorisms or unravel the tangles of his allusions, but to explore more fully an intriguing and powerful mind and talent.

[1972]

Grime on the Glitter:
Hollywood and McCarthyism

*The Inquisition in Hollywood:
Politics in the Film Community, 1930–1960,*
by Larry Ceplair and Steven Englund.

Heyday: An Autobiography, by Dore Schary.

Creative Differences: Profiles of Hollywood Dissidents,
by David Talbot and Barbara Zheutlin.

The 1950s were a time of codes—dress codes, behavior codes, moral codes, es-thetic codes, codes for individuals, and codes for groups—every *is* turned into an *ought* by elected, appointed, or self-appointed arbiters fearful of any deviation from the pure norms of cold-war America. The political consensus of the war had broken apart with victory and the death of Roosevelt. It was a time of fear when self-seeking could easily assume the guise of national interests and put up for grabs the definition of what was truly "American."

In this contest over what it meant to be an American, the most emblematic battle was fought between right-wing Washington (in the shape of the House Un-American Activities Committee) and left-wing Hollywood. The story of the Hol-lywood Ten, who went to jail rather than answer questions about their beliefs and associates, has been told before. But many of the earlier accounts were either *ex parte* pleas for the victims of the blacklist or written by what Larry Ceplair and Steven Englund characterize as anticommunist liberals intent on disparaging the talent of the blacklisted even while they attack the right-wing publicists and poli-ticians who aimed to destroy them. It is the achievement of *The Inquisition in Hollywood* that it is the first book on the period to take a historical view of the campaign against the Hollywood Left, treating it not only in terms of postwar politics (the usual approach) but also in relation to the long history of political activity in the movie industry.

This activity began in the early 1930s with such Popular Front organizations as the Hollywood Anti-Nazi League and the Joint Anti-Fascist Refugee Committee. But it is the Screen Writers Guild (SWG) and the growth of Hollywood unionism that are at the center of the story Ceplair and Englund have to tell. Screenwriters, they point out, were more than half of those blacklisted (and more than half of those who informed). Seven of the Hollywood Ten were screenwriters (plus two directors and one producer), six of the seven had been officers of the SWG, and two (John Howard Lawson and Lester Cole) had been president.

If one issue could be said to have forced the SWG into existence, it was credit— credit for what was written, credit for what was filmed. The contemporary celebration of the director as the most important creator in a film was far in the future, and the writer had even lower status. Both were employees, and the writers especially were entirely at the mercy of producers and studios who might hire them to do original work or rewrites, then fire them and leave their names off the finished film.

The Screen Writers Guild was therefore that strange phenomenon in unionism— a group of individualist creators banded together for collective support in making their personal work known to an audience. From the first, then, the problem of integrating artistic individuality (and the competition for freelance jobs) with political philosophy (and the belief in collective goals) intensified the general problem of Hollywood: where does art leave off and industry begin?

Ceplair and Englund have no answer to this perennial American problem. But through their command of statistics, their pioneering use of sources often ignored by more impressionistic accounts, and their large number of interviews with participants from all political perspectives, they maintain a balance between the changing shapes of political action, the more rigid forms of theory, and the individual careers that crystallize what would otherwise be contradictions. Most strikingly, Ceplair and Englund approach the actual issue of communist involvement with firm evenhandedness, emphasizing especially the breakdown of the New Deal coalition and tracing with some delicacy the confusion felt by many Hollywood leftists, who were attacked by HUAC for subverting the movie industry even while they thought they had accomplished little or nothing at all.

Unfortunately, the sophisticated political and historical account of *The Inquisition in Hollywood* is not matched by any clear sense of what films can or have actually accomplished. Ceplair and Englund accurately point out that the ultimate test of a film's politics is its impact on an audience, and they condemn the rigidity of the Communist Party's view of the relation of art and politics. But their own comments on specific films are often rudimentary and simplistic, and they fail to see the genuinely subversive nature of many films of the 1950s, more intricate (and interesting) because they were unable to speak directly. Like many of those they discuss on both left and right, Ceplair and Englund often seem to think that only specific content is truly political, and they condemn the ways even liberal producers would often remove a film's direct references and substitute vague generalizations.

But one person's smudged glass might be another's new window on reality. As Abraham Polonsky, another formerly blacklisted writer and director, has pointed out, form—a new perspective on the world—is often more politically influential than any specific content. The lines between causes in art and effects in an audience are very hard to draw, let alone predict. Traditional left-wing critics have often attacked *Viva Zapata* (1952) for its jaundiced view of the uses of power, even in a good cause (as well as for the fact that its director, Elia Kazan, became a HUAC "friendly" witness). Yet a few years later, in a different political atmosphere, the film became an inspiration to the early leaders of the New Left.

The great paradox of the blacklist was that, after being in the forefront of efforts to achieve credit for their scripts, the blacklisted writers thereupon lost it and had to masquerade under the names of others. As the years go on, it turns out that more and more of the most striking films of those times were credited to "fronts." The late Michael Wilson, for example, who with Carl Foreman had coauthored *The Bridge over the River Kwai* (1957), once recounted how Pierre Boulle, the non-English-speaking author of the novel, who had received the actual script credit (and the Academy Award), began to give interviews about how he had managed the adaptation. When Wilson was finally nominated in his own name for *Planet of the Apes* (1968), also coincidentally adapted from a Boulle novel, he could hardly resist wiring Boulle, "You've done it again." For *Friendly Persuasion* (1957) Wilson received no credit, but neither did anyone else—the only Hollywood film whose story and dialogue, at least according to the credits, emanates from the characters themselves. To compound the insanity, Richard Nixon, a distant cousin of Jessamyn West, the author of the original novel, frequently showed the film at the White House during his administration, no doubt to show what true Americans were like.

Such ironies are available everywhere in the accounts of the blacklist and underline the way the conditions of creative work in Hollywood make even the barest personal expression difficult, let alone the expression of one's politics. In the more open atmosphere of the present, it might seem to be easier. But in *Creative Differences,* David Talbot and Barbara Zheutlin merge career sketches and interviews to depict the continuing struggle of some 16 Hollywood workers—from the visible and highly paid (like Jane Fonda and Haskell Wexler) to less prominent executives, directors, technicians, and secretaries—as they try to mediate the peculiarly intense Hollywood tug-of-war between the individual and the system. It's a valuable book, especially for the way it reveals the often minute and personal ways the struggle for social justice is carried on in an industry more often noted for its surfaces than its depths.

Dore Schary, in *Heyday,* promises to be an equally intriguing witness. Schary—who began as a screenwriter in 1933, became a producer in 1941, and headed production at several studios until being fired and leaving Hollywood in 1956—was one of the first writers to try to get leverage for his work by becoming a producer. A strong liberal, Schary details the fight he (along with Walter Wanger and Sam Goldwyn) had with other studio heads about knuckling under to HUAC. He claims credit for suggesting the First Amendment defense to the Hollywood Ten and generally agrees with Ceplair and Englund that the Ten's hostile attitude toward the Committee (a strategy suggested by their lawyer) was responsible for a massive loss of support, although he personally refused to fire Adrian Scott and Edward Dmytryk (strangely referred to as "Dymytryk" throughout *Heyday*).

Schary generally characterizes himself as a humane person trying to realize his ideals and aspirations in the midst of a rapacious and corrupt Hollywood. In fact, some of the best parts of *Heyday* deal with the fitful ups and downs of a project before it becomes a finished film, as Schary bucks front-office resistance to such films as *Crossfire, Bad Day at Black Rock* (the great liberal *mea culpa*), *Blackboard Jungle,* and *Red Badge of Courage.* For Schary, talent is unrelated to moral and political character, and unions can be militant without being political—attitudes that are easy enough to argue with but were rare for an executive to hold at a time of witchhunting and guilt by association.

Yet, despite its interesting angle on the same period covered more historically by Ceplair and Englund, *Heyday* is finally unsatisfying because it is primarily a scrapbook. Held together by the invincible cheerfulness of Schary, who acts according to principles, gets fired, and yet always seems to wind up on his feet, it moves easily from talk of the blacklist to family jokes about his son-in-law's name. So intent is Schary on demonstrating that he was unscathed by Hollywood that he includes a good deal of trivial detail about his children, as if to prove that here are some Hollywood kids who grew up all right.

Even in 1980 the fog has hardly lifted. Budd Schulberg, in a recent article on the making of *On the Waterfront* (1954), talks about everything but the political context of the film's central theme of informing. So too Schary, for all his frankness in some areas, often sounds like a survivor glossing over the difficult times he lived through except to celebrate his own escape. Like all autobiographies, *Heyday* is as remarkable for what it leaves out as for what it includes. Schary is at pains to distinguish himself from the old buccaneering studio executives and the new cost accountants, modeling his own liberal paternalism on that of his hero FDR. But for all its emphasis on his liberalism and his Zionism, *Heyday* sheds little light on a crucial but hardly discussed thread in the cold-war fabric: the extent to which many Jewish studio chiefs, who had strongly supported liberal and leftist anti-Nazi groups before the war, feared that opposing HUAC's demands would only feed the anti-Semitic identification of Jews with communists.

Yet whatever their partialities, all three books are essential to the continuing dialogue about the place of Hollywood in American life, and its often confusing role in shaping and being shaped by American values. The secret codes of the cold-war period have hardly been completely cracked. But Ceplair and Englund have made a giant step forward in our understanding of the place of politics in the history of Hollywood, Schary furnishes the brief of an actively involved witness to the past, while Talbot and Zheutlin survey the attitudes of the present and the possibilities for the future.

[1980]

◻

We Are Your Sons
by Michael and Robert Meeropol

Perhaps we know an era has passed when we can look back and see that everything that happened in it has a symbolic quality. A fashion or a movie, a president
or a baseball player, an advertisement or an execution—any detail will evoke all
the rest. The period following World War II has recently become such a seamless
place, a land with its own self-consistent rules and demands, in retrospect revealing an absurd coherence.

To trace the secret continuities of the 1950s is especially ironic, because the
public rhetoric of the period was filled with demands for clear choices—opinions
were clearly right or wrong, the spirit of either/or imposed itself everywhere:
capitalist or communist, believer or atheist, patriot or traitor. The world was a
battleground of totally opposed forces, not light and darkness but America and
Russia, which seemed to amount to the same thing. We were expected to purify
ourselves for the coming apocalyptic battle, to purge ambivalence and become
one thing or another; for underneath the public clarities there was a fascination
with secrets, with loss of identity, the stealing of minds, and the washing of
brains.

The clearest enemy in this drama of national purgation was the communist—
cold, unemotional, ready to sacrifice every personal relationship for an abstraction. Humanity was reserved for Americans. Like the science-fiction monsters of
the 1950s, communists were totally alien. They might on occasion look human,
but that disguise was only a sham to entrap the decent but politically innocent
American. "We are all monsters in our subconscious," says a character in the
film *Forbidden Planet* (1956); "that's why we need laws and religion." In the
face of such allegorical politics, the rebels of the 1950s—the juvenile delinquents,
the beats—had to be without a cause. So they wandered, searching for some
vague revenge, hoping to restore some meaning to their lives, perhaps by meeting
a foe in single combat—but always ignoring the forces that had determined the
place of the contest and sold the tickets.

Michael and Robert Meeropol, the sons of Julius and Ethel Rosenberg, would
seem to have more reasons than most to seek revenge on the 1950s. Charged with
conspiracy rather than actual treason or espionage, the Rosenbergs were convicted

in 1951, on evidence that has become more and more suspect over the years and by legal procedures that received widespread criticism at the time. They were finally executed in 1953, on their 14th wedding anniversary, still maintaining their innocence, after Attorney General Herbert Brownell had requested a special session of the Supreme Court to vacate a stay of execution ordered by Justice Douglas.

On June 19 [1975] the Rosenbergs will have been dead 22 years, yet their case and its meaning are still being explored and argued, most recently by an excellent P.B.S. television documentary, "The Unquiet Death of Julius and Ethel Rosenberg." Now with secrecy in government being itself heavily criticized, we may finally be able to look at the trial of the Rosenbergs (and the sentence by Judge Irving R. Kaufman that blamed them for causing the Korean War) as a show trial like the Soviet trials of the 1930s, designed to convey more about their ideology of the government than about the guilt or innocence of the defendants.

But *We Are Your Sons* actually spends little time going over the issues of evidence and procedure that have preoccupied so many past commentators on the Rosenbergs. The book is less an argument than an attempt to recapture the true identities, not only of the Rosenbergs, but also of Michael and Robert Meeropol (they take their name from the stepparents). Discarding their privacy, they seek to assert themselves as the sons of their parents and in some final way to reconstitute a family divided when Michael was six and Robert three, brought together only for brief moments under the auspices of the warden at Sing Sing. The Meeropols call themselves "orphans of the cold war." Their book, they write, was born in response to Louis Nizer's "The Implosion Conspiracy," a self-important analysis of the case published in 1973, which they claim contained "false, fictitious and distorted writing about our parents, us, and our relations with them." It was this attack against the Rosenberg family itself, the most recent in a series of such attacks, that finally impelled Michael and Robert to reveal their true identities by bringing suit against Nizer for infringement of copyright, defamation, and invasion of privacy.

Family is in fact the heart of *We Are Your Sons,* as family was at the heart of the values of the 1950s. Communists, said the mythographers, couldn't have families like Americans because they sacrificed everything to ideology. The Rosenberg family, where the parents supposedly only valued the children for purposes of political manipulation, was the evil family that the good American family could measure itself against. The "good brother" David Greenglass testified against his sister Ethel Rosenberg to serve America. Evil Ethel not only did not testify against others but even dared to say she was innocent. The Rosenbergs, according to contemporary writers such as Robert Warshow and Leslie Fiedler, were not like real human beings. "The ideal Communist responds only to the universal," wrote Warshow." "Their relationship to everything, including themselves, was false," concluded Fiedler, although he thought they should not have been executed for this lapse.

Many of the over 150 letters collected in *We Are Your Sons* are the "deathhouse" letters to which Warshow, Fiedler, and others reacted so savagely, but many more have never been published before. A little over half the book is composed of these letters and a connecting narrative written by Michael who, as the older, took on himself the job of facing the outside world. His tone is undramatic and so the horror of the situation appears in more relief.

In the letters the urge of both Ethel and Julius Rosenberg is to try to make everything seem normal, but their tone gives them away. Long before they decide to use the letters as part of their appeal to the world outside, they have forced their language to create a world of relationships that would sustain them despite separation and possible death: they rehearse what to say to the children when they appear; they describe in minute detail the contents of their cells and their daily routines; they continually compliment each other on their ideas, their looks, their ability to get along with fellow prisoners and guards.

Ethel's language especially is oddly but appropriately reminiscent of the words of the confined heroines of the gothic novels of Ann Radcliffe. On August 16, 1951, she writes "I have the curious feeling of living in a world beyond whose walls no other exists." Only the bond with the invisible Julius sustains her, the thoughts of the children, and the self-objectification of her "case."

Michael's own language connecting these letters is not argumentative, but more melancholic and groping, an effort to recapture every detail of this Dickensian world he saw as a child. He records many events that seem normal and even bland on the face of it, but are all touched by some ironic resonance, as if fate would not leave him alone—inside the most common event there was always the secret of who he was.

Robert Meeropol continues the narrative after the execution, describing the lives of his brother and himself from that time to now—the constant question of whether or not to tell who they were, the efforts to hide, and the speculation about who knew. He describes the similarities and differences between his political development and that of his brother, familiar odysseys for those of their generation but made fascinating by the added knowledge of who they are. In an appendix Michael Meeropol offers a political and economic interpretation of the cold-war period, but his discussion is finally too abstract except for those places where he writes about his parents again.

As Michael and Robert Meeropol are aware, the power of *We Are Your Sons* lies not in its analysis and argument, but in the way it allows a different America to come to its own conclusions about the Rosenbergs and about the era in which they were condemned. The question of the Rosenbergs' guilt will, one hopes, be settled by suits now pending against the prosecution for subornation of perjury (of David Greenglass) and against the F.B.I. under the Freedom of Information Act. But the legal case against the Rosenbergs may have done less harm to America than the ideological case leveled against their human nature. Although it bears many signs of hasty writing and sloppy editing, *We Are Your Sons,* through its directness, its awkwardness, its sincerity, encourages us to make sure such cruel distortion does not happen again.

[1975]

Regiment of Women
by Thomas Berger

Twenty-nine-year-old Georgie Cornell, the hero of Thomas Berger's new novel, was born in 2096 and lives in New York City. The doorwoman of Georgie's apartment house, "in the jungle of the East 70's," womans the front-door anti-pollution airlock with a shotgun. Georgie's psychiatrist, Dr. Prine, wears a self-adhesive nylon beard and has been treating Georgie for frigidity with a dildo. She tells him his complaint that it hurts is merely a "defense"—as Dr. Daisy Rudin explained so well in her new book on the superiority of the anal orgasm, recently published by the giant firm where Georgie works as a secretary, unsuccessfully avoiding the attempts of his bald-headed boss, Ida Hind, to steal glances into Georgie's blouse at his newly siliconed breasts.

Through such details of satiric reversal, parallel, and extension, Berger first sketches in the background of his future America. The novel's title is taken from John Knox's 1558 attack on "Bloody" Mary Tudor, *The First Blast of the Trumpet against the Monstrous Regiment of Women,* and quotations from Knox, Martin Luther, Christabel Pankhurst, Grover Cleveland, Olive Schreiner, Confucius, Virginia Woolf, and others, including a final comment from Friedrich Nietzsche ("Woman was God's second mistake"), preface each chapter.

Georgie Cornell's America is governed entirely by women ("regiment" in Knox's title means "rule"); and in Georgie's New York men swear by Mary rather than Christ (whether Bloody or Virgin is unclear), admire Leonarda's Mono Liso, celebrate Columba's Day, and look forward patriotically to their six-month service at Camp Kilmer, where they are milked daily by sperm machines to insure the continuance of the species. (Normal intercourse in Georgie's world involves women taking men anally with dildoes, and the troubles for which Georgie is seeing Dr. Prine seem to have begun during a disastrous Junior Prom date when he was 18.)

The ruling women of 2125 haven't done very much better than the ruling men of today. The city and the society in *Regiment of Women* are basically chaotic and inefficient rather than inhumane or totalitarian. The George Washington Bridge collapsed years before into the Hudson Sewer during a rainstorm, and the general decay of 22nd-century America seeps into every part of the novel. Unlike the antiseptic dreams or nightmares of the future usually displayed in science-fiction

novels, the atmosphere of *Regiment of Women* is incredibly seedy, as if Berger
envisioned the world of the future as an extension of the back alleys of Dashiell
Hammett and Mickey Spillane, or of Ross Macdonald's decaying southern California towns.

But *Regiment of Women* isn't merely an extended tour through a turnabout
world that readers will view with disgust or approval according to their prejudices.
To paste up a collage of the details of *Regiment of Women* falsifies the actual
effect of the novel, which convinces almost in spite of the details. In Berger's
novel *Little Big Man* Jack Crabb tells how he first couldn't stand the smell of the
Indian village: "But, like anything else, living in it made it your reality, and when
I next entered a white settlement, I missed the odor of what seemed to me life
itself and felt I would suffocate."

Berger's imaginative power makes us live in Georgie Cornell's reality until it
becomes our norm, and the arbitrary rigidity of the sex roles in Georgie's world
makes us aware not of our "normality," but of our own arbitrary distinctions.
There is more compassion than bitterness in *Regiment of Women*. Berger's subject
is not so much the specific nature of sexual roles as the categorical severity with
which roles are enforced and deviations punished. The decay of Georgie Cornell's
America implies that the more politically and socially fragile a society, the more
severely it attempts to police and define individual nature.

Berger's settings and characters in all his novels are plausible rather than apocalyptic. His satire refuses to make an alliance between reader and author against
an oppressive, ugly "them." Paul Krassner once wrote that "the ultimate object
of satire is its own audience," and Berger's integrity arranges that no reader—
male chauvinist, militant feminist, or anyone in between—can emerge from *Regiment of Women* unscathed. All of Berger's main characters—Georgie Cornell
here, Jack Crabb in *Little Big Man,* Carlo Reinhart in *Crazy in Berlin, Reinhart
in Love,* and *Vital Parts*—are moved more by circumstances than by some passionate belief. Berger's clearest outrage is reserved for anyone who presumes to
sit in moral judgment on another, and his central characters are all slammed about
by beings more certain than they about the location of truth.

Consequently, there is little ideological significance to Georgie's journey from
the New York in which he is a brow-beaten secretary to the Maine lake where he
discovers he can put his penis into a woman's vagina without killing her. Along
the way Georgie is manipulated as much by the underground men's liberation
movement as he is by the female government. "Everyone he encountered was a
monomaniac of some sort, working compulsively to affect someone else: to alter
their personality, change their mind, catch them out, set them straight. Everybody
else always knew better about sex, society, history, you name it." Georgie's
resolution of his problems is purely individual, the affirmation of personal identity
that for Berger must precede the definition of sexual identity.

Like all great literary satirists, whose art gets at the root of imperception and
self-delusion, Berger is concerned with the way language can falsify reality. ("I
was never an aggressive boy," says Georgie. "I certainly don't think I could be
called effeminate.") By disorienting us through its language, *Regiment of Women*
indicts the society that uses language as a tool of oppression, making purely verbal

differences into codes and categories—rhetoric asserting and experiencing itself as truth.

Berger's own style, with its tendency to absorb the speech rhythms of his characters and its unwillingness to stand apart from them, is especially suited for such themes. Since *Little Big Man,* especially, he has concentrated on exploring the possibilities and revealing the secrets of everyday language with a deep wit and feeling that transform our awareness of the language we really use much more than does the flamboyance of a writer bent on asserting his personal style. *Killing Time* may be Berger's most successful effort to engage in this most truly poetic task of renovating the language we speak. But *Regiment of Women* is a flame from the same sources of energy.

Regiment of Women is in many ways a difficult book to talk about because, like the popular novels it imitates, it has few of the philosophical nuggets or technical tricks that professedly serious novels kindly include for the reviewer's convenience. But Berger doesn't use popular forms archly, as does, for example, Donald Barthelme. He finds in them energy, action, and simple decisions that are motivated more by self-preservation than by abstract moral or intellectual imperatives. Berger also concocts this combination gothic-horror, science-fiction, and detective story to explore and reveal a theme such works have always been fascinated by—the masculine fear of the domination of women. Berger uses these forms in the service of what I think is a compelling and finally humanizing fiction about male and female weakness perceived as human weakness, and about the potential strength of individual identity that the official and underground institutions of society equally ignore.

Regiment of Women is a brilliant accomplishment by one of our best novelists. *Little Big Man,* and perhaps *Killing Time* and *Vital Parts,* are among the best novels of the past 10 years. Next to these larger achievements, *Regiment of Women* may be more a fable, a deceptively simple romp through current prejudices. It isn't great in the way greatness has been defined by the novel since Joyce: each one a block-buster containing, as far as possible, all knowledge and experience. None of Berger's works is suitable for taking to the moon with matching toothbrush. They are novels that help you maintain a fresh response to the world around you.

With Joseph Heller and Ken Kesey seemingly stilled—and Richard Condon plunged into self-parody—Kurt Vonnegut may be closest to Berger in style if not sensibility; but Vonnegut lacks the edge of Berger's wit and the variety of his insights. Each of Berger's novels is an expression of an esthetic presence that continues to grow in strength and importance. *Regiment of Women,* for all its exaggeration and grotesque parody, has been imagined with such ferocity and glee that we assent to it almost in spite of ourselves, celebrating with Berger that anarchic individuality that outlasts all the forms that language and society attempt to impose upon it.

[1973]

Winter Kills
by Richard Condon

The most original novelistic style of the 1960s was the style of paranoid surrealism. As created by such novelists as Joseph Heller, William Burroughs, Norman Mailer, Thomas Berger, Ken Kesey, and Thomas Pynchon, the paranoid novel drew equally on the facts of national life and the clichés of popular fiction to create a world where technology, politics, and history had run wild and the only possible humanism was gallows humor. The dream of community that had inspired the Popular Front (and the literary methods of Dos Passos, Farrell, Bellow, and the Mailer of *The Naked and the Dead*) had been replaced first by the enforced order of the World at War, then by the annihilating solace of postwar Togetherness.

In the 1950s everyone—the Rosenbergs as much as Judge Irving Kaufman, Arthur Miller as much as Sen. Joseph McCarthy—seemed to believe that the system was fine; only individuals were at fault. It was a strange new American life which the novelists who were still working a naturalistic vein, still intent on cataloguing and thereby understanding the American wilderness, could never encompass. It remained up to the paranoid novel, drawing its energies more from American popular culture than from Kafka, to level its attack on the anonymous and inhuman orders the system had created.

Richard Condon was one of the most distinguished members of this group and through the controlled corrosiveness of his two great early novels—*The Manchurian Candidate* (1959) and *Some Angry Angel* (1960)—has some claim to being a founder. But something seemed to fall apart in the five novels that followed *An Infinity of Mirrors* (1964). Condon became a cult novelist, a little paranoid epicycle of his own, cutting easy slices from the same chunk of multicolored, hyperdense imagination, producing novels without any real qualities of invective and intelligence, stuffed with in-jokes and obvious parodies, a kind of virtuoso shoddiness.

Winter Kills, Condon's eleventh novel, begins in much the same way. Condon's hero, Nick Thirkield, is the half-brother of Tim Kegan, the rich, young, charismatic, handsome, womanizing, liberal Irish President who had only begun to deliver on his promise of America when he was assassinated by a lone fanatic in Philadelphia's Hunt Plaza in 1960. Now, almost 15 years later, a man who claims to be the second gun has made a deathbed confession and Nick is on the trail to find the power behind the gun, whoever it is: the right-wing Texas oil billionaire; the head of the Tubesters union; the film studio chief upset that his greatest star (and one of Tim's hundreds of mistresses) has committed suicide; the prostitute turned Mafia capo; or some other shadowy figure from the maze of stories, rumors, half-truths, and myths that pass for reality in America.

But *Winter Kills* is not a commercial ripoff of recent events in the style of Harold Robbins and Irving Wallace (themselves the butt-end of naturalism), nor is it another Condon novel like the last few, filled with the forgettable frenzy of a mechanical satirist. *Winter Kills* is instead a triumph of satire and knowledge, with a delicacy of style and a command of tone that puts Condon once again into the first rank of American novelists. Condon's hero is the lineal descendant of the ineffectual avengers who stalked the movie world of the 1950s. But while they were trying to hold on to a warped dream of individuality, Nick Thirkield is merely trying to find a fact. And Condon goes with him, less interested in facts than in nonfacts and superfacts, not historical truth but the Macy's parade of history, the overblown images from which we have each manufactured our own paranoid vision of the true connections of American society.

Until I read *Winter Kills,* I thought that Condon had been trapped between his perception of paranoia and his love of facts. The drabness of the 1950s ignited imaginations all over America. But how could a writer satirize the already nightmarish world of Paris under the Nazis *(An Infinity of Mirrors)* or America in the 1960s *(The Ecstasy Business, Mile High, The Vertical Smile)?* How does one use surrealism to attack the evil in a society where every newspaper reader has to believe three impossible things before breakfast? How can the paranoid intensities possible in art compete with the normal paranoias of everyday life?

Like one of his villains in *Winter Kills,* Condon seemed to believe that ''information is the key to everything.'' Data on wine and food and weapons technology tumbled out of his novels until what might have begun as a parody of modern acquisitiveness turned into a James Bond-like wallowing in it. The free-wheeling crime capers, seemingly so anticapitalist in their nose-thumbing attack on riches and respectability, disclosed their roots in the myths of romantic individualism with which the corporate capitalism of the 1950s nourished itself.

Winter Kills succeeds so brilliantly because the Kennedy assassination furnishes Condon with a familiar mythic landscape through which his Gulliver-like hero can wander, simultaneously prey to Lilliputian politics, Brobdingnagian physicality, Laputan science, and Houyhnhnm moralizing. The form of the novel has always implied paranoia: the reader and writer alone with each other and themselves, the plot that organizes the world for your benefit. Joyce reestablished what Laurence Sterne already knew: the added paranoia of the writer trapped with his words, the closed moment of history and language he believes it is his mission to re-create.

Joyce finally withdrew into his words totally. But novelists like Condon and Thomas Berger have completely moved away from the modernist obsession with literary language and are experimenting instead with the ability of the rhythms of daily speech and popular culture to embody the plain-speaking clarity of their satire. By destroying the gap between "serious" and "popular" culture, they make us realize that the myths and images we may consciously disdain affect us more deeply for our ignorance of them.

Winter Kills then, is "some kind of bummer through American mythology," in which almost all of Condon's characters, from highest to lowest, are driven by the American dream of being someone, making a difference, having power and control. *Winter Kills* isn't the world; it's the way we think about the world, the distortions and how they are created, "the application of the techniques of fiction playing like searchlights on a frenzied façade of truth." Condon has created a paranoid novel that does not leave us trapped inside its world, but functions instead as a liberation, exposing through the gentler orders of fiction the way we have been programmed to believe anything in print. By mingling historical reality with his own fabulous invention, Condon savagely satirizes a world in which fiction and reality are mingled to manipulate, exploit, and kill.

I said in a review of Berger's *Regiment of Women* in these pages that Condon's satiric power had lapsed into self-parody. *Winter Kills* proves me wrong and happy to say so. The joy in seeing Condon recover his former strength, the pleasure I take in *Winter Kills,* the intricacies of its style and construction, and especially the masochistic pleasure in its cauterization of so many national wounds, spring finally from that feeling of optimism in darkness that only healing satire can truly bring.

[1976]

The Difficulties of *Little Big Man*

In many of the films of Arthur Penn there appears a minor character who is a kind of chronicler, tagging after the main story, trying to get his hand for a moment on some of the truth and some of the glory that the heroes have absorbed from their own contact with fame and history. In his first film, *The Left-Handed Gun,* this character is the dime-novel writer Moultrie, who is outraged that Billy the Kid's real life doesn't live up to his own heroic fantasies. He even thinks that this disappointment is reason enough for his willingness to betray Billy himself in search of a better story. Similarly, a groupie played by Shelley Plimpton in *Alice's Restaurant* wants to sleep with Arlo Guthrie because he "may be an album some-day." Such characters are trying to suck a little permanence, a little glory, into their own lives by linking with what they believe to be true permanence and fame outside themselves. In their turn, the heroes themselves often believe that only such a chronicle can truly validate their identities: Bonnie and Clyde want to see their names in print as much as the reporters who follow them want to write their story. When Bonnie's poetry is printed in a newspaper, she says that for the first time she feels like she exists (a detail stolen by *Butch Cassidy and the Sundance Kid*). Print makes eternal the human assertion that otherwise quickly vanishes.

Penn pursues this theme in *Little Big Man* by emphasizing the framing character of the history graduate student with his tape recorder all set up to interview Jack Crabb about the "primitive life styles of the Plains Indians." Like the photogra-pher who takes the picture of Jack and his new wife, Olga, in front of their general store, he wants to "preserve the moment," using a phrase that is the title of a book of photographs by Penn's elder brother, Irving.

Both still photography and the chronicling common to newspapers and Ph.D. dissertations in history can try to restore the erosion worked by time, turning corruption and decay back into vitality and innocence, the old Jack Crabb in his hospital ward into young Jack Crabb once again. But in many of his films Penn seems torn between preserving the fleeting past through the clarity of photographic detail and revising it through the romantic permanence of heroic myth. All the critical complaints that in *Bonnie and Clyde* two killers were romanticized and heroicized were in this sense not complaints at all but clear visions of what Penn was doing. The implied question for Penn was whether or not one film could contain both the realism and the romance of their lives. But Bonnie and Clyde were not separate enough from the corrupt society that surrounded them and on which they fed. Their rebel roles, the fame and heroism they sought and projected for themselves, were sham. They were compromised because in fact they were guilty, and their slow-motion deaths are less a beatification than another effort to preserve the moment, to preserve the possibility of heroism that once existed, to stop time in its inevitably reducing and debunking rush forward.

With *Alice's Restaurant* and *Little Big Man,* Penn's uneasiness with the heroic vision of the past has become more and more acute. Both films have a kind of compelling openness and inconclusiveness after the tighter and more closed worlds of the earlier films. The hermetic posturings of *Mickey One* give way in some sense to the violence and directness of *The Miracle Worker.* To counter the romanticized heroes of *Bonnie and Clyde,* in *Little Big Man* we are faced with George Armstrong Custer, the demythologized hero. And such a figure is no longer the central character. That role belongs to Jack Crabb, who resembles the C. W. Moss (Michael J. Pollard) of *Bonnie and Clyde,* watching with telephoto distance as his two heroes ride out to their deaths. And it is no coincidence that the chronicler at one remove, the history student who comes to interview Jack, bears an extraordinary resemblance to Arthur Penn.

Penn's variations on the problems of romantic versus realistic heroism seem closely related to the way he presents the relations of youth and age in his films. In somewhat traditional terms, youth frequently has the energy of naturalness and innocence, while age brings corruption and cynicism. But anyone who remembers *The Left-Handed Gun* or *The Chase* could not call *Alice's Restaurant* an unambiguous paean to youth culture or see in *Little Big Man* a youth's clear-eyed condemnation of the lies and venality of America's barbarous treatment of the Indians. In one brilliant scene in *The Left-Handed Gun,* Billy and his gang have a mock fight, throwing flour sacks until they are coated like masquerading children; later, in a fiesta scene, Billy chooses to dance only with a little Mexican girl. Through such scenes Penn clearly implies that Billy's kind of rebellion is a fight against growing up, a pastorally based innocence that refuses to come into adult society. In *The Chase* the relation between Jane Fonda, Robert Redford, and James Fox constitutes the same kind of childhood world, a relation that no adult in the film, even the sympathetic sheriff, can really understand. The two worlds seem separate, like the adjacent houses in *The Chase,* one holding an adult party, the other a teenagers' party. For a while they remain distinct, but ultimately the adult world crushes the world of the children, as Redford is shot on the courthouse steps, as Pat Garrett kills Billy, who has considered him his father, as Anne Sullivan must tame and socialize the anarchic energies of Helen Keller, as the deaths of Bonnie and Clyde are engineered by C. W. Moss's father, supposedly to protect his son.

With *Alice's Restaurant* and *Little Big Man* the balance has shifted. The adults— Alice and Ray Brock, Marjorie and Woody Guthrie—are more sympathetic. Instead of being the betrayers of youth, the observing adults have become their victims. Arlo's bland screen presence and the feeble characterizations of many of the other young characters force us to look more closely at the adults. Only Alice and Ray really hold together the youthful Utopia of the Stockbridge church, while Woody, lying in his hospital bed, unable to speak, hardly able to move, implies a cannibalization of age by youth. Woody's music may live on, but his own end is still death. The grim possibility that Arlo himself may have the same disease that Woody suffers from underlines the fact that youth will fall victim in its turn. Both *Alice's Restaurant* and *Little Big Man* end with images of loneliness: Alice in a foreground of shuttering trees; Jack Crabb in the dark hospital ward. "Songs for Aging Children" is the real theme song of *Alice's Restaurant*. And the nervous final sequence, in which the camera tries to look at Alice directly but constantly shifts its angle, is an image of the uncertainty of the film itself, trying to focus on Alice's problems directly, but succeeding only in getting waylaid by youth culture and cheerful songs against authority.

Little Big Man tries to reconcile youthful iconoclasm and freedom with the wisdom and weariness of age by emphasizing the continuity between the young Jack Crabb on the screen and the old survivor in his hospital ward. In the novel Jack tells his story in the first person. We match in our heads the timbre of his voice with the nature of his adventures. But in the film the narrative voice with its cracked quavers constantly reminds us that the young face on the screen has somewhere in his future an old decayed body. From the crowded life of his youth as a participant in so many different communities, Jack will finally come to a time when the only interest in him any community will show is to put him away to die, like the forgotten Woody Guthrie who, in a scene left out of the final *Alice's Restaurant* but in the original script, sits unnoticed in a wheelchair in Washington Square, while nearby guitar players sing his songs.

With this kind of continuity in Penn's interests, why then does *Little Big Man* fail to hang together? Why does it seem more sprawling than rich, more scatter-shot than pointed? The answer, I think, lies in the character of Jack Crabb himself and how that character is conceived by Penn. Jack Crabb's inadequacies as a central consciousness or a conscienceless picaro seem to be artistic failures intimately related to Penn's themes. The gap between the youthful Jack and the 121-year-old Jack in the hospital is never really bridged. Penn, like his surrogate, the graduate-student historian, finally stands outside his central figure, without making the imaginative entry into Jack's character that could have given the film some needed coherence.

In Thomas Berger's novel, and in the retrospective or picaresque novel generally, this problem of main-character continuity rarely comes up because the narrative voice is enough to give an aura of unity. But when a film of such a novel is made, the events of the main character's life are objectified on the screen; they are no longer so intimately his; they have separated themselves from his point of view and his character and now exist as an independent reality. Only the voice-over narration remains to bridge the separate events, and with the loss of the continuity of personal reminiscence, such a device only emphasizes the many gaps. Jack's story in the film therefore becomes a series of vignettes: some handled well, like the Gunfighter period; some lamely, like the Religion period; and some poorly, like the Down-and-Out period. The purported structure seems to be a variation on Ford's *Three Godfathers*. In his different guises Jack will act out all the possibilities for a man in the Old West, and the width of his perspective will then be a model for a wider view of man and society that no individual—not the Indian Old Lodgeskins, the preacher's-wife-turned-whore Mrs. Pendrake, the itinerant con man Allardyce T. Merriweather, or the soldier George Custer—could have on his own. With such experience, Jack might then be the conscience and the hero of his society. Having experienced all, like some frontier Tiresias, he could gain wisdom and understanding: "It was no adventure. I knew Custer for what he was and the Indians for what they was."

Almost all the events in Jack's life that find their way into History, he observes from a privileged position: the death of his wife in the Washita massacre; the death of Shadow That Comes in Sight; the Sand Creek Massacre in which he and Old Lodgeskins walk out as though invisible; and the Battle of Little Big Horn itself, where he stands, wounded but uninvolved, watching Custer rant on the battlefield. Jack's place in the film is always behind or apart from the main action. When Custer vaunts before Little Big Horn, Jack sits behind him on a rise, while Custer postures in a little natural stage between rocks; when Old Lodgeskins goes up on the mountain to die, Jack helps him and then stands aside again. The grander heroes, good and bad, must have center stage, and Jack the observer lets them step forward.

This kind of a pose could be the best way to view history. It could be the main element in a kind of historical satire: the great men as seen by the little man, the outsider, who can reduce the pride of a Custer and make Old Lodgeskins into a true hero because he has an irony about himself and his pretensions. One figure behind Penn's Jack Crabb could thus be "Lyndon Johnson's dwarf alter-ego," that clownish "Mailer" who finds himself unwittingly at the center of great events in *The Armies of the Night.*

But Jack achieves none of these possibilities. He cannot play the role of the common man caught in History, because there seems to be little inside him that can bring together the many faces of his experience. Nothing seems to hold Jack together and therefore nothing seems to hold the film together. Merriweather says that Jack likes Old Lodgeskins because "he gave you a vision of moral order in the universe and there isn't any." And Old Lodgeskins says late in the film, "A world without human beings has no center to it." Jack Crabb could have been the moral center of *Little Big Man,* but he is not. Amid all the certainties of the other characters, he could have been the one who knew all at their proper value and could act wisely and well. But he never seems to come to terms with the warring parts of his own nature. If he has learned anything from his experience, he has not been able to act on his knowledge. All the great spectacle of *Little Big Man* is basically compromised because there is no vital center from which it is observed. Dustin Hoffman's acting in fact increases this episodic feeling. It is a versatile performance and that is its greatest fault. With Hoffman's ability to mime Jack's different states so accurately, Jack more and more separates into an incoherent handful of selves. And because he is not strong, the other characters have only a weak consistency: Custer slips into the shrillness of some superimposed ideology; there is no tension or release in the reappearance of Jack's sister Caroline; the death of Wild Bill Hickock, one of the few well-conceived characters, slips too easily into a checked-off vignette.

Penn's basic difficulty in *Little Big Man* is to have conceived the character of Jack Crabb as an imitation of a lack of moral authority rather than an expression of it. Jack may be the archetypal American liberal who knows and sympathizes so much with every side of the question that he becomes incapable of acting. Jack has lived for 121 years to wind up in a charity hospital. When he rests his head in his hands at the end of the film, he may be mourning more for his failure than for his loss.

But for all these fascinating possibilities, Penn has not finally worked out the structure and the images that will fully and complexly express these themes of age and wisdom, youth and vitality, historical involvement and artistic detachment. Authentic life exists in many parts of *Little Big Man,* but the film remains only fragments. Yet Penn's grapplings with these themes are more moving in their failure than the easy and limited success of most other directors. For all its faults, *Little Big Man* does embody a palpable sense of loss—the loss of youth, of time, and of opportunity. And if the ultimate emptiness of Jack Crabb is echoed by the final incoherence of the film, it is only the mark of how difficult it is to dream clearly of Eden when one lives in a fallen world.

[1971]

AFTERWORDS

Democracy and the Humanities

This is going to be essentially an optimistic talk, filled with praise of the humanities and what they offer students, along with praise of ourselves for being involved in this venture. But to make praise energizing rather than lulling, we have to know the attacks. As Milton remarked, only uncloistered virtue is truly virtuous, because it has been tested and still survives.

Therefore I'll also touch on the attacks on the humanities, not only from those who are upset with secular humanism, as they call it (without pausing to define or to praise religious humanism in contrast), but also from those, like William Bennett, our Secretary of Education, who attack literary theory and say that it prevents students from knowing the literary classics, as well as from those, like Jonathan Culler and other literary theorists, who attack the idea of a canon of great works as an elitist concept unsuitable either to learning or to democracy, and claim that there is a necessary disparity between literary criticism and literary education.

By the humanities I mean those studies—literature, language, philosophy, history, and art history—that have to do specifically with the ways human beings have tried to depict the world through visual and verbal rather than mathematical and quantitative languages, those studies where voice and authorship, individual perspective and audience understanding, are more important than a quest for an invariable and objective truth.

When most of us took our first courses in literature and the humanities in high school and college, the prevailing method was a combination of New Criticism and History of Ideas: read the language of the works carefully and analyze the themes and ideas. The recent expansion of interest in literary theory—the study of literature as a special case of language—goes hand in hand with an unprecedented self-consciousness about what it is we do as teachers and how it is we do it. Because language can never be merely a transparent vehicle for what it says, reading is no longer a question merely of dictionary definitions and their nuances.

This speech was delivered in 1986 to senior high school principals and heads of English departments as part of the "Year of the Humanities" organized by the Los Angeles Unified School District.

Questions of literary theory—the difference between spoken language and written language—therefore influence questions of composition training: should we encourage students to approximate the ideal essay that exists in our heads, or should we somehow support the particular mode of expression that they are developing for themselves? And if somehow the answer is *both* the social ideal and the individual aspiration, how is that integration accomplished?

The interest in these unsettling issues comes, intriguingly enough, at the same time as an increasing number of attacks from all quarters upon teaching and upon the humanities themselves—or at least upon different conceptions of the humanities. The links between elementary and high school, high school and college, have been questioned, as have the links between school itself and the outside world, along with the efforts of schools to connect students with the larger society and therefore, say these critics, to separate them from family and tradition. In response, some critics have advocated a consumer-centered learning in which students take only those courses that are deemed directly relevant to getting a job, while others have insisted on a return to a basic canon of Great Works.

Without being a Pollyanna, however, I do think that it is just as easy to read what is happening now as an occasion for ferment and change, rather than as either a forecast of oncoming gloom or a description of already rampant corruption. Aside from those individuals, like the fundamentalist families in Tennessee, who seem to be against the whole idea of public education, the critics of different trends in humanistic education do not see the benefits in what they attack, nor do they seem aware of the connections between their aims. Despite the dire conclusions of Secretary of Education Bennett, for example, literary theory has had the effect of allowing branches of the teaching profession to talk to each other. For the first time in many years, the rhetoricians and the literary critics have common ground. Pedagogy, a subject previously left to education journals, is now relevant to both literary criticism and literary theory. The history of teaching is considered to be part of the meaning of what is taught. All in all, a healthy professional self-consciousness has been born that should have the effect of making sure no one takes their professional training entirely for granted.

At the same time there is a great freshness, a ferment of ideas about education and learning, that has the potential to democratize the closed guilds by which older disciplines established themselves. A new spirit of interdisciplinary study, for example, has come into the university. Administrators at many schools now boast about hiring people with a joint appointment in English and law, or philosophy and medicine. Here at USC, a Center for Study in the Neurological Sciences will bring together talent from biology, psychology, linguistics, and other fields— for what is a greater disrespector of artificial categories than the brain itself? Many disciplines are in this way developing what they call lower fences. Fields of learning are questioning the rigid boundaries of what they consider to be an appropriate question and seeking instead for those areas in which they overlap with other fields, rather than those where they are pure and distinct. A spirit of what I like to call *amateurism* is more apparent: not "amateur" in the English sense of a dabbler but *amateur* in the French sense of one with an emotional affinity for a subject or subjects, where the connection is made through a sense of shared questions rather than a rigorous logic of professional development—*amateur,* that is, not opposed to the professional sense of depth of knowledge in a field, but *amateur* in the fascination with how that field is inseparable from others.

This is of course nothing new to you. Every day high school teachers must move back and forth between professional and amateur, specialized training in a subject and connecting that subject to the variety of the student's world. Or at least this is my fantasy, although many high school teachers I know start laughing whenever I say this—and point to lessons plans and curricula and other forms of institutional rigidity that they consider to be worse than anything a college teacher has to put up with. But let me keep my fantasy—or let me at least paint an idealized picture of high school teaching as an intellectual model, the bedrock of an integrated humanistic education rather than a preliminary workout or the farm team.

By the time students come to college and certainly by the time they arrive at graduate school, they have become too goal-directed, either economically, intellectually, or both to be totally receptive to the virtues of a general humanistic education. The National Center for Educational Statistics says that, between 1963 and 1983, the number of students majoring in foreign languages and literature fell 58%, philosophy 60%, and English 72%. And the natural sciences lost as well. As Andrew Hacker points out, though, the intriguing aspect of these statistics is that the loss was greatest not between 1963 and 1973, the era of unparalleled university expansion, but between 1973 and 1983, the era of the shrinking economy.

Although it may offend the purity that some would like to ascribe to the humanities, the evidence is now beginning to mount that a humanistic education is practical as well. Between one-third and one-half of the six or seven hundred corporations that recruit every year at USC now ask for humanities majors rather than business or some more obvious job-oriented major. Their explanation is that they can always teach a new employee the specifics of their business but they can't teach the skills of conceptualization, the verbal problem-solving, the style of attention, and the ability to discuss and dissect ideas that are the essence of courses in the humanities. Similarly, business schools are becoming aware that graduates who snag those high-paying jobs lack the training to get any further.

As these experiences show, and as our intuition surely tells us, humanistic study is a core for other study, and an essential in any interdisciplinary program. By "interdisciplinary" I include everything, for, except for those few researchers who push deeper into specific subject areas, we are all involved in interdisciplinary work and we all live interdisciplinary lives. "Interdisciplinary" is of course a humanistic concept, opposed to the parochial professionalism of individual disciplines, an indispensable aid to whatever else the student is doing, and a connection between the individual and the community—not necessarily through specific shared values but through the ability to be a critical and aware citizen.

Since the question of citizenship in a democracy automatically brings up the question of what a citizen is and who may be a citizen, let me turn now to the criticism of the humanities and of humanities courses, as well as the criticism of the humanistic "values" (on which conservative defenders of the humanities set so great a store) as in fact being based on a canon of Great Books that is anti-democratic, elitist, and exclusionary.

To a great extent I agree with this view: a small canonical group of texts has too often been the only subject matter of humanities courses. Alternative voices have *not* been included as much as they ought to. But I disagree that therefore those texts should be totally replaced by another new canon, which will be similarly invariable. To the extent that we are a society with a history in which individuals have had to grapple with the never-settled meaning of what it means to be an American, we have obligations both to traditional subject matter and to expanding the idea of what subject matter can be, in other words, to both the old and the new canons. The experience of reading is always to become Another, to enter into that other's consciousness, to shape one's own in sympathy and in contrast. In the exploration of alternate views of the world, a student, whoever he or she is, can learn as much from a book by a southern black woman as from one by a New England white man. But only if that student has been taught *to read* with understanding and empathy.

The word "privileged" is often used in literary criticism these days and it usually means "falsely or illegitimately considered centrally important." It's a useful word because it forces us to be aware of the number of books and ideas we teach primarily because they were the ones we were taught, or because we can easily find them in anthologies, or because they suit the shape of the semester or of the curriculum. But privileged works, works to which we return because of their continuing freshness and relevance, should not be considered separate from other works that strike a particular chord at a particular time. We are not setting up a hit parade. We are teaching how to read and how to understand. Part of that teaching is to interrogate standard works and an equally important part is to undercut any sense of ideal order and unchanging values they may embody or imply. If we emphasize learning as a continuing quest for understanding, we will better be able to see the so-called canon not as works chiseled in stone, but as ways individuals attempted to use language to create meaning.

In this way, I think we have to temper our training in delineating the aesthetic forms and teasing out the ideas expressed by language to consider language more generally *and* explicitly as a social act. The politics of language is around us every day, as the success of the recent antibilingualism initiative makes clear. But that politics is embedded in all works of language, even the seemingly most rarefied and aesthetic.

In one aspect, the humanities study historically validated works, the ones that have survived. In another, they study humanistically relevant works that may have been created yesterday. In the first aspect they affirm the continuity of human concerns through time. In the second, they affirm the variety and complexity of the human community, with its frequently time-bound and discontinuous preoccupations. And of course both of these aspects, the timely and the timeless, usually can be found in any single work.

To affirm the social nature of language is to affirm language as a form of action, a shape of human will, not passive before Great Works but engaged with them. Thus an authentic humanistic education does not teach theorists or works as canonical, nor does it teach ideas as exclusive or totalizing truths. It teaches instead how to respond as fully as possible to the experience of the separateness of the world as expressed in language, creating a stepping back that is sympathetic without being detached or aloof.

Now I must confess my prejudice: I believe that the study of literature is the core of all humanistic education. Whether that study is of imaginative or philosophical or historical literature, it involves a sense of knowing *how language works* to convey meaning from one person, called an author, to another, called a reader. In other words a good teacher, like a good story, must be defined not only in himself or herself, but also in relation to an audience.

Especially at the high school level, but all the way through the education system, a teacher of literature in this expanded sense is not just a teacher of history, or American studies, or movies, or political science, but a teacher of all discursive practices—all the ways language links us to other people and to the world.

This view of humanistic education as an education in the learning of the many languages human beings have used and are using to make sense of the world is clearly not immediately applicable to becoming a doctor, businessman, or computer programmer. But if we don't see its importance we will be in the danger, described by Robert Pattison in his book *On Literacy,* of creating a two-tier society in which a cultural underclass is trained in functional literacy, to work in a system where the executives and people in power come from schools in which language arts are the center of curriculum.

That possibility may offend our sense of education because our nineteenth-century legacy dictates that specialization and expertise in the practical, not education in the old-fashioned arts of reading and interpretation, are the way to success. But as Alexis de Tocqueville remarked, the ambitious in America choose immediate, practical goals because they were "much more in love with success than with glory," and by "glory" he meant an ambition that was not for oneself alone but for the community as well.

The great paradox of the humanities is that this area of study, which is most professedly about the values that unite us, is the subject most usually pursued by solitary individuals. As seekers and expositors of humanistic learning, therefore, we have a special relation to American individualism with all its virtues and faults. Our professional responsibility is to be aware of the culture and be connected to it. The exploration of the coherence of cultures is a humanistic topic, as is the training in being both inside and outside one's own. Without such training, the citizen is only a passive participant, pursuing private goals and only sporadically aware of his fellow citizens and his obligations to them.

The challenge in teaching this material and this approach is the difficult one of simultaneously establishing and undermining the absoluteness of authority. This is a particular problem of democratic education, and we all know how often students only want to know the right answers, and how upset they get when one tries to focus on the right questions instead. The idea of a canon or a right answer should be in constant interplay between the accepted classics and the need for their constant revision, the interpenetration of new and old. Just so the society itself should be viewed not as an invariable hierarchy but a community in flux, an amalgamation of individuals with differing traditions, whose values can yet be understood and absorbed into the whole, while strengthening it with their fruitful difference.

Thus the self-consciousness about the humanities that we as a nation are going through right now is tremendously important to our survival as a culture. Our task in part is first to distinguish acculturation from indoctrination, and then to turn the pragmatic effort to be acculturated, which everyone goes through in entering the education system, into the more expansive effort to be cultured and responsive to the differences that give America its vitality.

The old Europe-centered view of the world that was the basic standard for humanistic education and values for the last several hundred years is clearly being transformed. Into what, I'm not sure—and I certainly think that many of those values will be reaffirmed, although their connection to a narrow and historically determined definition of nationalism is definitely outmoded. But a different world is emerging—bound together economically and culturally, if not yet politically. It is a world in which nationalism of the old sort doesn't quite work anymore, although no one is very clear about what new nationalism or internationalism is ready to replace it.

The only thing that is clear is that it is an important part of our role as teachers to prepare our students to be citizens of that world. The key is not to learn particular things, I would say, so much as to learn about the nature of learning itself. The distinction William Bennett frequently makes between "skills" and "content" is therefore a false one. By "skills" he means techniques and by "content" he means values. But he doesn't see the values that are embedded in a sensitivity to the way language itself creates meaning.

It is hard to say what constitutes "advance" in a discipline like English or philosophy—if "discipline" is the right word. Perhaps the question is not so much "advance" as "renovation" in exploring whatever methods and values are both prior to the expertise of more professional disciplines and the source to which they should periodically return.

In order to do this, we must recall and reaffirm ourselves as students. In an important sense, we all learned much more when we were students than we do as teachers because as teachers we concentrate on our fields and our institutional places, while as students we were free to take courses in many subjects—and those courses overlapped, cross-fertilized, and meshed with one another—WITHIN US. The nature of the student I would like to stress here is again not the student as potential professional but the student also as *amateur,* the bee gathering from many flowers to create one nectar. We should be not so much creating the interdisciplinary curriculum as devising means of enhancing the interdisciplinary self.

An unavoidable part of education in a democracy is that each student, with rare exceptions, will assume a necessary distinction between personal knowledge (the knowledge with which one grew up, the ways of knowing the world that are taught before and beyond school) and school knowledge, those special ways of knowing and seeing the world—usually connected with learning particular languages—that must be taught by professionals in different fields of learning. What I would argue against here is the usual assumption that we have to put aside one to learn another. This assumption has been fostered by the basic democratic idea that education is a passport of social and economic movement, and it seems to be part of an assumption, once again, that connects specialization, profession, and occupation with "growing up."

But I wonder if someone who is only a good teacher, without being a good student, can still be a model of learning. I'm not talking about the need to do professional research so much as the ability to convey a curiosity not just about one's own discipline but also about its connection to other disciplines and to the world in general—the world that is an object constantly being offered to us for our understanding and interpretation.

I still have never quite gotten over—and I'm sure this is the experience of most teachers—the shock of discovering that students aren't as interested in the subject as I was when I was a student. Of course I think that way because I became a teacher, and inside almost every teacher is a former good student constantly raising his hand. But that otherwise depressing thought preserves a crucial desire to reawaken or keep awake in ourselves the freshness with which we first learned, the experience of being a student and what it means, especially the pain of confronting ideas that upend our most cherished assumptions. Perhaps an essential element in being professional is exactly the cultivation of this *amateur,* student habit of mind, once we realize the gap between the way we were trained and what we have to do and know once we are on the job. If our own students do not see us as continuing students and the educational process as an unendingly refreshing. part of life, then we can't blame them for wanting to make their own education as narrowly relevant to employment and status as so many of them do.

We have heard a lot in recent years about widespread self-consciousness and narcissism and the supposed ill effects on our moral culture they have brought. But I would like to stress instead the opportunities that that self-consciousness might bring. We will never again be able to be the country we were two hundred or even twenty years ago. And one essential element of the change is the increased awareness of "the world" with which our students come to us—an awareness usually accompanied by an almost invincible innocence about the relation of their awareness to that of others.

If we consider anyone's nature or actions, there is virtually nothing that we can't "explain"—and I'm putting "explain" in quotation marks—about them, nature or nurture, family or environment or ethnic background or DNA. But what IS unique about each person is the way they put all those influences together—the way they tell the story that is themselves.

Thus we might say we have three selves: a self that is conditioned in its beliefs by our pasts, however that past is defined; a self that acts, sometimes directly in the light of those conditionings and sometimes not; and a self that observes itself in action, judges itself, and then changes. It is this third self—the self-conscious self, the self-aware self—that it is our role as teachers of the humanities to foster. Or perhaps a better way of saying this is that our role today, in this media-swollen world, is to transform self-consciousness into self-awareness.

A basic goal of humanistic education should be to develop that critical sense of distance from the socially conditioned self. No one can purge it; so learn how to use it, instead of being used by it. The self-awareness thus developed is primarily the awareness of oneself as a member of not so much a society as a culture, that is, not a social system but a system of interpersonal understandings, beliefs, and values that—in the nature of American democracy—is constantly shifting, simultaneously self-celebrating and self-criticizing.

In democracies as much as in dictatorships, the classroom is frankly a place for cultural processing. The difference should be that a democracy educates for change by teaching the different languages we use and the different uses we put each language to, while a dictatorship educates for complacency by teaching the one language that is said to suffice for any situation. Too often we don't rise to this challenge. It's always easier to use last year's lesson plans and last decade's notes.

But we may also be prevented from perceiving the challenge at all, because we don't often enough consider how the classroom processes cultural values, believing it instead to be a place of purer truths, a hermetic laboratory of understanding where students along with ourselves should find a respite from the complications of actual life.

I agree with this latter view in the sense that I do think the classroom is a place where we teach how to pay attention and what to pay attention to. And paying attention requires a certain amount of screening out what for the moment at least is extraneous. But we also need to consider and to expose the ideology of what we do in the classroom, its social and political implications. Otherwise there will be a tremendous fallout in mistrust and alienation from our unwillingness to say what it is we are actually doing. The problem in exposing these assumptions and showing that learning must proceed from some assumptions about what is important is that a large part of our training in the humanities or the sciences has stressed that there is NO implicit ideology or hidden assumptions. We just give "the facts" or "the truth."

In the humanities especially, this seemingly "natural" or "innate" or "human" insight is itself a powerful ideological tool. But students need to understand the ideology of method in all areas of study. "Reading" is never a neutral term, because there are always many things we bring to what we read. Frequently a good number of them are not germane to interpreting what we read, but students should be made aware of the process, NOT so that we can say every truth is relative or subjective, but to demonstrate the necessary interaction of reader and work in the creation of meaning—the student as active participant rather than passive receptacle. We should try therefore to expose to students what they bring to the text that they themselves are not aware of. Then the work itself can be redefined not in terms of its "greatness" but as a vital and sufficient web whose interest comes from its ability to take in, turn, and transform so many of those readings for such a length of time. It is impossible to teach originality and innovation, but we can teach how to speak of matters of common interest yet with an individual voice. The experience of reading ought to be both a revelation of assumptions along with an undermining or expansion of them—a process that is often simultaneous. "Aha" is a revelation of prejudice as well as insight.

Much modern literary theory has argued that texts have no determinate meaning, that is, there is no one ultimate way finally to understand them. That, I think, is true, and the sooner students do not believe that there is only one way to understand anything, the better off we will be. But the lack of a single meaning does not mean that any meaning is valid. The openness of texts to the world and to alternate readings makes their meaning not indeterminate but complex.

The crucial element is less the final meaning than the willingness of teachers to let their own readings be permeable to the world. Virginia Woolf in her essay "Craftsmanship" spoke of the way the multiple truths in language are imaged in the multiple meanings of words (and, I would add, stories). Whose life has been really enhanced by being told that Shakespeare's basic theme is appearance versus reality? But whose sense of the relation between theater and life has not been expanded by appreciating the way in which Shakespeare focuses on this central question of social life and public affairs? Rather than a passive relation to a master work, reading should be an activity that draws out and develops the will of the student in a way that will make him or her a better citizen and understander of the world in general.

As teachers, therefore, we should strive to be models of a full understanding of the world, giving our students a sense of not only integrated knowledge but also an integrated LIFE. Only in this way will the classroom be made permeable to the world and the world to the classroom. The crisis we face is not so much a crisis of education as a crisis of attention—what to pay attention to and how much to give it. To make an analogy between rock lyrics and Renaissance poetry, or MTV and storytelling, is not necessarily pandering, but performing a theoretical act that unites something students think they know to what they don't know, defamiliarizing the familiar and familiarizing the strange. Thus we may hope to create an engaged and aware audience that doesn't just know the great works and the great examples, but knows in some way how to sift and winnow the tremendous amount of information we get every day.

In conclusion, let me return to Tocqueville, with whom so many discussions of democracy begin. He said, "When there is no more hereditary wealth, class privilege, or prerogatives of birth, and when every man derives his strength from himself alone, it becomes clear that the chief source of disparity between the fortunes of men lies in the mind. Whatever tends to invigorate, expand, or adorn the mind rises instantly to a high value." It is my hope that the humanities, considered as a way of knowing and understanding, might make those words come true for students not only in the classroom but for the rest of their lives.

[1986]

California Criticism: From Tweed Jacket to Wet Suit

California has always had an ambivalent significance in American mythology. Positively, it means life on the edge, improvisation, change, and flexibility. Negatively, it is fashion, faddishness, narcissism, and uncertainty—a land in which history and fable are hard to disentangle, the unconditioned nightmare.

One might therefore reasonably ask whether "California" may just be a handy name for whatever happens away from the East Coast. When I first visited 25 years ago, there was a good deal of looking over the shoulder to the example of the eastern schools. Academic wit and self-esteem required a certain condescension to the environment, just as they had for the writers and journalists who migrated to Hollywood in the 1930s and 1940s. This ambivalence was part of California–American literature as well. Its traces are apparent in Jack London, John Steinbeck, Robinson Jeffers, and William Saroyan. All in their different ways were uneasy about the superior or at least older culture to the east, and they worried about having sold out to fame and wealth and even to literacy.

But the novelists and poets who found in California a freedom from conventional literary expectations also discovered that the world of the eye engendered a different sense of narrative and storytelling. *The Last Tycoon* and *What Makes Sammy Run?* may be Hollywood novels written by men who had been scriptwriters, but *Absalom! Absalom!* is an American novel whose narrative shape has been heavily influenced by the experience of writing scripts.

The study of popular culture and film, though it may be Californian in tendency, was not so in origin. Does the idealism of Josiah Royce mirror Californian romanticism or does the positivism of Rudolf Carnap react against it? The salient cause may not be solely the environment, but also who chooses to come here (or leave). There are native California growths along with California-fostered tendencies that already existed elsewhere. Some are born California, some achieve California, and some have California thrust upon them. *Surprised by Sin* may have been written in Berkeley, but it also bears the unmistakable mark of its author's upbringing in Providence.

What then constitutes "California" as it influences literary theory and criticism? When I was a graduate student at Yale in the early 1960s, I went to a party at which one senior professor denounced several people who had taken jobs in California and unfortunately not at Berkeley. The attack was simple: they had ruined their careers. Berkeley was the one accepted outpost of East Coast rationality and professional discipline, just as San Francisco was the only place one was allowed to visit and even like a bit. All else was darkness or Lotusland.

What was missed or willfully ignored in this denunciation was that the choice of California was a personal choice, especially in contrast to what this established eminence implicitly considered to be more important: a professional choice, i.e., one that should have been impersonal.

Yet a crucial "California" idea is the connection of criticism and autobiography, in which the barriers between collective historical time and personal history are collapsed. "California" disdains the rigidities of form: rejecting hierarchy and "the prisonhouse of language" (the title of a book engendered in La Jolla), it is given over to the affective. Suitable to the climate, the distinction between indoor and outdoor is minimized, as is that between the life of the mind and the life of feeling, or between culture and nature. (I might as well go all the way.)

Before exploring the proposition that there is a peculiarly California school of literary criticism, I should point to one virtually unremarked effect of the rise of literary theory, that is, the demographic and sociological decentralization of the American academic world. This is a recent phenomenon. In the beginnings of the American critical "schools," neither, say, the New York critics nor the southern Fugitives were ever noted for their association with higher education, prestigious or otherwise. If anything, their allegiance was to magazines. Those with college or university connections tended to downplay or even mock them.

Then with academic expansion (underwritten first by the GI Bill of Rights and later, in the 1960s, by increased government funding) came a national competition that promoted existing university presses and academic journals, while it spawned new ones. With growing confidence, university presses began to break away from primarily printing the works of their own faculty members and looked to see what was new, nationally and internationally.

By the early 1970s the older university presses, for whose favor academic authors had competed for the past hundred years or so, had solidly selling back lists. Where were the new presses to go for new authors and new ideas? Luckily history, in the form of critical theory, was waiting in the wings. Since the student upheavals of the late 1960s, midwestern and western universities had begun to sense new intellectual opportunities, and more or less eagerly made space in the curriculum for areas of study that were either marginal or nonexistent in the East. With theory and the new perspectives, ideas could bloom anywhere. Epistemological regionalism was born. No one place now has a monopoly on innovative thinking. Sure, the *New York Times* tries to identify a "Yale School," but what it describes is the coherence of opportunistic hiring rather than organic growth. In fact, there are many more significant scholars, critics, and theorists outside the Ivy League (and away from the eastern seaboard) than there are inside. When there are fewer psychic authorities to contend with in the neighborhood, a fresher urge to discover has been born.

My favorite metaphor for this change is the Federal Highway Act of 1956, which projected the system of interstate freeways. Attacked ferociously at the time for its potential to homogenize America, in fact it created a two-tiered world: for those who like to eat exactly the same food and sit in the same decor for three thousand miles, there is an interstate culture of fast food and motels; but the same superhighways led these anxious adventurers away from the small towns, preserving something of their endangered individuality.

Disciplinary boundaries continue to be much more fluid in academic centers away from the East Coast. This fluidity is certainly coordinate with the ways in which literary theory has drawn upon philosophy, psychoanalysis, anthropology, art history, and other disciplines. But it is a practical matter as well. In traditional colleges and universities, exchange between departments and joint programs are often met with hostility. But socially as well as intellectually, as you move from East to West, a system of feudal estates is replaced by entrepreneurial opportunity.

Let me then attempt a little periodizing. The first phase might be called "Tweed Jacket," when California academics looked back on the East with a sense of deprivation, and often became more-East-Coast-than-thou. The only nod to the physical and the idea of work were the elbow patches on their jackets, a style still most characteristic of Berkeley, intent on creating "schools" of thought. For the next phase I might take as my text a line from Bruce Chatwin's *The Songlines:* "I had been sitting on my arse for a couple of weeks, and was beginning to feel the disgust for words that comes from taking no exercise." This, the "Sweat Suit" period, marks the point when the 1960s entered the academy, and with it much thought about the interlacing of the personal and the political, the physical and the mental.

Finally there is the "Wet Suit" phase, in which we plunge into the destructive element wholeheartedly. The world of the feeling and the affective become paramount, as does the body: align the self with nature and find its form. The influence of the East here reaches its lowest ebb. There's no place to kick against when you're in the water; just go. *The Body in Pain* is rooted in the East, just as *Renaissance Self-Fashioning* exhibits its California transplanting proudly.

None of these phases is so separate from the others, and phases two and three are especially compatible. Similarly, there are lags. Why, I wonder, are the Freudian models still so influential in literary study, when in daily life the insights of Jung, Winnicott, and Alice Miller seem much more pertinent? Perhaps the answer is that there can be no monolithic criticism in a state built on a fault, no matter who tries to be the Fissure King. Just as the death of the author was being announced in France, a counterrestoration was going on in California, to revive both the author's and the reader's personal nature through literary feminism. Without trying to discern the California and midwestern strains in the collaboration between Sandra Gilbert (University of California at Davis) and Susan Gubar (University of Indiana), it should be noted that attics are pretty rare out here, perhaps because many of the nineteenth-century "madwomen" who weren't locked up were sent out west to found dynasties.

As David Hockney, a California transplant from another field, has often remarked, surface is an illusion, but so is depth. This seems to me to be a quintessentially Californian perspective, thumbing its nose at the traditional (East Coast and European) assumption that depth is better, and more moral, than surface, when in fact both are part of an illusionism dating from the Renaissance, incidentally reflected in the outworn Marxist metaphor of economic base and cultural superstructure. As Chatwin, in *The Songlines* again, would have it, "Regardless of the words, it seems the melodic contour of the song describes the land over which the song passes." The myth of California is characterized by the restlessness that creates a story different from that of the established settlements. No matter how entrenched or traditional the new patterns eventually become, the California perspective involves the world of the ear and the eye as well as that of the mind. It may distinguish high culture from popular culture, but rarely with any hierarchy of social or aesthetic value. At its best, it searches for some new sense of narrative and explanation, more akin to story than to logic, to movement than to stasis. To conclude Californianly then: the recognition of impermanence is itself a spiritual discipline and a glimpse into the eternal, a California within, happier far.

[1989]

Credits

Text

"Popular Culture and Personal Time"
Reprinted from *Yale Review* (Summer 1982). © 1982 by Leo Braudy.

"Succeeding in Language"
Reprinted from *The State of the Language*, ed. Leonard Michaels and Christopher Ricks (Berkeley: University of California Press, 1980). © 1980 by Leo Braudy.

"The Rise of the *Auteur*"
Reprinted from the *Times Literary Supplement* (London), November 11, 1975.

"Hitchcock, Truffaut, and the Irresponsible Audience"
Reprinted from *Film Quarterly*, vol. 21, no. 4 (Spring 1986). © 1968 by the Regents of the University of California.

"*Maidstone: A Mystery* by Norman Mailer"
Reprinted from the *New York Times Book Review*, December 19, 1971. Copyright © 1971 by The New York Times Company. Reprinted by permission.

"*Stargazer* by Stephen Koch"
Reprinted from the *New York Times Book Review*, October 7, 1973. Copyright © 1973 by The New York Times Company. Reprinted by permission.

"The Double Detachment of Ernst Lubitsch"
Reprinted from *Modern Language Notes*, Winter 1983. Copyright © Leo Braudy.

"*Fanny Hill* and Materialism"
Reprinted from *Eighteenth-Century Studies (ECS)*, Fall 1970, with the permission of the American Society for Eighteenth-Century Studies.

"Zola on Film: The Ambiguities of Naturalism"
Reprinted from *Yale French Studies*, vol. 42 (1969). © Yale University.

"Lexicography and Biography in the *Preface* to Johnson's *Dictionary*"
Reprinted from *Studies in English Literature (SEL)*, Summer 1970.

"Daniel Defoe and the Anxieties of Autobiography"

Photographs

Index

Abortion, 22
Abstract Expressionism, 65
Acculturation, and humanities education, 284, 286
Adulation, and revenge, 133
Alice's Restaurant (film), 271, 272–73
All about Eve (film), 208
All that Jazz (film), 213n5, 218
Amateurism, 280–81, 284–85
Ambition, 219
American identity, 23–24
American Zoetrope, 244, 245
Annie Get Your Gun (film), 207
Anthropology
  culture and, 13–14
  film and, 235
Anticommunism
  McCarthyism and, 258–61
  Rosenberg trial and, 262–64
Antoine, André, 99
Antonioni, Michelangelo, *Blow-Up*, 244–45
Apocalypse Now (film), 222, 243, 244
Apuleius, Lucius, *Golden Ass*, 112
Art
  nature and, in *Fanny Hill*, 90–91
  politics and, in Sontag, 128–29
Artistic tradition, and genre film, 215
Art-within-art, 201–3
  as contrast vs. doubling, 203, 205
  as Renaissance technique, 202–3
Assassination, 22–23, 132–34
Astaire, Fred, 217, 218
Audience. *See also* Reader
  art-within-art and, 211–12
  catastrophic time and, 22–23
  genre and, 214–15, 223–24
  as knowing, 21–22, 215, 287
  relation to character, in Zola, 100–101, 103
  television and, 20–22
  Warhol and, 65

Audience-director relation
  Hitchcock and, 51–59
  Lubitsch and, 72
  Mailer and, 60–62
  Truffaut and, 48
Audience-performer relation
  assassination and, 132–34
  crime films and, 231
  in *42nd Street* vs. *Persona*, 208
  television and, 215
Augustine, *Confessions*, 112
Austen, Jane, 177
Auteur theory of film, 43–50, 242. *See also* Truffaut
Authoritarianisms, 33–35. *See also* Canons of literature; Control
Authority
  artistic, 237
  cultural, 23–25
  democratic education and, 283
  of director, 205–6, 210, 245, 248–49, 251
  legal, 115
Author-work relation
  in eighteenth-century novel, 174
  in Mailer vs. Pynchon, 145–50
  in sentimental novel, 169–72
  Sontag and, 130–31
Autobiography. *See also* Biography
  confessional, 112
  criticism as, 8, 126–31
  didacticism in, 112–13
  in fiction, 111–24
Avant-garde, 65–66, 127–28

Bacon, Francis, *Advancement of Learning*, 181
Bacon, Lloyd, 205. *See also* *42nd Street* (film)
Barth, John, 150n4
Bataille, George, 92n4
Bateson, Gregory, 167n10
Baudelaire, Charles, 64

Bazin, André, 44, 45, 47, 52, 54, 240–41, 251
Beardsley, Monroe C., 30
Beatty, Warren, 217–18, 221
Benjamin, Walter, 126
Bennett, William, 279, 284
Berger, John
  G., 146, 255–57
  Picasso, 256
Berger, Thomas
  compared with Vonnegut, 267
  Killing Time, 267
  literary language of, 269
  Little Big Man (novel), 266, 267, 273
  Regiment of Women, 265–67
Bergman, Andrew, *We're in the Money*, 69
Bergman, Ingmar, *Persona*, 204–12
Berkeley, Busby, 205, 206–7, 209, 212, 217
  42nd Street, 204–12
Bête-machine, 84, 85, 94n15
Biography, 107–10, 190. *See also*
  Autobiography
Blake, William, 196
Blow-Out (film), 247
Bogart, Humphrey, 48, 232
Bonnie and Clyde (film), 271–72
Bossuet, Jacques Bénigne, 181
Boston Draft Resistance Group (documentary),
  225, 226, 228
Boswell, James, 107, 108
Boulle, Pierre, 260
Boussinot, Roger, 69
Braive, Michel, 98
Brunette, Peter, 251n1
Bryant, Louise, 217–19
Bunyan, John, *Pilgrim's Progress*, 16–17, 139
Bussey, Gertrude C., 93n9
Byrd, Max, *Visits to Bedlam*, 193–94, 195–96,
  197–98

Cahiers du Cinéma (magazine), 44, 45, 47
California, in American mythology, 288
California perspective, 288–91
Camera
  mediation of seeing by, 244–45
  in Newsreel documentary form, 226, 227
  sexual role of, 210–11
Canons of literature, 8, 279, 280, 281–82
  "high" culture and, 13
  humanities study and, 283
  Sontag and, 127, 128
Capek, Karel, 80
Carné, Marcel, 1953 version of *Thérèse Raquin*,
  102
Catastrophic time, 18, 20, 22–25
Catholicism
  Defoe and, 123–24
  Italian-American directors and, 240–52
Ceplair, Larry, 258–60
Chabrol, Claude, 59
Chadwick, Owen, 184

Champion, Gower, 213n2
Chapman, Mark, 133
Character
  in Defoe, 111, 112–13, 114–21, 122, 185–87
  in film, 73–74, 248–50, 273–74
  in literary history, 162–63
  Lubitsch and, 73–74
  New Wave and, 47–48
  in post-World War II fiction, 256–57
  relation of audience to, in Zola, 100–101,
    103
  Scorsese and, 248–50
Chariots of Fire (film), 219–20, 221
Chatwin, Bruce, *Songlines*, 290, 291
Chicago (documentary), 228
Chomsky (documentary), 225
Christianity. *See* Catholicism; Religious
  viewpoint
Cinéma vérité, 62
Citizenship, 281–85, 287
Clarens, Carlos, 230, 232, 233, 234
Cleland, John
  Fanny Hill, 79–94, 178n2
  foreign activities of, 93n11
  influence of La Mettrie on, 83–84, 86–87
  life of, 83
Clément, René, 102
Cocteau, Jean, 49
Columbia University, literary study at, 6
Commercials, television, 20
Condon, Richard, *Winter Kills*, 268–70
Continuity
  irony and, 20, 21
  main-character, 273–74
  1950s era and, 262
  soap-opera time and, 214
  television and, 18–20
  Warhol-Morrissey connection and, 66
  in writing tradition, 169–78
Contrast, 203, 205
Control
  aesthetic and political, in Sontag, 129–30
  cultural awareness as means for, 15
  by giant corporations, 147–48, 233
  interpretation and, 15
  paranoid stories and, 17–18
The Conversation (film), 244–46
Cooperatives, documentary on, 226
Cooptation, 38
Coplans, John, *Andy Warhol*, 66
Coppola, Francis Ford, 240, 247
  Apocalypse Now, 243, 244
  The Conversation, 244–46
  Finian's Rainbow, 243, 244
  genre in films of, 243
  Godfather II, 243, 244
  Outsiders, 243–44
Corman, Roger, 242–43
Cowper, William, 196
Creative Differences (Talbot and Zheutlin), 260
Creativity, anxiety of, 216–17

Crime film, 230–34
Cruden, Alexander, 194
Cukor, George, *It Should Happen to You,* 45
Culler, Jonathan, 279
Culture
  anthropological concept of, 13–14
  contemporary, and literary study, 5–8
  high vs. popular, 13–16, 216, 269–70, 288, 291
  humanities and, 283–86
  present period of evolution in, 24
cummings, e. e., 31

Dean, James, 48
Death. *See also* Permanence; Time
  appeal of horror film and, 221–24
  denial of, and genre film, 219–21
Decline and Fall (Gibbon), 179–84, 187–91
Defoe, Daniel
  Captain Singleton, 116–17, 120
  Colonel Jacque, 113, 114
  Conjugal Lewdness, 114
  didacticism and, 112
  disguise and, 117–21, 122
  Dormer's News-Letter, 118
  experiences of, 117–18
  Farther Adventures of Robinson Crusoe, 115
  first-person narrative and, 111, 113–14, 174
  history of the novel and, 111–13
  Journal of the Plague Year, 116, 122–23, 124n9, 185–87
  Memoirs of a Cavalier, 119
  Mist's Weekly Journal, 118
  Moll Flanders, 116, 120–21, 122
  names in, 118, 119–21
  New Voyage round the World, 122
  personal identity and, 114–21, 155
  Robinson Crusoe, 16–17, 115, 120, 173–74
  Roxana, 116, 121, 123
  Serious Reflections of Robinson Crusoe, 113, 118
  Shortest Way with the Dissenters, 117, 118
Delany, Paul, 124n2
Democracy, and humanities study, 281–87
DePalma, Brian, 240, 246–48
  Blow-Out, 247
  Dressed to Kill, 247
DePorte, Michael V., *Nightmares and Hobbyhorses,* 195, 196–97, 198
Descartes, René, 81, 83, 85–86, 90, 163
Director. *See also* Audience-director relation; *specific directors*
  auteur theory and, 43–50
  authority of, 205–6, 210, 245, 248–49, 251
  detachment of, 245–46, 247
  Hollywood system and, 242–43
Director-performer relation, 213n3
  in *42nd Street* vs. *Persona,* 205–6
  Italian-American director and, 249–50, 252n7
  Lubitsch and, 73–74

Director's Company, 244
Documentary film, 225–29, 241, 252n2. *See also* Neorealism
Dos Passos, John, *USA,* 140–41
Draft resistance, Newsreels about, 225–29
Dressed to Kill (film), 247
Dryden, John, 177n1
Dualism. *See* Mind-body distinction
Duchamp, Marcel, 64, 65
Dunciad (Pope), 153–54, 173, 197
Durkheim, Emile, 194
Duvivier, Julien, *Au bonheur des dames,* 99–100

E. T. (film), 219, 223
Eavesdropping, in Zola's novels, 97–98
Eccentricity
  Defoe and, 114
  English view of, 195
  Sontag and, 127, 129, 131
Education. *See also* Graduate study; Teaching
  culture and, 37–39
  humanities in, 279–87
  language arts in, 283
  postwar pedagogical style and, 30–31
  student as *amateur* and, 284–85
  trend toward specialization in, 4–5
Eliot, George, *Adam Bede,* 145
Eliot, T. S., 127
Elliott, George P., "Among the Dangs," 14
Emerson, Ralph Waldo, 24
Empiricism, 31, 138
Engel, Arthur, 35n2
English Civil Wars, 138–39
Englund, Steven, 258–60
Enlightenment
  fiction and, 189–90
  image of madness in, 194
Epistemological regionalism, 289
Epistle to Dr. Arbuthnot (Pope), 153, 165, 172
Esterson, A., 161
Ethnicity, 3, 4–5, 250–51
Euripides, *Iphigenia in Aulis,* 181
Expatriate, 67–70, 71, 147. *See also* Lubitsch

Fame
  artists and, 130
  assassination and, 132–34
  history of, 9
  permanence and, 219–20, 221, 271
Familiarity
  education and, 287
  genre film and, 21–22, 236
  horror film and, 222–23
Family
  disruption of, and horror film, 222
  history and, 190
  in postwar America, 142
  in Richardson, 156–57, 161

Family (*continued*)
  Rosenbergs and, 263
  as security, 142, 156–57
Fanny Hill (Cleland), 79–94, 178n2
  Beggar's Benison performance of, 83, 93n11
  "scientific" language in, 94n18
Federal Highway Act of 1956, 289–90
Feeling. *See also* Mind-body distinction;
    Paranoia; Personal identity; Sentiment in
    literature; Sexuality
  languages of, 27, 34–35
  in postwar thought, 31
  visual arts and, 209–11
Femininity, 162–63. *See also* Sexuality
Fiction
  autobiography in, 111–24
  Gibbon and, 179–92
Fiedler, Leslie, 263
Fielding, Henry, 90, 182
  Amelia, 176
  Joseph Andrews, 184
  Tom Jones, 176, 184
Film. *See also* Genre
  American, in 1950s, 48–49
  analogy of, in novel, 147–48
  credit in, 259–60
  "entertainment" vs. "art," 204–12
  nonsync, 226
  politics and, 259–60
  postwar, 240
  silent vs. sound, 67–69, 203–4
  social psychological study of, 235–39
  stereotypes in, 237
  Zola's novels on, 99–105
Film criticism
  simple films and, 46–47
  Sontag and, 129–30
  Truffaut as critic-reviewer and, 43–50
Film history
  early sound period in, 68–69
  "film noir" in, 232–33
  Scorsese and, 248
  self-consciousness and, 233–34
  silent period in, 67–68
*Film Noir: An Encyclopedic Reference to the
    American Style*, 232–33, 234
Les Films de ma vie (Truffaut), 44, 45–50
Finian's Rainbow (film), 243, 244
Finian's Rainbow (stage musical), 141
First-person narration
  Defoe and, 111, 113–14, 174
  Gibbon and, 184
Ford, John, 68
Formalism, 64–66, 235
Forman, Milos, *Ragtime*, 219
42nd Street (film), 204–12
Fosse, Bob, *All That Jazz*, 213n5, 218
Foster, Jodi, 132, 133, 134
Foucault, Michel, 92n6
  L'Histoire de la folie, 194–95

Four Americans (documentary), 226
Foxon, David, 83
Framing
  42nd Street vs. *Persona* and, 204–12
  structure in sentimental novel and, 170–72
French film industry, 99
Fuller, Samuel, *Verboten*, 46
Fussell, Paul, 179, 180

G. (novel), 146, 255–57
Gallipoli (film), 220, 221
Garbage (documentary), 228
Garland, Judy, 207
Gauthier, Guy, 98
Genre. *See also* Crime film; Documentary film;
    Horror film; Musical film; Westerns
  audience for, 214–15
  Cahiers critics and, 47
  Hitchcock and, 54
  Italian-American directors and, 240–51
  nature of, 230
  self-consciousness about, 203–4, 215, 216,
    236
  sequels and, 215–16
  social beliefs and, 238–39
  tradition and, 21–22, 257
German film industry, 67–68
Gibbon, Edward, 179–92
  Autobiography, 188
  Decline and Fall, 179–84, 187–91
  Defoe's work and, 185–87
  domesticity and, 190
  early works of, 180
  Memoirs, 180, 181, 188
  narrative form and, 179–82
  *Observations on the Sixth Book of Vergil's
    Aeneid*, 180, 182
  study of Blackstone, 167n7, 182, 183
Gilbert, Sandra, 290
Gildon, Charles, 118
Godard, Jean-Luc, 44–45, 46, 47, 106n7, 222
  A bout de souffle, 43
  "Défense et illustration du découpage
    classique," 44–45
  Le Mépris (Contempt), 49–50
  Weekend, 62
Godfather II (film), 243, 244
Goethe, Johann Wolfgang von, *Sorrows of
    Young Werther*, 169, 171
Goode, William J., 34
Goodman, Paul, 126
Gothic novel, 170, 171–72. *See also* Sentiment
    in literature
Graduate study, 27–28. *See also* Education
Graham, Martha, 140
Gravity's Rainbow (Pynchon), 141–42, 145–50
Griffith, D. W.
  Drunkard's Reformation, 102
  Musketeers of Pig Alley, 230, 231
Gubar, Susan, 290

Gulliver's Travels (Swift), 16–17, 161–62, 163, 164, 173, 196
Gun control, 133, 134

Hacker, Andrew, 281
Hall, Edward, *Beyond Culture*, 7
Heller, Joseph, *Catch-22*, 143
Herodotus, 183–84
Heroism
  in Berger's *G.*, 256
  Penn's films and, 271–72
  Sontag's idea of the avant garde artist and, 127–28
Heyday: An Autobiography (Schary), 260–61
High Sierra (film), 232
Hinckley, John, 132–33
Historical film, 218
Historical novel, 256–57
History
  Berger's *G.* and, 255–56
  crime film and, 231–32, 233
  fiction and, in Gibbon, 181–85
  and myth, 236
  Penn's *Little Big Man* and, 274
History of ideas, 237
  fiction and, 189–90
  views of madness and, 193–98
Hitchcock, Alfred
  comedies of, 54
  I Confess, 143
  The Lady Vanishes, 54, 55
  North by Northwest, 54, 143
  Notorious, 54
  Psycho, 52, 54–59
  Rear Window, 143, 244, 245
  Thirty-Nine Steps, 53
  Truffaut's interview with, 51–54, 57, 58, 59
Hitler, Adolf, 128–29
Hobbes, Thomas, 138, 139, 154, 237
Hockney, David, 290
Hoffman, Dustin, 274
Hollywood, 231, 258–61
Hollywood studio system, 68, 147–48, 233
Hopper, Edward, 217
Horror film
  appeal of, 221–24
  conventions of, 223–24
  as dominant genre, 214
  relation to tradition, 21–22
House Un-American Activities Committee (HUAC), 258–61
HUAC. *See* House Un-American Activities Committee
Humanities
  American individualism and, 281–87
  attacks on, 279, 281–83
  conceptions of, 279–81
  future of, 37
Human nature. *See also* Personal identity
  materialist view of, 79–83

permanence and, 109
sexuality and, in *Fanny Hill*, 85–88
Hume, David, 154–55
  Enquiry Concerning Human Understanding, 155
  Treatise of Human Nature, 155

Identity. *See* American identity; Personal identity
Ideology
  in the classroom, 286
  crime film and, 232
  ethnicity and, 250–51
  literary criticism and, 31–32
Imagination, and sexuality, 81–83
Inclusion vs. exclusion, 37–39, 233
Incompleteness, and literary form, 176, 177
Individual. *See* Personal identity
Individualism
  crime films and, 232, 233
  humanities and, 281–87
  security of identity and, 143
Inquisition in Hollywood (Ceplair and Englund), 258–60
Intellectual, itinerant, 126
Interdisciplinary study, 280, 281
Interpretation
  authoritarianisms of, 33–35
  cultural, 13–18
  objectivity and, 30
Irony, 20, 21, 22, 216
I.S. 201 (documentary), 227
Italian-American directors, 240–51. *See also* Coppola; DePalma; Scorsese

Jacobs, Lewis, 69, 72
Jaque, Christian, 99, 100
  Nana, 100
Jasset, Victorin, 99
Jazz Singer (film), 203–4, 205, 212n1
Jeanette Rankin Brigade (documentary), 227
Jewish culture, 3, 27
Johnson, Samuel
  Dictionary, 28, 29, 108, 110
  Gibbon and, 182, 187–88
  language and, 29
  madness and, 196, 197
  personal rigidity of, 165–66
  Plan of an English Dictionary, 107–8
  Preface, 107–10
Jolson, Al, 212n1
Jordan, David, 179, 180
Journal of the Plague Year (Defoe), 116, 122–23, 124n9, 185–87
Joyce, James, *Ulysses*, 140

Kafka, Franz, 150n2
Kalbus, Oskar, 71
Keeler, Ruby, 213n2
Keynes, Geoffrey, 185

King of Comedy (film), 248, 249, 250
Koch, Stephen, *Stargazer*, 64–66
Kolb, Gwin J., 107
Kracauer, Siegfried, 69, 71, 218
Krassner, Paul, 266

Laing, R. D., 161, 167*n*11
La Mettrie, Julien Offray de
  English translation of, 93*n*9
  *Histoire naturelle de l'circ*ame, 81
  L'Homme Machine, 79–83
  L'Homme plante, 86
Lang, Fritz, *Human Desire*, 102
Language
  Berger's use of, 267, 269–70
  Cleland's use of, 90
  Condon's use of, 269–70
  creation of meaning by, 282–83, 284, 286–87
  Defoe's use of, 173–74, 175
  distortions worked by, 180–81, 266–67
  Johnson and, 108–9, 110
  partial meaning and, 173–74, 175
  power and, 31–35
  precision in, 29–32
  professional, 28, 33–35
  Richardson's use of, 156, 164, 174–75
  role of, in modern period, 138–39, 149
  social nature of, 282–83
  Swift's use of, 164–65, 175
Lapp, John C., 106*n*2
Lennon, John, 133, 134
Lévi-Strauss, Claude, 236
Lexicography, 107–10
L'Herbier, Marcel, 103, 106*n*5
L'Homme Machine (La Mettrie), 79–83
Libertine, 255–57
Literary criticism. *See also* New Criticism
  California influence in, 288–91
  film and, 7–8
  ideology and, 31–32
  in postwar period, 29–32
  privileging and, 32, 35, 282
  in 1950s, 4–5
Literary form. *See also* Narrative form
  American, and nineteenth-century novel, 140–44
  in eighteenth century, 169–78
  fiction as, 181
  loss of providence and, 137–40
  paranoia and, 139-140, 268, 269, 270 (*see also* Berger; Condon; Mailer)
  in Pope vs. Swift, 172–73
Literary history, 137–50. *See also* Literary form
Literary theory, interest in, 279–80
Literature, sociological views of, 237
Little Big Man (Berger), 266, 267, 273
Little Big Man (film version), 271–75
Locke, John, 89, 138, 154, 194
Logan, Joshua, *Picnic*, 46–47
Lubitsch, Ernst, 67–76, 218
  criticism of, 69

director-work relation and, 72–76
as expatriate, 67–70, 71
German films of, 71–72
Passion, 67–68
Trouble in Paradise, 70–75
Lukács, Georg, 103

Machine, usage of term, 84. *See also* Man-machine
Mackenzie, Henry, *Man of Feeling*, 91, 169, 170–71, 175
McCarthyism, 258–61. *See also* Rosenberg trial
Madness
  eighteenth-century views of, 193–98
  French vs. English views of, 194–95
  literary form and, 175
Maidstone: A Mystery (Mailer), 60–63
Mailer, Norman, 123
  Advertisements for Myself, 62
  An American Dream, 150
  compared with Pynchon, 145–50
  "A Course in Filmmaking," 61, 62
  Deer Park, 147–48
  Maidstone: A Mystery, 60–63
  Naked and the Dead, 145–50
Malcolm X, documentary on, 227
Male stars, and gangsters, 231–32
Man-machine, 80–83, 87
Man of Feeling (Mackenzie), 91, 169, 170–71, 175
Marcellinus, Ammianus, 180
Marcus, Steven, 90
Marginality, 127–28. *See also* Eccentricity
Marriage, 157
Martin, Steve
  in *The Jerk*, 217
  in *Pennies from Heaven*, 217
Masculinity, 162–63. *See also* Sexuality
Mast, Gerald, 69
Materialism, and *Fanny Hill*, 79–94
Matrice, 81–82
Meaning. *See* Language
Mean Streets (film), 248, 249
Meat Cooperative (documentary), 226, 228
Meeropol, Michael, 262–64
Meeropol, Robert, 262–64
Melancholy, 129, 130, 216
Memoirs of an Oxford Scholar (1756), 94*n*21
Metaphor
  in La Mettrie, 81–82
  of running, 219–20
Milton, John, *Paradise Lost*, 139, 150
Mind-body distinction
  in *Clarissa*, 159–62, 163
  Fanny Hill and, 79–92
  madness and, 193–98
  Sontag and, 128–29
Minimalism, 7, 8
Modernist vs. naturalist, 141, 143, 145–50
Mohammed, 187, 188
Moll Flanders (Defoe), 116, 120–21, 122

Montaigne, Michel, 123
Moral Majority, 22–23
Morrissey, Paul, 65–66
Moulin Rouge (film), 201
Murch, Walter, 244, 246
Murrow, Edward R., 31
Musical film, 203–4, 217, 218–19
Myles, Linda, 244
Myth, history and, 236

Naked and the Dead (Mailer), 145–50
Names, 118, 119–21, 145, 148
Narrative form. *See also* Literary form
    in Defoe, 185–87
    Gibbon and, 179–82, 190
Naturalism
    in *Fanny Hill,* 89–90, 94n17
    film versions of Zola's novels and, 99–105
    vs. modernism, 141, 143, 145–50
    Zola's novels and, 95–98
Neoplatonism, 167n13
Neorealism, 240, 251
New Criticism, 6, 30–32
New Wave, and *auteur* criticism, 43–48
New York Newsreel, 225–29
Nightmares and Hobbyhorses (DePorte), 195,
    196–97, 198
1950s
    American film in, 48–49
    Hollywood and McCarthyism and, 258–61
    novel form and, 140–44
    public rhetoric in, 262
    views of American system in, 268
1960s
    American culture and, 24–25
    literary criticism in, 4
    novel form in, 268
1980s, anxiety of creativity in, 216–17
Nixon, Richard, 31, 143
Nizer, Louis, 263
No Game (documentary), 226–27
Nonguet, Lucien, 99
Nonsync film, 226

Oates, Titus, *True Narrative of the Horrid Plot,*
    138
Observation. *See also* Documentary film;
    Voyeurism
    by character, 274–75
    cultural interpretation and, 13–15
    as motif in Hitchcock, 57
    Renoir's *Nana* and, 101–2
    Zola and, 96–98, 102
Oedipal relationship, 142
On Photography (Sontag), 127–28, 130
Outsiders (film), 243–44

Pacino, Al, 233–34
Paramount Pictures, 75
Paranoia
    critical theory and, 148–49

novel form and, 139-140, 268, 270 (*see also*
    Berger; Condon; Mailer; Pynchon)
    in postwar America, 141–42
    storytelling and, 17–18
    as term, 150n1
    of writer, 269
Parfit, Derek, 166n4
Partridge, Eric, 84
Pascal, Blaise, 138
Passion (film), 67–68
Past. *See also* Time; Youth vs. age
    genre film and, 214–24
    in popular vs. historical novel, 143–44
Pastoral mode, 237. *See also* Naturalism
Pattison, Robert, 283
Pedagogy. *See* Education
Penn, Arthur
    Alice's Restaurant, 271, 272–73
    Bonnie and Clyde, 271–72
    The Chase, 272
    Left-Handed Gun, 271, 272
    Little Big Man, 271–75
Pennies from Heaven (film), 216–17, 218, 221
Pentagon, documentary on, 226–27
Performer. *See also* Audience-performer
    relation; Director-performer relation; Male
    stars
    New Wave and, 48
    social psychological view of film and, 238
Permanence. *See also* Death; Time
    fame and, 219–20, 221, 271
    human nature and, 109
    time and, 214, 271
Persona (film), 204–12
Personal Best (film), 220
Personal identity
    art-within-art and, 212
    Defoe's characters and, 113, 114–21, 122
    in history of philosophy, 154–55, 166n4
    language and, 164–65
    literary history and, 152–54, 155–56
    madness and, 193, 194
    marriage and, 157
    masculine and feminine aspects of, 162–63
    Puritan conception of self and, 166n1
    Richardson and, 155–66
    in Thomas Berger's novels, 266, 267
Photography. *See also* Camera; Sontag
    permanence and, 271
    Zola and, 98
Pickford, Mary, 67, 68, 73
Pilgrim's Progress (Bunyan), 16–17, 139
Platt, Gerald, 157–58
Pleasure, in humanistic education, 38–39
Plot, and westerns, 238
Poirier, Richard, 150
Police militarism, documentary on, 227
Politics, and film, 259–60
Poltergeist (film), 223
Pope, Alexander, 139
    To Augustus, 172

Pope, Alexander (*continued*)
　compared with Swift, 172–73, 177*n*1, 195
　Dunciad, 153–54, 173, 197
　Epilogue to the Satires, 172
　Epistle to Dr. Arbuthnot, 153, 165, 172
　Essay on Criticism, 173
　Essay on Man, 197
　Moral Essays, 153, 165
　poetic form and, 172–73
　Rape of the Lock, 152–53, 177
Popular culture. *See* Culture
Pornography. *See Fanny Hill*
　as didactic form, for Cleland, 85–86
　eighteenth-century beliefs and, 93*n*10
　function of, for Cleland, 85–86, 88–89
　origins of, 92*n*1
Pouctal, Henri, 99
Professionalism, 7, 33–35, 281
Propaganda, 29–30, 226, 252*n*2
Providential order. *See also* Authoritarianisms;
　　Catholicism; Religious viewpoint
　Defoe's characters and, 123
　language and, 124*n*9
　loss of belief in, and novel form, 137–40
Pseudonyms, 145
Psycho (film), 52, 54–59
Pye, Michael, 244
Pynchon, Thomas
　compared with Mailer, 145–50
　Cry of Lot 49, 146, 148
　Gravity's Rainbow, 141–42, 145–50
　V., 146, 148

Racine, Louis, 93*n*8
Raging Bull (film), 249
Rape of the Lock (Pope), 152–53, 177
Reader. *See also* Audience
　erotic literature and, 88–89
　Gibbon and, 181, 182–83, 187–89
　Thomas Berger and, 266–67
　Zola and, 100
Reading
　active process in, 286–87
　teaching of, 282
Reagan, Ronald, 132–33, 134
Realism, 47, 128. *See also* Naturalism;
　　Neorealism
Reds (film), 217–19, 221
Reed, John, 217–19, 221
Regiment of Women (film), 265–67
Religious viewpoint. *See also* Catholicism;
　　Providential order
　fiction and, for Gibbon, 182–83, 185, 190
　New Criticism and, 31–32
Remakes, 216. *See also* Sequels
Renoir, Auguste, *Le Moulin de la Galette*, 102
Renoir, Jean
　Nana, 106*n*5
　1926 film of *Nana*, 100–102
　1938 film of *La Bête humaine*, 102

Resist and the New England Resistance
　(documentary), 225
Resurrection, 167*n*13
Richardson, Samuel
　Clarissa, 85, 89, 152, 156–66, 174, 176
　as father of psychological novel, 112
　Gibbon and, 184
　Pamela, 156
　personal identity and, 155–66
　sexuality and, 85, 89, 160
Richetti, John, 116, 124*n*1
Riefenstahl, Leni, 128–29
　Triumph of the Will, 130
Riot Weapons (documentary), 227
Ripoli, Roger, 106*n*2
Ritual. *See* Italian-American directors
Rivers, Larry, *History of the Russian
　Revolution*, 18–19
Robinson Crusoe (Defoe), 16–17, 115, 120,
　173–74
Rosen, George, 194
Rosenberg trial, 262–63. *See also We Are Your
　Sons*
Rosselini, Roberto, 44, 240, 241–42, 250
Roxana (Defoe), 116, 121, 123
Running metaphor, 219–20

Sacks, Oliver, 8
Sadoul, Georges, 99
Sainthood, in Scorsese, 248–50
Satan imagery, in *Clarissa*, 167*n*15, 168*n*22
Satire, in Sontag's essays, 129
Schary, Doré, *Heyday: An Autobiography*, 260–
　61
Schulberg, Budd, 261
Scorsese, Martin, 240, 248–50
　King of Comedy, 248, 249, 250
　Mean Streets, 248, 249
　Raging Bull, 249
　Taxi Driver, 248, 249, 250
Screen Writers Guild (SWG), 258–59
Scriptwriting, influences on novel, 288
Secular humanism, 279
Security, self-willed isolation and, 158
Self-awareness
　self-consciousness and, 202–3, 223–24, 285–
　　86
　Sontag's heroic avant-garde and, 127, 129,
　　130
Self-consciousness
　in art, 201–3
　in audience, 21–23
　in Bergman's films, 209
　in fiction, 257
　film history and, 233–34
　genre film and, 215, 216
　in Gibbon, 188
　humanistic education and, 280, 285–86
　Italian-American directors and, 243–44
　in Lubitsch's work, 73–74

New Wave influence and, 43–44, 204
  self-awareness and, 202–3, 223–24
Self-definition, in *Clarissa,* 156–66
Self-justification, usage of term, 167n6
Sentiment in literature
  Fanny Hill and, 91, 178n2
  novel form and, 169–78
Sequels, 214, 215–16. *See also* Remakes
Sergeant Pepper's Lonely Hearts Club Band
    (film), 219
Sexuality
  in Berger's *G.,* 256
  in *Clarissa,* 85, 89, 158–63
  Cleland's treatment of, 84–86, 87–88, 92
  in film dialogue, 209
  in *Gravity's Rainbow,* 146
  incompleteness and, 176
  in Mailer's novels, 146
  materialist view and, 79–83, 85–88
  in postwar American novel, 146
  Regiment of Women and, 265–66, 267
Sheffield, John (Holroyd, Lord), 190–91
Shoemaker, Sydney, 163
Shoot the Moon (film), 222
Silver, Alain, 232–33, 234
Singin' in the Rain (film), 208
Sixguns and Society (Wright), 235–39
Sledd, James H., 107
Smollett, Tobias, *Roderick Random,* 140,
    150
Soap-opera time, 18–20, 22–25, 214
Social psychology, and film, 235–39
Social role of critic/artist, 129–31, 145–46,
    238–39
Society, and self, 193–95, 196, 197
Sontag, Susan
  Illness as Metaphor, 128
  On Photography, 127–28, 130
  "Pornographic Imagination," 92n4
  Under the Sign of Saturn, 126–31
Soul. *See Matrice;* Mind-body distinction
Sound film
  advantages of, 203–4
  crime genre and, 231
  early period of, 67–69
Soundtrack, in Newsreel documentaries, 225,
    226–28
Speech, in Newsreel documentaries, 227–28
Spiritual autobiography, 112–13
  Defoe and, 116
Stargazer (Koch), 64–66
Starr, G. A., 124n3
Star Trek II (film), 219
Star Wars (film), 21
Stereotype, 237
Sterne, Laurence
  compared with Swift, 175
  Sentimental Journey, 176
  Tristram Shandy, 91, 147, 169, 174, 175–76
    177, 196–97

Storytelling
  cultural interpretation as, 16–18
  Gibbon and, 181–82
  moral, and DePalma, 246–48
  paranoia and, 17–18
Strick, Joseph, 102
Structuralism, 236–39
Studio system, 242
Style
  Defoe and, 114
  Gibbon and, 189
  for Lubitsch, 70
Stylization, in film, 47, 101, 240
Subjectivity, 175, 195
Superman (film), 219
Sutherland, James, 117, 119, 122
SWG. *See* Screen Writers Guild
Swift, Jonathan
  Battle of the Books, 173
  compared with Pope, 172–73, 177n1, 195
  compared with Sterne, 175
  Gulliver's Travels, 16–17, 161–62, 163, 164,
    173, 196
  literary form and, 172–73
  Tale of a Tub, 164, 165, 173–74, 175, 177,
    179, 197
Syberberg, Jürgen, *Our Hitler,* 129–30

Talbot, David, 260
Tale of a Tub (Swift), 164, 165, 173–74, 175,
    177, 179, 197
Taxi Driver (film), 248, 249, 250
Teaching. *See also* Education
  adversary style of, 37
  language of emotions and, 34–35
  of reading, 282
Technique
  Hitchcock and, 51–52, 53
  Lubitsch and, 73
  Truffaut's focus on, 51–53
Television, 18–22, 214–15
Terminator (film), 223–24
Theater, art-within-art in, 203–4, 205, 212
"Théâtre Libre" group, 99
Thérèse Raquin (Zola), 95–97
Thucydides, 183–84
Time. *See also* Death; Past; Permanence; Youth
    vs. age
  catastrophic vs. soap opera, 18–25
  in musicals, 218
  permanence and, 214, 271
Tocqueville, Alexis de, 283
Torn, Rip, 61–62
Total Work, 127–28
Toulouse-Lautrec, Henri de, 201
Tractarians, 35n2
Tradition, and eighteenth-century novel, 169–
    70, 173, 174–75, 176–77. *See also* Canons
    of literature
Trilling, Diane, 123

Tristram Shandy (Sterne), 91, 147, 169, 174,
    175–76, 177, 196–97
Trouble in Paradise (film), 70–75
Truffaut, François
    American film and, 48–49
    L'Enfant sauvage, 49
    Les Films de ma vie, 44, 45–50
    interview with Hitchcock, 51–54, 57, 58, 59
    La Nuit américaine (Day for Night), 50
    Les Quatre cent coups, 43
    "Une certaine tendance du cinéma français,"
        44

Uncertainty
    in Defoe's works, 112, 115
    film self-consciousness and, 207–8
    in Penn's films, 273, 274
Under the Sign of Saturn (Sontag), 126–31
Unionism, 258–59

Vadim, Roger, 102
Vartanian, Aram, 81, 87
Vergil, 184
Vidal, Gore, 150n6
Visits to Bedlam (Byrd), 193–94, 195–96, 197–
    98
Visual arts, and emotional isolation, 209–11
Visual imagery, and genre film, 217–18
Visual world
    Catholic filmmakers and, 242–51
    Richardson's *Clarissa* and, 159–60
Vonnegut, Kurt, 267
Von Sternberg, Joseph, 75, 76n11
    Underworld, 231
Voyeurism
    in films about performers, 209–11
    in Hitchcock's work, 53–54, 55, 56–57
    in Warhol's work, 64
    in Zola's work, 97–98, 100

Walpole, Horace, *Castle of Otranto*, 171
Wanderer, in Zola's novels, 97–98
Ward, Elizabeth, 232–33, 234
Warhol, Andy, 64–66
Warner Brothers, 205
Warshow, Robert, 263
Warton, Thomas
    History of English Poetry, 182

*Observations on the Faerie Queene of
    Spenser*, 182
Watt, Ian, 167n9
We Are Your Sons (Meeropol and Meeropol),
    262–64
Weinberg, Herman G., 70, 71, 72
Weinstein, Fred, 157–58
Weir, Peter, *Gallipoli*, 220
Welles, Orson, 244
    Citizen Kane, 44, 148
Wendt, Alan, 167n10
Westerns, 230, 236–39
White, E. B., 30
Whitman, Walt, 223
Wilde, Oscar, 8, 126
Williams, Raymond, 92n3
Williams, Robin, 217
Wilson, Michael, 260
Wimsatt, William K., 30
Winter Kills (Condon), 268–70
Wolff, Cynthia Griffin, 166n1
Woman, as main character, 162–63
Woolf, Virginia, 287
World War II, 18, 29–30, 141, 146
Wright, Will, *Sixguns and Society*, 235–39
Writer. *See* Author-work relation; Social role of
    critic/artist
Writing, act of, 163–65

Yale University
    literary study at, 6, 26–27
    Mailer at, 60
Youth vs. age
    for Coppola vs. DePalma, 246–47
    in Penn's films, 272–73

Zecca, Ferdinand, 99
Zheutlin, Barbara, 260
Zola, Emile, 95–106, 102
    L'Assommoir, 102
    La Bête humaine, 97
    film versions of novels by, 103–5
    Germinal, 102, 103
    Le Roman expérimental, 97
    La Terre, 97
    Thérèse Raquin, 95–97